MEDIAMAKING

For Eleanor Blum

MediaMaking
Mass Media in a
Popular Culture

Lawrence Grossberg
Ellen Wartella
D. Charles Whitney

SAGE Publications
International Educational and Professional Publisher
Thousand Oaks London New Delhi

For information:

SAGE Publications, Inc.
2455 Teller Road
Thousand Oaks, California 91320
E-mail: order@sagepub.com

SAGE Publications Ltd.
6 Bonhill Street
London EC2A 4PU
United Kingdom

SAGE Publications India Pvt. Ltd.
M-32 Market
Greater Kailash I
New Delhi 110 048 India

Printed in the United States of America

Library of Congress Cataloging-in-Publication Data

Grossberg, Lawrence.
    MediaMaking: Mass media in a popular culture / by Lawrence Grossberg, Ellen Wartella, and D. Charles Whitney.
        p.   cm.
    Includes bibliographical references (p.   ) and index.
    ISBN 0-7619-1176-6 (acid-free paper). — ISBN 0-7619-1177-4 (pbk.: acid-free paper)
        1. Mass media and culure. 2. Mass media—Social aspects.
    I. Wartella, Ellen. II. Whitney, D. Charles (David Charles), 1946- .
    III. Title.
    P94.6.G76 1998
    302.23—dc21   98-8875

This book is printed on acid-free paper.

98 99 00 01 02 03 10 9 8 7 6 5 4 3 2

Acquiring Editor:	Margaret H. Seawell
Editorial Assistant:	Renée Piernot
Production Editor:	Astrid Virding
Editorial Assistant:	Denise Santoyo
Book Designer/Typesetter:	Janelle LeMaster
Indexer:	Paul Corrington
Cover Designer:	Candice Harman

Contents

PART II. Making Sense of the Media

PART IV. Media and Public Life

Preface

Communication is perhaps the most human of all human activities. Humans have been seeking new media through which to extend the possibilities of communication—their ability to transcend time and space—since the invention of writing, paper, and much later, the printing press. Although communication is one of the oldest objects of study in human societies, the formal study of communication is relatively young. Concerns about the new electronic media have motivated both public debate and scholarly research since the introduction of the telegraph and the telephone. However, it is only since the 1920s that a unified body of knowledge has begun to take shape, and only since the 1950s that a formal discipline has existed. This body of knowledge, the discipline of mass communication (sometimes called media studies), attempts to understand the significance, not only of particular communications media, but of the general processes of media communication in contemporary society. The need for such a broad-based approach to the study of mass communication can in part be understood as a response to the changes that have taken place in society during the twentieth century and especially since the end of the Second World War. These changes are commonly described as the transformation of culture into a media culture. No place in the world can escape entirely the power of contemporary media, although different places (and populations) experience that power in different ways and to different degrees.

The expansion (and subsequent legitimization) of the field of communication has been fueled and supported by that postwar generation, the "baby boomers," which is often characterized and defined by its relationship to the media and to the popular culture that is distributed through the media. In fact, all three of the authors of this book are baby boomers. We are part of "the television generation," and each of us remembers when the first television set was brought into his or her home; we ranged in age from 1 year to 10 years old. This generational identity has influenced the way we have written this textbook in at least three ways.

First, we are part of the first generation to grow up on an entirely commercially defined but domestically located (and hence, family oriented) system of mass media. But we are also part of "the rock and roll generation," a generation of kids bound together in a common identity as youth, an identity that was defined less by shared experience than by a shared popular culture, which we claimed as our own despite the fact that it was commercially produced. We are part of the first generation that has lived its whole life immersed in media culture. We are part of the first generation for whom the media (along with education) were dominant institutions of culture. In addition, we were all in university during the late 1960s, when questions of the relationship between politics and culture, especially media and education, became part of the agenda of a movement that challenged the directions of society. The counterculture of the 1960s, built upon and alongside the civil rights movement, was the first national (and even international) political struggle that understood the significance of the media and popular culture and incorporated them into its analyses and strategies. Thus, one of the unique features of this book is that we refuse to separate the study of mass media from popular culture.

Second, we were all in graduate school, either in journalism or communications, in the early 1970s. As strange as it may sound, we were part of the first generation of scholars studying communications who actually saw themselves as *communication* scholars. Like any discipline, the study of mass communication was defined not only in terms of its object of study but also in terms of its perspectives, theories, and frameworks. Originally, these were drawn from a number of other fields, including literature, psychology, and sociology; but over time, these borrowings were modified to meet the demands of studying the media. And by the 1970s, the field could claim to have its own theories and models, which were, in turn, being taken up and used by other disciplines. No longer simply psychologists, or sociologists, or literary critics who were studying the media, communication scholars were defining their work both in relation to and independent of those other disciplines, so that the discipline of mass communication could no longer simply be reduced to them. As a generation, we argued that whereas the study of the mass media had to be interdisciplinary, it had to declare its own independence and that it was already more unified than people had assumed.

We do not mean to deny that the field of mass communication was, and to some extent still is, divided and even fragmented. From the very beginning of the discipline, the study of mass media drew upon both scientific and humanistic theories and research. These two versions of scholarship have very different notions of explanation, evidence, and progress. At the same time, the field is divided between those attempting to make the processes of communication more efficient and effective and those committed to criticizing the forms and practices of the media in contemporary society. A number of fundamentally different languages are used by communication theorists: languages of measurement, experimentation, experience, and aesthetics; languages of description, explanation, evaluation, and criticism. But this is not different from most disciplines that talk about human social and cultural life. Communication scholars have begun to address the relationship between these languages, to debate the kinds of knowledge about communication that each produces, and even to bring them together. Although the organization of disciplines and knowledge in the U.S. educational system discourages such efforts, it is becoming more important to draw the lines between science and interpretation, between description and criticism. We firmly believe that our understanding of media and media power can only be adequately described if we constantly work to bring the multiple languages of and perspectives on communication to bear on the media and popular culture. Furthermore, we believe that over the past century, a sophisticated body of knowledge about the media and media culture has been developing, a body of knowledge that transcends the diverse languages, traditions, and theories upon which it has been built.

Sometimes this is not always obvious. After all, there are still significant disagreements about some of the most basic questions concerning the media and their effects. Sometimes it seems that the emergence of every new generation of communication technologies (magazines, film, radio, television, video games, computers) leads us to ask the same questions over again: What is this new medium? What kinds of messages is it offering? Who is using the medium? How are they using it? What are its effects? What is its power? That these questions are constantly being re-asked should not be taken as evidence that we do not have the ability to begin to answer them. The fact is that new technologies appearing in new contexts in new historical situations demand that we re-ask the questions of media power, that we refine our knowledge and reassess our theories. But in fact, we know a great deal about the answers to some of these questions, and we know a great deal more about the complexities that make other questions so difficult to answer. There are questions that are still be explored, and there are new questions constantly emerging.

Hence, in this textbook, we propose to pay rigorous and explicit attention to the accumulating and burgeoning research on the media, at the same time that we draw attention to and examples from a wide range of modern media. This represents a sharp break from the approach taken by most introductory textbooks in the field. Most texts approach the field of mass communication as anything but a unity; instead, they begin by dividing the field into the various media of communication and treat each independently of both other media and of the broader processes of communication and culture. Typically, textbooks in the field are organized around isolated discussions of the different media: newspapers, magazines, radio, television, film, and so on. Moreover, because they cannot cover all of the significant ground simply by considering specific media, they are forced to introduce some topics that describe forms of popular culture (music, comic books) rather than actual media. We reject this framework in order to present a sense of the interrelations, not only among the media themselves, but between the development of a media culture and the broader social context within which the media are always located. Thus, this book is likely to appear much more theoretically and analytically oriented than the typical descriptively and empirically based approach of most textbooks in the area. We take this perspective because we believe that a broadly based and theoretically grounded understanding of the nature of media communication processes is an absolutely necessary part of any real understanding of contemporary life. And only with such an understanding will people be able to confront the rapidly changing and largely unpredictable future role of the media and popular culture in society.

Third, like so many members of the baby boom generation, we have continued our relationship to the media and to popular culture as fans, and in our case, as scholars. Although our tastes differ, and the role that popular culture plays in our lives differs as well, none of us would voluntarily renounce the place of the media and popular culture in our lives. Hence, we assume that there is a certain kind of media literacy, developed outside the classroom, that people bring with them to a class on mass communication. People have experience, knowledge, even expertise about the media from their own lives, from their use of the media. We hope to draw on those experiences and relate them to the theoretical and critical understandings of scholars of the media.

We assume that contemporary students are reasonably media literate, and not merely in the sense that they know what they like and where to find it. Rather, we assume that they have a very real and sophisticated "tacit" knowledge of the media, which enables them to use media in very specific and concrete ways to satisfy some of their needs and desires in the context of their lives. On the other hand, this does not mean that they are entirely in control of the media or its effects or that they have an explicit awareness of how the media are working or even of what they are doing when they use it in particular ways. This is important because it defines the pedagogical intention of this book: we do not think that the media are some evil powerful force against which we need to inoculate our students. Nor do we think that the function of a better understanding of the media is to educate our students' palate, to wean them off of the culture they like and, with our new critical tools in hand, lead them to the higher pleasures of more legitimate cultural tastes. Rather, our goal is much simpler and much more complex.

We recognize that different people are drawn to the study of mass media for many different reasons: The media occupy a central space and a great deal of time in all of our lives; they are interesting, attractive, exciting. Some people hope to work in the media industries—as creators, artists and producers, advertisers, or journalists. Many people suspect that the media have significant power, if not over their own lives then over the lives of others, or perhaps over society more generally. For whatever reasons, all of these motivations challenge us to know more about the media and how they are made and to know what we know in structured, systematic ways.

We want to share with students the knowledge and thoughts that scholars have developed about the relationships among media, culture, and society so that they will have a better understanding of how the world is shaped by human actions and decisions. What they choose to do with this knowledge, whether they will work to change that world, and whether those changes will be for their own advantage, for better or for worse, we cannot control. But it is always better to have more knowledge, more understanding, about the nature of human life and society, especially when, as today, we confront so uncertain a future.

Putting all of this together, we can say that the basic assumption of this book is that the media can only be understood in relation to their context, a context that is simultaneously institutional, economic, social, cultural, and historical. We have called this book *MediaMaking* because our basic assumption is that the media are actively helping to produce the context in which they exist, even as they are themselves the product of that context. In fact, in the contemporary world, it is becoming increasingly difficult, if not impossible, to separate the two parts of what is more and more a single process: The media make the world even as the world makes the media. Descriptions of the media, and discussions of the meaning, impact, and effects of media cannot be separated from a broader discussion of culture, history, and changing relations of power. It is not merely a matter of adding the context in all of its dimensions and complexity, or of treating the context as a secondary question, an afterthought, a footnote, or even a separate chapter. We will treat communication and its context as intimately interwoven. We cannot study communication apart from the other institutions in the society, or from the other dimensions of social life. The media are part of the economy, the history, the social relations of power, and the forms of identity, meaning, and experience of contemporary life; each is shaping and defining the others. Thus, this is a text about contemporary culture and society as much as it is a text about contemporary media. Although the book is designed primarily for courses in mass communications and media studies, we hope it may be of interest in courses focusing on such issues in other departments as well, including cultural studies, American studies, American literature and history, and sociology.

In this book, we attempt to explore the variety of ways in which mediamaking is involved in our social lives. We explore the different relationships between the media and the systems of social value and social differences that organize power in contemporary society. We examine how the media are produced and consumed and what they produce in turn. Thus, we have chosen to organize this book on the basis of the most important dimensions of this mutual process of making. The book is divided into four parts. Part I, Placing the Media, begins with an introductory chapter that defines our basic assumptions and approach. Chapter 2 considers different narratives of human history and the history of the media. Chapter 3 focuses on how the media function to produce particular kinds of products and how they are influenced by their interactions with other institutions. Chapter 4 looks at how the media, as economic organizations, both require and produce money and how this in turn influences the way they function and the kinds of messages they produce.

Part II, Making Sense of the Media, looks at how the media produce meaningful messages (Chapter 5), which people interpret (Chapter 6) to make sense of their lives and experience and to represent the world in which they live (Chapter 7). This section considers the role of the media in what we will describe as the social construction of reality.

Part III, The Power of the Media, considers the major dimensions in which the media affect people's lives: how the media produce social identities, contributing to people's sense of who they are and who other people are (Chapter 8); how people relate to and use the media in their everyday lives, especially in relation to questions of pleasure, desire, moods, and needs (Chapter 9); and how the media influence, shape, and affect people's behavior (Chapters 10 and 11). Finally, Part IV, Media and Public Life, explores broader issues about the relationship between the media and society, including questions about: news and information and their impact on politics and public behavior (Chapter 12); the "public" as the political face of the audience (Chapter 13); and different systems for judging and evaluating media systems (Chapter 14). Finally, a concluding chapter (Chapter 15) will consider the challenges raised by the increasingly global nature of the media and their relation to power in the contemporary world.

Ironically, even a book like this cannot escape the very issues that it raises, for it too is part of the very media culture that it purports to describe and interpret. Two examples should suffice. First, writing a text about media and popular culture poses at least one problem that other disciplines do not face. Given the time lag between writing and publication, almost any example of its objects of study that might be offered is so ephemeral and transitory that it is likely to be not only outdated but forgotten by the time the book is actually read. Textbooks on literature can use the classics; textbooks in sociology can use typical interactions or structures. But the media do not lend themselves to such appeals. Hence, unlike other media textbooks, we shall not use lots of extended examples, leaving it to readers to insert their own examples. Second, our negotiations with various publishers exemplified many of the arguments we will make, especially in Chapter 4: Publishers, like other media corporations, are driven to maximize their profit. Because the easiest way to do this is to increase the size of the audience, many publishers wanted us to decide what to include in this book on the basis of its difficulty (on the assumption that the more difficult the book, the smaller the audience). But the importance of mediamaking in the contemporary world and the possibility, if not inevitability, that it will matter even more in the future, seems to compel all of us, scholars, communicators, and consumers alike, to think about the enduring questions of mediamaking and the kind of world that is being made with the best and most rigorous concepts and tools that we have available.

This book was begun when the authors were colleagues at the University of Illinois at Urbana-Champaign. We want to acknowledge the influence and contributions of our colleagues and students, in particular James W. Carey, and through him, his teachers, Jay Jensen and Ted Peterson, both of whom have recently passed away. We also want to thank the Program in Cultural Values and Ethics for providing us with a semester free from teaching to begin work on this book. In many ways, this book reflects the singular culture surrounding the study of communication at the University of Illinois in the 1980s. That culture allowed three scholars with very different perspectives and commitments to come together as friends and interlocutors. The result, we hope, demonstrates the worth of reading and thinking beyond one's own necessarily narrow education.

PART I

Placing the Media

Media in Context

Human beings have always lived in a world of communication, but we live in a world of *media* communication, where we can travel great distances and across centuries, all in the comfort of our own living rooms. We can "see" what is happening across the globe or out in space or even in unfamiliar neighborhoods of our own cities. We can re-create the Civil War or picture life after a nuclear holocaust. We can vicariously experience enormous suffering and great joy. And we can hear the sounds of other cultures and sense how different peoples experience the world. We may discover that others in the world live very differently from us. We can learn that not everyone lives in the world of media communication and that not everyone who *does* lives in the same way.

The media have become an inseparable part of people's lives, of their sense of who they are and of their sense of history. The media provide an ever larger part of the imagery and soundtrack of people's memories. Some of our most powerful, most intensely emotional, and most important moments are intricately bound up with the media: the 1963 Kennedy assassination and funeral, the urban riots from 1965 to the present, the Watergate hearings in 1973 and 1974, the 1986 Challenger disaster, the Persian Gulf War of 1991, the 1995 O. J. Simpson trial, and Princess Diana's funeral in 1997.

From a less subjective point of view, the media seem to dominate and demand more and more of people's attention. For the media seem increasingly to have become the news. More and more political issues and debates revolve around the media themselves: there have been numerous cover stories about rap music and violence, about pornography (in cyberspace and on television), about digital television, about the role of the media in elections, about staging the news, about new telecommunications laws and deregulation, and about new technologies.

If we live in a world of media, it is still important to remember that we do not live in a media world. The media bring the world to us and help to shape that world, but there is still a reality outside of the media. It is becoming harder all the time to tell the real world from the media world. But it is essential to know the difference if diverse peoples and nations are to live together in peace. This book is about the ways in which the world and the media make each other, about *mediamaking.*

Whereas the world has a kind of durability and reality that resists the media's ability to remake it, the media have a kind of ephemeral quality that make them hard to hold on to. Most stories are fleeting and short-lived, and they go out of date all too quickly. But some stories live on in popular memory. Nevertheless, we must choose examples if we are to study this relationship between the world and the media. The Persian Gulf War provides a recent illustration of the complexity and the power of the media in contemporary life as well as of many of the problems the contemporary media pose.

On August 2, 1990, Iraq—under the leadership of Saddam Hussein—launched a massive ground attack against its Arab neighbor Kuwait. On January 16, 1991, the United States, with the blessing of the United Nations and at least token participation from other nations, led a counterattack against Iraq aimed at driving its forces out of Kuwait. At the forefront of this counteroffensive was a massive air strike launched against both Iraqi troops in Kuwait and Iraq itself.

This occasion was the first demonstration of the impact of the Cable News Network (CNN) on the flow of information in American media. For the first 72 hours of the air war, the television networks, trying to compete with CNN, provided continuous coverage of even the most trivial and uncertain war news. For the first time ever, as a result of contemporary technologies, especially mobile satellite communications, people were watching a live "war." One of the results of this immediacy was that the audience got to see raw journalism. The evening news usually has a seamless presentation, but for Gulf War coverage, the traditional editing and verification process was short-circuited. We could see how television journalism is made. Rumor, inaccuracies, contradictions, guesses, and often the most trivial and redundant news briefings were reported in the heat of live and full coverage. Yet, millions of people all over the world were glued to their television sets, unable to cut themselves off from the endless flow of "information" about the war. Commentators talked about the psychological dependence of the audience on this continuous news coverage. It became known as the *CNN Syndrome.* Moreover, everyone knew that something significant about how war is waged had changed when it became clear that the military leadership (and intelligence) at home were as dependent on television news as the rest of the nation.

The coverage of the war raised unique and difficult questions about freedom of the press. Precisely because the coverage was live, the military had to go to extraordinary lengths to control if not censor the media's reports. (Compare this with the U.S. invasion of Grenada, when the press was effectively blocked from any presence in the war zone.) On the other hand, when CNN correspondent Peter Arnett broadcasted live news reports from Iran (by setting up a direct satellite hookup) "the enemy" was given direct and live access to the American and allied public for the first time in wartime journalism. Critics charged that CNN was serving as a public relations and propaganda conduit for the Iraqis; yet, Iraq's attempts to sway public opinion in America often backfired (angering the public rather than winning its sympathy), demonstrating that audiences are always somewhat unpredictable. But the larger point is that both the Iraqis and the Allies tried to control the ways the "real" war was translated into a media war. Controlling the flow of news was not only about controlling the enemy's access to information, but also about the strategic presentation of the war to the public at home. But the relation was even more complicated because the media's images of the war had their own impact on how the war was carried out and on the response to the war "at home."

Perhaps the most striking feature of the Gulf War coverage was the visual images provided by the Allied military command of the first truly high technology war in action. Smart bombs and sophisticated video and laser technology allowed people to see bombs aiming at and hitting their targets. But the most curious feature of these images was how closely they resembled the imagery of common video games. And the resemblance became overwhelming when everyone, from the press to the military, began using the language of such games to describe the war. Although the games may have originally been modeled on high-tech warfare, they now seemed to have become the model for describing that warfare. But the war itself became more than a news story; it was a multimedia event. Prime-time entertainment television incorporated the war almost immediately; books about the conflict were published very quickly; a number of popular songs were released even before the war was over. Later, television programs, movies, books, and electronic games continued to represent and remember the Gulf War.

Yet "behind" these images and descriptions of the war, everyone knew there was a real war. Kuwaitis were killed by Iraqis; Iraqis were killed by the bombs dropped with computer accuracy. American troops were similarly at risk from the horrors of war, and even the everyday life of Americans at home was occasionally disrupted by the departure of loved ones and threats of terrorism. In the long term, even populations not immediately involved in the war felt its impact, and the war certainly affected the status of the military and the formulation of policy for future military engagements. Everyone knew that there was a difference between the media war and the real war, yet there was no way to imagine or comprehend the war except through media images. And as time has passed, it has become even more difficult to separate the war from the media's images; even people who were there have had to negotiate with the representations and images that have bombarded them in the years since they returned. The problem of "constructing the war" in the thought, imagination, and memory of the population, then, extended far beyond the realm of journalism, across all the media.

The example of the Gulf War illustrates what we mean by saying that human beings live in a world of media but not in a media world. Communication has always been a crucial aspect of human life, but in the second half of the twentieth century, especially in the Western industrial democracies, the media have become so intertwined with every aspect of our reality that the line between the two, media and reality, has become blurred and even porous. To try to isolate the media from other parts of our lives—as if we could talk about media *and* politics, media *and* culture, media *and* society, media *and* economics, or media *and* audiences—even for the purpose of study is an oversimplification. For the media are already implicated in these other realms: the media are already involved in making them what they are, even as these other realms are involved in shaping the media.

Consequently, this book is based on a different model of the place and power of the media in contemporary life: the model of *mediamaking*. This term is intentionally ambiguous. It implies that the media are *themselves being made* while they are simultaneously *making something else*. Above all, it suggests that we must see the media and all of the relationships that the media are involved in as active relationships, producing the world at the same time that the world is producing the media. This means that the media *cannot* be studied apart from the active relationships in which they are always involved: We cannot study the media apart from the context of their economic, political, historical, and cultural relationships. Studying the media is not an additive process, as if we can first understand the media and then add their effects on politics and economics. But at the same time, we cannot study some real political or economic events and then hope to understand the role of the media in representing them. To repeat ourselves, the media are constantly being made by the very same relationships that they themselves are making. If this sounds circular and somewhat confusing, think about the relationships in your own life. Virtually by definition, relationships are matters of reciprocal influence.

Making is the primary activity of media: making money, making everyday life, making meaning, making identities, making reality, making behavior, making history. And it is in these various activities of making that the media themselves are made, that we can speak of the media as making media. Making, then, points to the fact that the world of human life is a world of practices. *Practices* are the various forms of human activity that transform some aspect of human reality. Practices are activities that change the world, such as political practices, economic practices, intellectual practices, social practices, sexual practices, and so on. We must always be aware of the complexity of the media in relation to human practices as we attempt to understand the contributions that the media make, both positive and negative, to the very form and substance of contemporary social existence.

7

MEDIA AND MEDIATION

DEFINING AND DISTINGUISHING THE MEDIA

Everyone is familiar with the term *media*; people see it and use it all the time. But what do they mean? Many people use the term media to refer to television. Yet the term cannot be limited in this way, although television is certainly one of the most important media of our times. (Note also that *medium* is singular and *media*, plural: *television is a medium; the media are* . . .). Some people assume that the media are simply technologies that can be described in terms of the hardware of production, transmission, and reception. Although technology is obviously crucial to contemporary communications media, they cannot be understood simply as hardware, as if they existed independently of the concepts people have of them, the uses people make of them, and the social relations that produce them and that are organized around them every day.

Let's begin by outlining how the media can be described and differentiated. There are many ways of categorizing media, precisely because they are complex and multidimensional structures or formations.

We can categorize the media according to the geography or type of social relationships they are designed to construct or used to support: *Interpersonal media* are primarily used for point to point, person to person, communication. *Mass media* are primarily used for communication from a single point to a large number of points, or from a single source to an audience that includes many people. Whereas interpersonal media usually give the communicator a good deal of control over the audience, mass media allow the communicator little power to select and little likelihood of knowing much about the audience. Whereas interpersonal media enable the sending and receiving of messages from both ends, mass media tend to separate the sender and receiver. The interpersonal media include the telephone and the telegraph. The mass media include newspapers, magazines, books, radio, broadcast, satellite and cable television, film, records, and tapes. There is a third category, *network media*, which can be used as either interpersonal or mass media; even more important, they can also be used to create a new geography of social relations, connecting many points to many points, all of which can be both senders and receivers. Examples of network media are teleconferencing, the postal service, and the new computer communications technologies.

We can categorize the media according to a number of different *modalities*. One modality is the channel used in communicating: print (books), electronic (television), chemical (film). Another modality is the sense experience on which particular media operate: visual (books), aural (radio), tactile (Braille), mixed (television). Economic modalities are important, as well: directly purchased media (books, records, magazines, and tapes), media that can be delivered to an audience without direct cost (network television or radio), media that charge for general access (cable television, Internet providers), and media that charge for the right to view specific content (pay television, films).

We can categorize media by the *institutions* that produce and disseminate them. For example, we distinguish network television from local independent television stations from cable systems. We can distinguish different *technological manifestations*, especially of what appears to be the same communication technology: Think of the difference between a family television, the large television in a sports bar, and the Diamond Vision screen behind the stage at a concert arena.

We can also distinguish different forms of *media content*, which often cut across the media technologies themselves, as when we talk about entertainment or fictional programming, news or journalistic content, and advertising content. We can make finer distinctions among these as when we separate soap operas from situation comedy shows from westerns and action adventure fare, all located within the category of television entertainment.

Two other distinctions are worth making in the effort to locate and define a useful concept of communications media. First, we can distinguish communications media from other kinds of *information technologies* that are also involved in processes of communication. These include patents, copyrights, photocopying, computer programs, and video games.

Second, we can distinguish media from culture. In fact, one of the most common misuses of the term media equates it with popular culture. People tend to confuse television as a medium of communication with the entertainment content that defines the vast bulk of its programming. Since the beginning of the twentieth century, the new technologies of communication have quickly evolved into the major sources of popular culture, and most of the major forms of popular culture are not only distributed by but have often emerged in one or more of the mass media.

This confusion and conflation has resulted in a persistent and common form of criticism of the media: that each new media technology threatens other, more traditional, forms of popular culture.

Likewise, even fans of a new form of popular culture, especially when it is made available through new media, often themselves assume that the new form is inferior to the older forms it is replacing. Criticism of new forms of popular culture may turn into criticism of the media that carry them. Parents fret that electronic games keep their children away from better activities, such as reading or exercising. It is true that the media have become the primary space for new forms of leisure activities and popular culture. The twentieth century has seen a transformation in older forms of culture as well as a redefinition of leisure and leisure activities.

Understanding the media requires acknowledging and accounting for the complexity of the media. Every medium comprises and is shaped by technologies, social relationships (institutions), and cultural forms. Each of these ways of thinking about the media is important, for each contributes something unique to how we understand the media and their relationship to society and social reality. These three aspects of the media are central to our discussions throughout the book.

Technologies

When we think about media, the first thing that comes to mind is the various technologies of communication. *Technology* is the physical means of producing, reproducing, and distributing goods, services, materials, and cultural products. In the case of communication, technology includes the physical media and techniques, the technical practices and machinery, by which we communicate. Communication technologies are expanding and proliferating at an increasingly rapid rate. When the three authors of this text were kids in the 1950s, television was just becoming a widely disseminated technology. Not until 1954 was television in the majority of American households; by 1960, seven of eight families had TV sets. Stereos were nonexistent. There were no

BOX 1.1

Sousa on the Menace of the Phonograph

Every new media technology is greeted with an alarmist rhetoric. Often, the most extravagant and dire consequences are predicted as the inevitable result of the introduction of the technology. In the early part of the twentieth century, the phonograph was widely disseminated, and the recorded music industry grew rapidly. Here is what John Philip Sousa (1906), perhaps the greatest American composer of marching songs (including "Stars and Stripes Forever"), said about the consequences of the phonograph's popularity:

Sweeping across the country with the speed of a transient fashion in slang or Panama hats, political war cries or popular novels, now comes the mechanical device to sing for us a song or play for us a piano, in substitute for human skill, intelligence and the soul. Only by harking back to the day of the roller skate or the bicycle craze, when sports of admitted utility ran to extravagance and virtual madness, can we find a parallel to the way in which these ingenious instruments have invaded every community in the land. And if we turn from this comparison in pure mechanics to another which may fairly claim a similar proportion of music in its soul, we may observe the English sparrow, which, introduced and welcomed in all innocence, lost no time in multiplying itself to the dignity of a pest, to the destruction of numberless native song birds, and the invariable regret of those who did not stop to think in time.

On a matter upon which I feel so deeply, and which I consider so far-reaching, I am quite willing to be reckoned an alarmist, admittedly swayed in part by personal interest, as well as by the impending harm to American musical art. I foresee a marked deterioration in American music and musical taste, an interruption in the musical development of the country, and a host of other injuries to music in its artistic manifestations, by virtue—or rather by vice—of the multiplication of the various music-reproducing machines. . . .

When a mother can turn on the phonograph with the same ease that she applied to the electric light, will she croon her baby to slumber with sweet lullabies, or will the infant be put to sleep by machinery?

Children are naturally imitative, and if, in their infancy, they hear only phonographs, will they not sing, if they sing at all, in imitation and finally become simply human phonographs—without soul or expression? Congregational singing will suffer also, which, though crude at times, at least improves the respiration of many a weary sinner and softens the voices of those who live amid tumult and noise.

The host of mechanical reproducing machines, in their mad desire to supply music for all occasions, are offering to supplant the illustrator in the class room, the dance orchestra, the home and public singers and players, and so on.

Evidently they believe no field too large for their incursions, no claim too extravagant. But the further they can justify these claims, the more noxious the whole system becomes.

BOX 1.2

Leisure in "Middletown"

One of the classic studies of American social life is Robert and Helen Lynd's (1929) *Middletown,* the study of an American small town in the 1920s. The Lynds examined the changes that modernity brought to Middletown between the 1890s and 1920s, looking at such activities as making a living, making a home, training the young, using leisure, and engaging in religious practices and community activities.

Of particular interest to us is their examination of how the automobile and movies—both new technologies in the early 1920s—changed how Americans spent their leisure. The automobile was important for spreading the idea of vacation when families could travel relatively cheaply away from home. Moreover, and for the first time, ordinary Americans could go for a ride on any day of the week. Thus, the automobile helped make "leisure time enjoyment a regularly expected part of every day and week rather than an occasional event," the Lynds wrote.

Like the automobile, the motion picture is more to Middletown than simply a new way of doing an old thing; it has added new dimensions to the city's leisure. To be sure, the spectacle-watching habit was strong upon Middletown in the [1890s]. Whenever they had a chance people turned out to a "show," but chances were relatively fewer. Fourteen times during January, 1890, for instance, the Opera House was opened for performances ranging from Uncle Tom's Cabin to The Black Crook, before the paper announced that "there will not be any more attractions at the Opera House for nearly two weeks." . . . Today nine motion picture theaters operate from 1 to 11 p.m. seven days a week summer and winter; . . . twenty-two different programs with a total of over 300 performances are available to Middletown every week in the year. . . . About two and three-fourths times the city's entire population attended the nine motion picture theaters during the month of July, 1923, the "valley" month of the year, and four and one-half times the total population in the "peak" month of December.

cassette tapes, no videos, no cable television, no satellites, no personal computers or personal data assistants, no video games, no cellular phones. Today, even as we write, new technologies are being announced all the time. We anxiously await the arrival of high definition television, of recordable compact discs, and of home information systems that combine computers, telephones, television, and other electronic forms of information dissemination and entertainment.

Institutions

Technologies are not an independent part of society. Technologies are often created within, shaped by, and controlled by institutions involved in their production and use. *An institution is any large-scale entity, embodying a range of social relationships and social functions, created by humans to perform an essential function for a society.* An institution, then, is a specific social organization where particular decisions are made and can be carried out. For example, organized religion, the military, the school system, and the government or state can be seen as institutions. Their functions and relative power vary over time. The institution of contemporary mass media comprises industries (such as the television industry) and organizations (such as the National Broadcasting Company) that use professionals—people who are trained in and paid for specific skills to produce and distribute media products to a market or audience. In addition, other organizations, such as government regulatory agencies and universities, may also play a role in the complex institutional existence of the media.

More specifically, the relationship between communication technologies and institutions has varied over time as well: In Western Europe, through the Middle Ages, the Roman Catholic church controlled the technologies of writing and manuscript production. Only the church was allowed to teach writing, and only the church had the resources to control the labor (of monks and priests) necessary for the arduous reproduction of manuscripts. Because of this, the church was able to control what was written and, hence, disseminated. When Johannes Gutenberg, with the backing of his banker, Johann Fust, coupled the printing press with movable type (individual letters of type that could be moved around and reused) in the fifteenth century, he challenged the power of one institution, the church. But the printing press was created within and became part of other institutions—medieval institutions such as guilds and later modern commercial institutions such as banks and mass media industries. And these in their turn controlled how the technology was used and what sorts of things could be written, printed, and distributed.

13

Cultural Forms

Many organizations in contemporary American society produce and distribute things; often, these items are meant to be sold and purchased to make a profit for their owners. Media organizations are no exception (although in some cases and in some other societies, media products are distributed freely). Yet, media organizations produce something closer to the products of educational organizations than to the typical products of business. The products of media organizations are also distinct cultural forms. *Cultural forms are the various structures of languages and meanings and the uses that are embodied in the products of the media technologies and organizations.* In many cases, new media technologies simply borrow cultural forms from older technologies, as when film appropriated the melodrama from the theater or when television copied the serial program format from radio or when radio and television borrowed news stories from the newspaper.

MEDIATION

What holds the three aspects of media—technology, institutions, and cultural forms—together, what provides the unity of the concept of media, is the idea of *mediation.* According to *Webster's New World Dictionary, Third Collegiate Edition,* a medium is "something intermediate . . . a middle state . . . an intervening thing through which a force acts or an effect is produced." Although the meaning of this complex notion of mediation has changed over the centuries, there is still a certain common theme running throughout this diverse history. A very old and commonsensical sense of the term is "to occupy a middle position or intermediary" as in interceding between adversaries in an attempt to reconcile a dispute. We still talk about mediating labor disputes between business and workers. Similarly, in Christian doctrine, mediation describes the role of Christ interceding between God and humans. A second sense of mediation contrasts the mediated with the immediate or the real, for example, when we contrast the media world with the real world, or when we think that there is a difference between objective knowledge and information that has been mediated through the interests of some party. The modern sense of mediation combines these two meanings to produce a notion of the space between the individual subject and reality as a space of experience, interpretation, and meaning.

Finally, there is a fourth sense of the term mediation that refers to a formal relationship necessary to connect previously unconnected activities or people, as that between the producer and the consumer of some message. In this sense, mediation refers to how messages are transmitted from one person to another.

The notion of communication is complex because it embodies all four of these senses of the term mediation: reconciliation, the difference between reality and an image or interpretation of reality, the space of interpretation between the subject and reality, and the connection that creates the circuit of the communication of meaning. This complexity helps to explain the apparently contradictory effects of communication in society; but it also helps us understand why it is so difficult to arrive at a singular understanding of the process of communication.

TWO MODELS OF COMMUNICATION

Any attempt to describe, explain, and understand the media must presuppose something about the nature of the process of communication, for it is assumed that this process defines the essential function or nature of the media. This task is made more difficult because communication is something that we take for granted all of the time. Yet, the things that are most familiar are frequently the most difficult to notice, to say nothing of appreciate and comprehend, for we "know" them so comfortably and tacitly. The word *communication* comes from the Latin term for *common*. The question is, what is it that is made or held in common through the process of communication?

Communication is not only taken for granted in our society, it is often seen as a magical solution for many if not all of our problems. Some people assert that undesirable situations can be significantly improved through more effective communication. People write books claiming the key to success is better communication skills. People may act as if all of our problems were merely "problems of communication" and not real differences of opinion and values, skill and desire, resources and power. But improved communication may not be enough to relieve the racial tension in our society, or for that matter, to end a war. It may not even be enough to guarantee success in a career, a relationship, or life.

15

There are two different answers to the question of what constitutes the commonality implicit in communication. These have given rise to two fundamentally different perspectives on the process and practice of communication. The first perspective is grounded in the idea of *transportation*, in which some *thing*—a message or meaning—is transported from one place or person to another. Based on the image of transportation, scholars have developed a transmission model of communication. The second perspective depends on the idea of the *production of a common culture* through which the concept of communication is closely tied to notions of community and communion. Communication, like communion, is a process by which a particular community is bound together. This common culture surrounds everyone and everything in its commonality; it is the groundwork upon which both community and every specific act of communication are built. Based on the assumption that a common culture is the basic context of communication, scholars have developed a cultural model of communication. These two models have played a central role in the development of the discipline of communication studies.

THE TRANSMISSION MODEL

Modernization is closely tied not only to industrialization but also to the development of new technologies that facilitated the movement of goods, people, and information. In the eighteenth century, modernization was crucially dependent on the development of modes of transportation, such as all-weather roads and canals. In the nineteenth century, modernization included the advent of the railroad, the telegraph, the elevator, and the telephone.

Among the earliest attempts to develop a theory of communication in the twentieth century, the most successful reproduced the commonsense assumption that communication looks exactly like transportation, that is, that *communication is the process of moving messages from a sender through a medium to a receiver.* The analogy to transportation is straightforward. In transportation, something—wheat, for example—is moved from a source to a receiver by a certain agency or medium—for example, a train. In communication, a message—a certain sentence or meaning, for example—is moved from a source to a receiver by a certain agency or medium—for example, a linguistic code carried through a telephone. By the time the discipline of communication had been established in American universities in the early twentieth century, this transmission model had become the dominant model among communication theorists. Here is a typical diagram of this view of communication:

$$\text{Source} \rightarrow \text{Message} \rightarrow \text{Receiver}$$

The transmission model of communication is based on the interpersonal context, in which the major concern is the fidelity of communicating, that is, the accuracy with which the message is transported from one person to another in a linear trajectory, although the model may allow for feedback loops. This model assumes that all communication operates like interpersonal communication. At its simplest level, whether you are talking on the telephone or watching television, your first concern as a receiver of communication is whether what you are receiving is actually the same as (i.e., reproduces) the message that has been sent. The model implies that the major challenge of the process of communication is to successfully transmit the content of a message as if from the mind of one person to that of another—the exact thought and meaning in the mind of the sender is what can, should, and will be placed in the mind of the receiver. This sharing of meaning is called understanding or intersubjectivity.

The transmission model was the basis of Harold Lasswell's (1948) famous description of the study of mass communication. Lasswell, who wrote about mass media in the first half of this century, described the study of communication as a series of questions: *Who / says What / to Whom / through what Channel / and with what Effect?* Indeed, almost all of the scientific research in the field of mass communication is built upon this model. Drawing upon research methodologies in sociology, psychology, and social psychology, researchers have studied each of Lasswell's questions. Researchers have studied the "who" in studies of communicators—the people and organizations that produce media messages and control what gets transmitted. They have studied the "what" in systematic analyses of media content. And they have studied the "to whom" and "with what effect" in the voluminous research on the effects of media on audiences.

THE CULTURAL MODEL

The second model of communication is more difficult to grasp. The cultural model of communication draws a very close connection between the processes of social communication and the production of a common culture. The notion of culture is one of the most complex yet powerful concepts in modern thinking. Raymond Williams, a British literary critic and communication theorist, has traced the changing meanings of this term.

According to Williams (1958), the oldest use of the term culture already combined two different senses: on the one hand, culture involved notions of honor and worship; on the other hand, it described the agricultural process of cultivation, "the tending of natural growth." By the nineteenth century, these two meanings were extended to human development, and culture came to take on new meanings. Now the term described the process of "cultivating" particular abilities, sensibilities, and habits in human society (such as when we think of a "cultured person"). It described a particular form of human association and existence (for example, in notions of "folk culture" and "images of the organic or natural community"). Increasingly, the notion of culture was used to describe a particular set of highly valued activities and the "creative practices" that produce them—culture as the set of artistic and intellectual activities and products. For example, one of the most famous definitions of culture was offered by the nineteenth-century English literary critic and state education bureaucrat, Matthew Arnold (1960): "the best that has been said and thought." Finally, in its most recent form, culture becomes synonymous with the whole way of life of a society or people; thus, we might talk about the culture of the Middle East or of Iraqis or of African Americans or even of the dominant American culture.

Williams suggests that even as this last anthropological notion of culture becomes prevalent in contemporary language, the earlier meanings of culture remain active in our commonsense uses of the term. He explains that the reason culture became such an ambiguous and important term in our modern lexicon may have been that it offered a way of both describing and judging the changes that have radically altered the nature of social life since the seventeenth century. These changes, commonly referred to under the general term of *modernization* or *progress*, were so sweeping that they challenged any attempt to describe them or to judge them. The theory of culture is based on the attempt to describe the pervasive changes captured in notions of modernization, and at the same time, to identify some criterion against which these changes could be measured.

Williams notes,

> Culture was not a response to the new methods of production, the new Industry alone. It was concerned, beyond these, with the new kinds of personal and social relationships: again, both as a recognition of practical separation and as an emphasis of alternatives. (p. xvi)

In his words, "The idea of culture is a general reaction to a general and major change in the condition of our common life. Its basic element is its effort at total qualitative assessment" (p. 295).

Williams makes an important addition to this history of the concept of culture. He argues that what connects the notions of a whole way of life and a privileged set of activities is a set of processes that can properly be called cultural and that are, above all else, ordinary. These processes are ordinary in the sense that they are routinely performed by everyone in their daily lives; they are the processes of language and meaning production, of sense making and interpretation, of communication. It is above all the ordinariness of communication that defines culture as art and that unites the various elements of a whole way of life. For Williams, the dilemma of modern life is not that there is a struggle between the creative (art) and the uncreative (popular culture), but that there is no way for the vast majority of the population to enter into more public and social processes of communication. To transform the culture of the society according to every individual's experience requires that people be able to use language and the media of communication to both speak within and transcend the already existing common or shared culture. This process is what Williams calls "the long revolution."

Individuals continually attempt to give meaning to their experiences. Interpretations are usually provided for them by the shared languages (verbal, literary, visual) of their culture. But people have to constantly struggle to find ways to interpret experiences that appear to have no place within the existing culture. They create such interpretations, Williams suggests, through their attempts to communicate their experience. Thus, communication is a constant process of balancing the possibilities of the culture (social languages, shared experiences, and meanings) with the needs of individuality. If culture remained totally within the already constructed social language, everyone would understand everything, but there could be nothing new in the world. If culture were limited to the innovative realm of the individual, then shared understanding would be impossible. Culture as communication is the process of producing new shared meaning out of the interaction of historically given shared meanings and individually created meanings.

At the same time, for Williams, culture is the set of activities in which this process of producing new shared meanings is carried in the various forms of art and media communication. Making the leap from culture as art and literature to culture as film and television is a simple one. Today's media have certainly augmented older forms of art and have become the dominant means by which culture is created and shared.

The cultural model of communication sees communication as the construction of a shared space or map of meaning within which people coexist. Rather than a linear model, which first isolates the message and then sends it from one place or person to another, the cultural model emphasizes the fact that people already exist within a world of shared meaning that they take for granted. Without this common reality, communication would be impossible, and in fact, the vast majority of our communication merely serves to ritualistically reproduce that system of shared meanings within which we live.

A number of writers have followed media scholar James Carey's (1989) ritual view of communication and suggested that one can look at media presentations as "rituals" to illustrate the ways in which the media function as a cultural forum. When we think of rituals, we think of ceremonies and religious events—a graduation, the swearing in of naturalized citizens, a wedding, a Holy Communion. Rituals are formal but emotional public events, endlessly repeated, with special meanings for their present participants but just as important meanings for the wider society that has established them. A ritual serves to remind the society's members of cornerstone beliefs for that society. The ritual's repetition serves as a marker, both of the importance of those beliefs and their durability. A cultural model of communication extends this notion of ritual to encompass all of the repetitive practices of communication, such as saying grace before dinner, answering the phone, or greeting a friend.

This system of shared meaning represents the world for us; it gives us a common picture of reality; this concept is often described as *ideology*. But picture is perhaps not the most accurate description of this process, for we live within these pictures of reality. Map may be a better term, although even that is too abstract and distant from the way in which, in this model, communication defines and determines our experience of the world. But communication as culture can never be limited to ritual, to the reaffirmation of what a community shares, for it must also allow for and even institutionalize the possibility of creativity, growth, and change.

In fact, the cultural model of communication lies within a broader set of theories of the social construction of reality. Such theories start out with the observation that human beings lack the instinctual relationship to reality that enables other species of animals to make sense of and respond to the world. Culture is for humans the compensatory medium of information without which we would be condemned to live in a chaotic reality. Without culture, reality would be available to us only as what William James called a "booming buzzing confusion"; with culture, reality becomes ordered and manageable. Culture exists, then, in a kind of space of mediation, the space between humans as incomplete animals and reality, the space of communication as the production of meaning. Human experience is defined in part by the contribution of the specific human culture that binds together a particular community or society. Human beings live in a meaningful world, which they have produced through their own culture. Culture is the medium in which human beings externalize (objectify) and internalize (subjectify) their meaningful experiences of the world. (Chapter 5 will consider these issues in greater detail.)

CONTRASTING THE TWO MODELS

Consider the relation of the media to the Gulf War again. Using a transmission model, the analyst understands news coverage primarily in terms of the "information" that is sent from military and government sources through correspondents to the audience back home. Researchers might study the relationships between the various organizations involved in producing various messages: They might look at how the messages are constructed and what correlations there are between features of the message and the audience's response to them; they might try to figure out how audience members process the messages, and what individual audience members do with them. But the transmission model cannot deal with the enormous amount of misinformation and redundancy in the coverage, or with the relationship between news and entertainment.

Using a cultural model, an analyst would ask very different questions and offer very different descriptions of the media war. The analyst might begin by pointing out that the language and images used in the news are already understood by the audience; thus, the war can be incorporated into already existing frames of reference. Because the bombing is presented in the images and languages of video games, the war is offered to its audience as a purely technological combat. The style gives the audience a way of understanding the high-tech weaponry that is new in the history of warfare—the video display of smart bombs moving toward their targets looks like a video game screen. Yet, the metaphor obscures the fact that warfare involves human lives and human suffering, very much *unlike* a video game. We might hypothesize that the metaphor works because it appeals to and reinforces a common American belief that technology can provide the solution to all our problems.

Similarly, if an analyst uses a cultural model, she might offer a different account of what has been called the CNN Syndrome—constantly viewing the war coverage on television. Rather than assuming that people are seeking information about the war, we might assume that television viewing in this crisis serves to create and reinforce our sense that we are part of a community that is sharing this highly emotional and dramatic event. This is indeed a *media event,* through which we ritualistically share the experience of being part of the American community. And in this ritual watching of television, we find a way of coping with the anxieties and fears of a people at war. In this regard, the CNN Syndrome can be compared to other instances of national grieving or celebration in front of the television set, as when U.S. astronauts landed on the moon in 1969, when the Challenger exploded after liftoff in 1986, and when O. J. Simpson was tried for murder in 1995.

A cultural model of communication might also begin by recognizing the enormous power of language, culture, and rituals, focusing its attention on the ways in which the war coverage reaffirms the shared systems of meaning and values that define American culture. In this light, we can view the presentation of Saddam Hussein as an evil threat not only to peace but to the fundamental values of liberty, justice, and the American way. The coverage continuously reaffirms our own sense of our moral and technological superiority. But a critic might also point out that in their efforts to use language to define the reality—or their version of it—the governments and the military came perilously close to George Orwell's depiction of "newspeak" in *1984.*

In his pessimistically prophetic novel, *1984,* the late English writer George Orwell (1949/1981) created the dystopia—a negative utopia— of Oceania. Here Big Brother not only watches everyone (with the assistance of the Thought Police) but also attempts to control what anyone can think and imagine by controlling what they can say. Two special languages—Newspeak and Doublethink—are mandated. In describing how the central character, Winston Smith, struggles against Big Brother and Oceania's totalitarianism, Orwell highlights the relationship between language and thought. He reminds us, by counterexample, that our power to think, to be individual and human, to be free and to rebel, is caught up in our language.

> The purpose of Newspeak was not only to provide a medium of expression for the world-view and mental habits proper to the devotees of IngSoc [English Socialism, the only allowable political party], but to make all other modes of thought impossible. . . . Its vocabulary was so constructed as to give exact and often very subtle expression to every meaning that a Party member could properly wish to express, while excluding all other meanings and also the possibility of arriving at them by indirect methods. This was done partly by the invention of new words and by stripping such words as remained of unorthodox meanings, and so far as possible of all secondary meanings whatever. To give a single example. The word *free* still existed in Newspeak, but it could only be used in such statements as "This dog is free from lice" or "This field is free from weeds." It could not be used in its old sense of "politically free" or "intellectually free," since political and intellectual freedom no longer existed even as concepts, and were therefore of necessity nameless. (pp. 246-247)

Cultural reaffirmation is a constant element of our relationship to the media. In light of the cultural view, we can understand most of popular culture in terms of its constant affirmation and reproduction of already taken-for-granted meanings and values in American society: the importance of the family, belief in the power of the individual, the value of competition.

There are a number of ways to distinguish between the two models. Many people assume that research carried on under the auspices of the transmission model is always quantitative (based on statistic analyses applied to data gathered through either experimental or survey research methods), whereas research within the cultural model is predominantly qualitative, based on either the researcher interacting with the people he or she is studying in natural settings (ethnography) or the interpretation of texts. However, this distinction is by no means absolute, and there can be qualitative work within a transmission model and quantitative work within a cultural model. The sociologist Edward Shils once made a similar distinction by suggesting that the transmission model had lots of answers, but the questions were usually so specific as to be uninteresting, whereas the cultural model had lots of interesting and important questions, but they were so difficult that no answers were possible. Underlining Shils's distinction is the fact that the transmission model develops by generating and accumulating specific answers from specific case studies, whereas research within the cultural model develops more as the result of theoretical argument. Rather than accumulating and averaging across specific results, cultural research develops increasingly sophisticated concepts to deal with its growing recognition of the complexity of the processes of media communication. In this book, we are concerned less with the specific findings of research than with the conceptual and theoretical tools that enable scholars and critics to understand the media in all their complexity.

The two models also have different relationships and responses to the idea of context. As we have already said, it is impossible to separate communication from its context, to isolate its forms and effects from its relations with other forms and institutions of practices. Researchers committed to the transmission model nevertheless make a choice to isolate specific aspects of the media and also to isolate the media from the various elements of the context. By focusing on particular relation-

24

ships between elements of the media and other similarly isolated aspects of the context of social reality, such as a particular political campaign or a particular economic trend or aspect of the audience's identity or response, researchers hope to address very important questions about the influence or effect of the media on local events and circumstances, such as the effect of certain kinds of war reporting on public opinion about the war. Choosing the transmission model allows researchers to study the impact of the media on individual members of society and the psychology of media impact on various subgroups in the audience according to the rules and methods of quantitatively defined science.

On the other hand, choosing the cultural model, because it highlights the context of media activity, allows the researchers to address questions about the ways in which particular media practices reinforce or challenge existing social trends and tendencies. Researchers do not use the cultural model to describe the immediate impact of a media product or message. Rather, because it places a particular media product or message in its context, this model will be used to identify the way in which such messages fit into larger structures of influence and effects. For example, a cultural study of war coverage would be likely to focus on the enduring images of militarism, moral purity, and belief in the power of technology to solve human problems. Some researchers are trying to find ways to reincorporate a commitment to context within the transmission model, and those committed to a cultural model often must limit the complexity of the context that can be taken into account.

Although many scholars assume that the transmission and cultural models of communication contradict each other—that they have to choose one model or the other—we strongly disagree. We believe that each model has something important to say about the complexities of communication in the contemporary world; the usefulness of each model depends on our particular questions about communication. Thus, we prefer to think of the two models as complementary perspectives. However, we must not forget that even when the two models appear to be addressing similar questions, there are likely to be significant differences: what each means by effects, how messages are identified, how the relations between messages and effects are described and "measured," the kinds of evidence used to establish such a relationship. Although the two models of communication suggest very different understandings of the process, it is necessary for us to hold both models of communication in mind constantly. The decision about which model is more relevant and useful in a situation depends upon the situation and our questions.

The relationship between these two models will become clearer as we proceed with this book, for we will draw upon the research and writing of both traditions of communication studies as we attempt to explain the power of communication in contemporary society. What unites these two models is that both help us gain a better understanding of the power of media communication. Identifying the relationships between media and power is pivotal to understanding contemporary society. The media have the power to engage and entertain, to create and destroy, to open spaces and to close them. Recognizing the context of the media reminds us that their power depends on their relations with other practices and institutions and that, consequently, they do not wield their powers alone but share them with these other practices and institutions.

MEDIA AND POWER

The notion of power operates at two levels: capacity or determination and control.

POWER AS EFFECT

First, in its broadest sense, *power refers to the ability to produce effects, to make a difference in the world.* In this sense, every practice has a certain amount and type of power. For instance, television has the power to reorganize how we spend our time whereas a magazine is less likely to reorganize our time. Television also has an impact on the spatial arrangements of our homes; one of the problems facing anyone who wants to purchase a new large-screen TV set is to find a room in the house big enough to accommodate this device. Magazines are unlikely to have the power to shape the spaces within which we live. In addition, every medium from printed books to electronic networking has significantly reshaped people's experience of time and their sense of history.

This view of power as the ability to produce changes or effects in the world is closely connected to the notion of *determination.* In its most common usage, *determination is thought of as causality.* For example, some people believe that the statistical relationship between education level and income level demonstrates a causal relationship: Higher education level necessarily brings about higher income. In this sense, education determines income. To use another example, many people have argued that exposure to pornography causes viewers to exhibit specific, demeaning attitudes toward women. Some people have even argued that pornography is responsible for its users' violent behavior toward women. If that is the case, pornography can be said to determine attitudes and even behaviors toward women.

Another sense of determination follows from the more contextual vision of social life that we have advocated here. In this view, the relationship of any practice to its effects cannot be isolated and identified because it depends on the entire context. What a specific practice or set of practices can do is limit and shape the outcomes; we then say the effects are *overdetermined.* Consider some examples: In this view, pornography cannot be isolated from a wider range of other media representations that portray women as objects to be used by men. (Think of many ads in popular magazines such as *Rolling Stone* or *Vogue.*) But the effects of even this broad range of media portrayals cannot be identified outside of the context of social relationships and other aspects of our culture that help to define, shape, and limit the construction of sexual identities and differences. These social relationships not only qualify the impact of pornography, they also help to explain its production: It is not surprising that pornography is a major product of a sexist society. That is why we can speak of the overdetermination of pornography's effects.

Let's consider again the relationship of education and economic success. How is this relationship overdetermined? Consider that access to education is itself dependent on many other factors, including social class, race, gender, and family income. Furthermore, the very meaning of education is constantly being challenged and rethought. Some ask whether life experience should earn credit in school or college; others debate whether the point of college is vocational training or general intellectual advancement. Similarly, current discussions around the question of multicultural curricula in colleges raise a number of crucial

27

questions: Does becoming well-educated mean learning about European-derived culture only, or should students be exposed to the broad range of cultures, ethnicities, and histories in the world? To the extent that education level is related to a whole host of other social factors in one's life that mediate its relationship to income level, that relationship is therefore overdetermined.

POWER AS CONTROL: CONSENSUS AND CONFLICT

There is a second meaning of the notion of power: *control* over people and resources. In this sense, power can be understood as producing, and then operating through or exploiting, social differences in the world. To begin to understand how media have power, we need a theory of how social differences are produced and of their importance in society. Some theories of society, commonly referred to as *consensus models*, emphasize the unity and harmony within society and the ability of different peoples to get along together. Typically, Americans think of their nation as a "melting pot" in which different groups come together in a common identity: We are all Americans.

One of the most influential examples of a consensus model of society in media theory is the work of John Dewey, the eminent philosopher, educational theorist, and communication critic of the first half of the twentieth century. Dewey (1925) offered a sophisticated cultural model of communication based on the idea that communication is the process through which different groups in the society come to understand and accept each other despite their differences. Communication is the means through which a nation forges a common identity, a common purpose, and a common resolve.

Dewey felt that the new media of communications were not meeting the challenge presented by the complex problems facing America at the turn of the twentieth century: vast immigration from eastern and southern Europe, shifts of population from rural to urban areas, increasing economic interdependence among the different regions of the country. These historical changes in American life meant that different groups in the society were unable to understand each other and to act together toward a common goal. Dewey thought the mass media of the day (including newspapers, magazines, films, and later radio) were failing to fulfill their essential purpose of creating a common language that would result in a sense of national community with which people could understand each other and which would enable people to act together. This enormous faith in the power of communication and its ability to create new forms of unity out of the chaos produced by historical change explains Dewey's belief that "of all things communication is the most wonderful." Although Dewey was writing in the second and third decades of this century, his argument has a modern parallel: Today, new media are often thought of as providing an opportunity to bring people together. The user groups and interest groups on the Internet, some argue, returns us to an era when community through communication was a realizable dream: The information superhighway is supposed to be open to all.

However, other theories of society, commonly referred to as *conflict models*, emphasize the conflicts and inequalities within social life and the difficulties different groups have in living together. These critical theories of society emphasize the fact that the various resources of a society are unequally distributed according to various structures of social difference. Every society has resources that are highly valued: force, money, meanings, morals, identities, political position, emotions, pleasures, and so on. Some of these are more highly valued than others. Each of them enables those who possess and can use the valued item to have certain powers or capacities to make a difference (the first sense of power described earlier) in the world. The case of money is quite clear: Money can produce more money—when you know how to use it—and it can enable its possessor to purchase many other things as well. But as the old Beatles' song goes, "Money Can't Buy Me Love." On the other hand, we might not think of emotions as a resource of value until we think about the way in which people use emotion to control other people or the fact that people need emotional bonds to remain healthy. By the same token, the power to influence meanings—a topic we explore in detail in Chapter 6—is the power to define questions, or the power to define what others view as important and how they think about them. This is power, indeed.

These resources are not equally distributed across all members of the society. Different groups have more or less access to resources and a differing ability to use them. Moreover, such groups are not randomly defined; the distribution of resources is organized hierarchically according to systems of social differences. Every society identifies a variety of features that differentiate groups, but only some features are considered relevant to the distribution of resources. For example, in American society, we certainly distinguish blond-haired, blue-eyed people from brown-haired, brown-eyed people. However, no one justifies segregation in schools according to such differences. On the other hand, we do organize the distribution of resources differentially by social class, race, ethnicity and nationality, gender, sexual identity, age, and differential abilities. And this is what critical scholars mean by a system of social differences.

For example, feminism is a theory of society that emphasizes the unequal distribution of resources by gender and sexuality: It describes a society that subordinates women and privileges men as patriarchal. Although almost every society in human history has been patriarchal, feminism argues that it is important to identify the particular forms of inequality that characterize contemporary society. Women, for instance, tend to make less money than men, and often they are expected to work in the home, without pay; women tend to be subject to verbal and physical violence by men; women tend to have less access to political power (in the United States, there has never been a woman elected president or vice president); women are often viewed and represented solely as sexual objects; and women are thought of in our society as being more emotional and less rational than men. You might think of many other ways in which women are subordinated to men in our society. Feminism is a theory of society that attempts to identify and challenge the subordination of women in these systems of difference. A feminist theory of communication examines the ways in which media communication contributes to these relations of inequality between men and women.

Other conflict theories of society look at the subordination of racial and ethnic groups relative to the White majority; of the working class relative to the wealthier elites; of children and the aged relative to young and middle-aged adults; of homosexuals relative to heterosexuals; of various religious minorities relative to the Protestant majority of America; and of the physically handicapped relative to the physically able.

In recent years, many of these subordinate groups in society have challenged their subordination—including their portrayals in and ac-

30

cess to the mass media. Increasingly, questions of culture and media communication have been central in such struggles. These struggles are transforming the political and cultural life of the United States and the rest of the world. And they have had a profound impact on the study of media, for they have placed questions of power as control at the center of the discipline.

It is difficult to choose between consensus and conflict models of society. Media theorists who favor a conflict model of society generally view the more consensus-oriented alternative as defending the status quo, the current way of life and all of its inequalities. On the other hand, media theorists who stress the consensus model of society tend to defend their vision by appealing to the liberal faith that society is continuously progressing and that the lives of all people within society will improve in the future as they have in the past. Moreover, they argue that conflict theorists give too much importance to the problems of power and overlook progress and harmony in human life.

In this book, we use both models of society—the consensus and conflict models—because we believe both theories of society describe important aspects of the media's role in making American society and people's lives. As we have said, the media do play an important part in making the structured inequalities of different groups in the society. But although we recognize that the media contribute to these relations of subordination, we also believe that the media have positive and beneficial effects in society. And we believe, like Dewey, that media help to make us a community. Many contemporary struggles have been addressed by the media in a variety of ways. Media have a vital role to play in transforming society and in producing a more equitable social structure.

Somewhere between the pessimism of the conflict model and the optimism of the consensus model, we have to find the space for an appreciation of both the positive and negative sides of the media's role in American society. To become a critic of media is to walk a thin line between these two alternatives. The danger of pessimism is that you begin to think that people are so vulnerable to the media's messages that every exposure to entertainment subordinates them further. However, the danger of optimism is to ignore the ways in which real people suffer as a consequence of the power of the media.

31

One final note: There is no correlation between social theories and communication models. Or to put it differently, there is no necessary relation between one's view of society and which model of communication one supports. Scholars who use a cultural model can hold to either a critical or a consensual model of society, as can those who use a transmission model. The questions facing communication scholars are too complex to reduce the field of possibilities before we have even begun.

Narratives of Media History

To understand how the media operate today, we need a better understanding of how communication media have shaped and influenced human existence. Will the Internet fundamentally alter culture and society in the twenty-first century? We can only speculate about the future. But we can ground such speculations and our understanding of contemporary media by considering the history of the relationship between communication and society. We believe that history is a useful guide to understanding the present and the future. In this chapter, we consider some of the narratives of media history.

Typically, media history is presented as a series of technological inventions, a story about great people and organizations, and an analysis of particular events shaped by communication technologies.

However, there is another way of thinking about the history of the media, which emphasizes the role of communication in shaping human existence. History is a retelling of the past, an attempt to explain how something that occurred in the past affects who or what people and society are now. But the story of the past can be told in many different ways. The French historian Fernand Braudel (1972) offers a set of categories for viewing the scope of historical events. First, there is the shortest unit of historical time, the *event*. An event is a thing like a war, a decree, a meeting, or the introduction of television. Second, there is the level of the *conjuncture*, which describes short periods of time, usually measured in decades. Conjunctures comprise many events. For example, we speak of America in the Postwar Years and the Roaring Twenties. Third, there is the level of *historical eras*, or a period that can be viewed as a whole, usually less than a century, such as the Industrial Age, The Nuclear Age, or the Enlightenment. Finally, there are historical *epochs* representing major and significant transformations of human life that often cross national boundaries and that encompass events, conjunctures, and eras. Braudel refers to these as the *longue durée* or the long term, a temporal unit that encompasses centuries: for example, the Middle Ages and the Modern Period.

Three different historical narratives offer accounts of the role of communication and culture in human history. The first historical narrative is conjunctural in Braudel's sense and focuses on communication, culture, and social relationships in modern life. The second and third offer grand narratives operating at the level of the longue durée, the epochs of human history. The second narrative theorizes the transformation from oral to electronic. It examines the impact of changes in the modes and technologies of communication across the longue durée. To what extent has the history of communications fundamentally shaped the directions of human endeavor and social life? The third narrative describes a different transformation in the long durée, the transformation from modernity to postmodernity. In this narrative, communication is seen as a part of a broader cultural transformation in history.

THEORIES OF THE MASSES

A second kind of grand historical narrative stresses the sociological nature and impact of the media in history. The most influential of these theories focus on the changing nature of social relationships and cultural products: a theory of mass society and mass culture. There are at least two versions of such theories. One starts with social relationships and moves to culture. The other starts with cultural products and moves to society.

FROM SOCIAL RELATIONSHIP TO CULTURE

In the late nineteenth century and early twentieth centuries, the emergence and development of the discipline of sociology was largely defined by the *theory of mass society*. Mass society theory held that as a result of various social changes, including industrialization, both the nature of social life and the form of social interaction were fundamentally altered for the worse. The Industrial Revolution had prompted a transformation from a rural, agrarian society in which people knew each other intimately and personally (in German, the *Gemeinschaft*) to an urban, mechanical society in which people did not know their own neighbors except in terms of their professional function (the *Gesellschaft*).

The social importance of the transformation is that in the Gesellschaft, rather than being bound to one another by tradition and custom, mutual regard, and understanding, people now constitute a society *only* by formal, contractual relations. Think about the current popularity of marital and educational contracts. Social relationships are thus anonymous, alienated, disconnected. The individual in the mass society is isolated and vulnerable to manipulation and coercion. He or she is denied the reinforcing support of primary groups, organized around family, church, work, and community.

The individual becomes part of a mass, undifferentiated, unsupported, and easy prey for authoritarian appeals. Such theories of mass society view culture as having become little more than a tool for manipulating the masses, for providing an artificial sense of security and belongingness, for appealing to people's irrational and lowest desires.

FROM CULTURE TO SOCIETY

The theory of mass society reappeared in a slightly different form after World War II in the United States, when a wide range of social and cultural critics attempted to define the unique aspects of postwar American society and to differentiate it from the totalitarian societies that had emerged in Germany under Hitler's Nazism and in the Soviet Union under Stalin's communism. Identifying these two societies as mass societies, critics then had to address the question of whether mass culture inevitably produces a totalitarian mass society, because both Hitler and Stalin made important use of the media to create and maintain their power. But because the United States also has a mass culture, could there also be a totalitarian regime here? What is the relationship between a mass culture and a democratic society?

By far, the most popular response to these questions defined American society as fundamentally liberal: Critics argued that the diversity of American culture and the plurality of audiences for a range of cultural products guaranteed America's ability to resist the manipulation of authoritarian appeals. During the 1950s and 1960s, critics attempted to draw distinctions between different sorts of cultural products and between the different audiences to which these products appealed. These distinctions—high culture, mass culture, popular culture, folk culture, middlebrow culture—continue to play an important role in contemporary attitudes about media products. Critics also argued that different audiences responded differently, based on their own cultural background and resources, to the same media messages.

Such distinctions embody particular judgments about forms of culture and their legitimacy. To call something *mass* or *low* culture is to deny it value or prestige; for many years, it was enough to guarantee that such cultural products would not be the subject of serious critical scrutiny. Yet, it is important to try to define these terms, as they have been and still continue to be used in public and critical debates.

People often assume that high culture, or what we commonly call art, is both spiritually and formally (or aesthetically) more developed than other forms of culture, such as mass, popular, or folk culture. High culture is produced by specially trained professionals and/or uniquely inspired creative individuals. This is the art that is collected, that sells for ever-higher prices, that appears in museums and is performed in concert halls. Within music and the visual arts, high art is defined by very particular formal rules; it is largely the art of the European White male upper and middle classes since the birth of capitalism. It embodies specific values (individuality, the world as a set of objects to be possessed, etc.) that these classes fought to establish. These art forms themselves were often seen as quite revolutionary in their own time and were frequently suppressed and roundly criticized by the cultural elites of the day. Many of these forms, from the waltz to the novel, and many artists we now associate with "the best that has been thought and said,"

36

from Shakespeare to Beethoven, were initially considered "too popular" or "too radical" and thus denied legitimacy. Yet, over time, as these classes and their values have come to dominate our lives, the art too has come to define the norm of legitimate cultural expression.

Folk culture refers to those cultural products and forms that can be traced to a particular community or socially identifiable group. Folk culture is assumed to be an expression of the experiences of this group. Folk artists are not professionals; usually, they are not distinguishable from the rest of the population, and the interaction that occurs between artist and audience is informal because both artist and audience share a common life. Thus, bluegrass has always been seen as folk music, with its roots in Appalachian culture. On the other hand, country music is more problematic, for it is too commercial and too dispersed to be easily seen as folk music. Similarly, for most of the twentieth century, blues was seen as a form of folk music, always traced to its roots in the African American population. On the other hand, rap music, although it certainly started within a certain Black community, would likely not be considered folk music. There are many critics who would defend both high and folk art against what they consider to be mass or popular arts, both because of their broad popularity and their commercial base.

We might take popular culture to be that culture which, regardless of where or by whom it is produced, speaks to a large public audience that cannot be simply described by a single social variable, such as class or gender or age. That is, popular culture does not assume anything about the artist. The artist can be formally trained, a professional, or an amateur with little or no formal knowledge of the aesthetic forms he or she is using. Many rock musicians—the late Frank Zappa is one example—have extensive classical conservatory training, whereas others have never learned to read sheet music. The artist may or may not be part of any community. It is irrelevant in the end. Moreover, the audience for popular art is itself diverse and complicated. It is not a community with a shared common set of experiences. It is simply some portion of what might be called "the people." The people are not a class or a gender or a race or anything else; they are made up of different classes, races, genders, ages, regions.

In some sense, popular culture sees itself in opposition to high art, although it often shares many of the same values. Popular culture is often seen by its fans (perhaps mistakenly, given the economics of popular culture), as working from the bottom up, or as coming from the people and their interests. An enormous amount of exchange takes place between these two bodies of cultural work, popular and high. Pop art makes high culture out of popular icons: In the 1960s, Roy Lichtenstein made art out of comic strips; Andy Warhol made it of Campbell's soup cans. And numerous rock groups have attempted to appropriate techniques of classical music to produce what has come to be called "art rock" (for example, Genesis).

Finally, there is mass art. Is mass art something different from popular culture? Many critics would still argue that a distinction needs to be drawn. Popular culture, it is assumed, somehow speaks to people's experience or perhaps, as one critic argues, at least allows people the freedom to interpret the text to fit into their experiences. Mass culture, on the other hand, is assumed to be purely and entirely commercially motivated; it is assumed to come from the top down, given to the people whether they like it or not. It is manipulative, attempting to force its audience to interpret its texts according to the interests of those who have produced it for the masses. This is why critics of mass culture fear that it will inevitably lead to authoritarian political regimes.

Yet, it is difficult to sustain these distinctions. Just about all of popular culture (and even folk culture) is commercially produced. And experience has taught us that it is difficult to predict the ways in which cultural products can be interpreted by various segments of the population. Making distinctions between cultural products and giving them different degrees and kinds of legitimation is itself an expression of political and economic power (Bourdieu, 1984).

FROM ORAL TO ELECTRONIC CULTURE

In an oral culture, all interaction takes place in face-to-face situations. It is a preliterate society that has no shared form of fixing or writing messages. A print culture is a literate society in which a shared system of inscription, or writing, exists so that communication can take place outside of face-to-face situations, across time and space. In an electronic culture, communication can transcend time and space without physically moving the same object from one place to another. A variety of writers have described the general differences among oral, print, and electronic cultures, including Walter Ong, Havelock Ellis, Harold Innis, Marshall McLuhan, and Elizabeth Eisenstein.

THE ORAL CULTURE

It is difficult to reconstruct what it was like to live in a purely oral culture. Scholars of oral culture have had to base their understandings of this epoch on the anthropological study of nonliterate peoples (for example, Walter Ong has looked at oral culture in Yugoslavia) and on the epic poetry of Homeric Greece (in the work of Havelock Ellis).

Perhaps more than any other scholar, Walter Ong (1982) has characterized oral culture. First, Ong insists that there is a *different sense of time* in an oral culture. Because it has no records, its memory cannot be a recorded one; its history can only reside in the present moment, in the telling of its story. There is no way to go back and check the record to see if it differs from contemporary views of an event. There are no aids to recall the "facts" or even what other people have said in previous tellings. Ong says that "the past is indeed present but it is present in the speech and social institutions of the people, not in the more abstract forms in which modern history deals." Therefore, it is more likely that both myth and facts are intertwined in an oral culture's memory of its past, much like people's family histories: For many who desire to rediscover their family history, all they have is what has been passed from generation to generation orally, and not surprisingly, such stories are often conflicting and full of gaps that have to be filled in imaginatively.

Second, Ong argues that the *psychology* of oral cultures uses a different kind of memory system. Memory is not verbatim repetition; memory is thematic and formulaic. For instance, research on epic singers in Yugoslavia shows that they can repeat a song of hundreds of lines even though they have never heard the song before, but no single singer and no two singers ever sing the song in precisely the same way. Every singing is a different version of the epic. Yet, the general story varies little from telling to telling, although the specific words that are used in the telling do differ. Hearing a new song, epic singers break it down and memorize the themes of the song. They then verbalize it in the formulas they have in their own stock of epic stories. Different epic singers become known for different phrases and ways of telling stories. The epic singers use certain aids to recall particular songs, such as strong visual imagery and mnemonic devices.

Third, in oral cultures, performance is more important than authorship. Every time a work is performed, it is reshaped by the performer and provides a new model for future performances. The notion of composition as fixing the form and sense of a message in an original act of creation does not exist in oral cultures. Instead, those with the best memories and those elders who have become the repository of knowledge are likely to be the most respected members of the culture. There are no authors in an oral culture, there are only performances.

Oral cultures are likely to be relatively homogeneous with respect to their knowledge and social norms. A relatively small number of people are likely to possess and control the knowledge of and stories about the culture, as well as their distribution. Power is concentrated in these few people.

At the same time, oral culture tends to be very public and shared across generations. Education or learning involves a lot of demonstration and participation on the part of the student and less attention to abstract principles and logics. Hence, the world of children is less segregated from the world of adults. Children absorb the knowledge they will need during public rituals and public discussions. Notions of privacy and individuality are less important than a commitment to the social whole.

Social relations and social norms have to be more rigorously policed in face-to-face situations because there can be no recourse to some fixed text of rules or standards of conduct. It is the same with the very meaning of words and stories; meanings are always defined for the particular performance rather than in universal terms (i.e., there can be no dictionary).

For Ong (1982), oral culture represents a more personal and socially involved form of communication and consequently form of life. People rely on one another and operate collectively for the social good. At the same time, oral culture is rigid and extremely hierarchical, intolerant of differences and disagreements, and harsh on those who challenge or deviate from the social norm. Oral culture is resistant to change.

WRITING CULTURE

Walter Ong (1982) argues that the creation of the Greek alphabet (about 720 BC) changed how the Greeks thought and handled knowledge. It was now possible both to think abstractly and to create *canonical texts,* texts that could be used to measure the truth of any specific performance of a story. Writing allows the creators of a story to ensure that it is recorded just as they intend it to be. Thus, the function of memory changes from thematic and visual memory to verbatim memory. At the same time, the existence of writing meant that memory itself could be judged or held accountable to something else (the text or the written word). This is the advent of writing culture.

There is little dispute about the enormous impact of writing on human history. Writing changes the relationship between a communicator and the person with whom he or she is communicating. Audiences now can be remote in time and space, and the communicator can guarantee that the message received is identical with the one sent, without having to rely on the memory of a messenger. This means that a communicator can reach a much wider and disparate audience. To the extent that society was no longer dependent upon face-to-face communication, societies could expand their boundaries to encompass vast spaces and diverse populations. This was, as the Canadian economist and communication historian Harold Innis (1950) has argued, the beginning of empire.

According to the Canadian media theorist Marshall McLuhan (1964b), "It can be argued then, that the phonetic alphabet, alone, is the technology that has been the means of creating 'civilized man' (sic)— the separate individuals equal before a written code of law" (p. 86). In oral cultures, the community is the basic unit of social existence. Individuals within such a community are defined by their place in the ongoing performance of social life. In a writing culture, fixed, written, and permanent rules or codes of law develop. Individuals can appeal to and be held accountable to such codes. At this point, the individual emerges as a unique entity separate from the community. When we can say "Joe says" or "Mary told me," then authorship has created individuality.

The separation of the individual from the community, from society, entails a different conception of space and time. In an oral culture, neither space nor time has much meaning apart from the particular place in which the community lives and the particular moment in time that defines the community's sense of the present. Writing allows for an understanding of both space and time as continua that encompass other groups of people, other places, and other times.

Those who possess the skill of writing and reading, those who are literate, are also powerful. Writing enables knowledge to be hoarded, because knowledge no longer requires public performance. Knowledge is stored in private places out of public sight, and the ability to read and to write the texts of knowledge is itself of value and therefore not widely available. This allows for the development of rigid hierarchies and of formal institutions of power, such as the Church and the State.

PRINT CULTURE

But the revolution that McLuhan grounds in writing was only completed—and at the same time, transformed—with the invention of the printing press and movable type. The ability to mechanically reproduce a text freed writing from its reliance on an elite group of individuals (such as monks in the Middle Ages), and it guaranteed that each copy of the text would be literally identical to every other copy.

A number of consequences follow the invention of the printing press. It took control of writing out of the hands of the Church and the scribes assigned to copying ancient texts. With printing came the possibility of spending time to create new knowledge, new texts, and new interpretations of old texts. Increasingly, this search for knowledge, this ability to compare a variety of texts, to seek out new ideas and interpretations, could not be entirely controlled by any one institution, especially the Church. Thus printing was instrumental in the development of a secular society and a body of writing about nonreligious life. Secular writers challenged the authority of the Church on religious and nonreligious matters in favor of individual conscience. The historian Elizabeth Eisenstein (1978) has persuasively argued that printing and the book were instrumental in the establishment of democracy in the upper middle classes of early modern Europe.

Walter Ong (1982) suggests that with writing, things were not just given but could now be questioned abstractly. But even more, because writing allows backward scanning, one can revise a text, going back and eliminating errors and inconsistencies. Although one can't take back a word once it is uttered, one can look over a text and change written words to ensure the meaning intended. Therefore, Ong argues, with writing comes a mind-set that likes exactitude and precision, even in speech. This obsession with precision and exactitude gives rise to dictionaries embodying the desire to legislate the correct use of language.

Printing further reinforced the sense of individuality and privacy. Books, according to Ong, allowed for communication in private, reading by oneself, rather than in public settings. It also created a sense of the private ownership of words. Writing also separates the knower or speaker from what is known, therefore making possible introspection. "Opening the psyche as never before, not only to the external, objective world, [is] quite distinct from itself but also to the interior self against whom the objective world is set," Ong wrote (1982, p. 14). With printing, sight rather than hearing begins to dominate consciousness.

Printing enabled the emergence of the newspaper and novel. Although these forms of communication cannot be explained solely on the basis of the technology of printing (many other economic, social, and historical developments contributed to their emergence), it is fair to say that they could not have come into existence without the invention of printing technology. The merger of the printing press and movable type made texts cheaper because it cost far less to make a second copy of a text than to write and produce the first copy. Affordable reading material helped to spread literacy.

Raymond Williams (1965) has pointed out the ironic consequences of this spread of literacy in the seventeenth through nineteenth centuries. For example, the working class was taught to read so that they could read the Bible as well as manuals for the new industrial machinery, but it was difficult to control what a literate audience consumed. Workers often read political tracts and newspapers, which contributed to the growing political gap between the classes of workers and capitalists of the Industrial Revolution. This helped create new political forms of organization and power, such as political parties and democratic governments.

Marshall McLuhan (1964b) makes another claim for the impact of printing technology: Printing altered the very structure of human consciousness and thought. According to McLuhan, the physical relationship between the reader's eyes and the text comes to define a linear mode of thinking. Just as eyes move across the page, line after line, in a rigorous and necessary way, so too does one begin to think in similarly rigorously linear fashion, one idea logically connected to the next.

The result of such linear modes of thought is a different conception of time and space. It is in the age of printing that European powers explored and colonized the world, spreading their culture, their politics, and their religions across the globe. Time becomes a linear vector moving toward an indefinite future defined as progress. The belief in progress reinforced the drive for knowledge and discovery that printing had opened up. What followed was the age of scientific discovery.

ELECTRONIC CULTURE

When we think about electronic media, we are likely to think about radio, television, movies, and computers. But to understand these developments, we need to go back to the emergence of the telegraph in the nineteenth century. The telegraph had at least two important consequences: it reorganized people's perception of space and time, and it allowed for new kinds of organizational control. The telegraph enabled the almost instantaneous transmission of messages across space, and it fostered a rational organization of time. The need to coordinate the measurement of time around the globe gave rise to the establishment of standard time zones and the fixing of Greenwich Mean Time as the norm defining the correct time at any place in the world.

According to James W. Carey (1989),

> The simplest and most important point about the telegraph is that it marked the decisive separation of "transportation" and "communication." Until the telegraph, these words were synonymous. The telegraph ended that identity and allowed symbols to move independently of geography and independently of and faster than transport. . . . The great theoretical significance of the technology lay not merely in the separation but also in the use of the telegraph as both a model of and a mechanism for control of the physical movement of things, specifically for the railroad. That is the fundamental discovery: not only can information move independently of and faster than physical entities, but it

can also be a simulation of and control mechanism for what has been left behind. (pp. 213, 215)

The telegraph merely began a process that has continued to this day at an ever-increasing rate. Whatever one's opinions about the shape of the modern world, it is fair to say that the new electronic means of communication have revolutionized not only how people communicate but how they live as well. If print media centralized and made knowledge hierarchical and then the printing press began a process of dispersion and democratization of knowledge, then the electronic media have drastically accelerated both of these trends.

If printing enabled the transmission of messages across time, their ability to cross space was still severely limited. Although a ruler could now send a message to the far reaches of his or her empire and be fairly certain of the accuracy of the transmission, the process relied on the physical transportation of the written message. Even books that could be sent around the world, creating a single audience for an identical text, required the physical movement of the book as an object. But with the advent of electronic means of communication, instantaneous transportation of messages around the globe became a reality. A new form of empire, expanded across space, becomes possible, according to Innis (1950).

When information is beamed through the airwaves or through wires and cable, it becomes far more difficult to regulate and control access to it; many commentators have noted that the dissolution of the Warsaw Pact and the breakup of the Soviet Union were accelerated by the porosity of their borders to democratic messages from the West made available through the electronic media.

Furthermore, if print individualized and privatized what had been an essentially public oral culture, the effects of the electronic media have been both to reinforce the sense of individuality and privacy and to create new forms of what McLuhan has called the "global village."

Like books, the electronic media have become, over time, personal, mobile, and private. People no longer have to sit in large theater palaces or even in living rooms to watch movies or television programs; miniaturization allows them to carry music and television and computer networks in the palms of their hands. Furthermore, like books, the electronic media have developed in two directions simultaneously: They have created larger audiences for particular messages (the Bible and network television), and they have created highly selective audience segments organized around particular tastes, from philosophical books to the Home Shopping Network to thousands of bulletin boards and user groups in the cyberspace of the Internet.

Thus, as Carey (1989) argues, the electronic media have radically transformed our awareness and conception of both time and space. Space now can be measured in temporal terms: by the time it takes to transmit a fax, a television image, a computer file. Space no longer appears to be an obstacle in the organization of social, political, and economic relationships.

Time, too, has changed in people's understanding. The invention of computers has speeded up this process, leading to the introduction of almost infinitely small divisions. Can anyone imagine how short a nanosecond is? Time has become increasingly fractured and discontinuous. Printing challenged the stability and continuity of oral culture and created a commitment to change and progress; time in print culture was understood as continual, linking the past with the present. The electronic media seem to create real gaps between generations, and the time span of generational differences seems to get smaller and smaller even as the gaps become more and more pronounced.

There is a significant debate about the consequences of electronic communication for the exercise of control and power in the modern world. Some have suggested that the result of these technologies is the centralization of information and power; others argue that a countervailing tendency of the electronic media is to disperse and decentralize the control of information and power. The proliferation of regional television production centers (for example, Brazil and Mexico are major production centers for Portuguese and Spanish programming) and film production centers (Hong Kong and India) are examples of the diffusion or decentralization of power. Yet, there has also been a reconcentration of power. The globalization of film and television entertainment programming is a countervailing force to regional film and television production centers.

It is clear that with the electronic media, for the first time in history, the vast majority of the world's population can now participate in the dominant cultural forms and practices. There is some debate about whether the electronic media require literacy, whether the new media have introduced new forms of literacy, or whether they are creating an illiterate population. However, as Walter Benjamin (1969) argued in the first half of the twentieth century, the incorporation of the masses into the cultural arena as both consumers and potential producers of cultural products is a revolution. The effects of this are not well understood.

Some observers of the contemporary world have argued that the electronic media are transforming basic modes of awareness and thinking. If oral cultures are largely aural, emphasizing hearing and sound, and if print cultures are largely visual, emphasizing sight and the ability to read, then the new electronic cultures are multisensorial, requiring a constant monitoring and coordinating of a wide range of sensory experience and information. Moreover, although it is difficult to know how to describe the formal properties of today's electronic media products, one thing is clear: they are rarely linear in their logic and narrative form. The linear conventions of both time and space are constantly violated and played with, and the traditional logic of rationality seems irrelevant. And the impact of these technologies on the evolution of human existence is not at all clear. We are simply too close to the historical emergence of these technologies.

CRITICISMS OF TECHNOLOGICAL DETERMINISM

These grand narratives that lead from oral to electronic culture offer important insights about the role of communication in human culture, but they can be criticized as examples of theories of technological determinism. Technological determinism is the belief that technology is the principal if not only cause of historical change. Whether theories of technological determinism are optimistic or pessimistic about the present and the future, they assume that history is guaranteed in advance. Their proponents assume that the future is the result of the necessary and inevitable unfolding of the consequences of the past and present. Such theorists fail to adequately consider the ways in which people make history. When talking about the context of media power, one needs to recognize that the context is not stable and fixed; it is in fact constantly changing over and through time. Any discussion of media power must take history into account, both in the sense that the media themselves change through history and in the sense that the media's place and power in society are constantly changing.

It is perhaps easiest to identify technological determinism in the writings of Marshall McLuhan, who assumed that people's normal use of technology necessarily modifies their consciousness. McLuhan argued that the forms of communication technology (oral, print, electronic) available to people at a particular historical moment determine the ways they can perceive reality and the logics they use to understand it. To McLuhan, the content of the media, the actual messages, are irrelevant. This is the meaning of his aphorism "the medium is the message."

McLuhan's theory clearly assumes that technology determines everything else in history and, moreover, that communication technology is the crucial invention for humankind. McLuhan's is only one version of the common view that places the burden of historical change on the shoulders of communication technology. It is important to realize that on a smaller scale, many people make a similar assumption when they think about and often criticize "what television has done to society" or "how computers are changing the nature of work, social relations, and ways of thinking."

In his book, *Television: Technology and Cultural Form*, Raymond Williams (1975) offers a general critique of technological determination. Williams argues that all of the versions of determinism assume that technological invention is accidental and that it is the result of "an internal process of research and development," but he argues, these are both false. Communications technologies have always been sought in the context of solving particular social needs. These needs were often military and political, not economic and cultural. For instance, radio communication was first used by the Navy for ship-to-shore communication, and only later was it exploited for commercial purposes. Thus, Williams argues that we need to restore human motivation and intention into our understanding of how technologies are created and their role in history. Technologies are used in direct response to perceived social needs and problems. They are not merely symptoms but are intentional attempts at solutions. In this way, Williams attempts to recognize the complexity of the relationships among media, their contexts, and the production of history.

Technological determinism also ignores the active role of people (and social institutions) in making their own lives. It assumes that the use of a technology is prescribed by its own structure, rather than understanding that any technology can be used in any number of different ways and can be restructured according to the demands that different uses may impose. Depending on how people use them, technologies can have very different effects, not only on individuals but on society and history as well. That is, nothing essential to a technology determines its impact on its users.

FROM MODERNITY TO POSTMODERNITY

There is another grand narrative about the role of communication and culture in history: the description of the passage from modernity to postmodernity.

There is vast disagreement over just when the modern era begins—and ends. Some critics mark the beginning of the modern with the end of the Renaissance period in the sixteenth century. Others locate the beginning of the modern with the advent of Enlightenment philosophy in the eighteenth century; and still others distinguish between the Enlightenment and the modern, dating the latter from the mid- or late nineteenth century.

Discussions of the modern are quite dense and difficult, for they entail the relationship among three different concepts or domains: modernization, modernism, and modernity. In its simplest terms, these can be understood respectively as the historical processes, cultural practices, and social experience of change.

Modernization describes the broad spectrum of interrelated historical forces that radically changed the world since the beginning of the Industrial Revolution, capitalism, and colonialism in Europe and America. Thus, modernization is more than simply a question of industrialization, of the changing modes and relations of production. It includes as well new economic relations of distribution and consumption and new commodity markets. It includes new technologies and scientific developments, some of which contributed to changes in the patterns of social migration both within countries (urbanization) and across nations (diasporas). And it includes political (democratization, the modern nation-state, imperialism) and cultural events (public education and museums), as well as changes in the relations between them. For instance, Antonio Gramsci (1971) argued that with modernization, ideological consensus, rather than force, began to play a central role in the legitimation of power. And Michel Foucault (1977) argued that modernization brought new forms of power—normalization, disciplinarity, governmentality, and biopolitics—in which governments increasingly attempted to regulate the population by making people the object of knowledge and producing subjects who were responsible for policing themselves according to the norms of power.

Modernism refers to the cultural forms, discourses, practices, and relations, both elite and popular, both commercial and folk, with which people attempted to make sense of, represent, judge, rail against, surrender to, intervene into, navigate through, or escape from the New Worlds of modernization. These cultural practices and products were themselves shaped by the new forms of leisure and communications technology put into place by processes of modernization. That is, modernism usually refers to the cultural developments that began in the sixteenth and seventeenth centuries. And yet, it is more often used to refer to cultural developments of the late nineteenth century, which fully expressed in a variety of ways the pressures and consequences of modernization. It indexes all of the developments in art, beginning with the emergence of Impressionism and ending with Abstract Expressionism (Picasso, Gauguin, Duchamps, Renoir, Kandinsky, Klee, Georgia O'Keeffe). It included developments in literature, from the Bloomsbury group of writers in England (Virginia Woolf) to self-conscious forms of writing offered by Gertrude Stein, T. S. Eliot, Luigi Pirandello, Samuel Beckett, and James Joyce. It includes as well the architectural innovations of Louis Sullivan, Frank Lloyd Wright, and Mies van der Rohe. Modernism also has to include the new forms of mass media and popular culture—the dime novel, the Hollywood film, jazz, and the radio soap opera.

Modernity refers to the changing structure and nature of the lived social realities to which modernism and modernization responded and which were themselves shaped by both modernism and modernization. This is obviously an ambiguous and difficult concept to specify.

BOX 2.1

Modernism

Modernism is the generic name for a wide range of movements in the arts that developed at the end of the nineteenth century. It is difficult to characterize the enormous diversity encompassed by this term, and there are significant differences among critics who have attempted to define the term. Nevertheless, we can offer a number of characteristics:

1. Modernism was characterized by an emphasis on formal experimentation and a concern with the intrinsic properties of the medium (painting, language, architectural forms) rather than extrinsic criteria of judgment.
2. Modernism was fascinated with the new technologies and logics of industrialization and modernization, with the processes of urbanization, streamlining, efficiency, and so on.
3. Modernism emphasized unity and the totalizing power of art as a metaperspective on human reality. It sought a comprehensive metanarrative, whether at the level of the individual, the society, or history.
4. Modernism often constructed itself as a critique of the alienation produced by the modern world. In response, it emphasized the centrality of the power of subjectivity and consciousness as the basis of political, ethical, and aesthetic critique. And consequently, it placed great emphasis on the author as the source of the critical vision.
5. Modernism located itself as an avant-garde outside the center or mainstream of European and American culture. Because it assumed that it was criticizing the most fundamental values and assumptions of modern society, it assumed that its failure to be recognized was a sign of its success; it was often satisfied to "shock" the mainstream of society and assumed that its truth and value could only be recognized in the future.

Examples of modernism range from the literature of Kafka, Gertrude Stein, D. H. Lawrence, and James Joyce to movements in painting such as Impressionism and Abstract Expressionism.

It attempts to describe what it felt like to live in the new modern world, a world that attempted to break away from the customs, norms, and traditions of earlier generations. According to philosopher Marshall Berman (1982),

> To be modern is to find ourselves in an environment that promises us adventure, power, joy, growth, transformation of ourselves and the world—and, at the same time, that threatens to destroy everything we have, everything we know, everything we are. (p. 15)

As Karl Marx put it, in modernity, "all that is solid melts into air." Marx was suggesting that modernity is the experience of constant change, flux, or transformation, the search for the new, the turning away from tradition. Modernity is not just the fact of the development and change, but the yearning for change. Modernity involves the recognition that change cannot be stopped and that if one stops to rest, the world will pass you by or you will be swept away by these changes.

Many different intellectual traditions of the twentieth century can be seen as responding to the perceived historical rupture that was signaled in different forms in a vision of the modern. The modern in every instance always implies this rupture, an alienation from some past that served critics both as a measure of the change and a norm against which to judge the changes. Sometimes that past was defined by an image of community, of face-to-face communication, of pure art unsullied by the media and commercial interests, of traditional forms of value, rationality, and social relations. Think about how common it is for people who argue about the "past" to harken back to an idyllic time when "things were better," when life was simpler, when people were happier. Thus, the modern is defined on the one hand by the relations between modernization, modernity, and modernism. But on the other hand, it is also defined by its opposition to the old, to tradition, to the past.

Recently, some cultural and media critics have argued that another rupture in history has taken place sometime since the end of the Second World War, probably since the 1970s. Such critics argue that we are now living in a postmodern age.

Capitalism has changed. Transnational corporations, accountable to no nation-state or political ideology, have created not only global markets for goods and services but also global networks of production. New computer technologies have been applied to every stage of the economic process (such as manufacturing, financing, distribution, and exchange) resulting in decentralization and automation; markets and labor processes have been reorganized (emphasizing a multiskilled involved labor force); unions have declined, with increases in subcontracting and part-time labor; economies of scope have risen (consumption-driven small-batch production runs with high levels of product differentiation) to replace economies of scale.

If modernity is about mass production, mass culture, everything mass, postmodernity is about returning to the small and the flexible (flexible specialization of labor, flexible production). If capitalism in modernity is committed to maximizing profit by producing more for less and then attempting to persuade consumers to buy the products, capitalism in postmodernity is committed to maximizing profit by developing systems of production and distribution that can respond quickly to the different demands of smaller groups of consumers (obviously such demands may still be shaped by advertising). If modernity focuses on people as laborers, consumers, and family members, postmodernity constructs and celebrates identities as multiple, fragmented subjects defined entirely by consumer and lifestyle choices.

In postmodernity, there is no human activity that is free from capitalism, commodification, and the profit motive. No space in people's everyday life remains outside these economic processes. This is most apparent in the case of culture and communication, which have become totally commercialized. The result is that "no society has ever been saturated with signs and messages like this one," according to the American literary critic Fred Jameson (1991). This "omnipresence of culture" has important consequences for the experience of postmodernity.

Another mark of postmodernity is the increasing mobility, both voluntary and forced, of human populations around the world. The migration of whole societies, the problem of refugees, the incorporation of migrant workers, have created a global multicultural society that challenges the ability of any nation to define a reasonably homogeneous cultural identity or a set of cultural norms. The case of the failure of America's "melting pot" image is a telling example. Although the United States has always been a nation of immigrants, it managed, at least until the Second World War, to maintain a sense of itself as a whole, a European-derived, English-speaking nation. But new migrations— Asian, African, Latino—have challenged this image and made it almost impossible to define a central cultural identity for the nation. Moreover, the American experience has become the norm in other parts of the world as well. People's identities have become fractured, pluralized, and hybridized, and populations that were silent and marginalized in the past have suddenly moved to the center of the historical and cultural stage.

The rapid development of new communication technologies, in particular the computer and other information media, are essential to postmodernity. According to the French social philosopher Jean Baudrillard (1988), who echoes McLuhan's technological determinism, this is the most important factor bringing about the postmodern era.

Postmodernism as a set of cultural practices or a new aesthetic norm was first used in the field of architecture as a challenge to the high modernist form of the urban skyscraper, which typified most of twentieth-century urban building. Fred Jameson has offered the most commonly used description of postmodernism by describing features that cut across many cultural forms and media.

First is the *disappearance of depth*. By this, Jameson refers to the irrelevance of anything outside of the text, of the normal assumption that cultural texts refer to something else—such as deeper meanings or the expression of an author's intention or the representation of an external reality. In postmodern texts, only surfaces matter, only images are real.

Second is what Jameson describes as *pastiche*, which refers to the absence of any normative rules and definitions of coherent styles and forms. Perhaps the easiest examples to illustrate this are buildings by such postmodern architects as Philip Johnson and Michael Graves. Both of these architects combine elements from a wide range of historical architectural styles, from Greek arches to Gothic spires and modern glass walls, in one structure.

Third, Jameson points to the *schizophrenic* character of postmodernist works; such texts are frequently fragmented, both formally and temporally. Characters themselves are often inconsistent and seem utterly incapable of unifying past, present, and future into coherent stories, and authors seem unwilling to create coherent narratives.

Fourth, both history and the sense of history have been reduced to an experience of *nostalgia*, a romanticized longing for the past. The attempt to appropriate a missing past comes increasingly to resemble a search for a lost fashion, according to Jameson.

Last, and perhaps most controversially, is what Jameson calls the *postmodern sublime*. By this, he refers to that experience which cannot be represented in contemporary cultural codes. For Jameson, this unrepresentable dimension is the inability to construct maps of the contemporary spaces of everyday life within capitalism. As the world is changing so rapidly, under the influence of global multinational capitalism and decentered communication networks, it has become more and more difficult to locate oneself within the system of social relationships and political geography. Jameson thinks that people need "cognitive maps" of the space of their social lives, where they fit in some idealized social structure. But these cognitive maps are ever harder and harder to maintain, or even construct. If you have ever walked into a postmodern building, perhaps you can better understand this idea. One of the most common reactions to such buildings is that people often find it difficult to navigate—they can't quite figure out how to get from the lobby to their room, or from their room back to the lobby. Oddly enough, having made the trip once does not seem to make it any easier the second time.

Other critics have described the postmodern sublime in different terms. Perhaps the most important of these, and perhaps the most powerful description of the nature of the experience of postmodernity is given in the work of Jean Baudrillard (1983b), and in particular, in his notion of the *simulacrum*. According to Baudrillard, in the postmodern world, the difference between an image (or code) and reality is no longer important. In fact, if anything, reality is measured against images rather than images against reality. Consider the image of a Boston sports bar on the television show, *Cheers*. When the network wanted to go to such a bar during the World Series to interview local fans, what they ended up doing was going to the set of *Cheers* and interviewing the cast. Baudrillard would view this as perfectly reasonable and sensible in the postmodern age. How many times has someone seen a movie and said to him- or herself, didn't I read about this, or hear about this on the news, sometime in the past? And then a few months later, they read about it or see it on the news and say to themselves, didn't I see this in a movie? Baudrillard's point is that as the ability to distinguish reality from its images disappears, so does the difference between them.[1]

Consider Baudrillard's description of Disneyland:

Disneyland is there to conceal the fact that it is the "real" country, all of "real" America, which is Disneyland (just as prisons are there to conceal the fact that it is the social in its entirety, in its banal omnipresence, which is carceral). Disneyland is presented as imaginary in order to

BOX 2.2

Modernism and Postmodernism

Modernism	*Postmodernism*
romanticism/Symbolism	paraphysics/Dadaism
form (conjunctive, closed)	antiform (disjunctive, open)
purpose	play
design	chance
hierarchy	anarchy
mastery/logos	exhaustion/silence
art object/finished work	process/performance/happening
distance	participation
creation/totalization/synthesis	decreation/deconstruction/antithesis
presence	absence
centering	dispersal
genre/boundary	text/intertext
semantics	rhetoric
paradigm	syntagm
hypotaxis	parataxis
metaphor	metonymy
selection	combination
root/depth	rhizome/surface
interpretation/reading	against interpretation/misreading
signified	signifier
lisible (readerly)	scriptible (writerly)
narrative/grande histoire	anti-narrative/petite histoire
master code	idiolect
symptom	desire
type	mutant
genital/phallic	polymorphous/androgynous
paranoia	schizophrenia
origin/cause	difference-differance/trace
God the Father	The Holy Ghost
metaphysics	irony
determinacy	indeterminacy
transcendence	immanence

SOURCE: Hassan, 1982, pp. 267-268.

make us believe that the rest is real when in fact all of Los Angeles and the America surrounding it are no longer real, but of the order of the hyperreal and of simulation. It is no longer a question of a false representation of reality (ideology), but of concealing the fact that the real is no longer real and thus of saving the reality principle.

Finally, Baudrillard (1983a), drawing on McLuhan, argues that this historical transformation has significant implications for the very nature of media and the possibilities of communication:

> In short, the medium is the message signifies not only the end of the message, but also the end of the medium. There are no longer media in the literal sense of the term (I am talking above all about the electronic mass media)—that is to say, a power mediating between one reality and another, between one state of the real and another—neither in content nor in form. (p. 102)

Baudrillard's version of postmodernity depends on the power of the computer and other new information technologies to erase the distinction between the virtual and the real worlds. As a result, his theory of postmodernity is open to the charge of technological determinism. Other postmodernist visions, although not determinist, do tend to portray the future in rather apocalyptic and cataclysmic terms.

These narratives of media history offer insights into the role of the forms and modes of communication in human history. As we discuss the power and influence of today's media on modern life, we should keep these narratives in mind because debates about the power of the media are often debates about the future—about the futures we fear and the futures we desire. Every new form of communication has given rise to both optimistic and pessimistic visions of the future. The conclusions often depend upon conflicting definitions of what is important and what is trivial about the media, about what is fundamentally reshaping social life and what is a passing fad.

NOTE

1. Baudrillard (1983b) argues that there have been three stages of human history. He describes each stage by the nature of the assumed relationship between the image and reality. In the first stage, the image was seen as a counter-

feit, as the approximation of a world whose truth always remained outside of the image. Thus, there was assumed to be a natural truth, the law of god, for example, which images could only dimly copy. In the second stage, the image was taken to be the source of reality. Language produces reality, in much the way that we have described it in this text. But in the third, postmodern stage, neither term, language or reality, can be privileged, and the difference between them has disappeared or, in Baudrillard's terms, *imploded*. This is the simulacrum: the model against which both reality and its image are judged. The simulacrum is a model, like the genetic code.

Media People and Organizations

othing could be more important in understanding the processes of making media than understanding *who makes the media* and *how* they are "made"—the rules, practices, and procedures that govern what we see, read, and hear.

MEDIAMAKING AND LEVELS OF ANALYSIS

A key to understanding who makes the media is the idea of levels of analysis. By this, we mean that production of just about anything in an organized society involves phenomena at different strata, and at each of those strata or levels, variations are reflected in what is produced. As we ascend a "ladder of abstraction," we can think of media products as the creations of individual people, of media organizations, of media industries. Furthermore, the media together constitute an institution, and the ultimate shape of media is influenced by the interaction of the media institution with other social institutions. Finally, media are influenced by the culture in which they are produced: American media, for example, are similar to the media of other industrial countries, but there are important differences between U.S. media and those elsewhere. Understanding who makes the media, then, prompts us to ask different sorts of questions, and get different answers, at several different levels of analysis—the individual, the organizational, the industrial, the institutional, and the cultural.

MEDIA PEOPLE

More than a million people are directly engaged in the creation of media in the United States. Some—Sheryl Crow, Ted Koppel, or Jay Leno, for example—are well known and instantly recognizable, and they impart a particular flavor or spin to their products—a Sheryl Crow song covered by someone else isn't the same song, *Nightline* with Ted Koppel is recognizably different from other TV news and public affairs shows. What makes them different are individual differences among their creators—differences in talent, creativity, energy, and a host of other "individual difference" variables—the interests, values, gender, and ethnicities of the individuals creating them. Sometimes, in fact, even in very complex media organizations, the persona of the star becomes virtually identified with the product itself: For 30 years, when Johnny Carson starred in *The Tonight Show,* the show was popularly referred to as "Johnny Carson" (as in "I heard this joke on Johnny Carson last night . . . ").

MEDIA ORGANIZATIONS AND INDUSTRIES

However, *The Tonight Show,* starring Johnny Carson or Jay Leno, isn't just Johnny or Jay. Although Johnny or Jay (or David Letterman) is each obviously the linchpin of his program, the show would not go on without a hundred other people in different roles to get the show on the air. In addition to the star, we need an announcer, a bandleader and band, a producer and director, three or more camera operators, lighting and audio personnel, makeup artists, joke writers, researchers, and gaffers (electricians), not to mention the guests. Each performs a particular and essential role, and some clearly have more influence on the particular look or sound of the product than others. Moreover, *The Tonight Show Starring Jay Leno* is not just the product of these people *as individuals*; it is the product of an organization. The fact that media products are almost all created by complex organizations is important for several reasons. First, when something is the creation of a single individual, he or she has virtually total control over its creation and the shape the product takes. When products, however, are the creatures of organizations, "authorship" becomes more complicated, and interesting questions about creativity and control and coordination of production can be asked. And as we note below, we actually know quite a lot about rules and regularities that govern the processes of media created by organizations. In the *Tonight Show* case, several organizations are necessary to get that program on the air—starting with its production company and the NBC Television network (a corporate division of the General Electric Company, Inc.). The show is piped into homes via a local television station and possibly a cable television organization as well (and the local TV station and cable company are likely owned by larger media chains). Some of these organizations have a great deal of control over both the overall shape of the program and what is on any particular program, and some have almost none. Equally important, organizations are bureaucracies, which means that they are hierarchically structured so that some people are superiors, and others are inferiors; that they are governed by rules and routines that must be followed by all individuals; and that they strive for efficiency. We cannot account for how a particular program takes exactly the shape it does, even a particular Wednesday night *Tonight Show* episode, just by knowing all there is to know about the people preparing it. Characteristics of the organization, and of organizations in general, also help explain that. Put another way, a particular Wednesday night episode would be quite similar, although not exactly the same, regardless of whether the host was Leno or someone else, whether the first guest was Julia Roberts, Chris Rock, or Tori Spelling.

Still a third layer must be described to begin to talk about how the media product takes the shape it does. At the *industrial* level, we would note that certain elements characterize the products of an industry, regardless of the people *and* the organizations within the industry. We all have expectations about what a newspaper looks like, what it contains, that are different from our expectations about a book or a magazine or a television show. The differences are in content, style, and form, and they flow from the different expectations, practices, and routines that the makers of media products in each industry must follow. Each media industry, too, is characterized by different *genres* of product (see Chapters 5 and 6) that make the production of content predictable for both its producers and consumers. In the television industry, for example, we all have a very good idea what the "typical" television evening news program is like: *Channel 7 Eyewitness News* looks remarkably similar, whether we are watching Channel 7 in New York, or Boise, or Phoenix. It will open with a teaser of the top few stories and a brief tape clip, and after a commercial break, it will feature a half-dozen hard-news stories, all or almost all with tape; none of the stories will be longer than 90 seconds. There will be a male and a female anchor (the male will be older than the female), a weather person, and a sports anchor. One or two will be members of a minority group. Weather will be after the midprogram commercial break, and sports after the next break, and the "news team" will send us off with a "feel-good" feature. The form is set and so familiar that we rarely notice it, much less stop to ask *why*. A large part of the answer to why TV programs are so similar is that there are industrywide constraints—unwritten "rules" that characterize what TV is. Note that these rules are not chiseled in stone—they are not inherent in the medium itself but evolve from complex interactions over time. They maintain themselves because they are familiar, taken for granted, and usually unquestioned, by both those in the industry and the audience. The format allows for a degree of predictability that is an important characteristic of the mass media, both for the audience and the producers

MEDIA AS INSTITUTIONS

The media constitute an institution in their own right—that is, media share enough common characteristics with each other that we feel comfortable making statements that begin "The media are. . . ." What media are, the roles and functions they fulfill, what they say, is shaped or constrained by the relationships that the media institution has with other institutions. When we get to this level of analysis, however, we usually can only infer institutional influence from interpreting the real behaviors of individuals or organizations representing those institutions—by doing history as we describe in Chapter 2.

Let us point to an example from pop music. Although Americans value freedom of speech and in general believe that mass media should be free from governmental influence through censorship, institutions' influence—even from the government—over media can be direct as well as indirect—and powerful. In the late 1980s, a small group was organized as the Parents' Music Resource Center (PMRC). The PMRC, sometimes identified in the press as a group of Washington, D.C., housewives, was credited with forcing the recorded music industry into self-regulation. How could such a tiny organization exert such influence over a multibillion-dollar industry? A large part of the answer is *who* PMRC's leaders were: "Tipper" Gore, the wife of Al Gore, and Susan Baker, the wife of James Baker, who has served in several Cabinet posts. These kinships were sufficient to guarantee access to, and extensive coverage by, the national news media. These political connections suggested to the recording industry that if it did not undertake self-censorship, more direct and energetic intervention by the federal government might follow. In fact, large record producers did institute a labeling scheme to forestall government regulation. Moreover, we should ask *why* PMRC was able to force itself onto the public agenda *when* it did. After all, at least since the birth of rock 'n roll, objections have been raised both to the content and the style of pop music—in the late 1950s and early 1960s, some conservative ministers and even some radio deejays sponsored bonfires in which rock records were burned.[1] Why did PMRC leave its mark in the late 1980s? For the threat of government regulation to be taken seriously by the industry, record executives must have believed that the threat was credible. They did because the climate of opinion in the country was more socially conservative than it had been in the 1970s, and pop music sales were relatively flat. In sum, the fight to avoid censorship was not one they cared to risk, despite protests from a number of recording artists (for further discussion, see Grossberg, 1992). In short, the episode illustrates an example of the flexing of institutional power—an implied threat of governmental restraint.

MEDIA AND CULTURE

At the "highest" level of analysis, there are aspects of any culture, above, beyond, and outside its media, that are reflected in media content and form. The media do not reside outside their own society and culture but are a part of them, both influencing them and being influenced by them in turn.

BOX 3.1

Cultural Differences in Media:
U.S. and Italian TV News

An analysis of a week's worth of Italian and American television network newscasts during then-President Reagan's trip to Europe in June 1982 found that news broadcasts in the two nations varied dramatically, both in content and in *representational form.*

In both content and form, the differences are consistent with each nation's culture and institutions. The content of American television paid far more attention to international news and to the nation's chief executive, and slightly more attention to the national executive branch of government, compared to Italian TV news. Italian TV news, on the other hand, paid far more attention than American TV news to political parties and to labor unions (during the week, no American air time at all was given to unions). These differences reflect political reality: The center of national political power in the United States is the president and his administration, whereas in Italy, which has changed administrations slightly more often than once a year since World War II, the political parties and unions are the center of power.

One might have expected American TV news to devote more time to international news because it is an international power with extensive foreign interests and commitments, whereas Italy is not.

Even more interesting are differences in forms of representation. American network news programs tend to be thematic: TV news producers make a concerted effort to link stories together, to provide a common theme to keep audience attention. In the study by American scholar Dan Hallin and Italian researcher Paolo Mancini (1984/1985), Italian TV news tended to be disjointed, with one story wholly unrelated to the one preceding or following it. The same held true within stories: American stories tended to be unified by a common theme, and journalists tended to be interpretive; to our eyes, an Italian story would seem to be disconnected, and interpretation was usually left to the sources in the story, rather than the journalist. The unity, or lack of it, could be seen in the way each medium used visual images: in American TV news, the visual image was intimately connected to the spoken text; in Italian TV, the mov-

Probably the easiest way to see this is by using a comparative approach. If culture did *not* affect media, then media would be very similar in every society. TV news, for example, would be pretty much the same in, say, Italy, as it is in the United States. But this clearly is not the case; not only is TV news different, but most other media are as well,

ing image was usually literally background. The two also varied in their use of "the common man": In their study period, Hallin and Mancini found that one third of the people appearing on U.S. evening news programs were "nonofficials," selected by journalists to portray average citizens, for example, protesters or families of soldiers. On Italian TV news, virtually all sources were people deliberately selected to represent the views of organized social and political groups.

Finally, the relationship between the news organization and its audience differed. When an American TV journalist uses the first person, especially the first person plural (we), it is almost always to refer to the news organization: "Up the road at *our* foreign desk in London," Peter Jennings would say. But when an Italian journalist uses the first person plural, it is to refer to himself or herself *and* to the audience: "Let's see what is going on in Lebanon." Moreover, they note, first-person usage by American TV journalists is rare; for Italian journalists it is commonplace:

> The television journalist in the United States, in other words, will not normally "cross the screen" to put himself "on the side" of the audience in relation to events; while the Italian announcer routinely moves back and forth across that invisible boundary. (p. 215)

Why were the narrative forms in each so different? Hallin and Mancini argue that part of the explanation derives from economic differences: American network TV news is highly commercialized, and its producers must fight for an audience by presenting an attractive, visually engaging package; Italian network TV news was not so constrained. But perhaps more important is that the programs reflect very different political cultures. In Italy, the "public sphere" in which ideology and policy are debated is very much filled by political parties, unions, and industrial associations, and on Italian TV, it is their representatives who provide meaning and interpretation of the day's events. In America, political parties are no longer strong or central enough to do this, and most other organized political groups—trade unions, industrial associations, and other interest groups—generally pursue narrow, not broad, political agendas. In the United States, Hallin and Mancini argued, the press and the presidency are the only two institutions strong enough and able to serve as the interpreters, the arbiters of political meanings, and hence American TV news was more active and more autonomous than its Italian counterpart.

not necessarily in broad form (even in other languages, we would recognize a Japanese newspaper or magazine as a newspaper or magazine, a Russian news broadcast as a news broadcast) but in other ways—in content, in treatment of content, and even in the assumed relationship that writers have with their audience.

MEDIAMAKING IN CONTEXT

Our discussion of levels of analysis should make clearer that media are "made" in a specific context. Individuals and groups do creative production work, but that work is guided and shaped by the organizations they work in. The individuals and organizations, in turn, are shaped and guided by the industries they inhabit, and the individuals, organizations, and industries reside in a society that shapes and guides them as well.

At each of these levels, different influences operate on the making of media.

PEOPLE

The many individual characteristics of mass communicators can indeed influence the content and character of the products they create. For example, at least since the 1960s, women and minority groups have actively argued and worked against their underrepresentation in the media industries. For example, the American Society of Newspaper Editors (1997) reported that in 1996, only 11% of daily newspaper newsroom workers were members of minority groups (5.4% African American, 3.3% Latino, 2% Asian American, and .04% American Indian). Why is this a matter of concern? For at least two reasons—the desire of members of minority groups for equal access to jobs and fair consideration for promotion and advancement, and the belief that if minority groups are to receive fair and accurate portrayal in the news, minorities must be represented in newsrooms. In other words, this argument is that a personal characteristic of the journalist—in this case ethnicity or race—can make a difference in *what* news gets covered, and *how*.

Similarly, conservative critics of the news media have argued for many years that the media are liberally biased. Among the evidence they offer is survey data showing that American journalists, and especially "elite" journalists at the television networks and major newspapers, are more likely to identify themselves as political liberals than are Americans in general (see, for example, Lichter, Rothman, & Lichter, 1986). (We will see shortly that liberal critics argue that the media are conservatively biased, but their evidence comes from a higher level of analysis.) And several writers have suggested that the big-city and Jew-

BOX 3.2

Media People

In 1992-1993, the most recent year for which we have information, the U.S. Bureau of Labor Statistics estimated that more than 1.1 million people were employed—either full-time, part-time or as freelancers—in mass communication:

— 67,000 reporters and correspondents

— 232,000 writers and editors

— 67,000 radio and television announcers and newscasters

— 109,000 public relations specialists

— 427,000 marketing, advertising, and public relations managers

— 120,000 photographers and camera operators, about half of whom are self-employed

— 73,000 actors, directors, and producers

These numbers do not include many others who are employed by the media, from delivery drivers to business executives, from secretaries and printers to studio musicians. Further, it does not include many amateurs working in fanzines or as independent creators of Web pages.

SOURCE: Shoemaker & Reese, 1996.

ish backgrounds of Hollywood producers and screenwriters have shaped the content of American motion pictures and television programs (Gabler, 1988; Stein, 1979).

There are two views about how individual differences influence media content. First is that individual creators derive from their backgrounds and experiences the attitudes and ideas that shape what they create. This is clearly the case, for example, in fiction writing, when authors may derive their characters and stories from people and events in their own lives. Second is that to the degree that *groups* share a characteristic, then that characteristic may show up in much of the content produced by that group. In *The View from Sunset Boulevard*, for example, writer Ben Stein (1979) argues that big business is portrayed as corrupt or criminal on American television because the small number of TV writers and writer-producers (he estimates that no more than 200 people work steadily in the business) overwhelmingly share antibusiness attitudes.

These two arguments lead us in two directions. First, we need to divide values, attitudes, and norms that shape media content into two categories—those that are *general*, pertaining to someone's overall view of the world, and those that are *occupational* or *professional*, those sets of values related to a person's media job. In the latter case, for example, public relations specialists certified by the Public Relations Society of America subscribe to a code of ethics that requires them not to intentionally deceive others. Second, how much—and how—an individual can shape a media product depends a lot on the power-resources she or he can bring to bear when that product is created. Because most media are produced within complex organizations with hierarchical structures (that is, a boss makes and enforces the rules, and the subordinates follow them), we would expect that those higher up the organizational ladder should have the power: Presidents give orders, and those below carry them out, and this is the rule—sometimes. But the power to shape media products is not just top-down; media professionals do have some resources in making messages the way they think they should be made. In general, the power or autonomy that any worker has is directly related to that worker's indispensability to the organization in creating a media product.

Media scholar Joseph Turow (1984), borrowing from industrial sociologist Howard Aldrich, says that a useful way of understanding how media are made is a *resource dependence perspective*. By this, he means that we can better understand how media producers—individuals, organizations, industries—behave by understanding how their resources are allocated. Many resources are necessary to produce anything complex—time and money, talent and creativity, expertise and energy, raw materials and prepackaged components. The act of creating media is one of bringing these resources together, and anyone who controls a resource that a media organization or industry needs has some power over the shape of the finished product. In a case study of a California daily newspaper, sociologist Rodney Stark observed many years ago that reporters and editors could be divided into two groups, one of which—the "Locals"—supported the paper's conservative politics, and a second group which did not. The "Pros," the professionalized reporters, were able to keep their jobs and subvert some of the publishers' biases because they controlled resources upon which the paper depended. Among these resources were reporting and writing talent, a sophisticated knowledge of the paper's deadlines and editing routines, and expert knowledge of their "beat" specialties (Stark, 1962). In short, control of resources gave them a degree of power, independence, and autonomy; the greater the control over a resource on which a producer is dependent, the greater the power. In the recorded music industry, for example, established "track-record" artists can flex far more muscle in terms of creative control over their music than can newcomers.

The eminent German social thinker Karl Mannheim once observed that "strictly speaking it is incorrect to say that the single individual thinks. Rather it is more correct to insist that the individual participates in thinking further what other individuals have thought before" (cited in Shoemaker & Reese, 1991, p. 85). What this means is that in all we do, we operate inside social systems that predispose us to think and act in ways that are patterned by that social system. The newspaper example shows that whereas some control over the product resides at the individual or "people" level, the product must be described in an organizational context.

Likewise, in a study of the creation of *Freestyle,* an educational TV program for public television, James Ettema (1982) noted that three groups—educators, evaluation researchers, and television production professionals—were supposedly granted equal power in making decisions about the show's content, style, and format. On the planning committee to create the series, each had equal representation, and representatives of each group argued strongly to craft the show to suit its own interests. Over time, however, the TV production group, represented by the executive producer, won most of the arguments. He did so, Ettema argues, by appealing to his expertise about what makes "good TV," a subject about which the educators and evaluators were ignorant, and his knowledge of what could be done given a set budget. Although his knowledge was an individual characteristic, the rules concerning TV technique and budget constraints belong at the higher, organizational, level of analysis, and to that, we now turn.

ORGANIZATIONS AND INDUSTRIES

At this level, there is some blurring of the lines between organizations and industries. *All* organizations and all industries, media and otherwise, are characterized by roles, rules, and routines, as they attempt to cope with their environments, to bring order where there seems to be none: Where they vary is in their solutions to problems. Most TV production houses, for example, will have very similar structures and roles—people will have the same or similar job titles—and similar routines for writing and casting, production, and postproduction, but particular differences will show up in the shows they produce. Stephen Bochco Productions, from *Hill Street Blues* to *NYPD Blue*, are known to be gritty, "realistic" views of big-city crime, for example. We turn next to why and how rules, roles, and routines are used within organizations and industries, and how these ultimately shape the media, often in ways that are subtle and nonobvious.

Routines and Rules

For most of us, the first time we were assigned to write a term paper or research paper was a scary experience. What's a suitable topic? How long should it be? Where can I get information? How much do I need? How do I organize it? How much detail should I go into? How much of it should be my opinion, and how much should be "just the facts"? When do I need to use a footnote? The teacher could answer some questions fairly specifically. ("It should be 15 pages. It should open with a thesis statement stating a point of view, provide sufficient information to support the point of view, and close with a summary-and-conclusion."). Other answers were open-ended ("I'm not going to assign a topic; write on something you're interested in." [Yeah, right.]) Whereas writing that first term paper was hard, writing the second one was somewhat easier, and the third, a bit easier than that. That is so because we not only write the term paper but begin to learn the rules for researching, organizing, and writing them.

The same holds true for media organizations and industries. No creator ever sits down with a blank sheet of paper (or a blank computer screen) and says, "Now what am I going to create for the media today?" The creator sits down with a set of ideas (and, as Mannheim noted, these ideas are not new ones but rather ones that are inherited), and in these ideas are the rules and routines for getting to work. The rules and routines, then, are what make media creative practices *efficient*.

In putting together any particular *Tonight Show,* the show's production team begins not with a blank slate but with a lot of information—even before the first joke is written or the first guest invited—and a number of strategies for creating the show (for a more detailed discussion, see Tuchman, 1974). These unwritten rules and routines allow the team to organize its time productively: Months in advance, the producers and writers will know what nights the show will appear and what nights the host will be available or on vacation so that a replacement must be booked. At least 2 weeks in advance, the main star/guest must be booked so that her or his name will make the deadlines for *TV Guide,* newspaper television listings, and other promotional material. Lesser guests can be booked later, depending on availability and currency. Jokes for the monologue are written on the day of the show.

In one critical respect, TV talk shows are different from most other media products, in that "outsiders" who contribute to the show—guests—are not directly motivated by money, because the union-scale appearance fee is nominal. Most celebrity guests appear on such shows to further careers, to promote themselves and their latest products: "Celebrities," Marshall McLuhan (1964a) once commented, "are well known for their well-knownness."

How do guests make it onto the show? Not by chance. Established stars have established track records—they are familiar to audiences and "known" to the show's producers and host. Part of what they are known for, as sociologist Gaye Tuchman (1974) has noted, is for being "good TV." That is, they will, predictably, be humorous, attractive, nonpolitical, personable, and personal (but not *too* personal). All but the top few repeat talk-show celebrities will be "preinterviewed" by researchers and writers twice, once to steer them toward topics that the host can later ask them about and to steer them away from taboo topics such as politics and the details of their breakup with ex-spouses, and a second time to prepare them for the night's show: the "spontaneous" dialogue between host and guest is largely scripted. All potential guests who are not big stars are preinterviewed, to be sure that the potential guest will be "good TV."

How does the program staff learn about potential guests in the first place? Celebrity helps: The majority of talk- and news-show guests are already familiar, both to the producers and to the audience, largely because of prior performances in the media. But researchers and staffers are always on the lookout for "new" faces to add some variety. Where do they find them? There are two principal sources: first, bookers and especially agents who want to place their clients—comedians, actors, recording artists, and book authors—on the shows for the favorable publicity to be garnered. Second, *other media* are a rich source of the offbeat, bizarre, and unusual performer or character.

This extended example shows several aspects of media organizations' rule-boundedness: first, the rules and routines help to assure that production will be smooth, efficient, and *predictable*, with few surprises for the producers; second, the media end up being interdependent, relying on each other for the "raw material" that becomes their content; third, not everybody is treated in the same way, as "stars" are governed by different rules than are unknowns; and, finally, the rules and routines that make putting media products together easier, more predictable, and efficient for their producers also makes them predictable for audiences. However, intermedia "borrowing" and predictability hinder novelty, spontaneity, and creativity.

A second example from the organizational-industrial level is the decision making that goes into getting TV programs on the air in the first place. There is no way to guarantee that a new product will be a hit. Given this uncertainty, however, media organizations *do* have rules for deciding what new programs will air: first, "track-record" producers have a decided edge, and production companies with successful shows will have an easier time getting new shows on the networks than will newcomers. Second, spin-offs and shows that imitate successful shows will also have an easier time. Third, shows featuring established stars (Kirstie Alley, Tony Danza) are more likely to appear than shows featuring all new talent. Fourth, conventional and predictable shows will be most likely to air, in large part because the rules are enforced by cautious, risk-aversive network program executives. However, occasionally, unconventional shows do get picked up by the networks, and occasionally (*All in the Family* in the 1970s, *Hill Street Blues* in the 1980s, *The Simpsons* in 1990), they become hits. Turow (1982) has shown that even for unconventional TV shows, the conventional rules apply. In a study of how three conventional TV programs and three unconventional programs made it onto the network program schedules, Turow found that the conventional shows had conventional origins—they were the products of studios and production companies that already had shows on the networks,[2] and they were approved by network program executives who were well-established in the business. By contrast, the unconventional shows tended to be the creations of writer-producers whose track records, although extensive, were outside television, largely in films and theatrical productions. An important point is that established network executives and networks doing well in the ratings are not interested in unconventional, innovative shows: Truly new shows are championed by executives new to their jobs and willing to take risks to make their marks. CBS president Rob Wood told Turow that his ideas in his first few years as network president "were the freshest." Later, he said, "you learn the rules too well and don't think in new directions" (Turow, 1982, p. 121). And innovative shows tended to appear on networks either trailing in the ratings or anxious to appeal to attractive demographic groups to which that network was not presently appealing. Finally, Turow learned that unconventional shows took longer from their initial conception to airing—an indicator that networks were dragging their feet—and were far more likely to be placed in unattractive time slots than were more conventional shows. Thus, breaking the rules is difficult, and programming executives sometimes set up unconventional programs to fail.

Roles and Reference Groups

Within media organizations and industries, roles and reference groups serve important functions. A *role* is the set of attitudes, values, and behaviors expected of any occupant of a position. A role can be a job title or occupation. A film editor does certain kinds of work—splicing different segments of film into each other to attain a meaningful narrative. How the film is edited, however—what the narrative is supposed to mean—is dictated by the film's director.

Similarly, a reference group is any group of which one is a member and to which one orients his or her thinking and actions. We saw in the earlier example of the California newspaper that two sets of reporters (a role) allied themselves in two different reference groups, the Pros and the Locals.

Roles and reference groups are important for two principal reasons. First, doing anything as complex as assembling a media product requires people in multiple roles; each role carries with it different sets of behaviors and especially attitudes and values. Second, the existence of different reference groups helps us to understand the circumstances under which conflicts are more, or less, serious.

Role conflicts are inevitable because of the differences in values and attitudes implicit in different roles. In general, media production requires a three-tier structure. At the front end are "raw material" processors—the creative staffers such as writers, artists, or reporters who do the initial processing of media materials. In the middle are managers, editors, directors, and producers who coordinate the production and mediate between the front-end staff and top management. The top tier of executives sets budgets, makes corporate policy, sets organizational goals, and occasionally defends the organization's employees from outside pressures (Shoemaker & Reese, 1996). Most media organizations, and hence, their top managements, are most interested in making money: For a media enterprise to survive, it must do so, and thus, top management generally has the strongest and most direct interest in questions of profit. Management's vision of how to attain profit (or to meet other organization goals, such as respectability or prestige) may well not square with front-end staffs. As Turow found in his study of conventional and unconventional television programs, network programming executives tended to be conservative, being more interested in formulaic programs by track-record talent. At the other end, the writers and producers were generally interested in programs that stretched the creative bounds of the medium. Because the network executives generally had more power, they generally won in such conflicts.

However, as sociologist Muriel Cantor (1971) has shown, such conflicts are not inevitable. The *behaviors* implied by the role of television producer are fairly uniformly agreed upon, at least in the United States: The producer is the production boss, responsible for everything from writing the program or series (or assigning the writer) to getting completed shows "in the can" for airing to serving as the production unit's key negotiator with network executives. But the *attitudes and values* implied by the producer's role are not so uniform. In a study of American TV producers, Cantor found that three more or less homogeneous groups (reference groups) of producers existed. She called these groups Filmmakers, Writer-Producers, and Old-Line Producers. They varied in age (filmmakers were youngest, old-line producers the oldest), in previous professional experience, and in ways they became producers. Filmmakers came from film schools, got into TV and movie production companies in menial jobs usually associated with writing, and worked their way up. Writer-producers had more checkered backgrounds, with varied prior jobs in TV and films, and they were more likely to be independent, employed for individual projects; old-line producers had long prior records in radio and TV production. Most important, producer groups differed in the values and aspirations each espoused. The filmmakers, who were doing TV as a career path to being able to produce theatrical feature films, had few conflicts with network executives, because their primary definition of their role was "to give the public what it wants"—to entertain. Hence, they would make changes suggested by the networks both because they thought it was in their career interest to go along and because they thought the network executives had some sense of what was entertaining (and commercially successful) television programming. The old-line producers, on the other hand, had intermediate levels of conflict with network programmers: Although they tended to share with the filmmakers the "give the public what it wants" attitude, they tended to believe that they had a much clearer sense of what the public wanted than did network executives. Conflict was reduced, however, for these producers because they tended to produce the most successful shows, and network interference was least evident when shows were successful. The most protracted conflicts were between writer-producers and networks, because writer-producers fought the hardest to retain creative control, saw their jobs as creative work, and thought their work included making socially relevant and, if necessary, controversial, programs.

INSTITUTIONS

We noted earlier that within a society or culture, various institutions shape media content. And this is only half the equation: the media help influence the society and its institutions as well. If media content

75

did *not* have an impact on a society and its institutions, then those institutions would have no interest in shaping the media. But the constant barrage of criticism media face from government, the military, religious groups, and organized interest groups of all sorts is vivid testimony to the belief that the media have major impacts on public and private life.

The Nature of Institutional Relationships

In discussing the relationships between media and other institutions, we need to make two sets of critical distinctions.

First is the degree to which the nature of the relationships is passive—that is, how much do the media *mirror or reflect the societies in which they exist*—or active—how much do media themselves *shape and change the society?*

Second is the distinction between *formal* and *informal* constraints on media. Formal constraints are those codified into laws and regulations by the state. Informal constraints are all other mechanisms—ethical, social, economic, and cultural—that govern the media and shape their content.

In the comparison of U.S. and Italian TV news in Box 3.1, Hallin and Mancini (1985) argue that the cultural practices serve as *informal* constraints on the news people of each country: TV journalists' expectations of the implied relationship they have with the audience, for example, leads them to address their audiences in different ways. At the same time, Hallin and Mancini do not argue persuasively either way whether this relationship is active or passive—that is, whether the Italian media practice of addressing the audience in the first-person plural—*we* and *us*—results from a wider social practice, or whether it is actively used by journalists to encourage an audience bond, thus reinforcing a culturally familiar form of address. In large part, this is because extricating such practices from their context, and deciding whether one leads to the other or vice versa, is extraordinarily difficult.

The line between formal and informal rules is a bit clearer. Laws are codified, written down. We can tell a great deal about any society by seeing how the law books and court cases say things run. Moreover, this division points out several other important factors in the relationships between media and other institutions:

1. Formal, institutional relationships are perhaps the most important ones for understanding how the media operate. They account, in large part, for relationships between government and the media, and they explain how a society views the nature of the public.
2. Formal relationships change over time. Historically, the relationship between media and government has varied. In the United States, for example, the long-term trend has been toward less formal restraint of the media—at the same time that informal control of the media, especially by the economic institution, has grown.
3. Formal relationships do not in and of themselves explain how the media are regulated; we must consider informal relationships as well.

Government-Media Relations

Among all institutions that media confront, government is most important. This is true for several reasons. First, worldwide, government control is direct—the government is the only institution that can legitimately use force to assure compliance. In other words, if an enterprise breaks a law, it will pay a fine, or its officers or employees might go to jail. To ignore the commandment of any other institution usually means only that organizations within the institution censure or expel you—or use the law—the government—to punish the offender. Second, government exerts control not only over media, but other institutions as well, and control over other institutions may be indirectly reflected back into regulation of mass media. For example, the 1996 Telecommunications Law has enabled businesses previously not in mass media-related businesses—primarily telephone companies previously excluded from being content providers—to begin competing directly with television and cable; this provision was part of a complex lobbying effort with the Congress and the White House that also allows cable operators to compete with the phone companies for telephone business. Third, the relationship between the state, or government, and the media is undergoing radical transformation worldwide. Increasingly, formal governmental control of the media is being supplanted by informal regulation by other forces, primarily those of capitalism, as governments substitute market forces for regulatory pressures. Expanding on these themes suggests a brief history of the nature of the relationship between the government, or state, and the media.

Government and media have always—at least since the development of truly mass media—had a rocky relationship. In 1690, a Boston printer, Benjamin Harris, published the first issue of the first newspaper in America, *Public Occurrences*. As it happened, this issue included a story about brutalities committed by Indian allies of the colonial military. This first issue was also the last: Harris was forbidden by the colonial governor not only from printing any more issues of the newspaper but, for that matter, from printing *anything at all* without prior permission. Such *prior restraint* is unquestionably the most effective form of censorship, and it was typical not only in Boston but elsewhere in the American colonies, in Britain, and in Europe. It works not only directly—authorities can prevent the publication of anything critical of or offensive to the government—but also indirectly; as printers quickly figure out the sorts of material that censors are unlikely to allow through, they precensor it, not bothering to submit it to review.

A second and related form of censorship is *licensing*. Printers were granted a royal or governmental license to print, but the license could be withdrawn—effectively forcing them out of business—if they printed anything the authorities did not like. Unlike direct prior restraint, licensing does not directly prevent a printer from publishing critical materials, but the cost of guessing wrong about what the authorities will tolerate is so high—loss of one's livelihood—that licensing serves about as well as prior restraint in stifling free expression.

A third form of censorship comes in punishing the publisher after something is published. Two forms were powerful means of suppression in the colonial period—criminal prosecutions for treason or giving aid or comfort to an enemy of the state and prosecutions for seditious libel, or any published material that, without justification, cast blame on any public man, law, or institution established by law (see Rivers, Peterson, & Jensen, 1971). Both seek to punish publishers for material that to some people's eyes does no more than inform people about or criticize the government. Both were infrequently used. The mere threat of imprisonment or death was generally sufficient to keep publishers from being too critical. Printing presses were so scarce in colonial days that it did not usually take much effort for officials to find out who had printed something; today, of course, anyone with a computer and a printer or a two-way radio can be a publisher.

How could the government get away with these forms of censorship? The prevailing political ideology of the day was fully supportive. The authority of the state—the crown, colonial officials, governors—was absolute. Neither the press nor any other institution had any "rights" with respect to the state or governing authority. In the United States, development of the philosophy of libertarianism was intermixed with a steadily increasing desire among the American colonists to free themselves from British rule. The press ultimately freed itself from direct governmental control.

In 1735—still 41 years before the American Revolution—a New York printer, John Peter Zenger, was charged with seditious libel for printing a series of scathing articles about the governor of New York. Zenger did not write the articles, but because they were anonymous, the officials had no one to prosecute but the printer. As the law was written, Zenger was clearly guilty. Truth (the governor, history suggests, *was* a lying, pompous scalawag) was no defense under the law, and the judge instructed the jury that in fact, the greater the truth, the more the harm, and thus the greater the libel. But Zenger's attorney argued to the contrary, that the people should decide what is true and that a sovereign people should have the right to criticize those in authority. Zenger's acquittal technically did not change the law, but seditious libel thereafter was no serious threat to colonial printers, and the idea that a sovereign people could decide what was true became a part of the American ideology.

The 1791 ratification of the Bill of Rights brought with it the First Amendment, which says in part, "Congress shall make no law abridging freedom of speech, or of the press." Interpreted literally, this would mean that the press had become free from government interference. However, this was not to be, for several reasons, at several levels. First, from the beginning of the republic until the early part of the twentieth century, the First Amendment was a restraint only on the federal government, not on the states. Second, even at the federal level, Congress managed to pass laws, especially the 1798 Alien and Sedition Acts, which managed to muffle publishers and writers by threatening criminal prosecutions for sedition. Third, freedom of the press can mean different things to different people. True, the American press was in 1791, and is today, pretty much free from prior restraint or censorship by the government.[3] But courts have interpreted the First Amendment to say that some *classes* of expression are not constitutionally protected, including obscenity, libel and slander, and violations of national security.[4] This basically means that some things that could be printed are subject to subsequent punishment, which serves, as we've noted, as a damper on their publication in the first place. Nonetheless, the range of things that the government can prevent or punish through the application of law is quite narrow; virtually any criticism can be written, spoken, or broadcast; material that is tasteless, sensational, and even inaccurate (with a few exceptions[5]) is constitutionally protected as well. But for a clearer understanding of media-government relations, we need to widen the scope of our inquiry a bit. To repeat, the law—in the colonial period and today—covers only what the government can prevent or punish. As we'll see, that's only a small part of this important institutional relationship.

The key word in understanding how the media and government interact is *relationship*. In a relationship, each party typically has something to give and something it wants to get, and relationships are reciprocal: to get something you want from someone else, you give something you have in exchange. Recall our earlier cited resource-dependence perspective: What one party has to give is its resources; what it wants to get is the other party's resources. And by definition, in a reciprocal relationship, your resource is my need (if I didn't need it, it wouldn't be a resource for you, at least in dealing with me).

The major resource the media have is *publicity*, the ability to focus public attention on a topic or issue or person. The government and government officials need access to the public to focus public attention on problems and issues and especially to marshal public support for present policies and actions. This can be seen very clearly in election campaigns; a candidate needs media exposure to be seen as "viable," to have a chance of winning. The 1992 presidential campaign of Larry Agran, the Democratic mayor of Irvine, California, is a case in point. Virtually unknown to the national press and hence unreported on by them, Agran campaigned hard in New Hampshire but failed to attract much media attention: Why? Because he was an "unknown" and thus an "unviable" candidate. The evidence that he was unknown was easy to come by: Public opinion polls failed to find more than 1% or 2% of potential Democratic primary voters who expressed a preference for him. Early preelection polls always favor candidates with high name recognition. In the early 1992 Democratic primaries, New York governor Mario Cuomo, who wasn't even a candidate, was leading in the preference polls. Agran was frequently excluded from media events, especially debates among the contending candidates, because he was viewed as not being viable. In brief, voter preference comes from publicity, the media provide the publicity, and their decision rule about news coverage largely comes from their estimate of viability, determined by voter preference polls and election results.

If the media's major resource in dealing with government and political life is publicity, government and politics' major resources are the ability to supply to supply "raw material" to the media, especially the news media, and their ability to set the rules of the game for the way the media operate.

Clearly, those in political and governmental circles are interested not only in getting publicity but also in having it be favorable publicity, what has come to be known as *spin control.* Governmental and political officials attempt to influence what is said, and how it is said, by controlling the *access* that the news media have to them and their activities. The media's need—and the officials' resource—is news. Sociologist Herbert Gans (1979), in a content-analysis study of national TV news and newsmagazines, estimated that three fourths of all news came from government sources.[6] The dominance of the government as a source of news is understandable: The government acts on policies that affect us all, and hence its activities are news. Moreover, the media—and government—have adopted rules and routines that make covering government relatively efficient and predictable.

Government, political officials, and the military can control access in a number of ways. Getting favorable coverage means accentuating the positive and shrouding the negative by making access to symbols and messages that support your position easy and by making access to anything else difficult. Sources having great power—people such as the president, whom the press virtually must report on—enjoy a great resource advantage. The Gulf War of 1991 was another case in point. Although the nation's press corps complained bitterly over Defense Department restrictions on coverage, they by and large went along with these restrictions, for *not* reporting on the day's biggest news story was literally unthinkable, and Gen. Norman Schwartzkopf and his staff controlled all access to the field. By the same token, those who have no such guaranteed access simply do not have it as a resource.

We noted earlier that the First Amendment protects freedom of expression—of speech and of the press—but under current court interpretations, this freedom basically covers what Americans say and print but does not extend very far in covering anyone's ability, including the press's, to get access to information that the government, or other institutions, prefers to keep secret.

RELATIONS WITH OTHER INSTITUTIONS

We've noted before that the First Amendment grants the media substantial latitude in what they can say. It's important to remember, however, that it protects media only from government censorship; it does not apply to relationships the media have with other institutions or with members of the public, who remain free to censor what they will.[7] As may become clear from our discussions, whereas the history of formal control—control by government—of the news media is one of increasing freedom, the history of influence on the media by other social institutions shows no such pattern; the give-and-take pattern of fluctuating degrees of freedom enjoyed by the media depends on who has the upper hand in informal interactions between the media and other institutions.

The media clearly have important relationships with other institutions, and resource dependence marks these relationships as well. As is the case with government and the political sphere, the resources the media have are essentially publicity and legitimization, and the ones they seek are support, for attention, money, and content—the stuff of which media are made.

In the following pages, we look at media relationships with two other institutions—education and medicine. Two later chapters concern the media's interaction with two other critically important institutions —the economy and the public sector.

Education

The relationships between media and education are particularly close and complex. In the first place, much of our education is mediated; indeed, textbooks and educational materials account for almost a third of the $20.75 billion spent annually on books in the United States.[8] And if media are implicated in education, the reverse is true as well. Let's suppose that you're 20 years old and have watched—since you were 2—three and a half hours of TV a day, a little bit less than the national average of four hours a day. That means you've now watched about 23,000 hours of TV, or a bit under 3 years of 24-hour days; that's about 1.4 times as much time as the approximately 16,000 hours you've spent in school (as a matter of fact, if you're an average American, you've spent more time watching TV than engaging in *any* activity other than sleeping).[9] At least part of the time we're watching TV, we're also learning—education is not just the formal education we get in school.

At any rate, media may be used directly for education, with educators involved in planning and producing media, as the many programs of the Children's Television Workshop (*Sesame Street, 3-2-1 Contact, Ghostwriter*) attest. Media may also function incidentally as an educational outlet, as we learn much about the world beyond our immediate experience from the media.

Many educators are wary of TV and other media, feeling that watching television is negatively related to school achievement. Studies of the relationship show that it is neither simple nor straightforward. Some studies find this, but others don't; the best studies suggest that watching moderate amounts of TV has no relationship to how well students do in school, but watching 5 hours or more is hazardous to kids' grades. We may remind ourselves that the one nation in which kids watch more TV than in the United States is Japan, where students almost always score higher than American children on standardized tests.

A recent controversy, that over the use of Whittle Communications's *Channel One* in the nation's high school classrooms, illustrates one relationship between the media and education. *Channel One* represents a media challenge to the traditional structure of the schools, which until recently have not been commercialized. Because *Channel One* carries age-appropriate advertising during its 12-minute daily newscast, it has focused attention on American schools as a site for marketers to reach student consumers. The youth market, *Consumer Reports* estimates, is now $15 billion per year in direct expenditures, with young people influencing another $160 billion spent on kids by their parents (cited in Hamilton, 1997).

Education is, however, dependent on the media, most particularly the news media, for information and viewpoints about how schools run, from basic questions of educational policy to mundane matters of what the school cafeterias will serve.

Medicine

Medicine and health care make up one of the largest and most important sectors of American social life and its economy: health care costs now are almost one sixth of the Gross National Product, and the proportion of GNP devoted to health care is steadily rising. The monetary stakes alone, in what American health care is and what it will become, are enormous and likewise growing. Where do the media fit in? The networks and most large newspapers have correspondents who cover medicine and health as a regular beat, and a listing of magazines that accept advertising classifies more than 150 magazines under Health and Nutrition and more than 400 others under Medicine, Dentistry, and Nursing. (By comparison, Journalism and Writing has fewer than two dozen entries; see *Magazine Industry Market Place*, 1996.) While television news and newspapers tend to aim their coverage at explaining medicine and health to a mass audience and hence serve boundary-crossing functions (that is, they tell one institution, the public, about the workings of another), the vast majority of the magazines are specialized, or *intrainstitutional* media, informing an institution, or a specialized segment within it, about itself. But perhaps the most interesting place to look at the relationships between media and medicine is in television entertainment.

Doctor shows did not begin with *ER* and *Chicago Hope*. The genre has a history that predates the medium. *Dr. Kildare* began as a short story and became a radio show and series of movies (there were, in the

1930s and 1940s, fifteen Dr. Kildare movies) before it became the No. 1 television show in the 1960s. *M*A*S*H,* a variation on the genre, became the longest-running No. 1 show in TV history in the 1970s. Television studios and networks are attracted to medical shows because of their wide popularity, although, like shows of any other genre, not all succeed: Joseph Turow demonstrates that whereas 32 network medical shows ran for a full season or more from the 1950s through 1987, 22 others lasted less than a full season. TV writers and producers like medical shows because doctors and nurses (and even coroners, such as *Quincy)* are "good" central figures for a show. It's easier to write drama or comedy when the main characters are people who routinely and credibly come into contact with a wide and changing variety of secondary characters. Turow (1991) argues that this interaction helps explain why professionals in general—lawyers, writers, and teachers as well as doctors—are overrepresented in TV entertainment programming. Besides, medical stories almost by definition involve life-and-death situations, easy for high drama.

The popularity of the genre, moreover, has not been lost on the medical establishment. Early on, from the doctor movies of the 1930s to the 1954 debut of the series, *Medic,* the American Medical Association and the Los Angeles County Medical Association had enormous influence on the content of medical programs. The associations and the industry depended on each other: The TV producers got free technical advice to make shows accurate and realistic; in exchange, the medical associations were able to influence the portrayal of medicine on television—another example of the resource-dependence perspective.

The media do not exist "out there": they are *made.* And understanding how they are made is somewhat like peeling an onion—to understand mediamaking requires us to look at more than one level. People—individuals—make media, but they do so in an organizational context: that is, to make media requires rules, roles, and routines, and each of these influences what can be made. Moreover, organizations exist within industries that shape or constrain them. Furthermore, that understanding is fostered by paying attention to the way media people, organizations, industries, and institutions share resources with others, in what we label a resource dependence perspective.

BOX 3.3

Medicine on Television

In *Playing Doctor,* Joseph Turow (1991) makes a solid argument that the portrayal of medicine on television has been largely one-dimensional. Think about medical shows for a moment, and think about how most of them characterize medical practice:

Most shows are *set* either in a hospital or a doctor's private office. They're *not* set in insurance offices, health maintenance organizations, or "doc-in-a-box" walk-in clinics in malls. In short, medicine is portrayed only in its traditional locales, those favored by doctors.

Medical doctors are the central characters. This means that the *point of view* of the show about medicine is the doctor's point of view; when other characters introduce other points of view to create a dramatic conflict—the hospital administrator who worries about cost, for example—the conflict is almost always resolved in favor of the doctor-protagonist. In other words, the authority, legitimacy, and autonomy of the doctor is maintained.

Moreover, the doctor is thus depicted as the primary provider of medical care; nurses, orderlies, administrators, nutritionists, therapists, pharmacists, and psychologists are secondary, and their characters are relatively rarely fully developed, thus reinforcing a doctor-oriented view of medicine. Anyone, however, who's ever spent any significant time in a hospital appreciates the unreality of this characterization: Doctors spend considerably less time with patients and provide far less of the care patients receive than medical shows would suggest.

TV shows approach medical care from a massively interventionist, best-possible-care-at-any-expense viewpoint. This comports neither with how medicine is practiced among much of the public (here *ER* stands in contrast to most other shows), nor does it square with the painful decisions that public policy makers are debating about how much medical care the nation can afford.

On this last point, the failure of the Clinton health care package in 1993 owed much not just to the debate in Congress, but also to a core set of cultural expectations about what medical care should "look like," and mass media portrayals contribute very strongly to that set of expectations.

NOTES

1. When Elvis Presley first appeared on the immensely popular Ed Sullivan show on CBS television in 1956, the camera operators were commanded to shoot him waist-high and no lower, so that his gyrating hips would not offend the audience.

2. Until 1995, TV networks were barred by Federal Communication Commission regulations from producing their own prime-time entertainment programming. The regulations, aimed at fostering competition in entertainment production, meant that most prime-time network shows were purchased from Hollywood-based production companies, many of them affiliated with movie studios. In 1997, networks owned or had ownership interests in 29 of 80 prime-time entertainment programs (e.g., *Ellen* on ABC, *The Single Guy* on NBC), with the remainder produced by independent houses and studios (Sterngold, 1997). We must note that the formula for *All in the Family* was copied from a British sitcom, *'Til Death Us Do Part*, and *The Simpsons* was spun off from Fox's *The Tracey Ullman Show*.

3. Upheld most famously in the 1971 Pentagon Papers cases, in which President Richard Nixon's attorney general, John Mitchell, sought to keep the *New York Times, Washington Post,* and *Boston Globe* from printing excerpts of a secret Defense Department multivolume document on the origins and history of the Vietnam War. The papers had been surreptitiously photocopied by Daniel Ellsberg, who then made them available to the three newspapers. The U.S. Supreme Court said that prior restraints on the press were unconstitutional unless an extremely strong case could be made that publication would damage national security, and that the government had not been able to show that. It should also be noted that this "prior restraint" doctrine applies with greatest force to news; the Supreme Court as late as the 1950s was willing to say that local communities could pre-screen motion pictures and decide whether they were suitable for local showing.

4. In trying a case involving freedom of the press, a court must decide whether material is or is not obscene or libelous or slanderous; the publisher is protected if the material is found not to meet the legal definition but is subject to criminal prosecution, in obscenity cases, or to recovery of damages in libel cases. In theory, at least, prior restraints of material that would damage national security are still possible, although the government has not been able since the Pentagon Papers cases to prove any media publication would damage national security. It came close in 1979, when *The Progressive* magazine was prevented from publishing an article outlining how to make a hydrogen bomb. The government, however, dropped the case when the magazine was able to demonstrate that all the information contained in the article was already available in libraries and previously published articles, and the article appeared in the magazine.

5. The principal exceptions are in libel, slander, and deceptive advertising. Libel and slander are published or spoken, respectively, falsehoods that defame a person or corporation. Defamation, legally, is anything that exposes persons to hatred, contempt, ridicule; lowers them in the esteem of others; causes them to be shunned; or damages them in their business or calling. At present, the law of libel requires that for a private individual to collect damages for libel, she or he must show that a defamatory falsehood was published either with knowledge that it was false or with lack of due care for whether it was true or false. Reflecting the concern that public debate should be, in the words of the U.S. Supreme Court, "uninhibited, robust and wide-open," the standards applied to public figures (who presumably place themselves in the public eye on purpose) and government officials are even higher. To collect damages, they must prove that a defamatory falsehood was published with knowledge that it was false or with "reckless disregard" for whether or not it was. In deceptive advertising cases in the recent past, the federal government has moved largely against only flagrantly inaccurate advertising.

6. And fully one fifth of it came from the president of the United States. See Gans, 1979, Chapter 1. Virtually every subsequent content analysis of major news media has calculated similar proportions.

7. Legally, *censorship* applies only to restrictions by government.

8. Data for 1996 from the *Bowker Annual Library and Book Trade Almanac, 42nd ed.* (Bogart, 1997). Percentage includes elementary, secondary, and college texts, standardized tests, and subscription reference services but excludes audiovisual media.

9. In addition, let's assume that you'll go to work at age 22 and work a 40-hour week until you're 65, and that from 22 until age 72, you watch the national average of four hours a day of TV. That means that over the course of an average life, you'll spend about 98,000 hours watching TV and about 86,000 hours working. In other words, if you're an average American, over the course of your entire life, you'll likely spend more time watching TV than engaging in any activity other than sleep (unless you care to *add* the 16,000 hours of school to the 86,000 hours of work, which would make 102,000 hours of school/work compared with the 98,000 TV hours). TV use estimates from Nielsen Media Research, 1991, as cited on p. 737 of the *Information Please Almanac* 45th ed. (Boston: Houghton Mifflin, 1992). The school estimate is for 6.5 hours a day for 180 days a year from age 6 to age 20. Work estimate includes a two-week vacation yearly.

Media and Money

I t is not possible to think of the modern mass media without also thinking about money, economics, and profit. The media are, for the most part, made up of and controlled by corporations that both invest an enormous amount of money in their media operations and expect to make at least a reasonable profit. After all, the media are big business, one of the biggest in the world. In 1993, the most recent year for which we have an estimate, $295 billion was spent by the audience on American media—about $1,250 for each man, woman, and child in the country, and that amount is increasing at a rate of well over $10 billion a year. It is worth remembering, however, that there are millions of people, even in America, who simply cannot afford to purchase many media products.

In fact, how the media are organized institutionally and how they operate to produce the particular kinds of products they do are significantly influenced if not determined by their relationship to money and profit. In the United States, people take it for granted that the media operate within and are part of a capitalist economy, in which they must compete for profit in the marketplace. But people are not always aware of the differences the system makes. For example, scholars and critics persistently argue about the extent to which, and how, the organization of media as largely profit-making ventures influences what sort of media products are made available to the audience. On the one hand, there are numerous examples of media corporations producing messages that are critical of mainstream society and even of the capitalist economy from which they profit. Whether it is CBS records releasing records by the Clash advocating revolution, or the Italian media mogul Silvio Berlusconi publishing a Communist newspaper, the bottom line is money. On the other hand, there are many accounts of how media corporations have censored products (news stories, films) that were critical of their own actions (or those of their parent companies) and, more generally, of how they make products intended to defend their interests and points of view. In addition, critics commonly point out that the commitment to profit has, perhaps more than anything else, limited the range and quality of messages produced by the media. More generally, the question is whether the media's reliance on and commitment to profit conflicts with its important role in society.

This chapter will describe the economy of the media—what it looks like, how it behaves, how the money side of mediamaking influences the rest of mediamaking. Although there are significant economic differences among the various media industries, there are important similarities. We will stress the common economic factors that shape how the media operate.

A PRIMER OF ECONOMIC TERMS

From Adam Smith in the eighteenth century and David Ricardo and Karl Marx in the nineteenth century to John Maynard Keynes and Paul Samuelson in the twentieth century, we have come to accept a number of basic economic concepts and principles as fundamental. Because contemporary media operate within a capitalist economy, it is necessary to understand some of these basic concepts and principles.

The founding principle of any economy is the distinction between two forms of value. Every good has some *use value*, which describes its function in our lives. Most of the time, the use value of a product is obvious, but other times—think about designer jeans—it is not quite so obvious. Perhaps we wear designer jeans because they give us a certain status, or define for us a certain image and style. Every product also has an *exchange value,* which is its value (measured loosely in its cost) in the market. Notice that there is no necessary correlation between use value and exchange value. Water has a very high use value, but for most people, unless they live in desert, it has a very low exchange value. On the other hand, designer labels may have relatively low use value, but very high exchange value. Insofar as products are made primarily to be sold in the market, they are referred to as *commodities.* When people purchase a commodity, they treat it only in terms of its exchange value, its monetary worth, and forget about the fact that it was made by the labor of real people. *Money* is a kind of universal abstract measure against which we measure the exchange value of different commodities. Otherwise, it does not exist, and certainly, it has no value of its own, especially because the government no longer guarantees that it can be traded in for gold (the gold standard was supposed to guarantee the value of money).

People don't usually think about the production of the commodity, only about its place within the market. But it is precisely its production—or more accurately, the labor that goes into it—that gives a commodity its exchange value. This is known as *the labor theory of value.*

The aim of the capitalist marketplace is to sell the commodity at a higher price than the cost of the labor (and materials) necessary to produce it. This is profit or *surplus value.* The real aim of capitalism is to increase the rate at which profit is generated. Ideally, capitalists—the people who own the factories (the means of production), the banks, and so on—accumulate surplus value as capital to be reinvested, thus increasing both their profit and the rate of profit.

How does a capitalist create surplus value? The simplest way would be to create systems within which particular kinds of labor simply go unpaid: for example, think about the domestic labor of housework, which women have traditionally had to carry out "for free." But of course, this is not the primary way in which capitalism operates. On the contrary, a key feature of capitalism is that it makes labor into a commodity that can be bought and sold on a supposedly competitive market. Consequently, the most likely way for capitalists to increase their profit is to buy labor at the cheapest possible cost and to seek ways to increase the efficiency of labor.

The capitalist charges more for the commodity that is produced than he or she pays for the total labor, material, and machinery and thus

---

BOX 4.1

Ford and the Consumer Society

In the twentieth century, the relations between the capitalist and working classes have varied greatly. In the first third of the century, workers' attempts to form unions were often greeted not only with hostility but with violence from capitalists and the state agencies (police, national guard, courts) that were called upon to protect the capitalists' interests. At the same time, there was an early recognition that one way for industry to increase its profits was to increase its pool of potential consumers. Henry Ford is usually credited with the insight that he could significantly increase his profits if he could just sell cars to his employees. This meant that labor had to be paid significantly more than subsistence wages; employees had to earn enough money so that they could afford to buy the new consumer goods that American capitalism was going to make. It also meant that they had to want to buy these goods; this partly explains the enormously rapid rise of advertising in the early twentieth century (and partly explains the rise of psychology as a discipline as well).

By the end of World War II, this new compromise was firmly in place (and unions played a major role in this process): Wages increased sharply, in direct relation to the increases in the marginal productivity of industry (and hence of profits). Thus, workers were motivated to contribute to increased productivity because they were given a share of the increased profits, which enabled them to afford the middle-class comforts of American capitalism. This compromise, however, apparently ended during the 1980s, when both unions and high wages came under serious attack.

---

generates surplus value. It is as if the worker were contributing a certain amount of unpaid labor to the capitalist.

Profit is what's left over after one subtracts the cost of producing the product from the price one sells it for. There are two ways of increasing profit: lowering the cost of producing something and increasing the price at which it is sold. We have already discussed the most direct way of lowering costs. The latter is somewhat difficult to manipulate, for as economists like to point out, when a competitive market is working well, price is determined by the laws of supply and demand: As supply increases, price decreases, and as demand increases, price increases. Moreover, there is a complex relation in the market between supply and demand themselves. One of the most powerful ways of increasing profit is to participate in what economists call an *economy of scale*. In an economy of scale, after a very high initial cost of starting up, the cost of producing each unit of product declines rapidly as the number of units produced increases. That is, the more products that can be produced, the higher the *rate of profit* and the larger the profit on the last item that has been produced.[1] For items involving a lot of hand labor or very expensive materials, there are few economies of scale; it costs, per item, about as much to produce 100 television programs as it does to produce one. However, for products that can be mass produced, such as CDs, economies of scale are an attractive and powerful way to keep the cost down.

Of course, economies of scale only work to increase profits if one can increase the market demand for the product. And thus, once again, we return to the problem of trying to influence people's desire for specific products, a problem that has, as much as anything, contributed to the enormous growth of the media as industries responsible not only for promoting their own products but also for serving as the means of promoting the demand for other kinds of capitalist product as well.

ECONOMICS AND THE MEDIA

The media, particularly in capitalist societies such as the United States, operate to produce and even to maximize profit for their owners. Profit, generated from the sale of media products, can be increased in a number of different ways. The key to media profits is access, which can take either of two forms: selling products directly or indirectly to consumers or selling access to the audience to advertisers. Let us begin with the simplest question: What is the basis or source of the media's profits? In what different senses do the media exist as commodities? How are they economically supported?

THE SOURCES OF MEDIA SUPPORT

People in the industrialized world are surrounded by media almost everywhere they go. Every day, there are many occasions on which they use different media, both mindfully and absentmindedly. In every case, someone has to pay for the production and distribution of the media products. These different media are supported in various ways.

Some media products are paid for fully and directly by consumers. Most such media products are tangible physical entities that consumers take home with them, such as books, tapes, and compact discs. The price of the commodity covers its full cost plus a profit. You pay directly for the media product you consume; by controlling the price, the producers can make the product more or less affordable for the consumer. The producers are not entirely free to set any price. They have to recoup their costs;[2] at the same time, they have to recognize that higher prices are likely to reduce the total demand. Small demand may dictate higher prices, but higher prices may also lead to lower demand.

Direct purchases may come in a series of one-time sales, as when a consumer purchases records and books, or in the form of a longer commitment through subscriptions. In fact, in most media, subscriptions do not cover the full cost of the commodity, but in a few, such as community radio and some alternative newspapers, which refuse or seriously limit advertisements, subscriptions may in fact provide almost the entire income for the business. Similarly, some cable stations (such as premier movie channels) rely entirely upon subscription fees.

Other media products are sold as access instead of ownership. Control of access is by "turnstile": One pays to go through the gate, as with a movie or concert or Internet provider. As unlikely as it may seem given the costs of such tickets, the price of admission usually covers only part of the total cost and profit. Concessions and secondary merchandising (which we shall discuss shortly) often generate a significant part of the income. According to media economist Thomas Guback, some movie theater chains derive as much as 30% of their operating income from concessions. That helps explain why a few cents worth of popcorn costs $3. Similarly, although the price of admission to rock concerts has apparently gotten out of hand, rarely does the gate profit cover the cost of touring. Bands and promoters make profits largely by selling merchandise at the concerts.

Some media are delivered "free," so that there is no direct cost to the consumer at all. In the United States, at least, broadcast radio and television have developed as media that are supported entirely by advertising. Advertisers buy time in and around programming in hopes that the audience will be stimulated by the advertising to buy a product or service (or even to vote for a politician). Direct mail ("junk mail") advertising operates in the same way: the cost of producing and distributing it is borne directly by the advertisers. In the long run, advertising is not free to consumers insofar as the cost of advertising a product is usually added into the price of the product. Sometimes the advertising is paid for indirectly, as when bookstores get a commission for subscriptions to magazines entered with the ads they distribute with all purchases.

Some media are paid for in several ways combined: They may be purchased, but they are also subsidized by other means so that consumers share the cost with others. For example, the price of buying or subscribing to a newspaper or magazine is only a fraction of what it costs the publisher to produce it. In fact, the newsstand cost of a newspaper is just a bit less than what it costs the publisher to buy the paper on which one copy is printed. The rest of the money comes from advertising. Two thirds of a typical newspaper publisher's revenue comes from selling space in the paper to individuals and companies to print ads in hopes that consumers will see the ads and buy whatever goods or services they are advertising. Cable television is similarly supported: Subscription fees (both for basic services and for premium channels) are shared between the local cable operator and the various program suppliers. But increasingly, both the local cable system and the cable networks depend on advertising sales for their profit. Similarly, new developments of the Internet suggest that websites and even access will be increasingly subsidized by advertising.

Why would advertisers subsidize consumers' access to media such as television, radio, newspapers, and magazines? The answer is that, from the point of view of the advertisers, they are purchasing access to the consumers or audiences themselves. In television, for example, the advertiser buys something called "impressions" or the estimated number of people who see their television advertisement. In this sense, the television network can be said to deliver an audience to the advertiser ("We sell eyeballs," a Chicago television executive told a student) at the same time it delivers an advertisement and other programming to the audience. Television news is both subsidized by advertising and underwritten by the networks. Thus, for example, special news broadcasts are always difficult for networks to manage because of the complex negotiations necessary to cover the cost. Consider again the Gulf War:

BOX 4.2

Where Advertising Dollars Go

According to Standard & Poor's April 1997 *Industry Surveys,* estimated 1996 advertising expenditures in the United States were more than $173 billion, up 7.7% from 1995. According to the U.S. Bureau of the Census, U.S. population in 1996 was 264.6 million, and dividing population into dollars gives us the average expenditure per person in advertising dollars for each medium.

Medium	Total Advertising Dollars (in millions)	Advertising Dollars per Person
Newspapers:	38,595	145.86
National	4,335	
Local	34,260	
Magazines	9,180	34.69
Television	39,300	148.53
Cable	3,335	
Network	13,050	
Spot[a]	9,850	
Local	10,805	
National syndication[b]	2,180	
Radio	12,105	45.75
Network and spot	2,585	
Local	9,520	
Yellow Pages	10,845	40.99
Direct mail	34,840	131.67
All other[c]	28,355	107.16
National	21,185	
Local	7,170	
Total	173,220	654.65

a. Spot advertising is national advertising sold directly to local stations and groups, not through the network.
b. Nationally syndicated advertising is advertising sold within nationally syndicated, non-network programming (e.g., *Wheel of Fortune, Hard Copy*).
c. Includes, among others, weekly and business newspapers, newsletters, outdoor advertising, transit advertising, flyers, corporate event sponsorship.

by the end of the extraordinary coverage, the networks had lost millions of dollars, because extra programming costs were associated with the news coverage and especially because advertisers did not want to

Discussion

Until the 1990s, newspapers took the largest share of the advertising dollar, but the growth of cable TV advertising and of direct mail now means that television is the leading advertising medium and direct mail is a strong third. For newspapers and radio, local advertising predominates, a situation that is reversed for television. Nontraditional advertising media—media we generally do not give a lot of thought to, such as direct mail, Yellow Pages, Internet, and outdoor billboards—account for more than 40% of all advertising expenditures.

The last column of the table shows the average paid per person in 1996 for each medium; in the lower corner, the table shows that advertisers spent more than $650 to reach each man, woman, and child in America. This figure can be read as either the *subsidy* that advertising contributes to each medium or as the *hidden cost* for each medium, the amount advertisers add to the price of products to cover the costs of advertising. It is both.

advertise during the coverage, fearing their products would be associated with war. (That's just a little ironic, given the amount of violence on network television.)

Over the years, a number of different groups have argued that the underrepresentation of various social groups on television, for example, Blacks, Hispanics, and the elderly, is a consequence of this need for television programmers to deliver those audiences that advertisers most desire. Thus, the fact that until quite recently, advertisers did not see Blacks as a "most wanted" market segment for their specific products (because they were not thought to have a lot of disposable income) meant that the networks were reluctant to program shows aimed specifically at Black people. Programs about Blacks often are constructed in ways that are intended to attract both specifically middle-class segments of the Black population and White audiences as well (for example, *The Jeffersons, Good Times, A Different World, Cosby,* and *Wayans Brothers*). At other times, Blacks were kept off the air because programmers were afraid that their presence would offend other—White—segments of their market (this was particularly the case in the 1950s). Currently, however, advertisers are finding it necessary to define more and more specific market segments, and to redefine their often-taken-for-granted assumptions about which are the most desirable market segments for which products.

Traditionally, given the specific products that were advertised on television (household goods, food products, cosmetics), advertisers assumed that the best market segment was defined by housewives ages 18 to 49, those people who were thought to do the shopping for such goods for the entire family. Now network advertisers want even younger audiences, those 18 to 34. Moreover, as the number of available cable channels increases (some predict there will be as many as 200 channels per cable system), advertisers want to reach ever more specific target audiences for their products and are demanding programming geared to such specifically defined audiences (such as professional women ages 25 to 34 or upper middle-class male teenagers).

There are many new market segments available today as well. The structure of American families has changed significantly in the past 30 years. Fewer than 25% of American families fit the typical image of the nuclear family: a father, a mother, and some children living together. Furthermore, women's roles in the family have changed, and as income has been generally redistributed across the society, there are many new consumer groups of interest to advertisers: children, older people, single people, single parents, Blacks, and other minorities. In fact, advertisers find that they must develop strategies to identify who their potential markets are, where they can be found, and how best to appeal to them. This market segmentation has led to what is commonly known as *niche marketing* in advertising or *narrowcasting* in the broadcasting industry, in which the same product is marketed in distinctively different ways to different audiences, or different products (often only slightly different, with different brand names or labels) are marketed to different audiences.

Some "free" (and even some paid) media, however, are supported partly or fully by nonadvertising revenue. That is, they are literally subsidized. Many organizations—unions, universities, companies—wholly or partly subsidize their own publications, often called *house organs*, although they may also sell advertising to contribute to the costs. University publications, such as the telephone directory and the class schedule, were traditionally distributed free (although that seems to be changing). Similarly, universities subsidize their faculty's and students' access to the Internet. Public radio and television are supported through taxes, through corporate and foundation support, and by viewer and listener contributions solicited primarily by what some people in the business call "beg-a-thons."

Many countries in the world established state-owned and supported "public" broadcasting systems for both radio and television, rather than the competitive profit-making system put into place in the United States. In Great Britain, for example, the state-owned British Broadcasting Corporation had a radio and television monopoly financed by an annual tax on all television and radio sets. (Incidentally, taxing receivers limits access to over-the-air broadcasting.) British people could choose among several BBC-Radio and two BBC-TV channels. The tax—and the BBC—remain; but since 1954, private, advertiser-supported broadcasting has grown up alongside it. And the private broadcasting sector has put increasing pressure on the state to privatize the remaining public networks. More recently, this pattern has been repeated in most of Western Europe, and trends suggest it will be the pattern for most of the rest of the world.

Even in the United States, other forms of subsidy exist. Many magazines, particularly journals of opinion such as *The Nation* and *National Review,* often operate for long periods at a loss, a loss that must be made up by "angels" or wealthy individuals who underwrite the journal because they support its editorial positions. Government subsidy is more widespread: By issuing second-class mailing permits for printed matter such as magazines, the Post Office is using profits from the higher prices of other categories to cover the lower price of these subsidized permits. Various tax credits serve a similar purpose: More than two thirds of the states exempt newspapers from state sales taxes, and some exempt textbooks and magazines as well.

Many of the challenges facing companies that invest in Internet content involve questions of how to charge money and earn profits through this new medium. When people gain access to a particular site and download the latest album or magazine, or even video program, the whole issue of the nature of the media as economic institutions becomes central once again.

COMPETITION AMONG THE MEDIA

Capitalism assumes that any product enters into a freely competitive market. Whatever the reality of the degree of that competition in any particular market, any producer attempting to create and distribute a new media product has to consider the marketplace, where the product will almost certainly compete with other products. There are different forms of competition. First, there is direct competition for an audience: A new newspaper, for example, will compete directly with all the other newspapers already in the market. Similarly, a new album competes with other albums. When a single item, say a book or a compact disc, is brought on the market, it competes with other products much like it—other books and other CDs, especially those with the same target audience.

Second, there are forms of indirect competition both within and across media. Within a medium, products compete for resources necessary for their existence, for example, air time or advertising. A new newspaper has to attract advertisers that otherwise might have gone to another newspaper or to some other medium, such as radio. A new television program has to compete with other programs to find a place in a network's schedule so that it has the possibility of finding its audience.

In addition, a new media product has to find an audience, and sometimes that involves convincing an audience to buy that product (and spend the time necessary to use it) *instead* of buying and spending time with something else. After all, everybody's time and energy, and most people's money, are limited. Scholars analyzing economic data from the 1920s until 1979 argued that a *principle of relative constancy* was operating. After correcting for inflation, this principle suggests that over time, individuals spend a constant portion of their disposable income (income left over after taxes and essentials—food, clothing, shelter, and taxes) on media. If some media product is purchased, some other is not. In the more recent past, however, the fraction of disposable income spent on media has increased, largely because of increased spending on electronic and video media. In other words, people are spending relatively more on media and relatively less on other nonessential items than they did in the past. Hence, the attempt to introduce a new media product into an existing market may not face quite the same constraints as such endeavors did in the past. Instead, new products might be creating new markets and new categories of consumers (the traveler as a primary reader of *USA Today*).

Different conditions are involved when competition is between media themselves, when the new product is a new media technology. In discussing how media compete with other existing media, both for dollars and for attention, media economists have borrowed from population biologists the notion of an ecological *niche*, or a space that some entity successfully occupies because it has some competitive advantage over other, somewhat different entities. A local newspaper enjoys a couple of competitive advantages for its niche over competing media: It's a more efficient (cheaper and broader) vehicle for classified advertising (such as help-wanted, personal, and auto ads) and generally reports local news in more detail than television or radio. Television and radio, however, occupy slightly different niches and likewise enjoy competitive advantages over newspapers.

What happens when a new *medium* appears? Sometimes, a new medium wholly supplants or replaces an existing one: Motion pictures began life as peephole Kinetoscopes. People paid admission to a nickelodeon, a forerunner of the video arcade, where they, by themselves and for a nickel, watched a one-reel short subject on a single machine; for 100 people to watch a film at the same time required 100 Kinetoscopes. Enter the film projector: now 100—soon 1,000 and more—people could watch the same film at the same time using just one machine. This was a lot more economically efficient (cheaper) for exhibitors, and capital flowed away from the Kinetoscope and toward movie palaces.

The Kinetoscope and the movie projector occupied the same niche—popular light entertainment—and, in the process, helped to kill off still another "mass medium," vaudeville live performance. Furthermore, the projected movie altered the medium itself: film watching became a social experience; we watch films in groups, and we react not only to the film but to the other members of the audience as well. Groucho Marx of the Marx Brothers used to go to premieres of his movies with a stopwatch, and he would re-edit the movie if he found that too much, or too little, time had been left after punch lines for the audience to laugh: If too much time had been left, the movie dragged; if too little, the audience would be laughing too loud to hear the next line of dialogue.

Recorded music provides another dramatic and more recent example of media replacement. Vinyl records were supplanted by audiocassettes, which have since had to compete with the introduction of compact discs. Along the way, eight-track cassettes failed to find a niche. No one can predict what medium will replace CDs, but it is clear that something—digital audio tape (DAT) or some new form of multimedia digital disc—will. At the same time, although it appeared that tapes and discs would drive records off the shelves, it seems that vinyl is making a comeback. The point is that such media relations are too complex to predict in advance, and investment in media economies remains a highly risky business.

Some media continue on while the world changes around them. The American magazine began life in the eighteenth century, much as American newspapers did: a high-priced, locally circulated medium supported by and catering to the tastes and interests of elites. Only in the 1890s, half a century after newspapers went through a similar process, did magazines evolve to what they would become for the next 60 years: large, nationally circulated journals, supported by advertising and appealing to the widest, "massest" interests possible, with audiences that in some cases numbered in the millions. Cultural changes that made such magazines viable included increasing literacy in the population; increasingly efficient mass production, which allowed per-copy prices to drop dramatically; improved modes of distribution and communication; and the development of modern marketing. Not until about 100 years ago were there national brands of merchandise—before that virtually everything was generic—and without such national brands national advertising was literally unthinkable.

Magazines such as *Life, Look,* and *The Saturday Evening Post* dominated their niche: for a 35-year period, the mass circulation magazine had no competition as a national mass medium. Radio changed that a bit, but television changed everything. In 1950, *Life, Look* and *The Saturday Evening Post* each had a national circulation exceeding 5 million. As such, the magazines were important advertising vehicles, for no other visual medium reached so many eyeballs. Radio could *tell* you about a Pontiac or a Studebaker, but it couldn't show you one. TV could show (like magazines) and tell (like radio), and it added motion (like cinema).

More important, it could reach a larger audience. By 1955, TV reached 47.8 million American homes—78% of the total—and a modestly rated network television program was viewed by millions more people than any mass circulation magazine. Circulation of mass magazines, as one might expect, declined. The *Saturday Evening Post,* for example, slipped from 6.2 million at its peak in 1959, to just under a million when it ceased publication 10 years later. But more important than the readers deserting was that the advertisers deserted as well. TV was a more efficient (cheaper) media buy for advertisers; mass circulation magazines were driven out of their niche.

The magazine industry did not die. Magazines evolved. Of the 11,000 or so different magazines now sold in the United States, no more than 100 or so are classified as general interest magazines; the rest are intended for specialized or even hyperspecialized audiences. *The Baker Street Journal,* a semiserious quarterly publication for devotees of Arthur Conan Doyle's Sherlock Holmes, for example, was established in 1946, and 45 years later had a circulation of only 1,800. How could it survive, presumably making a profit, for so long? In two by now familiar ways: it charges for subscriptions, and it sells advertising. Presumably, people subscribe because the topic is of great interest to them. But what about advertisers? Given that the cost for a one-page ad in one issue is $175 and that circulation is 1,800, the cost per thousand readers (the measure of the efficiency of the cost of advertising) is $10.29. Who would pay such a high rate and why? Book publishers, purveyors of "Sherlockiana," makers of products that are probably of no interest or importance to anyone but serious Sherlock fans, the kind of fans who are likely to subscribe to the magazine.

The introduction of television as a commercial medium affected not only magazines but the motion picture and radio industries as well. Roughly one third as many people go to the movies in a typical week today, compared to the mid-1940s, for example, and only in the early 1980s did motion picture revenues surpass the industry's heyday of the 1940s. And this increase was largely the result of the sharp increase in the price of tickets, which more than tripled between the 1940s and the 1980s. The movie industry also adapted by specializing. Movie makers shifted from making films directed to a mass audience, in which adults and families were the primary market, to a set of genre markets—science fiction, martial arts, and especially horror/slasher films—aimed more at adolescents: In 1985, people ages 12 to 24 accounted for only 27% of the population but 53% of movie tickets sold.

As with movies, the advent of television signaled the end of radio as it had been known. Television appropriated not only the niche but literally the form of radio as well, and many of radio's most popular programs and performers migrated to TV: Jack Benny and Bob Hope, George Burns and Gracie Allen. Radio networks—CBS, NBC, ABC— became television networks. The result was that between 1949 and 1959, radio lost most of its mass audience and the national advertisers who marketed to this generalized audience. Radio adapted by specializing and reformatting: Instead of programming for everybody (conceived as a market of families), local stations began programming for more specialized audiences, initially almost exclusively along lines of musical taste—middle-of-the-road pop, rock, classical, country and western, rhythm and blues. By the 1970s, however, these musical formats were further fragmented and specialized (rock, for example, fragmented into dozens of different genres and formats), and other formats based on ethnicity or nonmusical programming (talk and all news stations) emerged. Many of these formats were available as relatively cheap prepackaged programming (Casey Kasem's Top 40 Countdown is a good example). Radio's survival was also made possible by two technological advances that broadened its audience: the development of the transistor, which allowed for smaller, cheaper, and more reliable receivers; and the opening to broadcasters of the FM spectrum, which enabled not only clearer signals but also stereophonic transmission, both of which were especially important for its increasing musical orientation. And so radio "downsized": expensive network-produced musical variety and dramatic programs were replaced with self-sufficient local stations and packaged programming. At the same time, radio expanded: More stations came on the air to chase after various specialized audiences.

Interestingly, as other media were specializing in response to television's threat to their market share, television's content between the late 1940s and the 1970s become less diverse, at least in the genres of programs it offered, (according to broadcast researchers Dominick and Pearce, 1976). In the early "Golden Age of Television," prime-time programming included many categories, such as quiz programs, westerns, serious drama, and musical variety, which had all but vanished by the

1970s, when TV programming consisted largely of situation comedies and action-adventures. This can be understood as a result of television's search for the largest possible mass audience: the result was that decision makers repeated the most successful genres, reducing much of the variety of early television.

Recently, network television's control of the broadly defined mass audience niche is being challenged by a host of competitors: cable and satellite systems (which now reach approximately 70% of U.S. television homes), video games (which compete with programming for the use of the television set), videocassette recorders (which can be used either to "time shift"—to allow viewers to record a program and view it at a more convenient time—or to play prerecorded tapes), and now even Web surfing. The network share of the television audience during prime time has fallen from a high of 91% in 1978-1979 to 40% in 1996-1997, which network executives attribute mostly to the encroachments of cable. These developments mark an interesting reversal in the history of media, for unlike other niche battles, what we have here are specialized formats challenging a mass medium, rather than a struggle between mass media.

PROFIT IN THE MEDIA INDUSTRIES

Media economics, like capitalist economics in general, focuses on efficiency and the generation of profit. There are significant differences across the various media industries: A large number of different factors help shape routes to profit in relation to each media. Still, one can identify the general economic principles that influence the content of media and the role of the media in society.

Many media industries, being capital intensive (they require large initial investments in fixed costs such as machinery), provide almost classic examples of economies of scale. For example, in the music industry, the cost of manufacturing each album declines as the number of albums manufactured increases. That is, the marginal cost of an additional album is small. Thus, it is to the company's advantage to produce and market only those records that can be expected to sell in sufficiently large numbers. Economies of scale are most pronounced for those media where materials and distribution costs are negligible. Think about media "hardware," such as CD players, VCRs, and personal computers. The initial prices on these items are always exorbitantly high; as demand increases, prices drop rapidly. The price change follows the law of supply and demand, but it is also the result of the economy of scale in the manufacture of these goods.

Yet, there are important ways in which media industries are more complex and significantly different from other types of industries, especially because some of them are involved simultaneously in two economic transactions: selling something to an audience and selling that audience to advertisers. In newspapers, for example, the initial investment is huge but the marginal costs of adding each additional copy are negligible. At the same time, one has to take into account the costs and profits of adding additional advertising pages against the additional profits. Radio, interestingly, is a slightly different case. There is no cost for adding any number of additional listeners within the broadcast area, but there are real material limits to the number of advertising clients that can be added. The larger audience does allow a station to lower their cost per thousand listeners and generate more income than a competitor, but there are serious constraints and limits. Finally, in some media, such as cable or telephone, the economy of scale is so strong that it tends to produce natural monopolies.

The profits of the media industries are constrained by a number of other factors that serve to both strengthen and mitigate the influence of economies of scale and the laws of supply and demand. One of the most important and powerful of these factors is audience size. In television and other media, two key measures are used to calculate the size of the audience; advertisers use these measures to estimate how many people will see their commercials, and television networks use them to calculate the popularity of their programs and thus how much they can charge advertisers to advertise on the programs—the larger the rating, the larger the charge. *Ratings* estimate the total number of households viewing any particular program. Ratings are expressed in *ratings points*, and each rating point is equivalent to 931,000 households with television. Hence, a program with an 18.8 rating is estimated to have been viewed in 17.5 million homes. *Shares* provide an estimate of the percentage of all households, among those viewing television, that viewed a particular program. Shares are expressed in percentage points. A program with a 31 share, for example, is estimated to have been viewed by 31% of all households watching TV at the time.

The number of people watching TV varies across the day. More watch in prime time (which is why it's "prime" for advertisers) than watch in the morning, afternoon, or late at night. Thus, both the ratings and share numbers are important measures. A program in the afternoon, for example, could have a large share of the audience but a modest rating; a soap opera with a 3.4 rating but a 38 share might be a smashing success. Yet, a prime-time show might have a much larger rating but a more modest share: A series with a 6.8 rating and an 11 share would be seen in twice as many households as the soap opera, but it would be a prime candidate for cancellation.

Because a television network's profits depend on its advertising revenues, which in turn depend on its market share (its proportion of the viewing audience), it needs to attract as large an audience as it can. But market share does not influence the production cost of making a television show. It costs about the same amount to produce and air each episode of *Home Improvement* (in general, half-hour sitcoms cost $500,000 to $700,000 per episode, one-hour dramas $900,000 to $1 million), whether it is watched by 25 million people or no one at all, although a network might be willing to make a larger investment (more per episode or more episodes) if it is confident about the future size of the audience. Similarly, the cost of producing a master tape for a record does not vary with the size of its potential audience, although a record company might be willing to invest more in the production of such a tape if they believe it is likely to sell well. Hence one of *the* most basic principles in media economics is: the larger the audience, the larger the income (whether from sales of the product, of advertising, or of admission) and usually, the larger the profit. For truly *mass* media, such as television, motion pictures, newspapers, and the like, this makes trying to reach the largest possible audience the primary goal.

A third factor that influences media profits is the specific shape of the profit curve in such industries, often described as the break-even point and the hit-to-release ratio. In the profit curve of a typical industry operating within an economy of scale, profits are calculated by subtracting marginal cost (the difference between the cost of producing the last and the next to the last product or good) from marginal price (the difference between the price of the last and the next to the last product or good). However, in many media industries, almost the total cost of the product is up-front; that is, almost all of the total cost is the cost of producing the first item (the actual television program or the master tape for a record or the first print of the film). Beyond the first item, the cost of subsequent copies or impressions is minimal and follows the principles of an economy of scale. This leads the media to calculate their profits on the basis of a *break-even point:* They attempt to recoup all of their initial costs as quickly as possible. Companies will often include the high cost of promotion and advertising media products in calculating these initial costs, because such promotion is necessary to begin the process of sales. But once a product becomes a hit, promotion costs decrease sharply. Thus, for example, all of what would be the profits from the sale of a record are charged against the initial costs of producing the master tape or the first copy. Once those initial costs are recouped, the record is said to have reached the break-even point, and every record sold after that creates pure profit for the company, minus the small marginal cost of producing the physical object itself. It is only after a record reaches the break-even point that the artists begin to collect royalties (their share of the profits).

For these reasons, the ratio of hits to releases is extremely important when a media corporation calculates its profits. The hit-to-release ratio simply describes the percentage of media products that reach and surpass their break-even points. It is not simply a matter of hits versus bombs, because a product with high initial costs might well sell a large number of copies, or do well in the box office, but fail to reach its break-even point. For a company releasing a large number of products, the profits from the hits (which surpass their break-even points) can be used to offset the losses from the other products. The result is that a company not only will attempt to produce as many smash hits as it can, but also will prefer to have a small number of mega-hits rather than a large number of smaller hits. Hit-to-release ratios are particularly important in the music, film, television, and book publishing industries.

One recent change has significantly affected the media industries: An increasing percentage of their profits come from *secondary markets*; these are profits derived from sources other than advertising or the direct sale of the product. There are a number of different ways in which such secondary profits are generated. One such source is the sale of merchandise associated with the original product: T-shirts and other clothing, toys, posters, and all manner of products with media logos. A second source involves licensing the rights to the product or its image to other media industries: Record companies license the use of their music to film companies for sound tracks, and sometimes original film sound tracks are released separately as records. Products can also be licensed to advertisers. In 1988, for example, the California Raisin Council made more money licensing its "California Raisin" characters than it did on its commission for marketing raisins. And the record company made money by licensing Marvin Gaye's "I Heard It Through The Grapevine" to the California Raisin Council. A third source involves the sale of the product to secondary markets, such as when television programs are syndicated, or when films are sold for broadcast or videotape distribution, or when any product is distributed outside the primary market of the United States.

The unique ways in which profits are generated and calculated in media industries mean that in general, media products are quite risky ventures; producers cannot know for certain in advance whether a particular product—a movie, a television series, a book, a record—will be popular or whether that popularity will translate into profits. In the case of most individual media products, as a matter of fact, the odds are against success. Nonetheless, a producer can, if sufficiently well capitalized (if starting out with a big enough cash cushion or credit line) underwrite a number of flops because successes can be spectacularly profitable. Thus, large and well-capitalized producers enjoy a decided advantage over newcomers.

One of the most important reasons for the high risk in these industries is that consumers have little brand loyalty in their media tastes. Rarely do people watch a program because it is the latest ABC offering or read a book because it is published by Random House or buy a record because it is on Polygram. There are exceptions, small companies that have developed specific identities—Harlequin in the field of romance novels, Merge for alternative rock. Rather, consumers are making choices for individual products from the wide range of offerings.

Warner Records's financial success in 1989 was largely due to the surprising and unpredicted success of unknown and largely unpromoted performers such as Tracy Chapman. Similarly, no major Hollywood studio would fund the production of Kevin Costner's financially successful and critically acclaimed *Dances with Wolves*. Only independent film company Orion Pictures—which subsequently went broke—was willing to invest the reported $40 million necessary to produce, distribute, and promote the film. In television, ABC's *America's Funniest Home Videos* was an afterthought spring-replacement program in 1989, which has gone on to become one of the most profitable and successful shows on the network in recent years. This uncertainty and inability to predict smash hits is an example of unique risks involved in mediamaking. The various forms of market testing that guide consumer products have not proven very helpful to the media industries so far.

The other reason for the high risk in media industries is that the industries cannot control the creative process. The songwriter, the screenwriter, the author, and the actor—all of them determine to some extent the success of the product. Yet, there is little the industry can do to guarantee the quality (and appeal) of what they produce.

Most media industries face similar problems of trying to manage the risk involved in producing hits, and they employ similar strategies. If the risk is the result of various features of the media economies in general, it is also the case that not all media producers or potential producers face the same odds. A number of strategies exist that allow a producer to maximize the chances of success; almost all favor the trends toward corporate consolidation—toward smaller numbers of larger media companies—that have marked the past few decades and that virtually all observers expect to continue into the future.

The first strategy is to maximize the investment capital. The more money available to invest in the product in the first place, the better the chance of making a successful product. Clearly, corporations with lots of their own money to invest have a competitive advantage. If a company is short on investment capital, there are a number of options. One can borrow it from someone else. But most lenders—banks, venture capitalists, investment groups—want assurances that the product will be a success. They are likely to look for a product that looks familiar— one that looks pretty much like other successful products in the niche— produced by people with successful track records. This formula favors already successful companies, superstars, and bland, imitative products. A second way to obtain capital is to sell one's company or part of it to a company with more capital or a better credit line. But often, the new parent company, like any investor, will demand some control over the product that is being planned. A broader, mediawide strategy may involve lobbying the government for favorable tax laws or regulations. This is a complex relationship because the increasing connections be-

---

BOX 4.3

How TV Producers Reduce Risk

Until 1991, federal law forbade networks from producing their own entertainment programming, and even today, the majority of network television shows are
purchased from independent producers in Hollywood, such as Carsey-Werner,
Aaron Spelling Productions, and Walt Disney Studios. For any given television
season, three to four times as many pilot shows are made as will be needed.
These pilots are chosen from dozens of scripts pitched to the network programmers by independent production companies. Because the networks commission and pay for the production of these pilots, they have a stake in developing
successful programs. Nonetheless, fewer than 10% of the pilots that become
regularly scheduled programs will be considered successful enough for a second season.

What strategies are used to reduce the networks' risk and increase the
chances of producing a smash success? The networks are generally committed
to controlling and rationalizing all aspects of the selection and production processes, from script approval to the choice of actors.

The networks use familiar formulas, themes, and genres; thus, they invest in
spin-offs (where supporting characters from one program become the stars of
another program) and copycats and crossovers (where successful movies or
books become television shows).

The networks use people with proven track records, including well-known
stars as well as production companies, writers, and directors who have been
successful in the past. Thus, Steven Bochco, after producing successes with *Hill
Street Blues*, *L.A. Law*, and *NYPD Blue*, can write his own ticket, as he did with
the dismal failure of the 1990-1991 season, *Cop Rock*.

The networks use different techniques for promoting new programs. They
might introduce a new program by staging a special pilot preview or by having
characters appear on other programs or by using a series of ads.

---

tween government and media result in both a reluctance on the part of
politicians to stand up to the media and, on the other hand, a reluctance
on the part of the media to do anything that might offend those in the
government who can pass such legislation.

The second strategy for reducing risk and maximizing success is to
integrate the production process. A producer who can control the entire
process of producing, marketing, and distributing the product enjoys
two principal advantages over a producer who does not. The first is
that it might give him or her some creative control. Suppose a group
wants to produce a record. The group might choose to turn the process

over to a record company or attempt to do it on their own, renting a studio, mixing the master, and designing the package and advertising themselves. The group would have to hire out the physical production and the distribution of the product. The album is more likely to turn out to be what the group wants it to be. This is the attraction of various do-it-yourself and independent record companies. But such choices also carry the risk of reducing the potential market for the product. Who's going to know about your music and who's going to buy it, and where? In attics and basements all over the world are unsold copies of bands' efforts to do this.

So the band opts for the more prudent course, taking its demo tape to a record company that is *vertically integrated.* A vertically integrated enterprise is one that controls the entire production and distribution process. A vertically integrated record company would control everything: the creation of the music, its physical reproduction and packaging, its marketing and promotion, and its distribution to wholesalers and retailers. When a young band goes to such a record company, its contract basically turns over complete control of the product to the company. The band may have to adapt its music to the company's ideas about what will sell. Until it is successful, the band may not get to choose its own producer or engineer, or the director of its music video, or the designer of its package cover.

A second advantage of vertical integration is profit. With the steps done separately, the recording studio makes a profit in renting the studio, the manufacturer profits in producing the tape or CD, and the distributor profits in moving the product to wholesalers. If a single company control all the steps, it gets to participate in additional sources of profit (and economies of scale) and to keep all the profits for itself.

Third, to maximize profits and minimize risks, a company can attempt to rationalize the consumption process. Although there are no guarantees that the public will buy any particular media product, there are myriad ways that a producer can increase the odds. Just as the production process can be integrated, so too can the consumption process. The company can try to maximize the potential market. The more people who have the opportunity to buy the product, the more who are likely to do so. For example, television networks are highly motivated to increase the number of stations affiliated with them. An affiliated television station is a local television station that has an exclusive agreement with one of the major networks to carry only that network's television shows. In return for carrying the television programs, the local television station—which is paid by the network a share of the network's advertising income—gives to the network an audience for the network's program. And because the size of the audience a network has across the country determines advertising revenues for any program, networks want to have as many affiliates providing audiences as possible. Thus, as recently as the 1970s, shows on the ABC television network were far less likely to be ratings winners than those on NBC or CBS, not necessarily because they were qualitatively worse or even less popular, but because they were seen in fewer markets; the network had fewer affiliated stations.

A company can also try to integrate the consumption process by creating a product that is assumed to have the best chance of appealing to the largest possible audience. As a former NBC vice president, Paul Klein, noted in the early 1970s, television programming proceeds on the L-O-P formula: Least Objectionable Program (interview in *TV Guide*, July 24, 1971, pp. 6-10, cited in Clark & Blankenburg, 1973). Programmers assume that people watch what's left over after they've rejected the other alternatives, rather than what they really want to watch: that attitude is hardly a strategy for innovative or novel products. The company can also maximize the potential market by rethinking the product itself. A product can be created for multiple media and at multiple sites of possible consumption. What, for example, is Charles Schulz's *Peanuts*? Is it the comic strip syndicated to a thousand U.S. newspapers, or the CBS television specials, or the characters licensed for stuffed toys, party favors, greeting cards, and Metropolitan Life Insurance commercials? The licensing of sports logos from professional and college teams and leagues and the use of sports endorsements is a multibillion-dollar-a year enterprise. Is George Lukas's *Star Wars* trilogy just the three movies that are among the 10 top-grossing films ever? No. More than $2.6 billion worth of *Star Wars* merchandise was sold before the re-release of the three movies in 1997.

The ability to profit by transporting products across media takes advantage of *horizontal integration,* or the control of markets across media. The 1980s saw an acceleration of media consolidations aimed at horizontal integration. In late 1989 and early 1990, Time, Inc. went into $10.7 billion debt to buy Warner Communications and thereby create the world's largest media company. A principal reason for this mega-merger was the synergy executives (and large lenders) thought it would produce. *Time,* for example, runs ads for its *Entertainment Weekly* magazine on Warner videocassettes; Warner Looney Tunes cassettes are now marketed through Time-Life's aggressive direct mail unit (the same folks who sell *Sports Illustrated* and all those home-repair and occult book series). The combined company is also the largest U.S. cable television operator, which, not coincidentally, owns Home Box Office and Cinemax and now owns Turner Broadcasting and its Cable News Network. This *synergy* can also be turned on competitors in an attempt to drive them out of the market. A year after the merger, the *New York Times* (Rothenberg, 1990) quoted a mid-level Time Warner executive, who understandably refused to be identified:

> We're saying that if a company normally spends $10 million on our magazines, let's get them to spend an additional $5 million on a bigger idea and force them to take that money from other media companies. We want to squeeze out our competitors. (p. 26)

Finally, the consumption process can be integrated by "rationalizing" the audience itself. This refers to the practices by which media corporations try to condition people to expect and desire certain kinds of products. Media corporations attempt to make audience choices or tastes more predictable. They may use familiar categories to guide them: For example, producers have at least some idea of how large the market for a particular film genre might be and can budget the film accordingly. Although staying within the genre increases the predictability of revenue, it also dampens both creativity and audience expectations. Media corporations may also attempt to use market research (a set of tools to gauge audience interest and taste, and thereby attempt to rationalize audiences) on potential products and audiences.

Given the high stakes in profits to be made, one might expect that large, vertically integrated corporations would try to control the market itself and thereby bring consumption under their control as well. Sociologists Richard Peterson and Charles Berger provide an historical example in the music recording industry. In the 1950s, through merger and consolidation, the industry became an oligopoly controlled by a handful of firms. The enormous growth of the music industry after the Second World War depended not only on the professionalization and industrialization of music culture but also on the industry's ability to change its primary audience from an affluent middle-class audience to youth. These companies competed by following standardized practices involving a handful of known stars singing standardized songs. If an innovative song did appear elsewhere (in the rhythm & blues genre, for example), it was quickly "covered" with one or more mainstream versions by established artists and distributed on the major labels. If an innovative and successful performer appeared on the fringes (Elvis Presley on Memphis's tiny Sun Records, for example), his contract could be bought out (by RCA Victor, for example). For more than 10 years, the major labels effectively controlled the audience for popular music by exerting control over its market (Peterson & Berger, 1975).

The mass media are implicated in these various structures of the capitalist market at a number of different levels. The media involve the production of goods for a profit: hardware as well as software. The media are a major source of advertising and thus of the promotion of other goods. And the media package and commodify the audience so they can sell it to advertisers. The audience has to be large, but it also has to be the right kind of audience, and it has to be in the right frame of mind.

Although the problems facing the media industries are, in some ways, typical of any capitalist industry, they also have unique problems that result from the fact that they are trading in taste and judgment. In many cases, this means that the industries can most efficiently control the process of distribution (rather than either production or consumption). That is precisely what the media are—a distribution system for culture, for communication, and for information. Media critic Ben Bagdikian (1997) has argued passionately through five editions of his book, *The Media Monopoly,* that the steadily increasing concentration of media ownership leads to increasingly tight corporate control over information and ideas; he estimates that 23 corporations control most of the business in newspapers, television, magazines, books, and motion pictures, and increasingly, too, ownership is not restricted to one of these media but radiates across several of them. Disney, for example, best known for its theme parks, cartoon characters, and motion picture production, now owns a television network and broadcast stations through its acquisition of Capital Cities-ABC and all or part of such cable networks as ESPN, Lifetime, and A&E, as well as daily newspapers, magazines, and book publishing interests.

Two other unique problems are worth mentioning here. First, although many of the media's products are sold to individuals or families, the industry cannot guarantee what is done with a product once it is owned. Television and radio programs can be taped and shared with others, just as the tapes and records we purchase can be shared with and even reproduced for other people. Books can be photocopied; magazines can be passed from one person to another. But what the industries can control is the production of hardware and consumable materials (such as blank tapes). These considerations have led corporations to integrate a wide range of media concerns into single corporations with diverse interests.

Second, most capitalist industries have to plan a certain degree of obsolescence into their products. Let's face it, it wouldn't do much for the auto industry if the car you purchased lasted a lifetime. One way of planning obsolescence is to emphasize the novelty of each new product, to focus on minor innovations that do not basically change the product. But too much novelty, too many innovations, are likely to act against the principles of mass production. These problems are particularly important in the media industries, where there has to be a continuous demand for, and supply of, new products.

Although large corporations dominate U.S. media production, it is important to acknowledge that there are a significant number of alternative media operating, even in the United States. These range from small and marginally capitalist institutions, for example, those that at times dominate the independent music scene, to explicitly noncapitalist media, such as pirate radio and TV, community radio, and alternative newspapers.

These are some of the problems facing the media industries. Moreover, the media play a central role in contemporary society: They shape our desire for goods, they control the information we receive around the world, they organize our leisure activities, and they provide many of the interpretations of reality we use in our everyday lives. The media help to create and shape our investment in certain lifestyles, images, and commodities.

NOTES

1. In fact, technically, when economists describe such relations it is in terms of the *marginal* rate of profit, which describes the profit made on the next to the last item produced.

2. The totality of the cost increases with the number produced, even though the amount of increased cost for each marginal product decreases.

PART II

Making Sense of the Media

Meaning

In 1985, President Ronald Reagan caused a minor sensation when he attempted to link Bruce Springsteen, and especially his song "Born in the USA," to his own conservative agenda and his own definition of patriotism. A national debate ensued, carried on not only in conversations but even in the national print and television press. What was the "real" meaning of the song? Many fans obviously interpreted the song as a celebration of American patriotism, carrying and waving flags at Springsteen's concerts. Others offered the lyrics of the song as "proof" that Springsteen was in fact quite critical of the way the United States, and its government in particular, had treated both the Vietnamese people and the military veterans who had fought in the Vietnam war. The issue was never resolved. "Born in the USA" today stands as both a patriotic anthem and an indictment of American injustice. In 1991, it was played on the radio in both contexts, supporting the war effort in the Persian Gulf and challenging the Bush administration to confront the inequalities of American society.

Competing definitions are not as rare as we might think. In the 1990s, debates over rap—especially gangsta rap—raised the same issue. Rap's critics claimed that it celebrated and promoted drugs and violence; its defenders claimed that it offered a critical portrait of the street life to which an entire generation of Black youth is condemned.

These cases point to the more difficult question of how we go about interpreting the variety of messages we receive through the media. More important, why do we even bother interpreting such messages? Consider the following examples:

> The President gives a speech and when it's over, news commentators describe "what he said" even though the audience already heard it. Do the news commentators do so just to make a living?

> A teenager has a fight with his parents over the CD he brings home because they're convinced that the lyrics are advocating Satanism or drugs or perhaps sexual abuse of women. Whether it is true or not, it probably had little to do with why the youth bought the album or what he hears when he listens to it.

> A couple goes on a date to the movies, and afterward, one of them starts analyzing the symbolism of Bruce Willis's bare feet in *Die Hard,* or perhaps starts talking about *Porky's* as a powerful metaphor for the difficulties of growing up in the contemporary world. Are these comments on the film just the result of taking a film class?

Failures of communication occur in the most common everyday interactions when we don't understand what we see or hear. Problems in interpretation, the process by which people understand or make sense of something, are not limited to problems of communication; they can occur in people's daily lives whenever they try to make sense of the world. For example, two people are struggling in the street. To decide whether and how to respond, an observer must first figure out what is going on. Are they simply fooling around or having a serious fight; is there a crime in progress?

Interpretation problems in mass communication are especially difficult. In interpersonal contexts, one can always ask for help. One can ask the teacher to explain what he or she is talking about. In any conversation or face-to-face situation, if one doesn't understand, one can raise questions.

Even if the President were speaking to 3,000 students in a campus auditorium, it is at least possible to ask a question, "Mr. President, what did you mean . . . ?" When the communication comes through mass media, help is not generally available. Even if we do talk back to the

122

television at times, we really don't expect to get a response. And although a fan might dream about asking Bruce Springsteen or Dr. Dre what his song is really about, most kids know better than to expect to do so. We could call a television station, or a record company, or a movie theater, but they are not likely to be able to explain the meaning of these various messages.

Most people are not aware that they are always interpreting messages from the media. For instance, people would say that most television programs present no problems of interpretation at all. Everything a viewer needs or wants to know appears to be right on the screen. *The Brady Bunch* is "a story of a lovely lady who was bringing up three very lovely girls. . . . " Yet, viewers are likely to recognize that whereas *The Simpsons* is also a good story, as easy to follow as *The Brady Bunch*, there is always something more going on. Its episodes seem to be commenting on society and social issues, or perhaps, the show says something about the difficulty of love and family in the 1990s.

Then, there are always some programs, such as *Twin Peaks* in the 1980s or *Northern Exposure* in the 1990s, that appear on first glance to be somewhat incomprehensible. Some viewers hated them because they were too "weird" and unstructured; other viewers became devoted fans. It is obvious that these shows were not simply, respectively, a soap opera mystery about who killed Laura Palmer and a story about a New York doctor stuck in small-town Alaska. Even the appearance of these shows was different from what people had come to expect from commercial television. There was, one might assume, some deeper meaning, something going on "below the surface." Not everyone understood the shows or cared enough about them to try to understand. After all, what many people want from television is entertainment, a chance *not* to think.

The conclusion that we want to draw from all of these examples is that we are always interpreting, although we are not always aware that we are doing so. The complexity of some messages makes it obvious that a variety of interpretations are possible. And we have to work harder to interpret some messages than others.

THE MEANING OF MEANING

Meaning is both the most and the least obvious of all the things the media make. In fact, the most difficult fact to grasp about human existence is that the world people live in is always meaningful or, if one prefers, that people are always involved in messages about the meaningfulness of that world.

WHERE IS MEANING?

One can begin to see the magic and mystery of meaning. For it is not only people's languages and their systems of communication that are meaningful. The world itself is also meaningful. Someone walks into a classroom and instantly knows that it is a classroom. All of the objects in the room—the blackboard, the chairs and desks, even the way they are arranged—serve as messages that tell the observer the meaning of this space. The same person would be dazed and confused if, on entering a room for a class, he or she found a stove, a bed, or perhaps a trapeze and a barred area all together. No one would identify such a room as "a classroom." It would not be clear what sort of room it was.

There are two domains of meaning. The world itself—at least to anyone beyond infancy—is meaningful. And the languages people use to describe it are themselves meaningful. In fact, language and the world are so closely intertwined that they are, for all practical purposes, inseparable. This is what distinguishes humans from other animals.

Certainly, in one sense, an animal's world is full of meanings. This is food, that is a friend, and that is an enemy. Animals must rely on their ability to understand, to make sense of their world. Yet, the information that enables them to make such meaningful distinctions is either innate (through such biological mechanisms as instincts) or learned by rather simple processes of behavior reinforcement, both positive and negative. For example, when a dog is repeatedly punished for doing something, it soon learns not to do that; it learns that the particular behavior is "bad".

Although some psychologists (known as behaviorists) have tried to explain human behavior through such processes of reinforcement and conditioning, most students of human behavior agree that instinctual knowledge and behavior reinforcement are not sufficient to explain the complexity of human action and experience. Instead, humans learn the meaning of the various parts and relations of the world through the messages that create their cultural and communicative environment. It is easy to ignore this important fact. For in most cases, the entire process is taken for granted. Understanding what is going on in the world, or what something is, or what some message means, seems to come as naturally as walking or talking or using the toilet, none of which actually comes very naturally to people. Everyone forgets how much effort it takes for children to learn to walk, to talk, and to use the toilet, and how much trouble their parents go to in teaching these tasks. By the same token, rarely do people have to stop and ask what something means.

Most of the time, the meaning of the various objects, places, and relationships people encounter seems so obvious, so natural, that only a very young child or a space alien or some sort of cave person would not understand. We can recognize a classroom when we see one.

Unless some dispute arises, there is usually no reason to make explicit our understanding of an event or a message. People take this meaning making for granted. But the meanings that surround us are not part of our genetic pattern: They are not fixed in place, once and for all. And it is this flexibility or *polysemy*—the fact that anything can have a variety of different meanings and interpretations—that may be the most human characteristic of all. And this underlies the human ability to laugh and to cry, to seek the truth of the world and the meaning of life.

Meaning organizes the human world. Human beings live in a world of meanings. That is, the maps they have "in their heads" that tell them how to survive in the world, that tell them what to do with different things, that tell them where to find the things they need and want, are maps of meaning. By telling people what things mean, these maps make the world understandable.

So how do people know what something means? Where do they find meaning? Or, in other words, where do the maps of meaning come from? Where do people get the meanings from which these maps are constructed? Are they out there in the world, to be picked up and collected like shells or cassettes? Or are they already inside people's heads, as the Cheshire Cat declares in *Alice in Wonderland*: "Words mean exactly what we want them to mean, no more and no less." Who is, after all, in control of the meanings of words, and of the world?

In a brilliant satire, Mark Twain describes Adam and Eve's arguments as they walked through the Garden of Eden. Eve wanted to give everything whatever name came to mind; Adam retorted that things were what they were and hence, that their names had already been assigned. Of course, it was Adam and not Eve who could "see" these correct names, who could read the correct use of words as if they were transparently written upon the face of the various objects and animals in the world. It is no coincidence that it is the male who claims to have this power (see Chapter 9).

The fact is that people do not find meanings in the world, nor are meanings already inside their heads. People *make* meaning. They make multiple and often competing meanings. But they are not entirely free to make any meaning they want. There is a history and a way of life behind the interpretations of the world and of languages that they make. This relationship between meaning, history, and ways of life is precisely what is meant by culture. People are not free to ignore the culture in which they live. There is a reality outside of language, even if they can only know it through their language and culture. The relationship between culture and reality cannot be easily grasped. It must remain something of a dilemma, for meaning is both something people find in the world awaiting them and something they imagine in their heads and project upon that world.

WHAT IS MEANING?

What precisely is this stuff called meaning? And how does it work? The most common way of thinking about meaning is that it is representational. To describe meaning as representational is to say that any language (or any system of meaning) always points or refers to the real world. Thus, the meaning of the word *dog* is obvious: It is a certain kind of object—a four-legged barking domestic animal—in the real world. In this sense, meaning always involves a process of naming. The word names that kind of object a dog.

But what about such notions as *justice* or *truth*? What do they mean? And what about *Superman*? Surely, none of these have any concrete existence in the real world. One can't hold truth or justice in one's hands, and Superman is only a character in a comic book. At this point, it becomes necessary to think of meaning as conceptual. That is, language refers to or points to thoughts inside our minds. The word dog means the particular image or picture or set of associations that come to mind whenever the word appears.

What is the relationship between two different people's thought objects (or concepts)? How is communication possible unless people know or at least assume that they share a common set of meanings when they talk with each other? After all, when Person A says "dogs are nice," she may be thinking of a cute, cuddly lovable thing, but someone else, Person B, may think that A is crazy because B's concept of a dog is a snarling, aggressive wolflike creature. Notice that one implication of this example is that communication may involve more than meaning understood simply as information; it also involves people's emotional and affective relations to whatever it is they are talking about.

Philosophers have pointed out that if meaning is conceptual, then every individual has a "private language," and any communication or intersubjectivity is really an illusion, for only the individual has access to the meaningfulness of his or her words. Moreover, the private language argument states that if meaning is conceptual, if the meaning of a word is a picture inside an individual's head, then how can anyone know that the picture referred to today by "dog" is the same as the picture referred to yesterday by "dog." That is, not only is communication with a private language impossible, but a private language itself is impossible; it could not work as a language even for talking to oneself.

The theories of meaning as representational and as conceptual both describe aspects of how meaning functions in the human world. But neither can explain the capacity, bestowed on people by their systems of meaning, to distance themselves from the world, to think and talk about things that are not present at the moment, or to imagine things that do not yet exist. Nor can they explain how communication between people is possible. That requires a theory that begins with the social nature of meaning systems: People seem to share common codes that provide common maps of the meaningfulness of the world. A code is a systematic structure or organization of signs, where a sign is something that stands in for something else; we shall return to these notions shortly.

Both meaning as representation and meaning as concept locate meaning in a direct relationship between the code and something outside of the code. To assume that meanings are either in the world (that is, representational) or in someone's head (conceptual) is to make the mistake of assuming that there is a simple and direct relationship between language and meaning, that there is an identity between the languages or systems of meaning people use and what meaning refers to. A representational or realist theory of meaning assumes that for every word, there is an object and for every object, there is a word. A conceptual or intentional theory of meaning assumes that for every word, there is a mental image or thought and that every mental image or thought has its own appropriate word. These two commonsense views of meaning assume that there is a necessary correspondence between a particular word or sign and its meaning. These theories assume that meaning is made up of discrete entities that are captured and embodied in systems of meaning but that ultimately exist outside of the system of meaning itself. Hence, using a language correctly involves learning what the proper word is for some visually perceived object (horse), or for some experience (soft), or for some thought (friendly).

Because people live within a particular culture's maps of meaning, it is easy to assume that every word has its own meaning (whether as an object in the world or a concept in our minds). But it is difficult to confront those situations in which the particular word or object has more than one meaning. If we talk about *democracy* or *art* or *rock and roll*, we will encounter disagreement over the meaning of these terms. And particular messages also often seem to have different meanings for different audiences. What is a love song for one person can be, for another person, a statement that love stinks. To one person, a news report on a drug bust can be proof of the effectiveness of the war on drugs, and to another, evidence of the failure of the government's policy. Ads for condoms can be viewed as advocating sex or addressing a serious social problem. The *Brady Bunch* can be an innocent program about an imaginary family, or it can be another example of male domination. How do we explain the disagreements that take place all the time over the meaning of different messages? Is Springsteen's "Born in the USA" a patriotic anthem? Does gangsta rap advocate drugs and violence? Is "death metal" music about Satanism? Why does your teacher want you to analyze the already obvious meaning of some television program?

SEMIOTICS AND THE MEANING OF MEANING

We can begin to answer some of these questions by turning to semiotics, the discipline that studies the nature of any system of meaning.

Semiotics begins by identifying the sign as the elementary unit of a code and a code as any system of meaning. A code can be very large, like the English language, or very small, like the system of traffic light colors. It can be simple (as in the code that says good guys wear white hats and bad guys black) or very complex (as in the world of fashion, where black takes on various meanings, from chic simplicity to mourning clothes).

CODES AND MEANING

A code is a systematic organization or structure of signs. This meaning is not very different from the everyday understanding of codes, especially codes as something to be broken. A code may appear to be different from a language, but in fact, they are both the same, although human languages clearly are among the most complex codes.

In semiotics, meaning has a certain autonomy, or independence, both from the world out there and from the pictures in people's heads. Meaning is located in the codes of society. Semiotics argues that this autonomy can be difficult to recognize because people live inside of their codes and thus take their systems of meaning for granted. According to semiotics, it is emphatically not the case that the languages or the systems of meaning people use provide a picture or mirror of their world and their thoughts. Rather, people expect the world to resemble the pictures that their codes create of it; in fact, they demand that the world mirror the codes of their language. Earlier in the twentieth century, two linguistic anthropologists, Edward Sapir (1921) and Benjamin Whorf (1956), argued that the world as people live and experience it always copies the grammatical structure of the language they speak. But semiotics goes even further. Consider the following example of a society and culture very different from the one most Americans live in today.

Anthropologists first studying the people of the Trobriand Islands in the South Pacific in the early twentieth century found that the Trobriand Islanders had a society built on what seemed to the anthropologists to be a rather odd interpretation of the water and its role in reproduction. These people lived in something of a tropical paradise. They apparently believed that sexual relations had nothing to do with reproduction. After all, sex was so pleasurable that it had to be a gift from the gods. If it were primarily serving a necessary biological function, it need not have been so pleasurable. And so they enjoyed rather free sexual relations. They also believed that when someone died, their soul lived on, swimming in the ocean. And when a woman went swimming, one of these free souls would enter her body and cause her to become pregnant. Hence, the Trobriand Islanders had strict regulations about when women could swim but few about sexuality. This system of beliefs, an interpretation of their reality, was real to them. It functioned well enough for them to survive for many centuries.

The issue is not whether the Trobriand Islanders were "correct" in their meanings of swimming and sexual relations. Their meaning code was both coherent and functional. In fact, as the impact of Western civilization increasingly forced the Trobriand Islanders to adopt new and, to them, alien maps of meaning, their culture and their society gradually disappeared. They did not know how to live successfully as a society in this new reality.

People in what are sometimes called "exotic cultures" (by which is meant cultures that are significantly different from our own) are not the only ones who make the world mean something beyond "rational" or "concrete" reality. Every society not only believes that its culture, its codes, are rational and coherent, it also believes that it can explain events that appear to violate the natural rational order. In the cultures of the Western industrialized nations, people commonly offer interpretations that make use of meanings such as *market forces* when the economy acts in ways they don't understand, or *quarks* when the universe acts in strange ways. And despite all the rationality and scientificity of these modern cultures, the majority of the people still believe in the reality of sacred and irrational events (such as miracles) or in the necessity of appealing to God.

Every society lives within the codes of meaning that it produces for itself. These codes produce the maps by which and in which people live their lives and through which they interpret the world as a rational place. And, to a great extent, every society is continuously forcing reality to fit into its maps, rather than face the more threatening possibility that its maps may be inadequate. Or to put it another way, every culture is made up of multiple codes and languages that are often incompatible and contradictory. Different people in the society may invest more credibility in one or another of these codes, but more often, people simply invest differently in any number of these codes. Sometimes codes are assigned to particular places, making those places into distinct "life worlds" as when people find that their work life or home life are quite different from their church life. And sometimes codes slip out of their places, as when a person appeals to God in the face of a tragedy.

What is crucial is how real people's interpretations are to them. Interpretations may have immediate and physical consequences. Consider a hypothetical woman anthropologist who plans to study the Inuit of northern Canada. She knows that when she arrives she will be invited to partake of a ritual supper of whale blubber, something that does not strike her as particularly appetizing. However, she also knows she cannot refuse the offer of food without insulting her hosts, probably ruining any chance of establishing the rapport she will need. And when she arrives, she is invited to supper and offered a bowl of what she takes to be whale blubber. The anthropologist eats the food that is offered and promptly throws up. Her hosts are confused and say to her: "We thought Americans liked chicken pot pie." Her interpretation of the food and not the reality of it made her sick.

Is this merely a case of expectations taking over? Well, in part. But it is the codes of meaning that define the structure of expectations with which people live their lives and act in the world and with others. In that sense, the codes of meaning not only represent the world, they produce it. Or, if you prefer, they produce another reality, a reality that is defined by its difference from the material world, a reality that is a world of meanings, a human reality.

MEANING AND DIFFERENCE

The semiotic theory of codes sees meaning as a function of absence and difference. Semiotics starts with the recognition that a sign is always about something else, that it represents something other than itself. The sign must always be different from what it represents. The chair one sits on is not a sign of a chair. But the word *chair* is a sign of what one can sit on. We cannot put the chair, the object itself, on this page. We can put the sign chair on this page. A sign is always a sign of absence. If people want to talk about a chair in their office, they only need a sign when the chair is not present in front of them. The sign *the chair in my office* allows them to talk about that which is absent; other-

131

wise they would have to pick up the chair and bring it with them wherever they went just in case they wanted to talk about it.

Because a sign must be different from what it represents, semiotics separates the question of meaning from that of representation. Semiotics in fact has little to say about representation because it is interested in how codes produce meaning, which in turn produces the reality people live in. But it has a great deal to say about the production of meaning in codes. Codes have a double reality. A string of numbers is only a code when it is assumed that there is another level of interpretation of the numbers in that sequence, that there is another string that can be related to the first. Similarly, when we see a red light, we know that it is red and that it is part of what the traffic code tells us. But the red light also tells us about something entirely different—namely, it conveys a set of legal constraints that demands a certain behavior from us: red means stop; green means go.

Codes depend, then, on two different systems, each made of different and differentiable elements, being brought together. Because codes are built upon these differences, they are able to construct meaning, and they enable us to see differences in the world. Without codes of meaning, we could not distinguish one sort of object from another, a man from a woman, an *Aedes vexans* (the common pest mosquito) and an *Aedes communis* (the northern common mosquito), because there would be no categories for such distinctions. We would not even be able to identify an object, because there would be no maps allowing us to distinguish an object from its background, a painting from the wall, or a tree from the forest.

A code is a system of signs, each of which is distinct from every other. A sign is itself made up of two different parts: *a signifier* and *a signified*. These are the two levels that make up any system of meaning or code. What is a signifier? A signifier is a material form—a sensuous marker like a sound or a visual mark. Obviously, a sign has to have some mark of its presence; it has to announce itself. But, not every mark, not every sound, not every squiggle on a page, functions as a signifier. *Qstk* is not a signifier in English. Similarly, while :-) is a signifier in a code in which it represents a happy face; ((((is not a signifier and thus, not part of a sign. For something to be a signifier, it has to be located within a code in which its uniqueness, its difference from any other possible signifier, can be recognized. Its uniqueness and its existence as a signifier are defined by its differences from the other signifiers within the code. For example, Americans have no difficulty distinguishing *cot* from *cat* when they hear them. Moreover, English speakers recognize them as signifiers, both written and aural. But *cet* is a different matter. These letters look like a typographical error or perhaps a new word. This "word" is certainly not a signifier in English. But if we were to hear the sound, we would probably assume it to be the same as cat. This kind of difference would not register the sound as a unique signifier, unless it signified a regional accent. Similarly, if you are driving and see a traffic signal that has a blue light on the bottom, you might reasonably assume that, as a signifier, it is no different from green. But if you saw a purple light, you might wonder whether it meant anything at all, whether it was a signifier. Thus, for something to be a signifier, it must already exist in at least one system of difference, within a code that makes its existence as a signifier possible. Public relations campaigns often recognize this fact. For example, when Standard Oil Co. of New Jersey wanted a new trade name, the company purposely chose one that was not a signifier in any known human language so that it could become a unique signifier in the code of trade names: *Exxon* was chosen because *xx* is a feature of virtually no written language.

Think about the line from the famous song by George Gershwin: "You say tom*ay*to, and I say tom*ah*to". In one code, there is no difference between the two signifiers, "tomayto" and "tomahto." They both mean a round, red fruit or vegetable, and they are the same signifier. But in the code of the movie *Shall We Dance*, with Fred Astaire and Ginger Rogers, the difference between the signifiers is crucial, pointing to class differences between the Astaire and Rogers characters and to a certain friction in their romance. Hence, "Let's call the whole thing off." In ordinary speech, the difference between "tomayto" and "tomahto" may identify no more than regional dialects.

Something is a signifier only by virtue of its location within a socially defined system of differences. There is a story commonly told about the armed forces' attempts to enlist the aid of the natives of the South Pacific islands in the battle against malaria. Mounting a large audiovisual campaign, including photographic blowups, the War Department had attempted to explain to these people how insects can carry the disease and why the mosquitoes therefore needed to be eradicated. After the war, investigators returned to try to understand why their media campaigns had failed. The local people told them that they did not have any insects that large; if they did, they would certainly think them dangerous. But they only had small, harmless mosquitoes.

Here is an example of the socially coded nature of a signifier. A picture is an example of an *iconic sign*—a sign that functions by virtue of its resemblance to its referent, what it refers to. Yet, even here, the natives who did not share the appropriate codes, never having seen a photograph, could not understand the manipulation of the signifier implicit in the blowup.

A system of signifiers, then, is an organization of any material or perceptual variables: It can be colors, sounds, spatial arrangements, shapes. The code tells those using the code where to draw the line between the elements. The code divides the universe of perception into a series of different elements. In that sense, the different elements do not exist as separable, identifiable entities except insofar as they are located within a code. The light spectrum is continuous, but we distinguish different colors in digital terms, separating, for example, red from orange, blue from violet. Similarly, we make distinctions (between b and p) to mark significant differences out of the spectrum of sounds. In other languages, b and p might not be marked as different.

But a code of signifiers by itself is not a code of meaning, for signs, language, and meaning are produced only when two such systems of differences are brought together. The second system of differences is the second level of a code or sign, the level of the signified or meaning. To use a simple example, the code of colors simultaneously establishes a system of different words (red, green, blue, yellow) and a system of differences within the electromagnetic spectrum. The differences are related to one another to create a single meaningful code of colors. The words can be a code of signifiers for the spectrum, or they can become a code of signifiers for another language of colors (red means love). Another example results from mapping a system of different sounds—words—onto the physical world of animals. Now we can label horses and mules, cats and dogs, cats and lions. Without the codes to mark the differences, there would be no way to think about the difference between a mule and a horse. People might certainly see a difference, just as they might see differences between different kinds of horses or between different horses, even if they had no signifiers for these differences.

Thus, the traffic code tells people that red is linked to stop, green to go, and yellow to caution. But what is the status of these so-called meanings or signifieds? Are they actual descriptions of our behavior? Obviously not, or we would not need traffic cops, and the protagonist of *Starman* could not have observed that yellow means "go very fast." Nor are they concepts within people's heads or real objects in the world. Like signifiers, they are the product of, and only exist within, the semiotic codes of the society. The meaning that is linked to a signifier is always another signifier. Think about it: whenever you try to come up with the meaning of a word or message, you can only come up with another word or message. It is like looking up a word in a dictionary: All the dictionary gives you is another word, which you can look up, to find another word. Sooner or later, you are led back to the original word you tried to look up. The meaning of a sign is always another sign; the signified is another signifier.

SIGNS AND MEANING

Thus, a sign is more than a signifier; it is a signifier linked to a signified or meaning, not as a concept or referent, but as another signifier, itself defined within its own system of difference. The sign is the interaction of two systems of signifiers. In the sign, the two signifiers are stitched together, one on top of the other as it were. The first signifier is the signifier of the sign, and the second signifier becomes the signified of the sign.

Within a code of meaning, the signified is always subordinate to, or conditioned upon, the signifier. The differences of the system of the signifier become a map or template for the system of the signified, defining its differences, in the same way that our color words are mapped onto locations of the electromagnetic spectrum. There is a classic example of this relationship between signifier and signifieds within a code of meaning, which will enable us to try a short experiment. First, think of the codes of meaning that make sense of the animal kingdom for us. Now, erase them from your mind and try to imagine living in a universe organized by a different code, the codes of a "certain Chinese encyclopedia" described by the Latin American writer, Jose Luis Borges:

Animals are divided into: (a) belonging to the Emperor, (b) embalmed, (c) tame, (d) suckling pigs, (e) sirens, (f) fabulous, (g) stray dogs, (h) included in the present classification, (i) frenzied, (j) innumerable, (k) drawn with a fine camelhair brush, (l) et cetera, (m) having just broken the water pitcher, (n) that from a long way off look like flies. (as cited in Foucault, 1970, p. xv)

Can you imagine what this world would look like? Can you imagine what it would be like to live in this world?

Codes organize the world into categories, telling us what is a significant relationship, what similarities and what differences are meaningful and matter. The organization of identity and difference (what things are to be considered the same and what are to be considered not the same) offered by the Chinese encyclopedia is very strange to us, but it is a viable code and it establishes a meaningful universe for someone. Recall now the codes of modern English-speaking culture that organize the animal kingdom. In fact, there are a number of different, overlapping codes. In American culture, we distinguish animals on the basis of size, danger, utility (domesticated pets, farm animals, game animals), and number (we mark extinct species), as well as by a hierarchical biological classification scheme of phylum, family, genus, and species (within which we distinguish mammals, reptiles, fish, birds). This system would no doubt strike the author of the ancient Chinese encyclopedia as weird. The Chinese encyclopedia categories define common identities that may be very different from the ones we are used to; similarly, they make distinctions that we do not normally make. But the code still establishes a system by which we could give meaning to the world and to our experience of it.

The codes of meaning tell people what events are worthy of note, what events can be said to exist at all, what is to count as an event. Most Americans or Europeans would be unlikely to take stories blaming our troubles on leprechauns very seriously, although many people are likely to live within codes that take the role of God in human history seriously. And even more people are likely to accept codes that explain the universe in terms of subatomic particles. No one has seen leprechauns, God, or subatomic particles. Why certain codes appear reasonable to particular groups of people is a matter we will take up in Chapter 7.

The ability to watch and understand television depends on an individual's knowledge of and familiarity with the relevant codes. Sometimes the codes are very simple. It does not take a lot of effort to explain the codes operating in a *Roadrunner* cartoon. There are two major characters: the bad Wile E. Coyote and the cute Roadrunner (a code of characters). Wile E. Coyote always attempts to catch Roadrunner and always fails (a narrative code). Usually, some gizmo such as rocket roller skates Coyote has purchased from the Acme Co. backfires on him (codes about technology), leaving Roadrunner to "Beep-beep" into the sunset. But imagine explaining this cartoon to someone who had never seen a cartoon. And how much work would it take to explain the necessary codes to understand what is significant and what is merely irrelevant detail on MTV?

Conversely, some codes of meaning that seem quite familiar and reasonable can seem quite strange when scrutinized. For instance, in almost all visual media—film, photography, television, news, commercials—black and white is used to signify documentary reality. How odd: most people see reality in color.

This example illustrates an important point about codes of meaning: They are arbitrary. To say that codes are arbitrary does not deny that there may have been—and continue to be—good social, functional, and historical reasons why specific codes were constructed in specific ways. Nor does it deny that, once an individual born into a social world learns to inhabit the world defined by the codes of meaning of that society, she or he sees nothing arbitrary about the codes. On the contrary, the codes (of signifiers, of signified, and of signs linking the two) appear natural, inevitable, logical, rational, commonsensical. Someone who refuses to accept the codes can only be an alien, or a threat. In fact, this is the theme of a number of popular films and television series, for example, *Men in Black* and *The Visitor*. The ubiquity of the codes is, unfortunately, often responsible for our attitudes toward people from significantly different cultures.

Codes (or any sign within a code) are arbitrary because they are the product of the joining of two systems of differences. No natural law says systems have to be linked (instead of colors, we could use shapes to control traffic flow). No natural law says systems have to be linked in just the way they were (red could mean go). No natural law says the world has to be divided up the way it is: A continuously changing system of colors could control traffic speed. Instead of dividing the world of water by size (oceans, seas, lakes, ponds; rivers, streams, creeks), the English language could have been more concerned with the content of the water (salty, dirty, full of fish) or the source of the water. There is no natural or inevitable correspondence between the two structures of differences that make up a code of meaning. It is not inevitable that the word *horse* refers to that particular animal instead of what is commonly called a cow. Similarly, it is not inevitable that the animal kingdom be divided up into Western scientific categories. In fact, the scientific system of classification has changed significantly over the past century, although the latest usages have not entered into common sense. The organization of differences, the maps of meanings that any culture's codes produce, are not some inevitable reflection of the way things are, but the product of human history and, as we shall see, of relations of power.

SEMIOTIC VIEW OF MEANING

A semiotic view of meaning has important implications for thinking about the meaning of any message or *text*. If a sign is always produced by temporarily linking together two signifiers, then it is perhaps not accurate to see this process as making connections between two independent chains or codes of signifiers. Rather, as C. S. Pierce (1958), the founder of both American pragmatism and semiotics, argued, a signifier is always sliding into another signifier in an endless production of meaning. The French philosopher Jacques Derrida (1981) calls this process *dissemination,* the endless movement and proliferation of signifiers. This notion opens up two possible misinterpretations. First, perhaps, dissemination implies that the movement from one signifier to the next is inevitable and natural, rather than social, as if the line of dissemination were determined in advance. Second, it might seem that the meaning of any signifier is not determined at all and thus is infinite. The line of signifiers extends into infinity so that, in the final analysis, there is no meaning.

Polysemy implies a different understanding of this sliding of signifiers. The movement of one signifier into another might be thought of as a game of musical chairs. It is only infinite and without meaning as long as the music doesn't stop, but, of course, the music is always stopped. (Asking how the music is stopped and who stops it raises real questions of power and points toward questions of ideology, to be considered in Chapter 7.) When the music is stopped, some signifiers find a seat—in other words, they slide into the position of signified (meaning). In this way, the potentially infinite sliding of signifiers into other signifiers (which is the process of language production) is transformed into the production of meaning by a particular articulation of signifiers.

Articulation is the process by which different elements are connected. In England, a 16-wheel semi-truck is described as an *articulated lorry,* referring to the link between the cab and the trailer. The cab and the trailer can be separated, although neither piece would be very useful alone. The two pieces can be linked to other cabs or trailers to form a different truck, but neither half is "a truck" itself. The production of signs, texts, and meanings can be seen in similar terms. Signifiers are linked to produce signs; signs are linked to produce texts; texts are linked to produce interpretations. When someone uses language, he or she articulates signifiers together and codes together; this is how language makes signs, texts, and meanings. Meanings involve the articulation of relations between signifiers, relations that are themselves described in terms of codes. This process, at a broader level, implies that texts themselves have meaning only in relationship to the codes with which they are articulated or located, and hence, in relationship to the broader set of other texts that carry those codes with them. The meaning of a message depends on the ways these codes are linked or articulated to other codes in and through texts. Hence, meanings are always *intertextual.* Articulation also implies that codes of meaning can transcend any particular message. Every message refers to other instances of the codes that have produced it. For example, as simple as the code of *Roadrunner* is, we would not recognize it except for the fact that it appears in so many other common texts in our culture.

If meaning does not exist outside of the structure of differences produced by the codes, then meaning is not movable from one language to another. *Translatability* becomes something of an illusion. In fact, the same signifiers, located within different codes, can become entirely different signs. For example, consider the following anthropological experience (Bohannon, 1967).

A woman anthropologist is studying an African culture in which storytelling is an important social ritual, normally reserved for the elders—always male—of the tribe. As a sign of their acceptance, the elders invite the anthropologist to tell a story. Searching her memory for an appropriate story, one that would demonstrate her wisdom and the wisdom of Western European culture, the anthropologist decides to recount the story of *Hamlet*. She tells it in great detail. But from the very beginning, she realizes that it is not going well. As soon as the tribal elders hear that Hamlet is visited by the ghost of his dead father, they become convinced that it is a story about witches. After all, the only explanation for ghosts is the spell of a witch. As the story continues, they become even more convinced that the story contains the wisdom of Anglo-American culture concerning the procedures for hunting and identifying witches. Despite the anthropologist's protests, they are not shaken from this interpretation and in fact, offer a cogent and coherent interpretation of the story. Furthermore, they are convinced that the fact that the anthropologist is unaware of the true meaning of the story is merely a sign that the elders of her own culture have kept it from her, not surprising given that she is a woman.

The African elders clearly articulated the narrative of *Hamlet* to a set of codes and texts different from those the anthropologist was taking for granted. This is not some unusual case. Although many critics would argue that it is precisely the very richness of *Hamlet*, its openness to many interpretations, that makes it a great work of art, a semiotic theory of meaning defines every signifier, every sign, and every text as polysemic. What differs is only the degree of ambiguity that is recognized and tolerated in the various institutions assigned the responsibility of policing the possibilities of interpretation and misinterpretation (such as the institutions of literary criticism). Any text can be articulated to a wide variety of codes and texts, but no society ever tolerates every possible articulation of every text. Consider the names of the Teenage Mutant Ninja Turtles: Donatello, Raphael, Michaelangelo, and Leonardo. For children, the names may signal a code of unfamiliar and therefore somewhat exotic names. For others, the names are part of the code of Italian Renaissance painters, and for still others, they are part of the code of famous artists who were gay. Each of these articulations changes the text and its meaning. Nor does anyone know for sure whether the creatures' creators intended people to notice all these codes; that is, whether they intentionally selected the names of gay Renaissance artists.

MEANING AND COMPETENCE

Concern about the making of meaning is not exclusively the province of a cultural tradition of interpretation. Psychology, and particularly an emerging branch of the discipline known as cognitive psychology, has more than a little to say about how humans interpret symbols.

Within cognitive psychology, the most prominent sense- and meaning-making model is schema theory. Schemas are knowledge structures—sets of beliefs or facts that people fit together in their heads to be able to organize experience (Graesser, Millis, & Long, 1986). An example of a schema might be a particular story schema. Virtually all Americans understand the crime detection story. A bad guy commits a crime—an initiating event; detectives come to the scene of the crime and follow the clues, which after some twists and turns in the plot line, inevitably lead to the detective's catching the criminal—the denouement. We even have schemas for kinds of detectives—the apparent bumbler (*Columbo,* Agatha Christie's Jane Marple), the sophisticate (Nick and Nora Charles from the 1930s *The Thin Man* movies), and the hard-boiled detective (Mickey Spillane's Mike Hammer). Just as there are schemas for detective stories, there are schemas for news, doctor shows, family comedies. Schemas offer a useful concept for a psychological view of how adults make sense of media messages. Schemas are activated as audience members make sense of the particular media message. A schema helps make the task of comprehending the specific narrative easier, and some media, like television, help the viewer by using formulas, which we discussed earlier in this chapter.

In this discussion of meaning, we have assumed an adult model of competence. Differences in interpretation are not thought to reside in the basic cognitive ability of the meaning maker. However, this is not the case for children. A substantial body of research examines how children come to interpret and make sense of media content, especially television programming. This literature draws upon theories of cognitive development, how children come to understand the world. In turn, the literature on children's interpretations of television has been used in the creation of educational children's television programs, starting with *Sesame Street.*

Children gradually become competent, and adult-like, in their meaning making of television programming. As they grow older, child viewers acquire the ability to understand the narrative contents, distinguish among program genres and formats, and correctly interpret the production forms (such as instant replays) of television. Chronological age is a fairly good gauge of children's competence, with children younger than ages 5 or 6 generally more idiosyncratic in their interpretations of the meaning of the television program than older children or adults.

Up to about age 5 or 6, young children tend to interact with television as though it were a "magic window on the world," not a construction acted out by actors. They are less skillful at recognizing the scenes of a plot adults consider central to understanding the story. They tend to focus more on the appearance of characters than the characters' behaviors in making interpretive judgments about the character and in forming beliefs about the outcome of a story. They have difficulty connecting events that are separated in time. And the production characteristics of zooms, fast pace, rapid cuts, for instance, influence their comprehension. Moreover, young children must come to understand the purpose of such content as advertising, that advertisers are trying to sell them a product and therefore may present the product in its best light. Preschool children typically have difficulty identifying which is the program and which is the commercial; where program characters such as the Power Rangers are also toy products sold in advertisements, distinguishing programs from advertising becomes more difficult.

Young children, however, can be aided in their meaning making. When adults and older children watch television with a preschooler, identifying important aspects of the narrative and making interpretive comments, they can aid the younger child's understanding of the program. Also, educational television producers have demonstrated that when there is congruency between the audio and visual tracks of a program, and even better, when there is redundancy between what is seen and what is heard, younger children understand the content better and learn more from television. Also, the use of program separators (such as "And now for these messages" or "And now back to our show"), required by the Federal Communications Commission during children's programs, help young children distinguish programs from commercials. That young children differ from older children and adults in their ability to understand and make meaning from television and other media is the underlying assumption of federal requirements that television broadcasters must identify their educational and informational programs for children. Young children are a special audience of meaning makers.

People live in a world of meanings and interpretations, organized by codes of differences. They do not make those meanings; they do not interpret their world for themselves. Nor does the world come already interpreted apart from human activity. People live within the codes, the systems of differences, and the articulations by which those codes have been stitched together in particular ways. They live within a culture, and the process by which that culture is produced, maintained, repaired, and transformed is communication. To speak of culture as produced and transformed is to also speak of reality as produced and transformed. People always live in a world made by the codes with which that world is made meaningful.

It is in and through communication that humans create the reality that they then inhabit. The codes of meaning that make up our common culture produce the very reality they represent. Communication cannot be separated from the world that it communicates, or from the codes that make it possible to communicate. For this reason, it is important to understand the codes and meanings that are communicated in the most public and visibly shared forms of communication in our society: the various texts of the mass media and popular culture. These texts clearly play an important role in producing the shared codes and maps of meaning that come to define the world we live in.

BOX 5.1

Children's Interpretation of Television

I sat down last Thursday to watch an episode of *The Simpsons* with my sons David, 8, and Stephen, 3. This episode was about the family's trip to a new Japanese restaurant for sushi where Homer ate *fugu,* a Japanese blowfish, which was presumably prepared wrong and therefore deadly within 24 hours to anyone who eats it. The rest of the episode revolves around Homer's likely last day of life and his attempts to say good-bye to the people he loves: his wife, Marge; his children Bart, Lisa, and Maggie; his father and his boss and friends.

Clearly, David, Stephen, and I were interpreting this show differently. Stephen had very little understanding of the plot of the show: He could tell me that Homer was sick, but he didn't know why or how. "Sushi" was lost on him. His favorite part of the show was when Homer showed his son Bart how to shave: Stephen likes to watch his own father shave, and Stephen particularly likes Bart. To Stephen, Bart is "cool." Apart from laughing when Bart is on the screen, Stephen shows little understanding of the program outside of a few scenes: He laughs when the policemen pull Homer over for speeding and when Homer runs home after his car breaks down. What's the show about? Stephen's not quite sure; his attempts to tell me about it or answer my questions suggest that he has a very rudimentary understanding of the plot—a lot of disconnected and discrete events are all that he can describe. What else happens? Stephen's not sure.

David had a much better understanding of most of the plot elements I thought were important for understanding the narrative: He knew that the fish Homer ate at the restaurant (he thinks it's a Chinese restaurant) was thought to be "deadly," he understood that Homer and Marge thought Homer was going to die and so Homer was planning all of the things he would do before he dies—"he has a list of stuff to do to make his family happy," says David. Here's David's description of the story: "He (Homer) went to a sushi place with his family and he ate something poisonous and he went to the doctor and he says he's going to die so he has a list of stuff to do before he dies to make his family happy. And so he does lots of things like play ball with his father, talks to Bart his son, listens to Lisa play her saxophone, makes a videotape for Maggie, and goes to the bar with his friends. And he doesn't die after all."

These differences between Stephen and David's comprehension of the narrative of *The Simpsons* illustrate that children have to develop an understanding of narrative and have to come to learn how to interpret television stories. Younger children, usually those in preschool or below age 5, tend to have difficulty understanding plot lines, particularly those events adults consider central or main points of the story. Consequently, younger children like Stephen tend to develop very idiosyncratic interpretations of the story. For Stephen, this episode of *The Simpsons* was about "Homer and Bart shaving." At Stephen's age, children have difficulty distinguishing reality and fantasy on television. (Stephen thinks that Bart and Homer live inside the TV set. He's not sure what happens to them when you turn off the set.) They have difficulty identifying the characters' motivations for their actions; they have difficulty understanding the plot lines; and they have difficulty distinguishing the different kinds of content, in particular commercials and programs, of television.

As children grow older, they become more adept at understanding narratives in general and television narratives in particular. David at age 8 and I agreed on the central events of what happened in the show. He is much better at distinguishing reality and fantasy, and he certainly knows the difference between the ads and the programs (on Saturday morning, he pays particular attention to the ads to decide which fast-food restaurant he should ask to go to for lunch; he chooses the one giving the best prize in their kids' meals). But even David has difficulty making sense of some of the characters' motivations, and he doesn't understand some of the more adultlike depictions, in particular, Marge, and Homer's discussion about "being intimate" is completely lost on David (for which both Mom and Dad are happy; they would rather address *that* question later). He brings a limited understanding about the social world and people to his interpretations of the television plot, and therefore he, too, compared to an adult viewer, has a different interpretation of the program. He sometimes looks quizzically at what I find funny about the show.

Children only gradually come to interpret television in the way adults do. That's why child advocates argue that children need programs specially designed with their needs and abilities taken into account. Adult programs, or shows that appeal to both adults and kids (such as *The Simpsons*) are interpreted differently by children of different ages and by adults.

(This essay was written by Ellen Wartella, an author of this text, as she watched a television program with her two children.)

The Interpretation of Meaning 6

I n this chapter, we consider ways to analyze and interpret the messages or texts of the media in all their diverse forms. People are interpreting what they see and hear all of the time, but they usually take their interpretations, and the ways they arrive at them, for granted. We will make explicit the kinds of questions people ask of these texts and the sorts of answers they expect. Then we will begin to develop analytic tools for examining texts.

Whatever the text—a film, an album, or a comic book—different readers are likely to have different interpretations and evaluations. Some people may find a particular text aesthetically progressive and engaging; others may find it boring, derivative, unoriginal. Some people will argue that a particular text is somehow subversive and rebellious, others that it is more of the same old message (about war, politics, money, or social relations of gender, race). Interpretation and evaluation are not the same thing, although they are often closely related in everyday practice. In the following discussion, we shall be less concerned with evaluation than with interpretation, with how people arrive at an understanding of a text.

Some people will focus on their relationship to the performer and his or her image. Others will approach the text more traditionally. They

147

talk about the text itself and consider how the artist may have intended it. Sometimes, people will refer to information beyond the text, such as interviews with the artist or their background knowledge of the history of the author, the medium, or the subject. Some people rely on knowledge or experience that most fans (and critics) would not think to bring to the text in question; their interpretations may seem particularly strange to others. Still others may be less concerned with the performer or the text than with the fans themselves and with their responses to the texts. Most people are familiar with the diverse forms of enthusiasm that have greeted such performers as Frank Sinatra, Bruce Springsteen, Michael Jackson, and Madonna, or such films as *Star Wars* and *Jurassic Park,* or such television programs as *Star Trek* or the numerous successful soap operas on daytime television.

In its simplest form, the transmission model of communication assumes that the aim of all communication is to maximize the likelihood that the receiver receives the exact same message (that is, meaning) as the sender sends. Hence, communication is assumed to function in such a way that the two ends of the process are somehow necessarily tied together; if they are not, the process fails. The British cultural critic Stuart Hall (1980), using semiotics, argues to the contrary that communication has to be seen as an articulation of two distinct processes, *encoding* and *decoding,* which do not have any necessary relationship to each other. Hall argues that although the two processes should be studied together, they are nevertheless distinguishable; and therefore, the process of communication, and its success or failure, cannot be judged by some comparison test. Audiences interpret messages by articulating them into their own codes. It is thus reasonable to assume that the decoded meaning will differ from the encoded meaning, which describes the ways the text is articulated within the institutional contexts of its production.

THE NATURE OF INTERPRETATION

We have shown that interpretation is itself a complicated and varied practice. Before someone decides what a text means, before he or she can interpret a text, at least three different questions must already have been answered, at least implicitly:

- What is the text to be interpreted?
- What question is the text answering?
- How does a text communicate?

WHAT IS THE TEXT TO BE INTERPRETED?

The task of interpreting a text is made even more difficult by the fact that, however simple a text may appear, it is actually quite complex. For the actual text—the signs and the codes—are themselves located in and cannot be separated from a complex set of relations: relations to the artist or author and his or her image; relations to the audience; relations to other texts and to the history of popular culture; relations to knowledge that people bring from a wide range of fields (including other media); relations to other forms of behavior (styles of dance, sexual attitudes, fashion); relations to the media (such as radio or MTV, which constantly repeat commercially successful texts) in which the text is itself communicated; and finally, relations to different audiences and their various structures of taste (for example, how a fan of Bruce Willis in the TV show *Moonlighting* sees the *Die Hard* movies will be different from how a fan of violent adventure films such as *Rambo* sees them).

In fact, one has to realize that there is no single text that can be isolated for the sake of analysis. There are the signifiers themselves, the sounds and words and images that make up any text, any song or film or TV program. But the meaning of these signifiers, and hence of the text, does not exist outside of the codes, the relations of difference, which the text produces, to which the text is articulated, and in which the text itself is located. In that sense, every text is an *intertext*. This characteristic helps to explain the radically polysemic nature of media messages. Every text, every organization of signifiers, is potentially a number of different texts, each with its own set of possible meanings.

WHAT QUESTION IS THE TEXT ANSWERING?

Let us turn then to ask what kinds of questions can be asked about a text. What kinds of things do people expect a text to provide them with or do for them? In different interpretations of a text, people are not always looking for the same thing, not always asking the same questions. There are two sorts of common things people might look for in a text, two reasons they might be interested in it: behavior and meaning. First, one can look for models of behavior, which might take the form of role models or "rules for living" or implicit instructions on how to do something. People learn everything, from dance steps to how to treat members of the opposite sex, to a variety of different poses and attitudes, from media texts. People can learn ethical maxims and illegal practices; they can learn how to make love, or use drugs, or even kill someone. Whether or not they act upon any of this knowledge is a different question, which we will take up in Chapter 9.

More commonly, when interpreting a text, one looks for some meaning that is not obvious to everyone, some meaning that is, as critics often say, "below the surface." In such interpretations, all of the obvious visible and audible signifiers are interpreted as if they point to some underlying, "deeper," and less obvious, meaning. This need not deny that many people can and do make sense of the text by taking its surface literally. And although they may even be aware of a deeper meaning, in many cases, this is because the interpretations of the deeper meaning of a text have already become so accepted and commonsensical that they no longer appear to be below the surface. Instead they appear for all practical purposes to be obvious and intentional. An example of this is the case of *M*A*S*H*, first a movie and then a television program set during the Korean War of the early 1950s. The show's popularity in the 1970s was built on an interpretation of it as a comment on the Vietnam War. This interpretation became so commonly held that most discussions of the program took at face value that *M*A*S*H* was "about" Vietnam. In the 1990s hit, *The X-Files*, this ambiguity is coded into the text itself: whereas Scully always sees scientific questions on the surface, Mulder always sees conspiracies and aliens hidden below the surface.

In many cases, including that of *M*A*S*H*, the deeper meaning of the text is identified with questions about the political and social organization of reality. Such questions need not be explicitly political— *M*A*S*H* was often read as an argument against war in general and against the United States acting as the world's police agency in particular. It could be about disputed values or attitudes (Christianity, capitalism, or drugs); it could embody the experiences, hopes, and desires of a community (for example, much of 1960s music is about youth culture); it could challenge or defend an existing set of social relations (those between Whites and African Americans); or in fact it could be about the way a particular culture has constructed an entire world.

HOW DOES A TEXT COMMUNICATE?

Sometimes when we interpret a text, we are not looking for its meaning. Instead, having already decided what its meaning is, we might be more interested in understanding how the text produces the particular meaning we assume it has. The question becomes less what the text communicates than how it communicates. Particular television programs might operate by using familiar clichés to demolish viewers' expectations of traditional television. Both Mad TV and David Letterman, as well as *Northern Exposure,* work precisely by violating the rules that normally enable television to communicate.

INTERPRETATION AND THE AUTHOR

Perhaps the most commonsensical view of the meaning of a text is that it means exactly what its author intended it to mean, no more and no less. Most people operate with this view most of the time, both when they have no problem understanding a text and when they do not understand it at all. (Two psychiatrists meet on the street: each says "Good morning!" As they pass, each asks herself silently, "I wonder what she meant by *that?*") Whether watching something that the viewer thinks makes the author's meaning very transparent, such as Steven Spielberg's *ET* or something completely opaque, such as David Lynch's *Wild at Heart,* people tend to assume that the task of interpretation is to identify with or get into the mind of the author to discover what is really going on. Understanding a text is taken to require that the interpreter become one with the author. Thus, when people look at and quite unself-consciously interpret a *Doonesbury* cartoon, they often assume that the meaning they find there (or is it the meaning they have given it) is what Gary Trudeau placed there for them to find. On the other hand, listening to a song by the Talking Heads, someone might assume just as easily that any inability to understand the song is a direct result of something going on inside the mind of David Byrne: he is too avant-garde (intentionally making it unnecessarily difficult), too crazy, or at least too serious.

There are, however, a number of problems with this view of media meanings. First, why should the author of a text have the last say regarding its meaning? Imagine that two people in love have a favorite film that they think is very romantic and hopeful. Now imagine that the director (who may or may not be the film's author, but we'll come to that in a moment) tells them that they have it all wrong; according to him, the film is really about the difficulties of sustaining love today. Do the lovers decide that they have been wrong all these years and that they have to give up "their" favorite film? Probably not, no more than Ronald Reagan could be convinced that because Bruce Springsteen's politics (and his statements) placed the singer in rather direct opposition to him, Reagan could not use the song as a statement of patriotism.

In fact, appealing to the author as if he or she could guarantee the meaning of the text contradicts the conclusions we have already reached: that texts are polysemic and intertextual. The fact that media texts are so widely and rapidly dispersed only magnifies the difficulties of trying to identify their meaning with the author's meaning. Often, authors do intend to, attempt to, and succeed in placing meanings in their texts. We have referred to this as the encoded meaning. But there is no reason to privilege such meanings. In most cases, people are simply unable to know what the author may have intended. The song "Yankee Doodle" was originally composed by British soldiers as a sarcastic put-down of the loutish American revolutionary soldiers. The Yankees, however, appropriated it as a patriotic song of their own. Today, it's mostly just a song that children sing. Similarly, Woody Guthrie wrote "This Land Is Your Land" as an angry socialist retort to—a protest against—the sentimental celebration of the country in Irving Berlin's "God Bless America"; now it has become merely another benign patriotic anthem.

The second problem with assuming that the meaning of a text is determined by the author is figuring out who the author is. Take a television program or film. Is the author the scriptwriter? The series creator? The director? The actors? The producer? The cinematographer? The studio or network executives who control the budget and who may often directly intervene into (censor) particular programs? Or is it the corporate owners, who also may intervene into the content of particu-

---

BOX 6.1

The Wizard of Oz

For almost all of us, *The Wizard of Oz* is a pleasant "family movie," and most of us know it from one of the frequent reruns of the 1939 MGM version featuring Judy Garland, Ray Bolger, and Bert Lahr. But it's more than that. L. Frank Baum's 1900 story, *The Wonderful Wizard of Oz*, was, according to writer Henry M. Little-field (1964), a political allegory of U.S. national politics around the turn of the century. The "yellow brick road," for instance, referred to the gold standard, which populist Democrats wanted overturned in favor of the free coinage of silver, represented in *Oz* as the magical silver slippers. The Emerald City was Washington, D.C., the cowardly lion was Democratic presidential candidate William Jennings Bryan, and so on. The *political* meaning of this story is now virtually completely forgotten, but we still enjoy the movie, and "understand" it with no reference at all to its politics.

---

lar programs (including the news)? Or is it the banks who are willing to finance some kind of media products and not others? Why are some films identified with their stars (for example, a Sylvester Stallone movie), others with their directors (for example, a Martin Scorsese film), and still others with their studios (for example, an MGM screwball comedy or a Disney animated cartoon)?

Can we isolate one single author? What if the different participants have different meanings in mind when they are working on the same text? Clearly, on a metropolitan newspaper or a feature film, hundreds of people contribute to the creative content of the product. The situation is not much better in a music album. People tend to identify the author with the performer, even when he or she does not write many of the songs. Many performers are groups, and writing credits are divided among them. Every performer plays songs written by others, including some ("covers") that have already been recorded. But in addition to performers and composers, there are managers (who often control the careers of all but the most successful stars), producers, engineers, and record company executives (not to mention all the people involved in video production and the marketing of other image paraphernalia). The traditional thinking that the creative artists are entirely responsible for their creations is no longer appropriate in the age of the mass media

153

and the mass production of popular culture. Today's "artist" is a group of people, all with their own intentions and responsibilities, all with their own agendas and constraints. In this rather chaotic context of creation, how can one possibly hope to identify the actual author?

Consider the big scandal in the popular music industry in 1991: the pop group Milli Vanilli, we discovered, was not what people thought it was. What exactly was discovered? Why did the two men lose their 1990 Grammy Award for best new group? In some sense, it was discovered that they were not the "authors" of their album. Stripping them of the award in effect said that they made no significant contribution to the production of the musical texts. Everyone knew that they had not written, engineered, or produced the text, or even played the music. Any astute fan already knew that they were not the creative force behind the music. But fans did believe that they *sang*: that is all they did. Then fans found out that they had not even done that. But did that mean that they had no authorial relation to the text? The media (and the Grammy committee) certainly seemed to think so. But some fans argued that the men did "front" the music; it was their presence, their style, and their image that gave the music its popular public face and, to some extent, its popularity. Just where does one draw the line? Who is responsible for a text? Who gets the credit?

Many questions can be raised about the relationship between authorship and the production of media texts; we will address these in other chapters. For now, the difficulty of identifying an author for most media texts makes it reasonable to assume that texts can be analyzed as if they had no author at all. After all, even if we are convinced that the real secret in understanding a text lies in what the author intended to say, in most cases, our only evidence will be what is available in the text. And if we give up the deeply held and romantic image of the creative artist, we are still left facing the text itself.

TECHNIQUES OF INTERPRETATION

There are many different techniques for interpreting the meaning of a text and for understanding how the text constructs and communicates that meaning. In this chapter, we are concerned with techniques that focus on the encoded meaning, that is, that start with the text itself.

Even if the text cannot be said to have a single, definitive meaning, the text does offer us certain organizations and structures of meaning that can be identified. We can understand the encoded meaning of a text to be what is "in" the codes and structures that can be identified in the text itself, putting aside all but the most obvious and culturally shared links between the signifiers of the text and other texts to which it might be connected.

Usually, people do not stop to analyze the system of signifiers that enable the text to signify in particular ways. Because they are quite familiar with the vast majority of codes employed in the mass media, people do not need to stop and inspect the text. But that is precisely what one must do to get a better understanding of how the media work to produce a meaningful world, and what specific meanings they produce. So we will explore some of the different techniques for interpreting or, as it is called, reading, a text of any type.

We are arguing that the author's meaning is not *the* meaning of a text. There is no *one* meaning of a text. However, it does not follow that just any interpretation of a text is valid. The signifiers of the text, their organization by and into particular codes, the intertextual relations of this text with other texts, and the questions and methods we bring to analyzing the text, all limit or constrain our interpretations. Not every text lends itself equally well to all methods of analysis.

Most of the time, when people reflect on their interpretation of a text, they focus either on the themes or on the symbols that are most obvious in the text. We look for a theme in the content or subject matter of the text; examples of themes range from love and family relations to war and social responsibility. *Cinderella* is a story about romantic love. *Twin Peaks* is a murder mystery: Who killed Laura Palmer? Or its theme might be seen as the story of life in small-town America. After identifying the theme, the interpreter's task is to describe the way the theme is presented in the text. For example, in *Cinderella*, romantic love is not only highly prized, it wins out over all obstacles. Love conquers all. In *Twin Peaks*, small-town life is presented cynically, and what appears to be a simple murder mystery becomes an exploration of supernatural forces.

Another way to interpret the meaning of a text is to look at the symbols that organize and give shape to the text itself. People talk about the various symbols of Christianity in Madonna and U2. Or in the classic film *Citizen Kane,* the entire film is organized around the symbol of the sled, Rosebud; understanding the movie might depend upon understanding the meaning of the symbol. Does Kane's memory of Rosebud signify the loss of innocence and youth? Is it an Oedipal rejection of his father? The task of symbolic analysis is to figure out how the particular symbol is working in the text: What is it doing or saying? The meaning of the text becomes the meaning of the symbol.

The problem with both theme and symbol analysis is that they are largely intuitive. They offer little in the way of new insights into how the text is constructing meanings, or into the range of possible encoded meanings that can be identified in the text. Both depend on prior assumptions the analyst makes about the meaning of the signifiers and symbols in the text. For example, in certain versions of psychoanalytic criticism, every vertical image refers to male sexuality. In an ad for Time-Life books, this kind of interpretive technique is used: A wife wakes up her husband and tells him she dreamed she was being chased. He offers to look up the various meanings of this symbol in his Time-Life book on dreams. Clearly, the strength of both theme and symbol analysis is to provide important ways of describing and clarifying people's taken-for-granted perception of the content and principal signifiers of the text.

It is important, however, to try to get beyond such intuitive approaches to interpretation. In what follows, we will consider four different ways of examining the text that go beyond intuitive interpretations to give us a better grasp of the encoded meaning of the text: content analysis, genre theory, narrative analysis, and semiotics.

CONTENT ANALYSIS

Content analysis is sometimes defined as a systematic and objective method of describing the manifest or surface content of a text. In its usual form, content analysis begins by defining a set of categories to describe the various elements of the content of the text. Next, the analyst counts the instances of each category that appear in the text. For instance, suppose we want to describe television programs. One way to describe them is in terms of how violent they are. To do this, we might count the number of acts of violence in each program. But first, an act of violence must be defined. Perhaps violence is "the infliction of

BOX 6.2

Content Analysis of TV Violence

In a three-year content analysis study of violence on network and cable television, the National Television Violence Study (1997) defined violence as follows:

> Our fundamental definition of violence places emphasis on three key elements:
> Intention to harm, the physical nature of harm, and the involvement of animate
> beings. Violence is defined as *any overt depiction of a credible threat of physical*
> *force or the actual use of such force intended to physically harm an animate*
> *being or group of beings. Violence also includes certain depictions of physically*
> *harmful consequences against an animate being or group that occur as a result*
> *of unseen violent means* [italics added]. Thus, there are three primary types of
> violent depictions: credible threats, behavioral acts, and harmful conse-
> quences. (p. 41)

This definition lays out the parameters not only for what the content coders
are to consider violence (credible threats of violence, actual violent acts, and
circumstances—such as finding a dead body with a gun next to it), but also, by
exclusion, what is *not* considered violence—accidents, disasters, and discussions of acts of violence without visual depictions. Elsewhere, the researchers
exclude from violence activities by animals that might be gory and perhaps fright-
ening to children, such as a hawk catching or killing and eating a rabbit.

Using this definition, the NTVS researchers found that about three of five U.S.
television programs contained one or more instances of violence.

harm by one person on another." We might further want to distinguish
between verbal and physical violence and between intentional and accidental violence. We would have to define each of these categories or
types of violence as well. However many categories there are in the
system, the task of the analyst is to identify the number of occurrences
of each category in the text. The problem is to provide a clear enough
definition of each category in the analytic system so that different analysts can agree on each instance of the category. For example, when Wile
E. Coyote's traps backfire on him, is that an example of intentional or
accidental violence? Is calling someone stupid an act of verbal violence?
These are questions of the definition of content analytic categories.

More typically, content analysts find it necessary to use a number of different category systems, each describing a different dimension, in order to more fully capture the content of the text. For instance, if they want to describe a television news story, they might begin by devising a coding system with several dimensions. They might consider: its location in the newscast, whether it is first or last or in between; its length in seconds; its overall topic—whether it's about war or government or sports; who produced, prepared, or delivered it—the anchorman reading it, a reporter on the scene; where the news depicted took place—in Washington, D.C. (such a story might be coded as national) or Paris, France (such a story might be coded as international or European or French, depending on why the story is assumed to be interesting in the first place) or Paris, Illinois (U.S., local, Midwest, or Illinois); who was quoted or cited in the story—and here there might be several dimensions as well—whether sources are male or female, Black or White, governmental officials or private individuals, and so on. There are obviously many dimensions and, within each, large numbers of categories that one might use to describe the content of a television news show. And so the content analyst has to begin by deciding which questions about the text he or she wants to answer and these questions in turn define which dimensions will be examined.

Another important part of content analysis is deciding what texts will be analyzed to answer the questions. For instance, if a researcher wants to know how violent television is, he or she must decide what is meant by "television." What will the sample be? That is, what television programs will be analyzed and for how long? Will the researcher analyze every program in prime time on every network and cable channel for a year? Does this include or exclude news programs? Imagine how large the sample could be. But if, for practical reasons, the researcher studies only a week's worth of prime-time programming on the three major networks (ABC, CBS, and NBC), can he or she claim to be describing "television"? Choosing the sample is often as pivotal as defining the categories of analysis. In fact, the most common criticisms of examples of content analysis often focus on these aspects: What does the sample represent? Can the study be generalized beyond this sample? After all, in content analysis, the sample should be representative of the object of study. Similarly, categories should capture the significant or important aspects of the texts, and categories should be defined specifically enough to capture all the important differences. (For example, would coding the order of presentation of a news story give a real measure or even an indication of the importance of the story?) These are questions about the *validity* of the study. Content analysts are also concerned about the *reliability* of their content analysis, that is, whether a different set of coders would code the content in exactly the same way, or whether the same set of coders would code the same content the same way if they did it a second time. Similar questions can be raised about every method of interpretation and analysis of texts.

   Unlike the other methods of interpretation, content analysis claims to be systematic and objective. It is made systematic by making the categories mutually exclusive (so that any element can be coded in only one way) and collectively exhaustive (so that every element can be coded in some way, even if it is only put into a general category called "other"). Content analysis is made objective by training different analysts to apply the same set of categories in the same way. This is called content coding. That is, any two people should *code* Tom slugging Jerry in the same category of the coding system for TV violence, as an intentional physical act of violence. Note that the word *code* is used in content analysis in a way that is different from its use in semiotics, although it is in some ways similar. Like a semiotic code, a content-analytic code uses one set of signifiers to mark the differences in a second set of signifiers. In semiotics, for example, colors mark different behaviors at traffic lights. In content analysis, one assigns numbers to categories and maps them onto another set of signifiers, the content.

GENRE THEORY

   A genre is a class of texts that have something in common. Genres are invented by people in the industry, by critics, and by audiences. For the industry as well as for writers, they are a way of defining, measuring, and sustaining taste. For instance, the networks may decide that westerns are popular again, or that family situation comedies are declining. This alerts programming executives to be on the lookout for proposed western series and to avoid new sitcoms. Similarly, record companies may decide that hard rock is not selling as much as dance rock and heavy metal. Fans often use genres to describe their tastes, although rarely is anyone a fan of every instance of a genre. Genres can be very broad, encompassing a great deal of diversity, such as the genre of westerns or war movies, or even heavy metal, or they can be narrow, as in spaghetti westerns, or speedmetal, or gritty police series (e.g., *NYPD Blue*). Genres are not simple and stable categories. Nor do they have any reality apart from the ways they are used by the industry, by critics, and by fans. They are constantly changing. Family sitcoms by Norman Lear in the 1970s, such as *All in the Family* and its spin-offs, *The Jeffersons* and *Maude*, changed the genre itself, by, for example, making dialogue more like the "real world" and introducing social-issue controversies (for example, Maude's abortion) that the bland sitcoms of the 1950s and '60s had studiously avoided. Likewise, the 1970s blockbuster sci-fi films, such as *Star Wars*, changed people's expectations about sci-fi films: the wizardry of George Lucas's Industrial Light & Magic technical crew made earlier sci-fi films seem amateurish, not "real" representatives of the genre. It is not always clear whether a text belongs in a genre. Many critics, for example, have argued that the *Star Wars* movies are more accurately seen as examples of the western genre, only set in space, than as science fiction movies.

The real challenge of genre analysis is to look at the relationship between a genre (as some general structure or set of expectations that describes a range of texts) and a particular example of the genre. One can explore how the particular text embodies the features of the genre, and also how it reshapes them, how it defines its own individuality and uniqueness within the genre, and even how it transforms the genre itself. But such an analysis depends upon developing a definition of the genre under discussion, and that depends in part on the analysis of the specific texts that make up the genre.

There are as many ways to define a genre as there are theories of meaning, but three are most commonly used. The first defines a genre by a shared set of conventions (such as conventions about narrative, characters, location, styles). The western, for example, is not merely defined by its setting in the nineteenth-century American West, but also by certain stock characters (the strong silent hero-gunfighter, the evil businessman or gang leader, the schoolmarm, the saloon girl) and by certain events (the card game, the swindle, the gunfight, the saloon brawl). In this sense, the genre specifies both the formula that is reproduced in every western and the limits within which each new example of the genre has to find its own individuality.

The second approach defines genre as the underlying structure of values that the genre puts into play. The western is often about the conflict between culture and nature, embodied in the competing images of eastern and western life. Similarly, heavy metal music might be thought of as the embodiment of the conflict between angry youth (sexuality, violence, and noise) and creative adulthood (musical mastery).

Finally, and perhaps most flexibly, genres can be seen as articulations of texts that define a particular set of intertextual relations. In this sense, genres tell us how to read a particular text by placing it into more familiar structures of meaning. For example, one can say that there is a genre of adult/children's programs, which brings together such programs as *Rocky and Bullwinkle*, *PeeWee's Playhouse*, *The New Adventures of Mighty Mouse*, *The Simpsons*, and *Beavis and Butthead*. Locating these texts in this genre would direct an analyst to compare these programs and find contradictory codes within them. The same signs may mean different things to adult and child viewers. These programs are double-coded; they are understood one way by a child and another way by an adult. This difference is crucial to the genre and to the way the individual programs construct meaning.

In any case, genre analysis is often a fruitful and powerful tool to describe the specific ways in which a text can both resemble many other texts and yet maintain its own sense of difference.

NARRATIVE ANALYSIS

One of the major ways in which a text can organize meaning—which is the same as saying one of the major forms of codes—is narrative. Narratives are the stories people tell themselves. They are usually, either directly or indirectly, stories about themselves and their world. Narratives tell people who they are and where they came from; they tell them about their possible futures and the forms of social relationships they value. They explain the structure of the world and the relations between different events within it. They tell people how to act in different circumstances, and about their own abilities to act within and upon the world. Narratives are the most common codes of the mass media.

161

BOX 6.3

Watergate and the News as Narrative

Media scholar Michael Cornfield (1988) argues that media coverage of Watergate, the 1972 break-in at Democratic National Committee headquarters in the Watergate office complex in Washington, which ultimately led to the 1974 resignation of President Richard Nixon, "became, through journalism, a real-life tale of crime and detection."

Cornfield underscores that journalists

bind the news into narrative forms through framing devices that specify a time sequence (beginning, middle, end) and a space for the characters to interact (setting). Framing devices surface in chronological sidebars and charts, in such phrases as "questions remain" and "only time will tell," and in references to time spans outside the one automatically established by the journal's periodicity (i.e., daily for newspapers, weekly for newsmagazines). (p. 184)

Moreover, the press, where convenient or appropriate, organizes stories around themes. Watergate becomes a detective story through repetition in the coverage of Watergate as a "caper," through the labeling of the firing of special prosecutor Archibald Cox and the resignation of Attorney General Elliott Richardson as "the Saturday Night Massacre," and through the discovery of incriminating evidence in the White House tapes as "the smoking gun."

What is the *importance* of the press's characterization of the continuing Watergate story as a detective story? We think there are two important outcomes. First, by labeling it a detective story, the press led itself to some sorts of coverage (looking for "clues" to unravel the mystery) at the expense of others. If Watergate, early on, had been framed, for example, as a beleaguered individual (Nixon) against a misguided society, the press might well have been inspired to look for other sorts of "facts." Second, because Watergate *became* in popular lore the prototypical news-as-detective-story case, subsequent events have been held to its standards: the political fallout of the Bert Lance affair in the Carter administration and of the Iran-Contra scandal in the Reagan presidency was considerably lessened because in each of those cases, no "smoking gun," or irrefutable evidence of presidential involvement was ever found. Before Watergate, the president might have had to resign just because such political crises occurred on his watch.

They are everywhere, in advertisements and just about every form of entertainment. Narrative structure is central to movies, television, comics, and most popular songs. Even the news transforms events into stories: elections become horse races, international crises become wars of nerve, riots become criminal adventures, and so forth.

Narratives are the easiest thing to take for granted, because everyone is always immersed in stories—stories about our family, about where we come from, about our country, and about our identity. Everyone is made comfortable listening to and following stories. Most conversations about particular texts in the mass media involve recounting the narrative—the plot—of some text or set of texts. When anyone walks into the room in the middle of a television show or movie or even the news, the first question is "What's happening?" Or even more directly, "What's the story?"

Narrative analysis goes beyond the simple and straightforward plot summaries that circulate among friends and even within the various media industries (for example, in *TV Guide*). It begins by making a distinction between the story and the *discourse*. The story is the actual progression of events through time that makes up the substance and the content of the narrative. The discourse is the way the text describes or tells the story.

The story is the content of the text: the events and the characters involved in them. Every story has a beginning, a middle, and an end. Presumably, there is some point—some conflict to be resolved, some goal to be achieved, some mystery to be solved. Some events will be more central and crucial than others, just as some characters will be more involved in the narrative. The events presumably are linked, and they come one after another. But also, in narratives, it is usually assumed that events are linked by some causal connections. That is, people assume that because someone did this, then that happened, and so on.

Narrative *characters* are not real people; they are only players or roles in a story. They serve a specific set of story functions by doing certain things. For instance, a function of the character Princess Leia in *Star Wars* is to create tension between Luke Skywalker and Han Solo. Characters have a variety of physical, social, and psychological characteristics assigned to them by the narrative, although not all of these may be necessary to the story. The fact that Lando Calrissian is played by a Black man, Billy Dee Williams, makes no difference in the story itself. Sometimes, however, the fact that a star is playing a particular character makes it more difficult to separate the character as a narrative function from the real actor playing the part. For example, in any role Harrison Ford plays, he brings the swaggering Han Solo along with him. And when he seems not to, critics always note in their reviews that he is "playing against type" and often the movie flops.

The mass media use and manipulate stories in many ways. Obviously, the story is one of the "hooks" that attract and sustain an audience's interest. Anyone who watches a lot of television, however, soon realizes that television programs often tell the same basic stories over and over. The programs spend more time on the minute differences within the same plots than on developing new plots. What becomes central in these repetitious stories are the characters and the relationships among them. This helps us understand why people might watch the same program or film again and again, and it partly explains the rapid syndication of successful programs: people *are* willing to watch the same program again.

In many series, the story is manipulated in ways to make it ever more suspenseful. One need only think of the preponderance of cliffhangers (where the program or even series ends with a major narrative question unanswered: Who shot Mr. Burns? Is Mulder dead? Who killed Laura Palmer?) Even on a popular children's show, such as *Ghost Writer*, cliffhangers are popular vehicles for maintaining viewer interest. Another way of manipulating stories is characteristic of soap operas: Many story lines interweave within the same program, each with its own narrative interest.

Stories can be used also to help set up an apparently real world within which the story itself exists. Thus, characters from one TV program will often significantly enter into the narrative of another, as when Mannix appeared on *Diagnosis Murder*. The 1970s sleuth and the 1990s doctor cooperated to solve a crime. In other instances, a series may make reference to another series, as when in *Alf*, the character Alf appears on *The Tonight Show* with Johnny Carson, or when a story line on *L.A. Law* has Douglas Brackman date Vanna White from *Wheel of Fortune*. CBS developed an advertising campaign "Come into our world," which exploited this capacity of narratives to construct an alternative reality. Within that alternative reality, events are often as predictable and meaningful as they are within the world of our own everyday lives. Think of how realistically the Bob Hoskins character, Eddie

Valiant, entered the world of the 'toons in *Who Framed Roger Rabbit?* Audiences sometimes get into the act, as in the case of Trekkies, fans of *Star Trek,* who often "live" within *Star Trek*'s universe during Trekkie conventions. And it is part of the folklore of television that many soap opera fans live within the world of, say, *General Hospital* and *The Guiding Light,* sending wedding presents and get-well cards to the characters.

The narrative is more than a story, however, because rarely is a story told straightforwardly. *Discourse* is the way the story is told in a particular text. The same story can be told in many different ways, depending on who is telling it and to whom. Narrative theory, then, is primarily a way of examining how a story is told and figuring out what difference it makes that it is told one way and not another.

Every narrative (the story in discourse) has a narrator, someone who is telling the story, and a *narratee,* someone to whom the story is being told. The narrator is always, in some sense, inside of the story. It is often, for example, the voice of a character. In *Star Trek,* the captain narrates the story, speaking into his log. The narrator defines the *point of view* that the audience has on the story, on what is taking place. In *Star Trek,* the viewer sees the world through the captain's eyes. This is certainly a common ploy in much television. Viewers see the story through the eyes and hear through the voice of the main character. Sometimes the audience does not know who the narrator is; such an anonymous narrator is not usually a major character in the story itself. Some narratives play off this feature of discourse by not revealing that the narrator is in fact a major character. For example, we find out at the end of Agatha Christie's *The Murder of Roger Ackroyd* that the narrator is the guilty party. In the dramatic film, *Sunset Boulevard,* the narrator dies at the end with the death of the narrator's character. Akiro Kurosawa's classic film, *Rashomon,* presents the same story narrated by four different characters to make the point that, told from different points of view, the "same" story is really four different stories.

In visual narratives, the narrator is almost always identified with the camera. That is, the camera's angle of vision, its perception of the world, defines the narrator's point of view. In that sense, the old adage that the camera doesn't lie is only partially true, because the camera may indeed lie by its identification with a single character and its consequent involvement in the story itself. The traditional Hollywood film uses the camera to establish a "third person" narrator who apparently exists outside the story. Occasionally, however, within such traditional films, the camera takes a position in the story. Viewers suddenly find themselves looking at a character (usually a woman) from a hidden position (outside a window or from a closet). They know someone is likely to enter into the action. This technique creates much of the suspense in films such as *Wait Until Dark* and many of Alfred Hitchcock's films.

Much of so-called avant garde cinema violates the tradition of a third-person or anonymous narrator by placing the camera in the position of a major character within the story. This is a typical strategy in most of Ingmar Bergman's films, such as *Wild Strawberries*. On Saturday morning's *Muppet Babies*, the camera presents a kid's-eye view of the world, and even when the only adult in the show, Nanny, appears, viewers hear her voice but only see her legs up to her knees, exactly as a small child would experience her.

Narrators can be described by their relationship to the story and by their knowledge of it. A narrator can be speaking as a character within the story (a *diegetic* narrator, such as Angela in *My So-Called Life*) or from outside of the story (a *nondiegetic* narrator, as in the news and most documentaries). A narrator can be telling us a partial story (usually if he or she is acting within it, he or she will have only limited knowledge, like Magnum) or the narrator can be framing the entire thing (as, for example, a detective who has already solved the mystery. A narrator can have more information than any character could possibly have: an *omniscient narrator* knows what is going on everywhere (as in many fairy tales). Narrators can have different degrees of reliability, which may or may not be intentional. The criminal, narrating his or her own crime, obviously has an ulterior motive in presenting actions in a certain light. On the other hand, perhaps the narrator has only been told the criminal's side of the story and, not realizing that this character was the criminal, recounts the discourse as if it were the truth.

Just as there is a narrator within the narrative, someone is there to receive the narration. Often, in television, this receiver is a live audience. Sometimes, the story itself makes it clear that the entire discourse is a conversation between two people, one of whom is narrating the story to another. Sometimes, the story makes it clear that someone is there but does not identify who it is. This is the effect, for example, of a canned laughter track. Or the internal audience may be identified but remain absent from the discourse of the text itself. For example, the captain of the Starship Enterprise is always telling his story to Starfleet command as he records his "captain's log."

The narrator and narratee are not the same as the author and the audience. In fact, insofar as the author and the audience are real people, the interpreter of the text can have little or no access to them through the narration itself. But the discourse does create what critics refer to as an implied author and an implied reader. We may decide, for example, that the narrator is a rather shady character; we can also infer that we are supposed to know that and, hence, mistrust what the narrator says. The implied author gives another perspective on the story. The *implied* author is the image of the author constructed from the information in the text; it is the reader's imagination of who the author of this text must have been. What does one make, for example, of Stephen King from his texts? Describing a movie as "a woman's movie" suggests that its perspective—not merely that of the narrator but of the implied author, as well—seems to represent women's feelings, concerns, and so on; it makes no difference whether the actual author is a man or a woman.

The implied reader, on the other hand, is usually assumed to be on the side of law and order, justice, and authority. The way in which both Captains Kirk and Picard (in the original *Star Trek* and *Star Trek: The Next Generation*) are cast as narrators suggests not only a very sympathetic implied author, but also, that their audience should be sympathetic to these authority figures as well. The *implied reader* or *audience* is then the audience that one imagines the implied author wants for his or her narrative. Feminists often argue that whoever the narratee may be, the implied audience of most commercial entertainment is male, judging by the way women are portrayed. Sometimes, the narrator will seem to address the implied audience directly, so that the implied audience and the narratee are one and the same. This is the case, for example, with almost all pornography.

The relationship between the story and the discourse is further complicated by the temporal relationship between the two. Is the narrative told while the events are unfolding, or immediately after, or at a much later time? The discourse of the narrative is free to change the organization of events within the story. Using flashforwards and flashbacks (when the future and the past, respectively, are represented in the present), the discourse can make connections that might be otherwise unavailable, or it can confuse and conflate events. Sometimes, these techniques are responses to the fact that simultaneous events cannot be represented simultaneously in a linear narrative, and discourses must always face the problem of how to represent such events. Events that recur in the story may be told only once in the discourse, whereas events that occur only once may be repeated for emphasis. The narration may take longer than the story (as when it is stretched out for effect), or the story and discourse may be told in the same time, or the discourse may merely summarize the events that occurred. Most discourses are summaries, and it is easy to forget that a selection was made. One of the most interesting things about the reporting of the Persian Gulf War in early 1991 was that the news was taking place in real time, not only as it unfolded but also lasting as long as the events that were being described. Occasionally, the discourse may simply skip over entire scenes of the story (an ellipsis), creating a gap in knowledge, for example, when the discourse skips from the protagonist's past to the present, leaving out what happened in between—as in *The Wonder Years*.

It is in these relations between the story and the discourse that we can discover the narrative and gain a more critical perspective on it. Narrative theory allows anyone to see how the telling of the story constructs the story itself and to identify the perspective that is taken on the story. In this way, it can give one a better view of how meanings are produced and communicated.

SEMIOTICS

We have already discussed many of the basic premises of semiotic analysis. Here we want to describe some of the analytic tools that semiotics makes available for the interpretation of specific texts. Remember that meaning is produced when one signifier enters into a relationship with or is articulated to another, and every signifier in a text implies another signifier, and so on. Through this process—which is referred to as *connotation*—chains of meaning are established: *a* means *b* means *c* means *d* . . . . This red, white, and blue cloth means the flag of the United States, which means the country itself, which means the love and respect one should feel for the country. As these chains of connotation are reiterated within a culture, they can become fixed and frozen, as if calling up the first signifier opens the door into which come rushing all the meanings that have been linked to it. Such chains become codes that then structure future texts and interpretations. When this happens, we can speak of *myths,* such as the Cinderella myth, and the myth of rags to riches.

A distinction that will prove very useful in semiotic analysis is that between *syntagm* and *paradigm.* These describe the two dimensions along which any text is organized. The syntagmatic dimension of a text describes its organization, how its signs are connected in time or space: This is next to that, this follows that. For example, in the previous sentence, *this* precedes *is.* If one were to reverse this order, so that *is* preceded *this,* this would change the phrase from a statement to a question. Changing the syntagmatic organization of a narrative, or a photograph, can seriously alter the ways in which meanings are produced, as well as the specific meanings produced. For instance, taking a photograph of the current president standing next to a portrait of Abraham Lincoln is most likely an attempt to connect Americans' positive associations with Lincoln to the president.

A paradigm is more difficult to understand and identify than a syntagm, for it describes possibilities rather than what is actually in the text. A paradigm describes the potential substitutions that one can make without changing the syntagmatic relationship. For any element, there are substitutions that can be made, that are allowed by particular codes within the culture. For example, watching a story in which a boy is bitten by a dog, one can imagine substituting a wolf, or perhaps a cat, for the dog. But could one substitute a horse? And what about an elephant? Or a train? In the example of the photograph of the president, would a picture of the president's family behind him work as well? What about a picture of Moscow's Red Square or of Bart Simpson? A simple paradigm within American culture says that one could substitute a picture of George Washington or John Fitzgerald Kennedy, because they have similarly positive connotations. On the other hand, one would probably be well-advised by our paradigms not to use a picture of Richard Nixon.

The existence of paradigmatic and syntagmatic codes can be useful in analyzing a text, especially through the *commutation test.* The commutation test simply asks whether a difference makes a difference. If this were changed, how would the meaning of the text be affected? Does it matter if the good guy wears black? If a heavy metal band does not play guitar solos? If Bart Simpson had ordinary hair? This is the power of semiotic analysis: to allow us to identify the ways in which texts establish meaningful differences that produce different meanings.

Let's consider a simple example of a semiotic analysis. Consider a portrait of the Simpson family. A number of iconic codes tell us that this is a cartoon. How do we recognize something as a cartoon? For one thing, notice that Matt Groening, the Simpsons' creator, observes a cartoon convention: The characters have four fingers (drawing goes faster). Cartoons simplify and exaggerate the iconicity of signs. What changes would affect our assumption about whether this is a cartoon? Could a supermarket tabloid doctor the cartoon to present a story on an extraterrestrial family?

What other codes are operating? There is a code of gender marking: Anyone (that is, anyone familiar with the codes operating here) can tell which are the male and which are the female figures (as one almost always can in all cartoons and animated films, even when the characters are small, cuddly animals). They are marked by a number of different signifiers: size (males are larger than females), hairstyle, dress, accessories, and eyelashes (apparently men don't have any). The presence of accessories and eyelashes on the females suggests as well that they are more concerned with their appearance. The adults are marked not only by size but by distinctive hairstyles, as well as Homer's ever-present 5 o'clock shadow.

The group is clearly a family. There are male and female adults with children (what would we conclude if there were no adults, or two women instead?), and there is a banner announcing "The Simpsons." Americans often reference a family this way—on mailboxes, welcome mats, holiday cards, and so on. The position of Marge's and Homer's hands (around each other) suggests either a self-conscious pose or a happily married couple. Each child is holding "horns" over the next child's head, a common childish prank in photographs. The fact that Homer is doing this to Bart suggests that he is rather childish. The childish gesture reinforces a broader interpretation of Homer's appearance as connoting stupidity: overweight, unshaven, an exaggerated overbite (notice the entire family has a pronounced overbite), nearly bald.

All the family members have the exact same smile—perhaps another sign of "family," but it also could connote more: a certain stupidity or perhaps the threat of irony. Perhaps something more is going on under the surface. Perhaps the family is not quite so normal.

The most obvious signifiers in the picture are the round bulging eyes—certainly warning any viewer that this family is not normal—and the hairstyles. The two girls' spiky hair may just be a cartoon representation of curly hair, although their appearance gives them other connotations as well: their starlike quality perhaps suggests positive (angelic) features. Marge's rather spectacular blue hair certainly stands out. Is it dyed? Presumably, at least one hopes. It resembles a grossly exaggerated beehive hairdo, popular in the 1950s. Certainly, this hairstyle tells the viewer something, not only about Marge, but about the class and tastes of the family.

Finally, there is Bart. In other images of the Simpsons, Bart is often separated from the rest of the family, signaling his difference and importance. (Although we have gone beyond the particular image, this is justified because most people in this culture will have seen other images of the Simpsons as well.) Bart is usually the only character allowed to speak (in the balloons that mark cartoon speech)—such phrases as "Hey, Dude," "Don't have a cow, man," "Ay Caramba," and "An underachiever and proud of it." Similarly, in the animated cartoons, Bart is frequently positioned as the narrator. Bart is often presented with or on his skateboard, an important sign in contemporary youth cultures.

The most central signifier in Bart is his hair. Like Marge's, it is not like the rest of the family's. Its spiked quality suggests punk culture, but its height makes it look more like a crown. It could even resemble popular African American hairstyles.

Two other aspects or possibilities of semiotic analysis are important here. First, semiotics often finds (or assumes, depending on your point of view) that texts are organized around a series of binary oppositions or binary codes: black/white, individual/social, good/bad, male/female, young/old, beautiful/ugly, strong/weak, work/play, nature/culture. Such codes create structures of meaning by establishing equivalencies between the terms of different binary oppositions (woman = young = beautiful = weak = play = nature) and then privileging one side of the opposition over the other. In this way, cultural codes create hierarchies or pecking orders—male over female, strong over weak. Think about the western, which often divides the world into good versus bad, white versus black, East versus West, culture versus nature, individual versus community, violence versus talk, civilization versus crime. Different westerns will create different systems of identity among these various binary codes and weight the two resulting systems of meaning differently. In *Shane*, individuality and violence are necessary to save the family and community, but in the end, they cannot be integrated into its harmonious existence. In *High Noon*, violence is only legitimated by its integration into the family and community. The binary oppositions that such a semiotic analysis identifies are themselves part of a code in which they are made meaningful. Notions such as bad/good or man/woman are only meaningful within the codes of society; they have no independent existence outside of people's maps of meaning.

Such analyses also fail to recognize and challenge the assumption that each of the terms within a binary opposition exists independently of the other, that each term has its own meaning and definition. Women exist, men exist; they can be defined independently of one another and then compared. Yet, by the very terms of semiotic theory, this is impossible. *Deconstruction*, the invention of the French philosopher Jacques Derrida, is a theoretical extension of semiotics and a critical practice that criticizes the tendency in semiotics to believe that codes are organized according to simple binary oppositions (or that such oppositions are simply equivalent to the semiotic notion of difference). Deconstruction undermines the ability to draw such simple dichotomies in which one side is made superior (male) to the other (female). Deconstruction argues that the terms in such binary oppositions depend on each other (as in a system of differences). That is, deconstruction extends the argument that difference is more fundamental than identity. The very meaning of the two terms, of male and female, depend upon each other; apart from their relationship, they have no meaning. The meaning of female is not-male, but at the same time, the meaning of male is not-female. The meaning of the terms is defined by the relationship between them and does not exist apart from that relation. Each term is tainted or contaminated by the other term, because the other term is already present and active within it. Deconstruction cautions us not to glibly assume that the western is about the value of civilization over violence or the individual over the community. Instead, a deconstructionist would argue that every western is about the complex ways in which nature and culture, civilization and violence, individuality and community, are always implicated together and constitute one another.

Second, because semiotics argues that the meaning of a text is the product of its articulation to and by a set of cultural codes, one can analyze a text by isolating the various codes that intersect to produce its most obvious readings. To put it another way, because the polysemy of any text suggests the possibility of many interpretations, one has to wonder (and explain) why most people (in the same culture) arrive at what are basically the same interpretations for the vast majority of cultural texts, especially media texts. If so many meanings are possible, why do people arrive at so few, and why do they usually arrive at the same one, a meaning that is not only taken for granted but is assumed to be obvious and transparent? According to semiotics, the answer is that a relatively small number of very powerful semiotic codes transect in the text itself and thus produce the accepted meaning. The classic example of such an analysis is that offered by the French critic, Roland Barthes (1970/1974), in his book *S/Z*. Barthes takes a classic realist short story (realism here refers to a aesthetic genre) and analyzes it by identifying the various codes, five in all, that construct it precisely as a realist text. The precise nature of each of these codes is not important here; the point is that a complex structure of codes constructs and produces the meaning of a text.

There is, however, a weakness in the analysis, and Barthes not only recognizes it, he makes it central to the analysis itself. It is the point where Barthes' analysis meets deconstruction. Like Derrida, Barthes argues that every text has a certain point where it falls apart, where it falls in upon itself, where its assumptions appear, if only by their effects. This *aporia* is a gap in the logic of the text, an absence on which it builds its entire textual edifice. This aporia disrupts the fluidity of the narrative and undermines the transparency of the taken-for-granted interpretation, even as it remains taken for granted. The point is simple: even when polysemy seems to be totally under control, there is always at least one point in the text when it is threatening to reappear, and that point can never be totally sealed up.

THE ANALYSIS OF VISUAL TEXTS

A lot of mass media is visual, and there are techniques of interpretation that can help us analyze visual texts. For the sake of time and space, we will focus here primarily but not entirely on semiotics. Semiotics is particularly useful in visual analysis, because people often assume that visual images are somehow closer to reality, as if they were less subject to manipulation and less structured by codes. Semiotics explains that this is not so.

As in any other text, one can begin the analysis of a visual text by examining the appearance of themes or repeated visual motifs and symbols. The depiction of a man with his arms outstretched (the crucifixion) is a common visual symbol in our Christian iconography. Similarly, the eagle flying overhead is commonly used as a symbol of freedom. We can describe the structure and the content of the visual image. Is the composition balanced? Symmetrical? Harmonious? What sort of contrasts appear? What is foreground and what is background? These differences describe visual codes: for example, in Anglo-European culture, people assume that what is in the foreground is more important than what is in the background. Different structures of composition direct people's eyes to see different parts of a picture in a different order with different emphases. A disharmonious composition often places its subject in a negative point of view to contemporary eyes.

We can also begin by examining the *mise-en-scene*, what is in the frame itself. We can describe the time and place, the appearance and spatial organization of the setting, and the camera's point of view. We can look at the way in which the scene is constructed, at the presentation of characters (their costumes and makeup). We can consider how the lighting both illuminates and hides particular aspects of the scene, and how it gives other elements a specific emotional tone (soft lighting is often used to present someone in a rather romantic light). We can see which characters are most frequently lighted and from what angles. We can observe the actions of the character.

A *shot* is a single frame of a moving image, or a single photograph. Every shot is framed in particular ways, defined by the manner in

174

which it has been photographed. Does it look flat or deep? Where is the line of sight, and where does the horizon appear? How is the shot focused? Where is the camera positioned? Is the hero, for example, shot from above, from below, or from straight on? Shot from below, for example, the hero will look larger than life. Are the characters shot from far away (long shot) or from up close? Returning to moving images, one can ask whether the camera pans (moves horizontally) or tilts (moves up or down), or whether the camera tracks—moves with—the action. Are the camera's movements rough or smooth, in time with the action or working against it?

Finally, we have to look at *editing,* the process by which shots are connected to each other. The editor chooses shots, their order, their respective lengths, and how they are joined. Shots can be connected by fading out into black, or by fading in from black, or by superimposition (in which one shot fades in while the other fades out), or by having the frame of the new image literally push the old image off the screen, or by simply splicing the two shots together in what is called the cut. For example, most Hollywood films are dominated by what has come to be called *continuity editing,* which ensures that the viewer feels the narrative continuity reproduced on the screen. In such editing, a shot establishing a scene is usually followed by a reverse shot of someone looking at the scene (the scene is now no longer visible, and the viewer assumes that the previous establishing shot was filmed from this position). Also, scenes can be intercut with each other at different tempos. Finally, editing can be organized according to various principles, including rhythmic, or spatial, or temporal relations among the images. TV journalists hate to use jump cuts (cutting from one shot to another shot of the same person) largely because this calls attention to the fact that the news film has been edited. This editing reminds the viewer that something has been left out, that the account is not verbatim, and that someone (the journalist) comes between the story and the viewer.

The issue of editing raises some obvious questions: Who gets to be the editor? On what bases do editors make their editing decisions? What effects do these editing decisions have on the "meaning" of the texts? What effects do these meanings have on the audience? These questions point to the role of the media, the role of power in the media, and the power of the media. Throughout this book, we will continue to try to get a better understanding of these complex processes of meaning and power making: Who makes meaning? Who is entitled to make meaning? Who makes this text apparently mean that? Who stops the endless flow of meaning? Are some people or groups more able to get their message across? Who are they and why do they have this ability?

We have introduced the notion of meaning as one of the primary products of media communication. Meaning is the process by which people organize the world into significant differences. This process is accomplished through the construction of codes (and of signs within the codes) that are socially, culturally, and historically specific. We have argued that there is no single meaning to any media text; texts are intertextual and polysemic. Every text can be located within a number of codes, and each articulation produces not only a different meaning, but a different text. The four modes of analyzing texts—content analysis, genre theory, narrative theory, and semiotics—are tools we can use to obtain a more reflective and rigorous reading of particular media texts.

Ideology

T his chapter brings together two notions that we have already introduced but left rather underdeveloped: power and the social construction of reality. Every society attempts to guarantee its own continuing existence. A society maintains itself by reproducing its institutions and its structure of social relationships. To do so, it has to continuously reproduce the things necessary for its existence, from the resources to produce food and shelter for its people, to the labor necessary to transform these resources into commodities, to the individuals willing and able to participate in the institutions and occupy their assigned roles in the social relationships. But we have been suggesting throughout this book that the institutions and relationships that constitute a society always embody structures of power and inequality. If a society is to continue existing, it must, therefore, ensure that its particular relations of power—its particular hierarchies of economic, political, and cultural power—continue to operate with some appearance of legitimacy in the lives of the general population. One way of doing that is to use force to control people's lives and to actively suppress opposition.

A less troubling and more efficient way involves getting people to accept a particular way of thinking and seeing the world that makes the existing organization of social relations appear natural and inevitable.

177

Although such *ideological power*—the attempt to define reality in particular ways—has always been part of social life, its importance increased significantly in the eighteenth and nineteenth centuries, as part of the processes of modernization in Europe and America. Historically, becoming modern involved the democratization of both political and cultural life. As "the masses" gained political power and cultural literacy, partly as a result of the development of new communication media, the use of force became more difficult, costly, and visible, and thus it became an instrument only of last resort. Instead, society came to rely more and more on the ideological possibilities of communication and culture.

IDEOLOGY, REALITY, AND REPRESENTATION

The issue of ideology is closely tied to the discussion in the previous two chapters: the media make meanings and organize them into various codes and systems. Implicit in these arguments is the assumption that these codes interpret reality; they make the world meaningful and comprehensible. The introduction of terms like *reality* and the *world* signals the move from questions of meaning to questions of representation, from culture to ideology. After all, there are lots of meaningful texts that do not necessarily claim to describe an actual reality. Much of the time, people assume they know the difference between fact and fiction, although as we shall see, this assumption is very problematic. Many meaningful statements explicitly describe a world that is not actual (for example, a world in which a man with super strength and X-ray vision constantly saves the world from bad guys). That world might be one that we can imagine; it might even be one that we assume to be plausible. Or there may be certain features of that world that we take to be descriptive of our own world. For example, we might agree that the legitimate law enforcement agencies need help, or that the difference between the good guys and the bad guys is obvious. Other meaningful texts describe fantasies that people may take to be describing impossible realities or at least realities that they would not want to see actualized.

People experience the world only through the cultural codes of meaning that enable them to interpret or make sense of the world. Yet, people are capable of understanding many codes of meaning that they

178

are incapable of experiencing as possible or even imaginable realities. In other words, certain codes of meaning are not only intelligible, they are also assumed to be descriptions or possible descriptions of the world. As descriptions or representations, particular codes appear obvious, commonsensical, and even natural. They are assumed to be objective descriptions of how things are, and more often than not, of how things have to be.

The word *representation* literally means "re-presentation." To represent something means to take an original, mediate it, and "play it back." But again, this process almost necessarily alters the reality of the original. Representation involves making a claim on and about reality; but it is not the same as realism. It is not merely a matter of realistically constructing an imagined world; it is not merely a matter of what critics have called "the willful suspension of disbelief." In this sense of realism, the producer of a text will try to maximize the experience and impact of the text on the audience by drawing the audience into the universe that the text has created. Hence, as we have noted, films use continuity editing to create the illusion, not that this is *the* real world, but that the world the film creates has a reality of its own, a reality that acts in much the same way as the reality of the world outside the text behaves. A reality in which contradictions abound, fish fly, and elephants talk marks itself as, in some sense, unreal.

To make a realistic text, producers have to try to hide their own presence in and operation on the text. As we have already suggested, a producer who is aiming for realism will avoid editing practices that emphasize his or her own interventions; for example, audiences notice such things as jump cuts, when cinematographers and video editors keep a camera and subjects in the same position but edit out a portion of a filmed or videotaped sequence. They not only notice that something is missing but are also reminded that the world they are seeing is not "real" because it has been produced. The illusion of realism is broken. And for just this reason, media producers seek to avoid jump cuts: they aim for a seamless, involving presentation that draws the audience's attention into the content. The audience must "forget" for a moment that the text is "just a text" producing meaning: its realism, which may or may not necessitate that the world of the text has specific relations to the audience's everyday reality, depends on the audience's ability to imagine the actualization of that world.

For example, when two of the authors were watching the first *Batman* movie in 1990, we were startled midway through the movie, as Batman is scaling a building, when a college student sitting behind us blurted out, "Cheez, is that fakey!" Up to then, we guess, he had found the portrayal of a grownup dressed in a bat costume and hopping off skyscrapers perfectly plausible. Or as Dennis Muren, the supervisor of special effects for *Terminator 2* and a six-time Academy Award winner in that category, put it, "Reality is so touchy. Everyone can tell if something isn't real. Once something is unbelievable, you've lost the audience" (quoted in Pollak, 1991, p. B2).

Representation, on the other hand, is not necessarily realistic, although it is always staking a claim on reality. Realism as a genre is only the most obvious way in which particular texts might attempt to operate ideologically, that is, to make claims about reality. But even the most fantastic texts—think of all the Disney animated movies—can still be effective ideologically. For ideology is not a characteristic of texts themselves but of the ways they are located and deployed in society. Insofar as a text, through whatever means, makes a claim about the world that its audience lives in—about what is real and possible—then a text is ideological.

Consider the following example: In April of 1992, "riots" erupted in Los Angeles after a Ventura County, California, jury acquitted four police officers on charges stemming from the beating of motorist Rodney King. Virtually every person in the nation, and many across the world, had repeatedly seen a home video of the beating, in which King was struck 58 times by police officers. No one challenged the "truth" of the videotape: it did capture real events. But to render a verdict, the jurors in the King trial had to interpret the reality of the videotape. The prosecuting attorneys pressed on them one version, that King was savagely beaten by police officers out of control; the defense's version of reality was that the police officers acted reasonably under the circumstances. One picture, two different ideological articulations, two different realities. But also notice that the very description of the events following the trial as riots—rather than as protests, or demonstrations, or even an uprising—is an ideological choice.

Ideology is not only a matter of meaning becoming representation; it is also about the question of power and inequality. Although the concept of ideology originated with the French *philosophes* of the Enlightenment in the eighteenth century, it was the German philosopher and political economist Karl Marx who developed the concept in its present form. Writing in the nineteenth century, Marx wanted to understand how minorities were able to maintain power and why the vast majority of people accepted a system and even acted in ways the consequences of which seemed to be against their own interests. Why did subordinated populations accept their subordination and even act in ways that continue that status? Quoting Marx (1975),

> In the social production which men carry on they enter into definite relations that are indispensable and independent of their will; these relations of production correspond to a definite stage of development of their material powers of production. The totality of these relations of production constitutes the economic structure of society, the real foundation on which legal and political superstructure arise and to which definite forms of social consciousness correspond. The mode of production of material life determines the general character of the social, political, and spiritual processes of life. It is not the consciousness of men that determines their being, but, on the contrary, their social being determines their consciousness. (p. 425)

Marx is concerned here with simple questions. How do societies maintain and reproduce structures of social difference and power? Why do some people see themselves as superior and thus justify their privileged position in society? More important, why do people who are subordinated *accept* their subordination? In some societies, hierarchy is maintained through the use of force; you may be surprised to learn that even less than a hundred years ago, factory owners often used force to subdue workers and to compel them to accept their exploitation (Ewen, 1976). Even today force is often used against illegal immigrants and in many Third World countries. However, most modern democracies eschew the use of force in favor of ideology. If those in power can succeed in constructing a dominant vision that justifies social inequalities, and they can win agreement to this vision, then their position of power is reasonably secure; force becomes unnecessary. The construction of such a consensus is thus always tied to the particular interest groups that struggle for power in society.

Let's take a simple example: In the nineteenth-century American South, the dominant ideology represented Blacks as inferior, often not quite human, beings. To the extent that both Blacks and Whites agreed to this ideology (and notice that this agreement was often unconscious because it seemed so commonsensical), the system of subordination and subjugation endured. Of course, not everyone—certainly not all Blacks and not all Whites—accepted race-based subordination as a natural fact, and some struggled against it. And often force was used to subdue such disagreements. Still, the ideology was largely successful for many decades. Paradoxically, this ideology often was more humane in its consequences than less discriminatory ideologies; in treating Blacks as not fully and rationally human, it allowed for interracial relationships of a fairly wide range, and it usually protected Blacks as if they were like children. For all of the horrors of this period, then, we should not forget that northerners who staked out the moral high ground often ended up treating Blacks worse than did Southern Whites. Nonetheless, and certainly by today's standards in the United States, any ideology that justifies the enslavement of any human by another is unjustifiable.

In the contemporary world, the media are involved in the production of ideology all the time. After all, they are, as we have suggested, perhaps the most important producers of meaning and the codes of meaning in contemporary society. Furthermore, they are often a central and important part of people's everyday lives. They have the potential, then, to become the site at which meanings become more than meaning. When the media become representations, when they make claims about the way the world is, they become powerful ideological institutions. And they are, therefore, potentially a source of great conflict and struggle.

Almost all media texts, from the news to *The Simpsons*, can be seen as ideological. Although it is true that not all media texts (whether apparently factual news reports or obviously fictional entertainment programs) support the status quo or the power structure, what is often presupposed or taken for granted is a set of relationships that usually do: The dominant codes of the media in the United States, for example, rarely if ever question whether a business enterprise should make a profit or whether politics is defined solely by the electoral system as opposed, for example, to organized protest. Similarly, the media seem to regularly present the world in a way that makes assumptions such as the primacy of the nuclear family, the necessity of working for wages, and the relative value of various segments of the population; in these media portrayals, these values seem commonsensical, universal, and even unquestionable. That is, the media, like other ideological operators, are constantly hiding the gap between reality and their representations of it.

But ideology cannot be understood simply in terms of particular unrelated acts of representation, or particular unrelated codes of meaning, applied to particular events, people, relations, or practices. It always involves *ways* of representing, seeing, and thinking about reality. In *Ways of Seeing*, John Berger (1972) gives a number of examples of the new ways of seeing the world that characterized the emergence of modern society in Europe. Berger points, for example, to artists' practice of representing people with their possessions as a new perceptual system for thinking about the value of individuals. Similarly, he points to the ways in which women are represented in visual arts (from painting to advertising) as the passive objects of an unseen man's gaze.

Another example of a "way of seeing" the world touches some of the deepest assumptions about reality in the United States, where the laws, economy, and value system all seem to be centered on the "natural" priority of the individual. Americans tend to see individuals as the most basic and valued unit of social life. Perhaps this in part explains Americans' hostility to socialism, as well as the effectiveness of negative rhetorical appeals that attack social alternatives (from single-source health care to labor unions) as socialist. It might also explain most Americans' suspicion of religious cults, because they are based on the community as the basic unit of social life.

Ideologies are not merely particular systems of representation or ways of seeing. They are also ways of excluding and limiting, for they set the boundaries on what we are able to understand as possible. Ideologies are also not neutral. For in defining the terms within which reality is experienced, perceived, and interpreted, they are always articulated or connected to the struggle of one group or another to maintain or challenge particular social organizations, particular relations of power. Ideology is then about trying to get people to see the world according to the terms or codes that have been set by one or more groups of people, usually those who control the power within a society. Although some ideological codes are explicitly linked to political positions and philosophies (think of the ideologies of communism and capitalism, or of the Democrats and the Republicans), ideology is a much more pervasive and common feature of social existence.

Capitalist societies, for example, need to have people who are willing to sell their labor so that someone else can profit from it. Capitalist ideology needs to have people believe that anyone can be economically successful who is willing to apply himself or herself. People who "fail" must have something wrong with them. (What must constantly remain hidden is the fact that there are structural inequalities in the system and that the system in fact needs such inequalities.) Similarly, the two-party system depends upon people's unshakable belief that the two-party system guarantees them a real say in the governance of their country. Patriarchy—the assumed superiority of men and the masculine over women and the feminine—requires that all people take as "natural and obvious" that men are stronger, more rational, better rulers, natural family heads, and so on. An example of an ideological or taken-for-granted assumption about the natural way of organizing television can be seen in the fact that American television programs are always interrupted by commercials. Whereas Americans find watching this unproblematic and have no problems connecting the segments into a single narrative, people from other cultures often complain that they find it difficult to follow the story and distinguish the program segments from commercials. As we shall see in Chapter 9, ideology is always involved in the way that the media treat various segments of the society.

REALITY AND THEORIES OF IDEOLOGY

Reality is a somewhat paradoxical concept because reality is what most people assume exists independently of any concept or representation. Reality is what exists, end of discussion. Thousands of years of argument in metaphysics (the theory of the nature of reality) and epistemology (the theory of knowledge of reality) quickly disproves the commonsense assumption that reality is not a problem. Even if reality is what it seems, however, the question remains how human beings can know and talk about it. The most common theory, and the most commonsensical, assumes that reality is a collection of material facts (what actually exists or happens), that human beings accurately perceive such facts, and that these perceptions (and the facts they correspond to) can be accurately described, captured, or even mirrored by the various verbal and visual languages of human culture. Every society assumes that its own perceptions and languages provide the only and most accurate représentation of reality. These sorts of realism have two great flaws: They are ethnocentric, and they cannot explain misperceptions, hallucinations, disagreements, and so forth.

A second theory goes back at least as far as the Greek philosopher Plato, who offered the following fable to describe humans' relationship to reality. Imagine that some people have always been prisoners in a cave, chained so that they can only see the back wall. Behind them, figures move and dance in front of a fire, casting shadows on the back wall. The prisoners, having never been out of the cave and never having seen the figures, assume both that the shadows are real and that they are all of reality. Plato was suggesting that people confuse appearances (which do have some causal or indexical relation to reality) for reality itself. Plato drew an absolute distinction between people's experience of the world—an experience of images and appearances—and reality itself. The latter exists behind the former as its cause, but without an understanding of the nature of this causal relationship, people are incapable of knowing reality itself. Such a "phenomenal" theory makes experience the other inferior half of reality.

A third theory asserts that reality is not real in any obvious and direct sense. It is, rather, the product of human invention—something people create and re-create (produce, maintain, repair, and transform). In this view, no independent reality is ever available to human beings; rather, the things that are taken to be real are real because they are socially constructed, or represented as real. According to this view, *reality has to be made to mean*. The claim that reality is socially constructed implies that communication is always doubly articulated: First, the chain or sliding of signifiers is stopped to produce meaning, and second, particular meanings are themselves articulated to other practices and events as their representations. The first is the production of meaning or significance; the second, the representation and construction of reality. And insofar as each of these articulations is possible only from a position of power, then, the social construction of reality is always a process inextricably related to the relations of power in a society. Notice that such a theory does not necessarily imply that there is nothing that

185

is not language or culture, that there is no material reality. It does, however, imply that insofar as human beings experience any reality, such reality is always the double articulation of culture, an ideological product.

Each of these theories of reality and knowledge offers a different account of the operation of ideology. Because human existence is always more complicated than its theoretical description, each of them has a certain truth and describes at least certain moments of the relations of power constructed within and by the cultural and communication environments in which people live.

A REALISTIC THEORY OF IDEOLOGY

The most commonly held theory of ideology, a realist theory, defines ideology as "false consciousness." For example, Marx claimed that the dominant ideas of a society are the ideas of the dominant class.[1] That is, the class that holds power (for example, the capitalist class) attempts to impose its ideas, its version of reality, on the rest of society. These ideas intentionally misrepresent the world, at least from the point of view of the real interests of the working class. The capitalist class tells the world that it is the natural order of things that labor power be sold as a commodity on the market, that the quality of one's being is measured by one's life, that the family is where one lives out one's real life, and so on. The fact that workers believe them means that, in one way or another (and Marx never quite figured out how), they are brainwashed. They are suffering from false consciousness because they are taking as true knowledge ideas that are false. (This formulation assumes that there must exist true knowledge and that there must be some way to tell the difference.)

This theory of ideology also implies that there is a direct correspondence between social position (such as class membership) and knowledge and interests. Thus, there is something called "the interests" of the working class, which can be defined independently of any particular social struggle and defined solely by the fact that workers sell their labor as a commodity. Moreover, there is a truth that would describe their reality. Similarly, the capitalist class has its own interests and its own truth. The problem comes when the truth of the capitalist class is universalized and naturalized, then offered as the truth for everyone, as if

BOX 7.1
Reality and the Issue of Child Abuse

As we investigate the emergence of child abuse as a social problem, we see that all three views of reality are at issue.

1. Reality as apparent. We can say indisputably that child abuse exists—that parents and others entrusted with the care of children on occasion willfully inflict harm on them, sometimes to the point of injuring or even killing them. Evidence of this reality occurs any time a child is admitted to a hospital for a broken bone or a ruptured internal organ and no one is able to furnish a plausible accidental cause for the injury. So child abuse is real. But a strong case may be made that child abuse has occurred throughout human history; as the eminent late French social historian Phillippe Aries (1962) showed in his book *Centuries of Childhood,* severe corporal punishment of children was commonplace in Europe for much of the past thousand years.

2. Reality and appearance. Why did child abuse become defined as a social problem in the United States in the past 30 years or so, when previously it was not? Clearly not because abuse was new. Was it becoming more frequent? Yes and no. It was perhaps more frequent because of the post World War II baby boom: The 1950s and 1960s saw unprecedented numbers of children and parents, hence more opportunity for abuse. But this would not necessarily lead to any change in the *rate* of abuse.

What did change in the 1960s and 1970s was the rate of *reported cases* of child abuse. Why did this occur? As Barbara Nelson (1984) documents in *Making an Issue of Child Abuse,* in 1962, the U.S. Children's Bureau, a federal agency within what was then the U.S. Department of Health, Education, and Welfare, formulated and circulated to the states a model statute for doctors and hospitals to report cases of suspected child abuse.

Between 1963 and 1967, every state passed an abuse-reporting law. Every state legislature is a busy place, working at any one time on hundreds of pieces of legislation. Why would all of them be compelled to pass this legislation? The answer to that is that child abuse was an issue whose time had come, despite the "fact" that no one could argue that more of it was going on than in the past, and despite the fact that the mass media in general routinely paid little or no attention to reports of parents killing or maiming children.

Why had the issue come of age? As Nelson tells the story:

Dr. C. Henry Kempe and his colleagues published "The Battered-Child Syndrome" in the AMA (American Medical Association) *Journal.* The article and its companion editorial caused a storm in medical circles and in the mass media as well. Indeed, the article and editorial are routinely used to date the rediscovery of abuse. In this instance, medical research and opinion did cross the

(continued)

187

BOX 7.1 Continued

bridge to the mass media, primarily through the vehicle of the AMA press release, "Parental Abuse Looms in Childhood Deaths." The message of the article and editorial was clear: Kempe and his co-workers had "discovered" an alarming and deadly "disease" which menaced the nation's children. (as cited in Protess & McCombs, 1991, p. 166)

In short order, Nelson notes, the problem of child abuse vaulted to the pages of the nation's news media and was picked up as a theme on televised dramas, soap operas, and talk shows. Child abuse had become a salient social problem, something that politicians could not help noticing.

Notice Nelson's use of quotation marks around "discovered." By saying that Kempe and coworkers "discovered" child abuse, she is saying that they found something already there, in just the same way as Christopher Columbus "discovered" the "New World." In short, the appearance caught up with the reality.

3. Reality as social construction. Notice also Nelson's use of quotation marks around "disease." She calls Dr. Kempe "inspired" in his labeling of child abuse as "The Battered-Child Syndrome." Why? By identifying child abuse as clearly dysfunctional and criminal behavior, he separated abuse from normal parental discipline, including "acceptable" corporal punishment. Indeed, Nelson argues, a large part of the reason child abuse had gone "undiscovered" although doctors, especially radiologists, had repeatedly seen children with broken bones, was that doctors had been reluctant to report cases because social and cultural values so strongly favor the "natural authority" of parents over children. Only when abuse was identified as a medical "syndrome" could journalists, entertainment producers, and legislators find ways to describe and, ultimately, proscribe it. As Nelson states flatly, "A social problem is a social construct," unrecognized as a problem until the right combination of values to give meaning to facts is found and the right agencies and organizations are in place to begin to solve it.

---

it were both the way the world is and the way it has to be. In other words, ideas, knowledge, and culture are simply a reflection of the social position of those who produce them. They are not real; they are nothing but the effect of more real and determining social and economic relations.

Such a view of ideology is common in the contemporary world. As we shall see in Chapter 9, it plays a central role in many discussions about the politics of identity, as when one member of a group accuses another of having bought into the mind-set of the dominant group. Equally commonly, some critics of contemporary society assume that the media are consciously and intentionally feeding the population false information and a false set of attitudes about the way the world is and has to be. In fact, some critics assume that, on the basis of the social identity of the producer of a particular text (by which they usually mean the board of directors of the responsible corporation), one can know the ideological bias of a text. Capitalists produce pro-capitalist texts that intentionally misrepresent reality to the audience for the sake of maintaining their own power. Male-run corporations produce pro-masculine texts that intentionally misrepresent reality to the audience for the sake of maintaining their own power.

EXPERIENCE AND IDEOLOGY

A phenomenal theory of reality adds a layer to the analysis of ideology. Experience is always in some sense false, only a shadow of reality; it always exists at a distance from reality. And yet, experience has its own sort of truth. It is at the very least the necessary starting point for any attempt to discover the truth of reality. Experience is the dimension through which human beings live the meaningfulness of their culture. That is, a phenomenal theory emphasizes the fact that human beings live in a meaningful world, but it still privileges the real world as if it could be accessed outside of the codes of meaning that define people's experience of it. A phenomenal theory of reality gives rise to a humanistic theory of ideology.

This theory of ideology emphasizes the more humanistic and less economistic side of Marx's (1975) writings. It refuses to reduce culture and knowledge to a mirror image of reality or to a direct effect of something else; it refuses to ignore the active role of meaning in human life. Instead, this theory begins with the assumption that people's position in the social world determines their experience of the world through the mediation of the cultural and communication forms that have emerged naturally and *authentically* from that position. That is, rather than assuming that there is a natural correspondence between social position and truth, a humanistic theory of ideology assumes a natural correspondence between social position, cultural forms, and experience. First, social position determines experience. By virtue of being working class, a worker is alienated from his or her labor, whether or not he or she knows it. By virtue of being a woman or a person of color, one inevitably has certain experiences of the world. For example, every woman has had the experience of being "sized up" by men, and any person of color has had the experience of being treated differently than White people. Second, left to their own devices, groups produce their own cultural forms and institutions, which accurately express and represent their experience.

However, precisely because these social groups are politically and economically subordinated, their culture is also subordinated to the cultural institutions and forms of the dominant class. The dominant culture tries, through any number of means, to replace and displace the authentic culture of the subordinate. It may simply drive or crowd their institutions out of business in the name of profit, in the way that the record and radio industries basically defeated and erased the music hall tradition of the working class. It may marginalize the cultural products and practices of the subordinate groups by constructing them as unworthy of serious consideration, or of social support. It may castigate them as vulgar, profane, obscene, dangerous, and even unpatriotic. Or it may appropriate them, incorporating them into dominant cultural codes so that these authentic expressions of subordinate experience are transformed from a challenge to the dominant values into a reaffirmation. For example, during the protests against the Vietnam War, dominant news media reporting on demonstrations would often emphasize that the very fact of such protests confirmed the unique privilege (freedom) of American society. In the process, the actual object of the protest (for example, the war in Vietnam or the disproportionate number of Blacks serving in the armed forces) was forgotten or ignored (Gitlin, 1980).

The result of this contest between an authentic culture and a dominant culture is that the subordinate group's ability to express and represent its authentic experience is negated. The dominant culture misrepresents and redefines other's experience. Thus, the subordinate group comes to experience the world in the codes of the dominant group; its experience is made inauthentic because of the mediating power of cultural or communicative codes. While the truth of knowledge (as an authentic relation to the world through experience) and ideological misrepresentation are still at stake, the key terms are no longer truth and reality but experience and culture.

The correspondence that such a theory assumes, a correspondence between one's position in and perspective on reality, experience, and cultural forms, is reflected in the assumption that there is a structural homology or parallelism that operates and can be read across these diverse dimensions. It is as if, everywhere one looks, one sees a particular message that can be taken to describe the structure of culture and experience, whether the authentic or the dominant. For example, consider Raymond Williams's (1975) discovery of the structure of mobile privatization. Mobile privatization, in its simplest terms, defines a structure in which the individual avoids the hostile world by retreating into the privacy and safety of the home. The outside world is beamed into the home via the mass media; no longer do individuals need to foray out into the world to gather information. Williams argues that this "structure of feeling" describes at least a significant part of the culture and experience of contemporary life and that it can be read from a wide range of texts and aspects of the mass media.[2]

SOCIAL CONSTRUCTIONISM AND IDEOLOGY

Both of these theories of ideology assume that ideology is in some sense a distortion or correctable misrepresentation of reality. In the end, ideology is a kind of bias operating within culture and knowledge. But social constructionism denies that there is any access to a reality outside of representations that would allow one to measure the truth or falsity of representations. Ideology is not "bias" because it cannot be measured against something that is not ideological, or that exists outside of ideology. One can only compare one ideological representation to another. Phenomenal theories of reality that contrast it to "mere appearance" assume that people (or at least the critic or scholar) have at some level an unmediated (nonideological) experience of the world that can serve as a normative yardstick against which to judge specific ideologies.[3]

People live within the systems of representation; they experience the world according to their codes of meaning. There is nothing outside of them that allows them to measure or judge their truth. Ideologies, then, are the systems of meaning within which people live in reality or, to put it differently, live their relationship to reality. They define how

191

people experience the world, what they take for granted. Ideologies define what is taken to be common sense; the truth of ideological statements appears obvious and even natural. But people are often unaware of many of these ideological codes, because the codes are unconscious and often unchallengeable.

If realist theories deny experience any significance, and humanistic theories make experience into the privileged access to truth, a social constructionist theory argues that experience itself is what ideology produces. It suggests that the most powerful and important effect of ideological representations is that they construct our most fundamental and basic experiences of the world. When Richard Nixon and even Robert Kennedy went hunting for Communists in the 1950s, they honestly saw such figures everywhere and viewed them as a real menace. There was no way to argue against this ideology by appealing to some experience outside of another ideology. In other words, an ideology is self-contained and non-falsifiable.

The twentieth-century French philosopher Louis Althusser (1970) was the leading proponent of such a theory of ideology, arrived at, he argued, by bringing the insights and arguments of semiotics and structuralism to bear on the question of ideology. Althusser defined ideology as the systems of representation in which people live out their imaginary relationship to their real conditions of existence. Notice: what is at stake here is not people's relations to reality, but their relationship to a relationship. What is this imaginary relationship, if not people's already meaningfully interpreted relations to the world? To put it simply, there is no way out of experience. Experience is the beginning and end of ideology. It is the world in which human beings always exist, and it is the product of ideological experiences.

If this theory is accurate, then it would seem to follow that the more obvious the truth of an experience is and the more certain people are of that truth, the more ideological that experience is. Consider the following analogy. Two people are talking. Person A says that his arm is broken. Person B says that it is not. Only one is right in this matter of fact. (Even judgments of such matters of fact involve relations of power. As Michel Foucault (1973) has demonstrated, the history of medicine is partly a history of the reorganization of power: for example, who has the power to diagnose such things?) But suppose Person A had said that he was in pain, and B had challenged this claim. There is an obvious

192

problem here, because Person A made a statement of experience and not fact; we assume that people do have some privileged empirical access to their own experience. I cannot be mistaken that I see red, although I can be mistaken that there is something red there. Yet, a constructionist theory of ideology seems to suggest that just such experiential statements, statements that seem to be the most secure, are in fact the most ideological.

How does this production of experience work? It works by pulling individuals into its signifying systems in such a way as to make them responsible for those representations; individuals become the authors of their own experiences. You know when you "see" a red car. That is, you *authorize* your own interpretation as the truth because you are the source and author of the statement and hence of the experience. Ideology works in just this way. It positions individuals as the subjects of their own ideological statements and hence of their experiences. People believe themselves to be the arbiters of an experience that is in fact constructed by ideological codes. Althusser (1970) describes this process as interpellation. Interpellation is ideology's ability to assign individuals to specific positions within its own communicative (semiotic) representations of reality.

We can further explicate this rather difficult notion by suggesting two experiments. First, pick up something that someone else has written in the first-person singular, such as a letter or a report. Now read it aloud. You will find that you begin to identify with the *I* in the text, that you feel yourself living what the person who wrote it lived, and that it seems to become part of you, or rather, you seem to become part of it. Through an identification with the *I*, it begins to become part of your identity, but of course, this will only be temporary because you know what is going on.

Now try a second experiment: The next time you go to a movie, imagine that the world that is represented on the screen is real and that you are in it. Ask yourself where are you standing in that world. Think about your field of vision, what you can and cannot see; that will pretty clearly define where you are. Now ask yourself if you could be standing anywhere else. Even if you can imagine other positions, you will still be unable to actually put yourself in them; you remain firmly rooted where you are. Why? You are positioned by the camera. Because the camera that filmed the scene is your only source of information about the world of the movie, you are basically forced to identify with the camera and to be in the place it defines for you.

Films represent a reality that does not exist outside the film. Viewers experience it according to the way they are positioned in relation to what appears on the screen. They can see only what the camera shows them. More important, in most commercial Hollywood films, the camera never violates people's sense of their perceptual position in the world by showing them something that it would be impossible for them to see. They cannot see what is going on behind a wall or in another place or behind their backs. The camera may turn around, but it must always do so in predictable ways that do not violate the viewers' sense of where they are standing in relation to the film's world.

These two experiments illustrate the process of interpellation. Interpellation literally means putting into the space. Theorists use it to describe the way in which different codes—the codes of language or the codes of the cinema, for example—place people into particular positions that define their subjectivity and experience of the world. It is a bit like walking down the street and hearing someone say, "Hey you." You turn around thinking that perhaps they have called to you. In that instance, you have been hailed and positioned—interpellated by that single simple utterance. Interpellation makes the individual into a subject (a speaker of language) responsible for every word that he or she speaks and for the reality that these words imply. Return to Chapter 5's image of a game of musical chairs: Meaning is created when the moving signifiers stop moving, and some signifiers slide below others into the chairs, taking on the function of signifieds. Interpellation answers the question of why the music stops. The individual speaker stops the music; it is his or her apparent intention that creates the meaning. To put it another way, it is the *I* who is both inside and outside of language that draws the line between the signifier and the signified.

If ideologies are somehow linked to particular power relations and interests, then it appears that one has to assume that ideologies somehow distort reality for the sake of the interests of those in power. Returning to the example above, it is in the interest of capitalists to construct an ideology of the free market of labor, but such a market does not actually exist, or so it would seem. But according to social constructionism, an ideology is not a biased view of a reality that can be described outside of ideology. This problem is known as *mystification*.

194

Ideology mystifies in two ways. First, because an ideology presents itself as natural and universal, it hides its connection to the interests of particular social groups or power blocs in society. By making the labor market, as it functions in capitalism, appear to be the only rational and natural form of labor, for example, the ideology of capitalism hides the ways in which this particular form of the labor market exploits workers for the benefit of capitalists. Second, ideology is mystifying precisely because it does create the reality it represents. For example, the ideology of patriarchy represents women as the weaker sex and thus continues the privileged position of men in society. Precisely because of the commonsensical nature of this ideological representation, parents often treat boys and girls differently. Boys will be encouraged to participate in activities that augment their strength, and they are allowed to be rough, whereas girls will be guided toward more passive pursuits. Or consider a different example. Marx said that the major figure of capitalist ideology is the commodity, something made to be sold. Capitalist ideology represents everything, including labor, as a commodity. Through the power of this ideology, everything in capitalism—including workers—*becomes* a commodity. The mystification arises not because things are not commodities (they are) but because they need not be. In a different ideology, such as the communism Marx envisioned, labor need not be rewarded on the basis of its value, but on the basis of people's requirements for a humane life.

Or, to return to the question of patriarchy, one can imagine a different system of child rearing that would, among other things, disprove the apparently natural differences between the sexes. But this new system would not actually disprove patriarchy so much as replace patriarchy with a different construction or representation of reality, which would in turn create its own reality.

IDEOLOGY AND STRUGGLE

One need not choose among these theories of ideologies, for each can be seen to have different uses. The social constructionist theory describes the broad terrain on which a society's communication and cultural life actively determine both the structure of social relationships (power) and their relationship to the world. Still, it has little to say about specific situations in which ideology becomes a more conscious and explicit site of struggle. A humanistic theory of ideology describes the struggle between attempts on the part of subordinated minorities to define a part of their life outside of the control of the dominant majority, a space of authenticity to which they assign a direct relationship to their subordination. It also describes some of the processes (such as incorporation) by which a dominant ideological code might attempt to deal with such moments that might escape or even resist its domination. Both of these theories are concerned with the way domination is achieved and maintained through the construction of a cultural consensus using the means of communication. But neither theory addresses those situations where the existing consensus is precarious enough that it can be maintained only by an explicit ideological war that often consciously dissimulates to the audience. A realist theory of ideology is often useful for describing explicitly political economic battles (for example, capitalism vs. communism).

A social constructionist theory maintains that ideology always involves practices of articulation. In Chapter 4, we argued that any event or media product can have multiple meanings or interpretations. The same media product can be read as telling a number of different stories. We argued that meaning was produced by linking or articulating signifiers or signs or texts. Similarly, there exist at any moment a number of different stories about reality or about specific events that occur. Ideology is then the product of a double articulation: first, a text is articulated to a certain meaning, and then a meaning has to be articulated to reality to become an ideological code. Consider any government scandal (from Watergate to Irangate to the latest one). Every scandal elicits a number of stories, each of which seems to make sense of the "facts." Each version has different consequences, and each is related to different political interest groups. For example, Watergate was a scandal of the corruption of a small group within the Republican Party; Watergate was a phony scandal invented by Democrats to embarrass the Republicans; Watergate was a sign of the corruption that has become pervasive in American politics; Watergate was a "nonevent," no different from the way politics has ever been conducted.

Notice that it *does* make a difference which of these stories becomes the accepted one, which becomes "knowledge" that most Americans share. It is this struggle to make specific meanings and stories into taken-for-granted representations of reality that defines the struggle over ideology. If articulation describes the way specific meanings can be attached to specific signs or texts, it also describes the way a particular set of meanings can be linked to material or nondiscursive practices and events. Remember the example of the Trobriand Islanders, who believed that sex has nothing to do with reproduction. As a story, it can be humorous and entertaining to Westerners. But as an ideology, that story had been successfully articulated to reality so that the islanders actually experienced the world in its terms.

The question of how reality is represented, the choice between different stories or pictures of reality, is not random. Nor is the decision freely made by each individual in isolation. Individuals do not get to decide that reality is this way, even though the rest of the world disagrees with them. The construction of a socially shared representation of reality is always implicated in society's attempt to reproduce its own existence and to ensure the continued viability of the particular relations of power characterizing that society.

On the other hand, although one ideology (or more accurately, an ideological formation, because it is composed of numerous statements that might not fit seamlessly together) is usually dominant, there are always competing stories about events and reality in a society. The *dominant* ideology defines the taken-for-granted or commonsense reality of the vast majority of people in the society. How does this work? For ideology can be effective only if it appears to be unquestionably true, so obvious and natural that any rational human would assent to its interpretations. Recreational drugs, for example, have become demonized by contemporary conservative ideologies, and increasingly the common sense of American society. To stand up and speak for *certain* drugs, to argue that they are not the evil force that we have been led to believe, seems almost impossible. Indeed, the demonization of marijuana is quite clear in the debates about the use of marijuana for medicinal purposes. In this way, specific ideological representations of reality become both natural and universal. Those living within an ideology assume that any rational being would share their commonsense perceptions; if they do not, then something must be wrong with them. The construction of "welfare queens" as lazy parents out to cheat the American public provides a further example.

There are always multiple ideologies within any given society. This is not quite the same as saying, as we did in Chapter 5, that there are always many meanings or stories. For an ideology is more than a story, it is a representation. An ideology embodies the claim by a particular group that this meaning or story represents reality. Consequently, ideologies are always in competition with each other. There is always a struggle between ideologies to achieve dominance. In that sense, people cannot be seen as passive "dopes" who unknowingly are manipulated by a single dominant ideology. Because there is no sure way to establish how reality will or must be represented, people are constantly involved in the struggle over ideology. The British media critic Stuart Hall (1985) tells a story about when his young son was learning the colors and simultaneously something about his own identity. The son could not understand why he was "black" because in fact he was brown. But a particular color has been articulated to a particular social identity. That color carries with it a particular set of meanings: In Western cultures, these are largely negative, as in black magic, black humor, the wearing of black at funerals. And these meanings are carried into the articulation. This articulation is part and parcel of a racist ideology that naturalizes and legitimates the subordination of Blacks. But Hall also points out that one of the most important parts of the civil rights struggle was the ideological struggle to disarticulate *black* from its negative connotations and to rearticulate it to a more positive image: Black is beautiful. Or consider another example of the articulation of color and race: When the authors were growing up, one of the crayons in the Crayola box was labeled *flesh*. Today that color is *peach*.

Many of the most obviously political struggles are often ideological. Consider the abortion debate. The very attempt to label the antiabortion forces "pro-life" already suggests an ideological strategy. After all, it is commonsensical to favor life, and it is quite difficult to speak against it. By the same token, the pro-abortion forces prefer to be called "pro-choice." Recent rhetoric from the antiabortion campaign has attempted to link or articulate abortion (as killing fetuses) with the Holocaust (the planned genocidal campaign against Jews by Nazis) and slavery. This is clearly an ideological project that, were it to succeed—that is, if it became consensually accepted, the dominant ideology—would make it quite difficult to defend abortion. If every time someone opened their mouth to defend abortion, the Holocaust and slavery followed close behind, the abortion rights movement would be finished. Culture involves constant struggles between competing ideological codes, each attempting to gain the upper hand, to somehow win people into seeing the world in terms of its particular meanings, to experiencing the world in its terms.

Ideological formations are not as coherent and systematic as the discussion thus far may have made it appear. As the Italian journalist and critic Antonio Gramsci (1971) argued, common sense is not a systematic structure. On the contrary, it is made up of contradictory fragments of meaning and understanding, assumptions about the world that a society inherits from any number of different sources. Often, no one can remember where these bits of knowledge originated, or how their truth was established. They are now, as Gramsci describes them, traces without an inventory; we have lost the ability to remember where they came from and why they seemed so reasonable at some time.

Thus, the ideological effects of a particular text need not be determined only by the totality of the program or narrative. One can watch the Batman movies, find many aspects of the films unacceptable and certainly unrealistic, but leave the theater finding notions of vigilantism and the incompetence of the police strongly articulated (or rearticulated) in one's common sense. Similarly, consider the Rambo films: looking at the narrative as a whole, one might argue that at least one possible ideological articulation of the movies makes the federal government into the enemy. But that is probably not the most common ideological effect of these movies, which were more likely linked to various notions of violence and individualism and even jingo-istic patriotism. More recently, *Independence Day* transformed the Cold War fear of communism by relocating the enemy as the feared Other into outer space. But as in the sci-fi movies of the 1950s, one can ask whether the film is really about new threats facing the United States here on Earth or is it, as some critics have suggested, less about particular enemies and more about the need to reassert a strong sense of identity against a common enemy in the face of political challenges to the established system of identities and differences. To put it simply, is the current revival of sci-fi movies about alien species really a backlash against feminism, antiracism, new immigrants, and the end of the Cold War?

On the other hand, *Men in Black* seems to undermine any ability to represent aliens as uniformly threatening others.

One of the most interesting recent public spectacles presents a good opportunity for thinking about the complexity of ideological struggle and the differences between the theories of ideology we have discussed here. On August 31, 1997, Diana, Princess of Wales, was killed in an automobile accident in Paris while fleeing with her lover from the paparazzi. The world media coverage was unrivaled, and the public response unprecedented. Over a billion people watched the funeral; millions of people sent flowers or waited for hours to sign books of condolences from all over the world. The death of Diana, the "people's princess," was the occasion for a worldwide collective act of public and private mourning. This event and its subsequent media coverage will no doubt give rise to many essays and books over the next few years that attempt to interpret its cultural meaning and ideological significance.

Let us begin by considering how each of the three theories of ideology might be used to enlighten our understanding of this event. An ideological realist might interpret this event as another media spectacle that distracts public attention from the serious problems of contemporary society by focusing on the life of another member of the rich and famous. After all, Diana's worldwide celebrity was itself a construction of the media. Diana's image as the people's princess is false consciousness, because in reality, she was a wealthy member of the ruling elite who used most of her time and money in conspicuous consumption of exorbitantly priced designer fashion.

A humanistic theorist might talk about the ritual aspects of her life and her death. Beginning with her marriage and ending, for the moment, with her funeral, Diana's entire life and image as Princess of Wales was a media ritual celebrating all sorts of common values and dreams. Like the mythic Cinderella, the fairy tale that was Princess Diana's marriage reaffirmed our faith in love, marriage, and the apparently happy ending suggested by the myth that Prince Charming is waiting around the corner for every woman. Diana's life reaffirmed our belief in the importance of compassion and charity and, in the contemporary political climate, of volunteerism. But the events leading up to her divorce and her death were a spectacle of another order, reaffirming our worst fears about dysfunctional marriages, unsupportive families, and the victimization of women in contemporary society.

The social constructionist might make a number of observations. First, he or she might raise the question of Diana's relationship to contemporary notions of royalty and the power of the monarchy in contemporary British life. Diana's death seems to have challenged the monarchy in new and powerful ways that threaten to either reform or end its power. Second, a social constructionist might want to inquire into the grounds for the very real and powerful emotional identification with Diana that marked the worldwide response to her death. Psychiatrists reported that women patients talked about her life and death as public parables about the changing nature of life for women in contemporary society: from eating disorder to abuse. Finally, the social constructionist could use Diana's life and death to talk about the changing nature and role of celebrity in the media; how the traditional and tabloid press are implicated in the development of the paparazzi and journalists who spend their lives stalking celebrities to provide the apparently insatiable demand for coverage. Are these changes in the media themselves related to other aspects of contemporary definitions of entertainment and news, and the blurring of the distinction between them. The question remains, *where* is ideology produced? Where is it found? Where are the struggles over ideology taking place? The answer is simple: wherever language, culture, and media are found. For it is in the shared culture of a society that ideology resides. And as the media have grown to be the most important and visible cultural institutions of the society, they have become the most important ideological battlefield. It is in the media that one finds not only the dominant ideology—from which people learn the commonsense view of reality—but also subordinate ideologies struggling to change that commonsense view.

NOTES

1. The major text of Marx and Engels here is *The German Ideology.*
2. In fact, Williams discovers this structure through an analysis of the economics, technology, and cultural forms of television.
3. See Marx's *Das Kapital,* volume 1, where he describes ideology as a necessary misrepresentation.

PART III

The Power of the Media

Producing Identities

People have always needed a sense of who they are and a place to
ground that sense of their identity in one or more of the institutions or activities of their lives: the church (and their soul or some core
values), their work (and their labor or skills), their families (and their
sense of a generational past and future), and, increasingly in the twentieth century, their leisure and consumption activities. (Thus, it seems
reasonable to work at an unrewarding job so that one can afford to enjoy the weekends.) Moreover, every person can be described as and has
a sense of himself or herself as both an individual and a member of
various social groups (which can range from the very broad, such as
Black and White or male and female, to the very narrow, such as a
graduate of a particular university or a member of a particular Greek
organization). That sense of individuality, whether grounded in the religious spirit or simply in some personal essence, involves some sense
of transcendence, some sense that we are not only the sum of the various social roles that we play, the various social groups to which we
belong.

By the 1950s, the issue of identity had become not only politically
and culturally but also psychologically dominant in American culture,
especially among youth. In fact, a new psychological "disorder" was
"discovered" among college students, some of whom began to feel anx-

205

ious about who they were. They apparently worried that their individuality, that which made them unique, was nothing more than the sum of the various social groups to which they belonged and the images they took on. In fact, many of the most powerful images from 1950s popular culture—James Dean in *Rebel without a Cause*, Marlon Brando in *The Wild One*, Jack Kerouac's novel of the "beat generation," *On the Road*, and even the later parody of a beatnik, Maynard G. Krebs, from the TV show *Dobie Gillis*—revolved around this common search by young people for a stable individual identity. By the 1980s, this anxiety had become a taken-for-granted part of growing up. Calvin Klein could even use it as the theme for his commercial with Brooke Shields: *Is there a real me? Or am I just what you see?*

This identity crisis was often assumed to be linked to the growing power of the media (and media images) in the lives of these youths. In fact, there can be little doubt that the strength of the traditional sources of identity—religion, family, and work—has declined in proportion to the growing power of the mass media, leisure activities, and the consumer lifestyles in which media and leisure are bound up even as they define and promote such lifestyles. More than anything, what nearly everyone in America shares, whatever school or church or job they go to, is the mass media. Despite differences in taste and access, there are significant commonalities in our shared experience of the most "mass" of the mass media, television, popular music, and block-buster movies. At the same time, the sense of unity among people, created by such powerful identities as were defined by religion, nationality, and work, have themselves been increasingly undermined by the powerful representations of difference that have come to define the media's cultural content, even as the media have come to shape social life. Ultimately, the media's ability to produce people's social identities, in terms of both a sense of unity and difference, may be their most powerful and important effect.

In this chapter, we will explore the ways in which the media produce people's sense of who they are and who others are. There are many dimensions on which people have a sense of themselves, a sense of their own identity.

- Politically, people exist as citizens and as members of a public.

- Socially, people exist as exemplars of social roles (fathers, children, teachers, and so on).

- Culturally, people exist as exemplars of social groups (often defined within semiotic systems of differences, such as Black and White, male and female).

- Economically, people exist as consumers and members of an audience.

But it would be a mistake to conceive of the concept of the audience as only an economic category, where the audience is understood as the *market* for media (and other) products. Not only is the concept of the audience intricately bound up with the dimensions of social and cultural identity, there is at least one other dimension that has to be accounted for: the audience as *fans* and members of subcultures.

A fan is not simply a person who uses or enjoys the media. Fans identify themselves with a particular media product, star, or style. They may be members of a particular subculture or followers of media fads or fashions. We shall postpone a discussion of the significance of fandom and subcultures until the next chapter.

In this chapter, we shall discuss the remaining dimensions of the audience and identity: the audience as market and as a set of social and cultural identities. We are ignoring the differences between social and cultural identities because we will be treating all of these in relationship to the media, as questions of audiences and representations, rather than of social relationships between people per se. That is, we are not going to address the ways in which one's identity is shaped in specific social relationships: You learn that you are a student, and how to be a student, in relation to the activities of teachers and other students in a classroom; you learn that you are a girl and how to be female in relating to boys and other girls and observing how they relate to each other). But you also learn that you are a student or a girl and what that means through the variety of cultural and media texts that represent such identities and place or interpellate you in specific relations to those representations. Thus, we are concerned with how notions of the audience and of identity actually involve an image of the entire process of communication; talking about the audience in a particular way already makes assumptions about why certain media products are produced, what those products do, and how audiences are affected by them. And the two dimensions of audience and identity discussed here—market and cultural identity—are all used by all of the groups involved in communication, including media producers, economic institutions, and the people who use media. At various moments, audience members may think of themselves as markets, and as having specific cultural identities.

CONSTRUCTING THE AUDIENCE

The *audience* as such does not actually exist except as an idealization. That is, the audience is itself constructed by people who use the term for a particular purpose. The chief executive officer of a television network may claim that he or she is simply supplying the audience with what it wants, even though only a fraction of the potential viewing population is watching (and even fewer claim that what they get is what they actually want). The Gallup poll claims, on the basis of an extraordinarily small sample, to know what the audience is watching; but pollsters cannot know what is actually taking place in front of the television set. Advertisers are not only trying to reach the audience, but to adjust their messages to fit the audience. *TV Guide* claims to speak for the audience, as do the talk show hosts who claim that "our viewers want to know . . ." Various political advocates from the political right and left make all sorts of claims about the viewing habits and desires of something called the audience. Different notions of the audience are the creations of different economic, political, and cultural groups. There are different audiences for different media and cultural forms. For example, ABC has never quite figured out why its prime-time special on the superstar band U2 (in 1997, while the band was enormously popular) failed to attract the band's fans.

The concept of the audience is a social construction, a concept that can mean and be made to do many different things. Yes, there are real people out there watching a television program, or reading a newspaper, or buying an album, who can be said to be *in the audience* for a particular media product. However, the idea of an audience is never merely an innocent description of the sum total of individuals. The fact of the matter is that the audience does not exist out there in reality apart from the way in which it is defined by different groups, for different purposes. How the concept of the audience is constructed determines how it can function and how the relationship between the media and their audiences can be described, measured, and evaluated.

THE AUDIENCE AS MARKET: CONSUMERS

The most common conception of the audience within the media industries is as a conglomeration of potential and potentially overlapping markets. *A market identifies a subset of the population as potential consumers of a particular identifiable product or set of products.* Markets may vary according to their size (the market for techno-dance is smaller than that for mainstream rock; the market for NHS speakers is smaller than that for all-in-one stereo systems), although often, the general population has little sense of the size of various markets (for collectible cards, or comic books, or *bhangra*—a mix of Indian film music and disco, for example). Markets may also vary according to their duration (the market for the latest hit film or album is quite fleeting compared to the market for films or albums in general) and to their stability and flexibility (the market for television is probably more stable and flexible than that for network television in particular). Markets can also have "identities" attached or articulated to them. In this sense, the market for heavy metal music is generally thought of as primarily composed of adolescent boys; the market for Saturday morning cartoons as preschool and grade school children, and the market for soap operas as adult women.

There are two basic ways in which audiences are constructed and function as markets: consumers and commodities. The most common way that those involved in the media industries think of the audience is as made up of consumers: to sell a book, a film, a record, a videotape, or any media product, or even to get people to watch, listen, or read something, a media producer has in mind the type of person who will purchase or tune in to that product. That "idea" of the media consumer is what is referred to as a *market type*. As we described in Chapter 3, the media industries spend a great deal of time and money in the search for more and more information about media consumers and the appropriate appeals to make to convince media consumers to buy a particular media product. The people who purchase and enjoy the products of the media often think of themselves as consumers as well. And insofar as they are successfully constructed by the media as an audience for the media, as a particular market type, people will often think of themselves in these terms. That is, by linking individuals together within the category of a market, at least a part of their identity is defined by their participation in this market.

It is not enough for the industries to simply be able to describe specific market types; they have also attempted to develop better ways of understanding what is going on in such consumer groups and better ways of describing and categorizing the various types of such groups. The three most common and persistent ways of describing market types are: demographics, taste cultures, and lifestyle clusters.

Demographics is the quantitative description of a population according to a set of social or sociological variables. The American population can be described by counting the number of people who fit into a set of demographic categories such as age, race, gender, income level, education level, employment category (professional, sales, blue-collar, pink-collar), place of residence (urban, suburban, rural), geographic region (Northeast, Southeast, Midwest, Southwest, Northwest, and West) and type of residence (home owner, home renter, condo owner, apartment dweller).

Assumptions about consumers underlie marketing categories. Media corporations invest a great deal of money in market research to identify the likely market for their product. This information helps them determine marketing and strategies and advertising styles. The Disney Channel is more likely to be marketed to families with children (say, through an ad in *Parent's* magazine or during *Goosebumps*) than to single individuals. And TV commercials for herbicides used in farming are more likely to be found in less populous areas of the Midwest than in the cities of the Northeast.

A second way of understanding a market type is as a *taste culture*. In this case, the demographic identity of the audience members is less important than the continuing commitment of a group of people to some type of product. For example, science fiction producers want to appeal to the science fiction fans out there, who are always seeking a new book or film to indulge their taste for this genre. Similarly, among music consumers, there are clear taste cultures that are not always easy to define demographically; yet, clearly, the market for classical music is different from that for country-western or Elvis Presley or Sinead O'Connor. In fact, among even a fairly homogeneous group of people—at least in demographic terms—a wide range of musical taste cultures is probably represented.

Whereas some taste cultures correspond to generic categories (the taste culture of science fiction fans), others are characterized by either multiple genres or by selective choices made from different genres. For example, radio programmers think of different formats as appealing to different taste cultures. Contemporary hits radio, the most popular format, comprises some heavy metal (Guns & Roses, Tesla, but not Metallica), some dance music (Madonna but not Prince), most pop music (Adam Schmidt but not REM), some rap (MC Hammer but not Public Enemy), and so on. Producers operating with an understanding of the audience as taste cultures construct media products according to their understanding of the features of the product that hold the taste culture together, rather than according to their image of a particular demographic group of consumers.

The most recent way developed to describe market types has been used extensively by advertisers: *lifestyle clusters* can be understood as a mixture of demographic categories and consumption habits or tastes. A lifestyle cluster represents a segment of the population that tends to purchase and use certain kinds of products or to make certain kinds of decisions, including voting. The best-known example of a lifestyle cluster is the *yuppie*. What's a yuppie? Originally, it referred to a small market segment of young, urban professionals (y-u-p) with a great deal of disposable income who tended to display their wealth through the purchase of particular brands of consumer goods. For example, *Newsweek* defined a yuppie as someone with five different kinds of mustard in the refrigerator.

A lifestyle cluster creates groups in the population whose members have several characteristics in common. Most important, the members of a particular group tend to spend their money and time in similar ways. The entire population of the country can be displayed as a number of lifestyle groups, according to systems of consumption patterns and values. The most powerful of such descriptions takes the project one step further, by attempting to correlate lifestyle clusters with geographic location (for example, as described by zip codes of home residences). Advertisers and media producers can then target a particular lifestyle cluster for their products: Sometimes this takes the form of producing different versions of the same magazine with different advertisements directed at different lifestyle markets. Direct mail advertisers often now tailor their mailings according to zip codes and even specific block addresses.

Implicit in the very notion of the audience as consumers operating in a market is the need to continually make people think of themselves as consumers. Many historians and media scholars have observed that this is one of the major effects of the media in the twentieth century: to help construct a consumer society by encouraging people to locate their identity in their leisure tastes and consumer practices rather than in other roles such as jobs and churches. The ideological message is that what we buy says more about who we are than other facts, including where we get the money. Media programs and advertising are all about this redefinition of self-identity. The media are both a part of any lifestyle and one of the ways such lifestyles are produced and promoted. The media reinforce the power of the market over identity, even as they themselves produce the very identities that locate people in the market as consumers.

In most countries of the advanced industrial world, people take the existence of a consumer society for granted. It appears natural that everyone in these societies is part of a national market and that their lives are defined and measured by, if not devoted to, the consumption of various goods and services. But in fact, the notion of a consumer society is a very recent invention, and it took a great deal of work—not only economic but political and cultural work as well—to establish it.

The origins of the consumer society can be found in the social changes that were the product of economic developments between 1880 and 1920. In fact, many of the basic features of contemporary society came into existence in this period. Society was changing as economic, political, and cultural questions were increasingly transformed into bureaucratic decisions for experts. Mass production came into being, as a result of the assembly line—using expensive single purpose machinery with cheap, quickly trained "single purpose workers" to inexpensively produce a large number of the same item—and Taylorism, a system for time studies, which enabled any production line to be broken down into identifiable movements that could be performed in certain specifiable times. These changes had two immediate and significant consequences.

First, the new glut of cheaper products had to be sold; thus, new and larger markets had to be discovered or opened up. As Henry Ford made more cars and made them more cheaply, he also had to find people who had the money to buy them and who wanted or believed they needed to buy an automobile. In one sense, the solution was obvious: Henry Ford is often quoted as having said, "If I could get my workers to all buy cars, I could make a fortune." And that is basically what happened. Higher wages allowed workers to become consumers of the goods they were mass-producing. And shorter hours allowed them the time and freedom to use their newly purchased goods. But higher wages alone were insufficient. Workers were often reluctant to spend their money on what seemed to be frivolous luxuries. The culture of many of those in the working class emphasized saving for a rainy day rather than spending. Moreover, it was not enough to convince workers and their families to spend their money. They had to spend it in predictable and controllable ways. It would do no good if all of Ford's workers decided they wanted Cadillacs when there were lots of Model Ts waiting to be sold. It is in this context that both advertising and marketing research were introduced as ways to maximize and rationalize the consumer habits of these new consumers who were apparently reaping the benefits of mass production. It is in the same context that department stores and national glossy magazines arose.

Advertising not only had to define the particular desires and needs of these new consumers, it had to make *them* think of themselves as consumers as well. People who for generations had lived on the edge of poverty, and whose identity was almost entirely built around their family and their work, had now to think of themselves as consumers rather than producers, as individuals with their own desires rather than as families. Work had to become less a source of identity and pride and more a means by which people could fulfill their desires through consumption.

But this new consumer society, and the communicative and cultural changes that helped to produce it, were responding as well to other serious changes and problems confronting the United States between 1880 and 1920: There was a sharp rise in labor protests, often aimed at the systems of industrial production and wage "slavery" themselves. New waves of immigration, especially from eastern Europe and the Mediterranean, challenged the apparent homogeneity of the society, creating the need to find ways of integrating these new populations into the American way of life. And finally, in the early twentieth century, there were a series of "Red scares" motivated by the fears of a domestic communist movement based in immigrant and labor populations.

Advertising, the mass media, and ultimately the new consumer society were placed into this crisis as a new source of social control and harmony. By giving all the people the sense that they had access to commodities that would improve their lifestyle and their social status, the new consumer society sought to undermine the conditions that led to social unrest. By bringing people's desires and needs under the control of the new culture of mass media, and hence, under the control of science and industry, the new consumer society sought to "rationalize" people's everyday lives. It was thought that the new culture could shape people's consciousness, leading them away from real social dissatisfactions toward individual desires, away from issues of class and inequality and toward questions of prestige, style, and status. In the new consumer society, apparently, all social problems could be solved by working on your "self."

In a sense, at least part of the function of modern mass media has been to change the way people have thought of themselves: to make people think of and even experience themselves as consumers. And it still remains part of the very effects of the media on audiences—to remind us that the value and purpose of our lives is defined by our existence as consumers, by what we buy and what we own. It is no accident that so much of the content of the media is directed to our consumer life, that the stage of the media's messages is always cluttered with products.

Notice that conceiving of the audience as consumers does not mean that people are entirely passive; on the contrary, the audience as consumer is very active. People must make decisions about which media to expose themselves to and which products to buy, then buy products, use them up, and buy more. A goal of the media is to constantly reproduce—and along the way, influence—this activity of desiring and buying, not only of media products but of other products as well. The audience as a market is constantly working, gathering information on what products exist, deciding what is best for them to buy, and eventually, going out and buying them. The audience need not always be consciously involved in such activity—except insofar as they choose to consume particular media messages rather than others—but they are always being reminded of their role as consumers and as potential markets for specific products and services.

At the same time, it is important to realize the limits of the claim that a part of people's identity is defined by their investment in consumption. People are aware of themselves as consumers, but there is far more to their self-conscious sense of their own identity. In addition, not every individual act of consumption necessarily defines one's identity. What we are describing is a general, culturally constructed sense of an economic identity, not a specific sense of lifestyle cluster or taste culture. For some people, the particular brand of jeans they buy and wear may be a part of their identity, whereas for others, it is a relatively minor issue in their lives. What we buy may reflect either our group identifications or our individual taste. Someone who refused to consume or who opposed consumption in American society would seem like an outsider if not a crackpot.

THE AUDIENCE AS MARKET: COMMODITY

The media not only created a consumer society by constructing the audience for its messages as a market, but it also constructed the audience as a commodity. Remember that a commodity is an object produced in order to be sold for a profit. It may seem odd to think of an audience as something that is produced and sold, something from which someone can make a profit. But think about how media work in their relation to advertising: The media produce an audience for their own media products and then deliver that audience to another media producer, namely, an advertiser. When people watch their favorite TV program, they are also watching the ads embedded in the show. Some people may enjoy watching ads for their own sake: For example, in Italy in the 1970s, the most popular prime-time show was a half-hour of commercials. In the United States, it is not uncommon for advertisers to advertise forthcoming advertisements or to give advertisements a story line: The early 1990s brought us a romantic narrative involving neighbors sharing Taster's Choice coffee, and each new episode of the commercial was announced in advance in *TV Guide*. Similarly, both Pepsi and Coke have mounted major ad campaigns to trumpet forthcoming series of commercials.

However, ads work only when their audience moves on to become the consumers of the product being advertised. Think about the discussion of advertising support for television in Chapter 4. Few people choose to watch TV programs for the advertising, and yet, viewers are inevitably an audience for the ads. As we said, this is why ratings are so important in the relationship between the television networks and advertisers. Each wants to know the size of the audience as a potential market so that it knows how much to charge or pay for this particular commodity. In fact, networks program a particular series precisely to attract a specific market type so that it can sell that audience as a highly priced commodity to an advertiser. And increasingly, advertisers (as well as other media producers) attempt to link their products to specific, highly desirable social groups and identities (consider for example the marketing campaigns of Pepsi or Toyota or Levi's).

Media producers have to think about whom they want to attract as an audience for their shows because this is the audience they are selling to advertisers. A television network may decide to leave a program on the air even though it has a relatively small audience if it is a particularly attractive audience to advertisers. A radio station may decide to change formats to one already overrepresented in the local market because, again, its demographics are the most desirable to the local advertisers. On the other hand, a program that has a relatively large audience may be taken off the air if the particular market it attracts is decidedly unattractive to advertisers. Programs such as *Gunsmoke* and *The Beverly Hillbillies*, although both were still relatively successful in the early 1970s, were nevertheless canceled because their audiences were primarily rural and old, not particularly attractive audiences to TV advertisers. One of the major reasons that popular musical styles such as heavy metal and rap are so underrepresented on radio is that their audiences are not particularly attractive to advertisers. The long-term underrepresentation in the media of certain social groups, such as Blacks and Latinos, might similarly be partly explained by advertisers' assumptions about the desirability of such audiences.

Advertisements attempt to transform the audience for a particular program or media product into the potential market for the advertiser's product. For example, a television network or radio station sells the audience for each program to advertisers. It delivers this audience as a commodity to the advertisers so that the advertisers can get their message—consume this product—to the audience. Advertisers are purchasing what they hope is the attention, the visual labor of watching, the labor of listening, of the audience. If the audience is not actually watching or listening and paying some minimal attention to the ad, then the advertiser has wasted money.

Television and radio are only the most obvious places where the audience is commodified. In the music industry, for example, the sale of actual musical commodities (records, tapes, CDs) accounts for a decreasing percentage of profits. Instead, music is increasingly used to deliver audiences to the sellers of other products and media, such as clothing with rock star insignia, and to films (where soundtracks are important). Also, music is used in advertising to sell other products. In short, even in those industries that we think of as not relying on "advertiser support," the audience is commodified indirectly.

Part of the reason audiences can be so easily commodified is because of audience loyalty to certain media celebrities and media products. Stars can supply their fans with a wide range of merchandise in addition to their albums; on the other hand, if an advertiser wants to reach a certain segment of the market, he or she might reasonably decide to hire a particular recording artist who has already proven to be attractive to the particular segment to provide the musical soundtrack for or even appear in its commercial.

Technology has created serious problems for advertisers and the media. Consider television: Advertisers cannot be confident that the audience of a program is actually the audience for the commercials embedded in the program. With remote control, audience members can move ("graze") from program to program and avoid all commercials while they watch parts of several programs at a time. And by videotaping programs, people can avoid watching commercials at all as they fast forward ("zap") past them. Recent audience research demonstrates that audience members turn off the sound during commercials. In response, advertisers try to devise means to keep the audience's attention (making commercials as short as 15 or 20 seconds, or making them more entertaining, more like mini-programs or mini-music videos).

REPRESENTING IDENTITIES

The audience is composed of individuals who are each members of one or more social groups that define their identity. In addition to characterizing the audience as market and commodity, then, we can think of the audience as *cultural identities* represented in the media.

A part of your identity might be defined by the fact that you are a college student; but this identity is already quite complex, and the way it is lived may vary depending on your age, background, income, and so forth. Nevertheless, you are part of an entire generation of college students, both past (all college graduates) and present (the particular graduating class). You are also part of the population of a particular university or college; your affiliation may be expressed in any number of ways (wearing school colors or clothes, sporting the school insignia, supporting the athletic teams). You may also be a member of various groups on and off campus ("greeks" or independents, commuters or dorm residents, different majors and classes).

Consequently, even something as apparently simple as your identity as a college student is itself the product of your particular position in a variety of social groups and social differences. In addition, everyone brings many affiliations with them to campus: religious, racial, ethnic, gender, and sexual identities, particular regional and economic origins (Midwest farming or Northeast working class or Southwestern suburban middle class) as well as particular interests (for example, sports and musical tastes). One of the things that every university tries to accomplish is to bind students together into a common identity with common loyalties. Recent events have made this task even more difficult, as many universities and colleges have experienced an increasing sense of fracture among various gender, racial, and ethnic groups, each of which is likely to have its own associations on campus.

In fact, many of the major social and political problems facing the contemporary world involve the relationships between and among different social groups: among racial groups (black and white, brown, red, and yellow, as they are so crudely described), gender and sexual groups (men and women, straight and gay), age groups (children, youth, adults, and the aging), economic groups (working, middle, or upper classes), religious groups, ethnic and national groups (whether Bosnian, or Bosnian American), and so on.

The problems that these relations impose on the contemporary world cannot begin to be solved unless one first begins to understand the relationship between an individual and the social group or groups to which he or she belongs. This relationship defines the problem of social identity. In fact, social identity is a very complex notion that involves at least three different questions: first, exactly where do such categories of identity come from and what do they signify? Second, what does it mean to belong to or be a member of a particular social group? In other words, how is such membership determined? Is one biologically assigned or socially positioned or culturally interpellated or perhaps a little bit of each? And third, what is the content or meaning of the categories and how are these meanings themselves determined? Implicit in all of these questions is the issue of the role of the media (and culture more generally) in the construction of people's social identities. What is the relationship between the images (visual and verbal) of the various categories of identity made available in the media and the ways in which people take up and live their own identities and relate to those inhabiting other identities?

There are two major schools of thought that respond to these questions, two major theories of identity, and each has distinctly different views of the role of the media in the politics of identity and of the relationship between media images and social identities. The first assumes that the categories of identity are natural and necessary and universal. This *essentialist* view assumes that every category exists naturally, in and of itself; Black-ness exists whether or not any other racial category or group exists. And the meaning of the category is always intrinsic to the category itself, determined ahead of time. That meaning, and hence, anyone's membership in the category, might be determined by genes, or by the anatomy and physiology of the body, or by some determining history (common roots in Africa or the common experience of a history of slavery). According to this theory, representation is a matter of accuracy versus stereotyping. The question then is how to contest negative images with positive ones, and how to discover and re-present the authentic and original content of the identity. Basically, the struggle

219

over representation here takes the form of offering one fully constituted, separate, and distinct identity in place of another.

The second theory of identity emphasizes the impossibility of such fully constituted, separate, and distinct identities. It denies the existence of authentic identities based in a universally shared origin or experience. Instead, it argues that the categories of identity are culturally constructed and can be understood only relationally. Consequently, they are always in process and incomplete. According to such an *antiessentialist* view, the very existence of such categories, as well as the specific ways they function, the specific differences they mark, and the specific meanings they carry, are all culturally constructed. Identity is always an unstable and temporary effect of relations that define identities by marking differences. The theory recognizes that there are differences between people but insists that which differences become important and visible (skin color rather than foot size), where the line is drawn (between Black and White, or male and female, or young and old), and the meanings of each category are the products of the communicative codes of a society.

There is no single, universal, or essential content to a category and consequently, the question of whether any specific person belongs to a social group must also be the product of cultural processes. Moreover, to say that such categories are relational is to say that categories are only defined by their relations to or differences from other categories. Or, to put it another way, the meaning of the categories of identity is largely the product of the ways that the members of the categories practice their relations to members of both their own category and to the members of other categories as well. The emphasis of the anti-essentialists is on the multiplicities of identities and differences and the interactions among identities. Obviously, representation is no longer a matter of accuracy and distortion but of identities that are produced and taken up in and through practices of representation.

REPRESENTATION AS STEREOTYPES

The media provide pictures of people, descriptions of different social groups and of their social identities. If someone has never seen any member of a particular group—an Azerbaijani, for instance—then it is likely that what they think such people are like will be the result of what they have seen, heard, or read about them in the media. But what does anyone make of the media's representation of a group of which they are a member? Walter Lippman (1922) referred to *stereotypes* as "pictures in our heads" of other people or more accurately, of the identity or nature of other groups of people. Stereotypes can define some people's expectations of how, for example, women, or Hispanics, or other groups in the society are supposed to behave. In this sense, stereotypes are neither avoidable nor necessarily bad. In the modern world, the media are obviously a major source of such pictures.

Typically, discussing the process by which the media re-present the various social identities in the world as stereotyping implies that there is some "correct" image of a social group's identity that is somehow distorted in the media's portrayal of that group. Sometimes, stereotyping is a matter of the absence of images of a particular social group; but it is more often a question of how the group is portrayed, of the content of the images themselves. We can take note of the extent to which various ethnic and social groups have been represented negatively in the mass media and how images of various groups have changed over time in accord to that group's changing position in the culture. Media images of women, minorities, New Yorkers, doctors, the handicapped, Southerners, and so forth are likely to elicit certain expectations about how members of these groups act. How social groups are portrayed in the mass media, particularly in films, on television, and in advertising, has been a long-standing concern of various representatives of those groups who feel they are being misrepresented or stereotyped.

In this sense, stereotyping is the process of distorting the portrayal of some social group in a media image. That media contribute to stereotypes (and even create stereotypes of groups) is assumed to be the result of systematic biases in the portrayals of social groups. One major research project in the United States, the Cultural Indicators Project at the University of Pennsylvania, has been systematically comparing the demographic profile of those who appear on prime-time television to national demographics as shown in the U.S. Census since the late 1970s. Over time, the research has demonstrated that the world of television is dominated by White males in traditionally powerful and adventurous occupations. Women, the old, children, and minority groups are systematically underrepresented (at least in terms of their numbers in the population) in the world of television (Gerbner, Gross, Jackson-Beeck, Jeffries-Fox, & Signorielli, 1978).

Perhaps the best example to provide here is the changing images of Blacks in the film industry and on television. In the very earliest days of film, Blacks were portrayed in a blatantly racist manner, perhaps best exemplified by the 1913 film *Birth of a Nation*. In the 1920s and 1930s, a few stereotypical Black roles appeared, such as Stepin Fetchit's "Black fool" and the "mammy" in *Gone with the Wind*. However, the majority of American films simply ignored and excluded the Black population. Similarly, the Hollywood studios ignored the work of a number of pioneering Black filmmakers (such as Oscar Micheaux), who produced all-Black films that have remained unknown to White audiences and often to Black audiences as well.

By the 1950s and 1960s, a few Black actors became Hollywood stars. Sidney Poitier, who won an Academy Award in 1963 for *Lilies of the Field*, opened the door to other actors, such as Bill Cosby, Ossie Davis, Ruby Dee, James Earl Jones, and Morgan Freeman. More important, as these actors became successful, they were able to demand less demeaning roles and less stereotypical images. Even in this period, however, Black actors did not fare particularly well: There were still few Black stars in the overwhelmingly White film industry, and the roles were still limited and racist. Even at the height of the civil rights movement in 1960s and 1970s, "blaxploitation films" (such as *Shaft* with Richard Roundtree), although they created Black stars, were overtly racist and stereotypical.

By the late 1980s, the emergence of major Black filmmakers, such as Spike Lee (*Do the Right Thing*), Mario Von Peebles (*New Jack City*), John Singleton (*Boyz 'n the Hood*), Matty Rich (*Straight out of Brooklyn*), and lesser-known filmmakers such as Charles Burnett (*To Sleep with Anger*) and Julie Dash (*Daughters of the Dust*) provided a vibrant and challenging alternative portrait of Black life in America and the racist currents of American culture. These filmmakers have opened the door, not only to new generations of Black actors, but also to Black participation in the various aspects of film production.

This shift from an absence of Black people in film and overwhelmingly stereotypical images of Blacks to the production of films about

Black life and racial themes by Black producers, writers, and directors has taken most of the twentieth century.

Television, too, has shifted in its portrayals of Blacks and has followed a somewhat similar course. In the early days of television, with the exception of *Amos 'n' Andy's* stereotypical representation of happy-go-lucky hucksters, Black people were absent from prime-time drama. However, Black entertainers such as Pearl Bailey, Louis Armstrong, Johnny Mathis, and Nat King Cole did appear on variety shows in the 1950s. It wasn't, however, until 1965, when Bill Cosby was paired with Robert Culp in the series *I Spy*, that a Black actor emerged as the star of a network drama series. The 1970s saw the rise of a number of situation comedies featuring Black family life, *The Jeffersons, Sanford and Son*, and *Good Times*. And Black stars such as Bill Cosby, James Earl Jones, Arsenio Hall, Keenen Ivory Wayans, and Oprah Winfrey—often with creative and financial control (and in some cases their own independent production companies)—continue to increase the participation of Blacks in a wide variety of television genres.

These shifts in portrayals of Blacks in American media cannot be understood outside of the real struggles over civil rights in American society and the changes that have resulted. Not until the rise of the civil rights movement in the late 1950s and early 1960s did stereotypes begin to change in the media. As well, pressure groups began to confront racist images and demand more positive representation in television and in film. Last, and most strikingly in recent years, Black professionals have moved into creative and economic control as producers, writers, and directors in the film industry, as well as owners of radio, TV, and media properties. The fact that larger numbers of Blacks have moved into higher economic strata has helped to create a Black market for advertisers and media programmers. Moreover, youth of all races have become a significant market for Black cultural products across many media and genres. All of these factors have contributed to changing the stereotyping of Blacks in mass media.

This doesn't mean that stereotyping no longer exists. Some people have criticized many contemporary Black films on the grounds that the emphasis on urban gangs and crime continues many of the stereotypes of Black people. Other ethnic groups, such as Hispanics, Arab Americans, Italian Americans, Asian Americans, and others, have complained over the years about their representation in the media. The rise of the feminist movement since the 1960s has made us increasingly aware of the stereotyping of women in media images. And the horrors of the AIDS epidemic has made questions about the stereotypical representations of gay men and lesbians an important social concern. In each of these instances, fighting media's stereotypical representations has become a crucial part of the group's struggle for social equality.

For the fact is that stereotypes, even if they are only images, do have real and important consequences. They can affect the self-esteem of those being stereotyped, and they can often come close to determining the way some people think of and behave toward members of the groups being stereotyped. And sometimes, if they are repeated often enough, people forget entirely that they are dealing with images; the images become the reality that determines the ways people, institutions, and even governments act in the world.

A good example of the potentially pernicious effects of stereotypes might be the representation of AIDS and of people with AIDS (PWAs). These images affect how many people think about this disease and those who suffer its consequences. Critics have documented the effects of such stereotypes on issues of education, funding, legislation, and even research and treatment. Remember the startling power of the image of the late Princess Diana holding hands with PWAs in a London hospital. AIDS activists have often complained about the way the disease is represented in the mass media. Thus, the disease is often represented primarily in its association with homosexuality, concealing other equally pertinent facts: for example, that the majority of AIDS cases in New York City are among people of color, with a rising percentage among women. This misrepresentation perpetuates itself, in that it affects the patterns of counseling and diagnosis. Moreover, they argue, the representation of PWAs as lonely victims passively awaiting death distorts the facts of the disease and how it is lived. And it also distorts the fact that PWAs are also suffering from government inaction, insurance companies' and corporate employers' greed, the unavailability of adequate health care, and institutionalized racism and homophobia.

Thinking of people in terms of stereotypes only enables us to ask whether a stereotype is an accurate portrayal of a particular group. But to ask this question already assumes that this grouping of people is inevitable and natural, that its identity is singular and stable and exists independently of how it is represented in cultural codes and the media. For example, to ask whether the image of Blacks on television is an accurate one assumes that all "Blacks" have the same identity, which can be compared to what is presented on television. But what happens if all Blacks do not have the same identity? Do we really want to assume that conservative Supreme Court Justice Clarence Thomas, Bill Cosby, Spike Lee, Dr. Dre, and a young urban unemployed Black man are really essentially and basically the same by virtue of being Black, that they are all representatives of the same identity? And what if Blacks' identity changes, as when, to use a simple example, heavyweight boxing champion Cassius Clay changed his name to Muhammad Ali? What if some Blacks do seem to fit the stereotype? For instance, what if there *are* kids out there who want to be like the stereotypical character J.J. from *Good Times?* or the violent and sexist gangstas of NWA? Does that make these kids somehow less real for how they behave?

Some critics have even argued that by continuously focusing on the question of race and stereotypes, other critics are reinforcing the tendency of our society to divide everyone into Black or White. After all, is it necessary that the world be divided up that way? Most people don't worry about stereotypes of people with big feet, and they don't assume that such people have some identity of their own or that they are suffering from the ways they are represented. Finally, as long as one is talking about stereotypes, it is too easy for some people to ignore that, for some people out there, the media are representing who they are, or to put it in other terms, the stereotype is not of someone else but of themselves. This raises one of the most important questions about the role of the media in people's lives, for it deals with how people come to understand who and what they are, to view their identities and identifications, the positions that they occupy in society.

REPRESENTATION AS CULTURAL CONSTRUCTION

By seeing media representations as actively involved in the ongoing construction of identities, one can begin to appreciate the complexity of the processes by which people's identities are produced by the culture they live in: How is a category of identity established? How are individuals assigned to it? How is its meaning determined?

Consider where the categories of identity come from. Aren't most distinctions found in nature? For example, people normally assume that racial and sexual distinctions are genetically based, but that is simply false. People do not somehow see through the body into the genetic code. What is being read as sex or race are signs on the surface of the body. Genetic diversity is much more complex and plural than our simple categories allow. Even physiology and anatomy cannot explain the systems of relations that define people's identities. Are all women capable of bearing children? If someone is not, is she then not a woman? Do all Black people have dark skin? Then how does one account for the history of "passing"?

To take one category, aren't all people born either male or female? Yes and no. Biologists used to believe that sex was determined by a simple combination of two chromosomes, creating only two possibilities. But they have discovered that there are more chromosomes and more possibilities involved; what remains true is that for purposes of biological reproduction, sexes can be functionally divided into two large groups. But biological reproduction among humans requires certain social relationships as well. People have to occupy certain social roles and practice certain behaviors. These roles and behaviors define what is called gender identity. Again, our common sense makes it seem reasonably easy to divide the world into two major gender groups—masculine and feminine—although many critics have argued that such classifications are too crude. In fact, much of feminist theory addresses the question of how certain characteristics, behaviors, and styles come to be thought of as either masculine or feminine.

The categories of identity are the products of cultural codes, which select some aspects of the body and make them significant (into signifiers) whereas others remain "mere anatomy." Such codes, as we described in Chapter 5, organize signifiers according to relations of difference, so that any signifier of identity is only significant insofar as its difference from other signifiers is provided by the code itself. Culture selects the relevant dimensions that will constitute people's identities and organizes them into relations of difference. It is not merely that to be White is to be not Black; it is also that being "not-Black" is itself part of the very meaning of being White. And, by the same token, being Black always includes being-not-White. The two categories are bound together, each always implicated in the very existence and meaning of

226

the other. This means that more than a set of biological characteristics determines who is included within each category—an Asian woman may suddenly find herself placed in the position of a "Black" person by the cultural codes of race in contemporary America.

At the same time, one term is always dominant within the culture; one term defines the norm. The norm is not only positively valued, it is treated as if it were neutral. It does not appear to be an identity at all. It does not need to be named; it remains *ex-nominated*. For example, although we think of Black as a race with its own characteristics, it is usually measured against an assumed neutral Whiteness that is rarely marked as a race. The same argument can be made for most of the other major dimensions of people's identity, including sex, gender, class, and ethnicity. We talk about Polish Americans and African Americans but rarely about Anglo Americans.

Everyone occupies some positions in these various codes of difference. What is the process by which individuals are given identities by being placed into one of a binary pair, by becoming identified with one term? This process of being placed is called interpellation. Recall the discussion in Chapter 7 (and the two experiments we proposed). The process of interpellation occurs when individuals are placed into (and take up) particular (social) positions by and within cultural codes. Who we are, in one sense, is answered by where we are. I am the person standing here, the one who can see you looking at me but can't see me looking at you. *Subjectivity* is a useful term to capture this sense of the relationship between who and where we are. Subjectivity is the sense of existing both at the center of and apart from any particular experience. Subjectivity lets people reflect on their experience and their place in the world; it lets us carry on a conversation with ourselves about ourselves, as it were. It is what lets people use language creatively to say new things, and to express their experiences. That is, part of what you are, your subjectivity, is defined by the fact that you occupy the center of your own field of vision and experience. You are always at the center of your experiential field. Because you are the subject of your experiences, because they are in fact your experiences, they seem quite natural and obviously true.

But what about someone whose experiences of the world are not legitimated, someone who is forced to see the world through someone else's eyes? What happens to someone for whom the world seems to

227

deny their experience of who they are, their subjectivity? Consider the way many women who were raped were treated in our society—we can hope that this is only rarely still the case—often, their own experience of having been violated, abused, victimized, was denied and the woman was treated as the cause of her own violation. She was not viewed by the society as the victim of violence (reinforced by systematic and structural sexism), but as the aggressor who—by how she dressed ("seductively") and by how she interacted with the man ("willingly")—asked for it. That is, her experience is recoded into the dominant codes of male experience. After all, if you are placed in the position of the subject through certain codes, then you can also be placed in the position of the object.

People occupy a variety of positions in language and social relationships depending upon how they are addressed and interpellated. A teacher says, "you have to . . . " A friend says, "we feel like going . . . " An older brother says, "Do I have to take it along . . . " Think about all the different ways people are addressed, even in the media, ways that may include them in or exclude them from certain identities? This same process works not only to produce people's sense of themselves as human subjects (capable of creativity and autonomy) but also to place people in the various culturally constructed categories of identity.

How is it that society interpellates people into these systems of cultural differences, guaranteeing that it reproduces the basic structures of its organization of power? Some media critics draw upon Sigmund Freud's psychoanalytic theory, which tried to explain how children grow up as social subjects, reproducing the sexual and gender roles of their parents. According to Freud, this is accomplished by the child's renunciation and repression of specific desires, which results in the formation of an unconscious. People become subjects because they reject part of who they are. (Boys defer their desire for their mother by trying to become their father; girls renounce their desire for their father by bonding with their mother). There are enormously powerful social processes at work interpellating individuals into their "proper" places as "normal" members of society. Some feminist film theorists argue that the basic plot structure of Hollywood cinema reenacts the process by which people are interpellated into and accede to their appropriate gender and sexual identities. Different media continually address differently gendered and sexed audiences (for example, Lifetime—the channel for women; various women's magazines; soap operas).

In the media, women seem to be largely defined or placed as the object of male pleasure—both visual and physical. Many classic Hollywood films, television programs, and even commercials feature rather gratuitous shots of women in various stages of undress, as if they were placed there only for the viewer's pleasure in looking. This coding of pleasure means that the camera's position defines and embodies a male perspective on the world. The camera is masculine. Similarly, in most narratives—at least until recently—it is the male characters who define the action of the story, although it is often the woman who, as an object of desire, makes the story move. The hero sets out to win, to rescue the woman, or to find some object required to win or save the woman. The woman is rarely allowed to speak. If a strong woman character threatens to disrupt the masculine universe of the story, she will almost inevitably be subdued in the end, by either death or marriage. Similar processes are at work in all of the cultural processes of identity including, for example, race. People are interpellated by other people's language and behavior, as well as by the media texts that address them.

However, the actual people receiving this message are not necessarily as passive as this makes them sound. Interpellation can define someone into a subordinate position, but the person has to accede to that interpellation. He or she has to take up the position. People can struggle against specific interpellations, struggle to reject the experience, or try to find alternative positions within the text. Consider the following rather simple example: Someone tells a racist joke to a group of people. Everyone in that group is interpellated as White and insofar as they remain silent, they accept that interpellation. But what if one person were to suddenly say: "You only told that joke because you assumed that I am White." What would that do to the normally assumed processes of interpellation?

Cultural codes, and especially the media in the contemporary world, also articulate the meanings of the various positions people occupy. In this way, we can think of the media as actively constructing the meanings and expectations that are associated with, or linked to, particular social identities. For instance, the meaning of "young Black man" as an identity in America is often linked to a host of threatening associations: juvenile delinquent, drugs, potential mugger. The result is that people in the United States are often more nervous near a young Black man than near a young White man; even the police follow more closely the behavior of young Black men on the streets. The civil rights movement can be seen in part as an attempt to challenge the meanings that the dominant cultural codes articulated to Blackness, meanings that were almost entirely negative, and to construct new articulations: "Black is beautiful."

For example, consider what meanings have been linked to the identity of woman in American culture. Women have been seen as weak, emotional, nonassertive, and illogical. But there is nothing inherent in the position of women that makes them less aggressive, more emotional, or even weaker than men. The fact that women have different hormones cannot provide a sufficient explanation of these meanings. These meanings are not necessary. There is nothing inherent in women that determines these connotations of the identity of being a woman. These meanings can and do change. But they are also powerfully effective in society. The fact that the articulations have been made has a strong influence over the way people, both men and women, think about women and the way they behave toward women. If people believe that women are weaker than men and that they are supposed to be less aggressive, this will certainly influence the way parents differentially treat boys and girls. The results will make the articulation even stronger, make it appear even more obvious, natural, and commonsensical. Because women "are" weaker, parents tend to discourage their little girls from rough-housing and playing in contact sports (although this is apparently changing). And because boys "are" tougher, parents are (often too) quick to discourage little boys from crying and to encourage their aggressive play in team sports. Parents encourage different cultural tastes, which reproduce certain articulations (and which also produce different interpellations). But these meanings are open to challenge; articulations can be dis-articulated, and new links, new articulations, can be made.

Moreover, the links are never made in either simple terms or in isolation of other identities. For example, Spike Lee's *School Daze* created a furor by opening up a debate about color differences, and the resulting racisms, within Blackness and among Black people. Identities are never simply Black or female, just as people never live their identities simply as Black or female. Real people are—they live their identities as—Black and female and middle-class and American and urban, and so forth. So the articulations that give depth to the categories of identities are always more specific, fragmented, and contradictory than theories of stereotypes assume. Sometimes, these different identities interact in a variety of ways to produce the particular, concrete identities that define who people are. Sometimes, these identities even conflict and produce competing demands on people. For example, Alice Walker's *The Color Purple* opened up a public debate within the Black community about the relationship between Black men and Black women, and among Black women.

The notion of articulation frees the struggle over representation from some stable and true external referent against which all meanings are measured. Rather, it makes the mutually determining conjunction of social reality and cultural representation the only game in town. The history of media representations is not a progression from stereotypes to truth but a struggle to constantly articulate the meanings of people's identities and the ways they can live those cultural categories. There is no single narrative that can be told. There are always competing meanings and articulations struggling to win dominance or at least acceptance.

The history of representations of women on network television shows a complex and contested play of meanings circulating around the category of woman. During the 1950s, the common history argues that women occupied a subservient role to men; that women were almost always little more than window dressing or support for strong father figures on such family programs as *Father Knows Best* and *Leave It To Beaver*. Of course, women could sometimes be zany and incompetent, as was Lucille Ball's character in *I Love Lucy*. When women appeared in nonhousewife roles, they were still subservient to the men they served as secretaries or nurses or saloon girls.

And yet, other critics have pointed out how much more complex this field of representations was: the comedian Lucille Ball was not zany and incompetent; she was assertive and brilliant (and it turned out, astute in business). Sitcom mothers often turned out to be the real strength in the families. And working class women, such as Alice Cramden on *The Honeymooners*, were important predecessors for contemporary images like Roseanne's. Not all the women of the 1950s were se-

231

ductively attractive (*Our Miss Brooks*), and not all the men were competent ideal mates (Jackie Gleason or Milton Berle).

In the 1960s and 1970s, as the women's movement gained national attention, women's roles began to change on television as well. During the 1960s, women began to occupy more positions outside the home, as police (Angie Dickinson in *Police Woman*), TV news producers, and more frequently on television news as correspondents and reporters. Yet, women were still young, attractive, and secondary to more powerful male figures. Mary Tyler Moore's role in *The Mary Tyler Moore Show* represented a significant advance over her earlier role as the at-home housewife and mom on *The Dick Van Dyke Show* (and certainly a very significant advance over her appearance in *Richard Diamond*, a detective show in which only her legs were shown and her voice heard). It was the first network program to focus on an unmarried working woman. Yet, the program continued to reaffirm many of the most common meanings of "single women" in our society. Mary was constantly looking for a husband, or at least a good date, and despite her growing power in the office where she worked, she always seemed subservient to Lou Grant in ways that the men in the office were not. (For instance, only Mary called her boss "Mr. Grant.") But such a typical narrative ignores the fact that there were many moments which out-lived the 1950s, and even some moments which foreshadowed the decades yet to come.

By the 1980s and 1990s, however, women's roles on television had changed and with new roles have come new images of the possibilities of what it means to be a woman in American society. It is impossible to answer the question of whether these new images reflected or brought about changes in society; the only possible answer is both. For instance, the success of the over-60 Jessica Fletcher character in *Murder, She Wrote* and of the *Golden Girls* validated new images of being old and female. Yet, Jessica is a highly traditional woman in many ways, devoted to the memory of her dead husband and to sexual abstinence. Also, the development of the aggressive newscaster *Murphy Brown*, and the less than perfect housewife and mother *Roseanne* have broken many of the old stereotypes of both women in work and women at home. Yet, Murphy Brown pays a price in sometimes being less than likable, and she still has to play male/female games, even as a single mother. And it is the case that, for each of these steps forward, one can point to programs that seem to have taken two steps back. Sure, Ellen came out as a lesbian, but there is more than enough homophobia on television. And what does one make of the success of programs such as *Married with Children?*

Identities never proceed in some linear and coherent story from falsity to truth, or from truth to falsity. The codes of identity are always complex and contradictory, defining a field in which different meanings battle to become the dominant articulations. The field is never entirely open, and it is often quite constrained, but it is often contested. Sometimes, the story is one of an expanding field of competing meanings; other times, the story is one of shrinking possibilities. Ideology is always a matter of struggle rather than simple domination. Victories are sometimes won and new meanings become dominant; sometimes victories are won when new meanings are simply allowed into the field. Just as women have advanced into new roles and occupations in American life over the past several decades, the cultural codes associated with the identity of woman in the media have developed, broadened, and become more complex. These changes are not simply the result or reflection of changes taking place in the "real world," for they are in part responsible for these very changes. As we have been suggesting throughout this book, the relationship between communication and reality is too complex to be described either as simply production or reflection.

We cannot talk about the image of women in television as if television were itself a simple homogeneous message, or as if it were somehow isolatable from other media. For the ideological struggle over the representations of woman takes place across all of the different cultural media, which have to be taken then as complex interactive systems of messages. Second, the struggle over the ideology of woman cannot be limited to images of women per se and the roles they play, for the meaning of woman cannot be separated from a complex array of other social roles and practices. Thus, the struggle over the meaning of woman can also take place in representations of the family and of domestic spaces (the household) and of the variety of practices that take place there. The ads on television in the 1950s, ads for new consumer goods usually marketed as labor-saving and convenience devices for the household, were all about "being a woman." But so were ads and programs about television itself. A number of media historians, most notably Lynn

Spigel (1992), have recently argued that families had to be taught how to watch TV, just as much as they had to be taught, as did architects and builders, about how to redesign domestic spaces to accommodate the new medium into the family living space. Thus, the ideological field of woman involves representations of issues as diverse as domesticity and domestic spaces, suburbia and the reorganization of urban spaces, the changing nature of labor in and out of the home, family relations and consumption, and the place and use of the new media such as television. But these are more than representations. Hence, ideological articulations always involve realities that are not merely cultural; they also involve social and material practices (like the actual spatial organizations of houses and the material design of television sets), which may themselves be the object of other ideological struggles.

In recent times, and partly as a result of the increasing importance of the media in constructing people's identities, people seem to have developed a much more fragmented and fluid sense of their own identities. Some identities even become so contaminated by other identities that it is difficult to tell what they refer to. For example, when the British Commonwealth sponsored a photography exhibit asking amateur photographers to document their sense of national identity within the "British commonwealth," the results were baffling to say the least. People's sense of their national identity was composed of fragments of tradition, of American commercial culture, of British symbolism, and of the media. There was no pure identity, only the articulations of the variety of identifications that people made in their lives (Goldman & Hall, 1987). In fact, there has been a long history (which has only increased with time) of debate about what it means to be "American," about whether schools and the media should present a coherent (traditional) view of Americans and American history or whether they should open the door to multicultural views of how various groups have come to be part of American life. People's identities are less stable and unified than they were in previous generations, and people tend to have less commitment to any single identity than did previous generations. Debates about multiculturalism may partly reflect the fact that the very nature of people's identities is changing as a result of the growing power of popular culture and the mass media.

Consuming the Media

I n the early 1970s, the novelist Jerzy Kosinski (1970) created one of
the most telling and powerful images of the omnipotence of television in our everyday lives: Chance, the gardener in *Being There,* lives
through the television screen. Television is not measured against reality; his reality is measured against television. All that he knows is what
he observes on television—who he is and what the world is like. But
even more startling, how Chance lives his life, how he reacts to and
with other people, how he feels, his pleasures and desires, and even his
moods place him inside a television world.

> Chance went inside and turned on the TV. . . . By changing the channel,
> he could change himself. He could go through phases, as garden plants
> went through phases, but he could change as rapidly as he wished by
> twisting the dial backward and forward. In some cases, he could spread
> out into the screen without stopping, just as on TV people spread out
> into the screen. By turning the dial, Chance could bring others inside
> his eyelids. Thus, he came to believe that it was he, Chance, and no one
> else, who made himself be. (p. 5)

> He did not know how to explain to her that he could not touch better
> or more fully with his hands than he could with his eyes. Seeing encom-
> passed all at once; a touch was limited to one spot at a time. She should

no more have wanted to be touched by him than should the TV screen have wanted it . . .

"I know, I know," she cried. "I don't excite you!" Chance did not know what she meant . . .

He turned and looked at her. "I like to watch you," he said. (pp. 94-95)

There are two ways of reading Kosinski's parable of modern life. Perhaps Kosinski is arguing that television defines reality in modern life. This interpretation raises crucial questions about the relationship between media and reality. Or perhaps Kosinski's parable is a description of the extent to which television—and by extension other media—increasingly occupy a central place in our everyday lives.

We have argued thus far that the media produce commodities (and money) and cultural products (meanings, ideologies, and identities). But the circuit of communication cannot end there. People have to purchase or acquire these commodities and then use (and eventually use up) such commodities. Media industries depend on the fact that people "use up" their products so that they will continue to buy new products. Similarly, meanings, ideologies, and identities can only be effective if they are interpreted and taken up by the audience members. In this chapter, we discuss the ways people make use of media products, that is, the ways they select them and attend to them, and especially the ways they locate them in different places and relations in everyday life. Understanding how we consume media in our everyday lives requires us to explore people's relationship to media and cultural products. Why do people choose to use certain media products, under what conditions do they use them, how do they use them, and what are the consequences of these choices and conditions of use?

Raymond Williams's (1965) image of the "long revolution" describes the enormous and significant changes that have produced the advanced industrial democracies. Williams traces these changes—economic, political, and cultural—to the moment when Europe was transformed by the emergence of capitalism, democracy, and mass literacy in the 1600s. In fact, each of these social forces fueled the others so that, Williams argues, developments in media, such as the advent of the printing press, are a crucial part of the emergence of modern society

236

and modern life. It would be a mistake, however, not to recognize, as Jerzy Kosinski does, that these social forces, including the media, affected not only the broader structures of society but the more mundane and immediate ways people lived from day to day, from moment to moment.

Williams's argument has enormous implications for how we think about the media and their effects on us. Common sense may lead us to link, in a direct and simple line, the media or specific media products with the visible or identifiable results that they produce: For instance, we talk about television's effects on violent behavior or the effect of pornographic material on sexual attitudes or the influence of journalistic practices on election behavior. But Williams would argue that this simple linkage is a mistake. Any attempt to understand the power of the media or specific media products requires us first to understand how these products are located within and operate within people's everyday lives: That is, the effects of the media depend on or are *mediated* by where, why, and how people use or consume them.

For instance, research has demonstrated the different effects on children of television viewing depending on whom they are watching it with: Preschoolers who watch *Sesame Street* with an adult tend to learn more from the program than those who watch the program alone (Lesser, 1974). Or you may have had the experience of associating a certain song with an old girlfriend or boyfriend or perhaps a particularly emotional time of your life. Every time you hear this song now, your response to it is colored by that emotional association. Or just think of the difference between watching music videos in your home and in a dance club. All of these are examples of the ways everyday life, the context of and psychology of media use, influence the effects of the media.

But there is an additional complication that Williams's argument forces us to recognize: The long revolution itself is responsible for shaping and changing people's everyday lives. To put it another way, the sociology and social psychology of media use are themselves historically influenced by the media whose effects they mediate. An obvious example of this interdependence comes from studies of how Americans spend their time. As sociologist John Robinson (1996) has pointed out, the advent of television has "colonized" leisure time in America, so much so that every additional minute of leisure (time not spent work-

237

ing or caring for family and household or sleeping) that Americans gained between the 1960s and the 1980s was spent watching television. Similarly, the new portable media technologies—transistor radios, miniaturized televisions, Walkmans, cellular phones, laptop computers—all make it possible to carry media into places and spaces of everyday life hitherto closed to media and culture. Thus, there is a reciprocal relationship between the media, everyday life, and the effects of media products.

The introduction of almost every new media technology in this century has immediately given rise to considerable concern and widespread public discussion about who is using it, how often, and under what conditions. That is, before people have worried about the effects of movies or radio or television on their audiences, they first take notice of the size, shape, and character of the consuming public.

Oddly enough, the process of consumption has received little attention in economic theories, although it is generally acknowledged that consumption is the necessary completion of the process of exchange on which all economic relations are based. The production of anything, from a widget to a television program, makes no sense unless someone consumes it—that is, buys it and uses it up. Every product is designed and made on the basis of certain assumptions about how it is to be used—under what conditions and for how long. Cars, for example, are produced with a certain life expectancy as well as with certain assumptions about the uses to which they will be put; most cars are not designed to be driven in races or demolition derbies. But, as we shall see, manufacturers cannot accurately predict how consumers will use their products.

As students of the media and culture, we need to ask to what degree the intended use of a product determines its actual use and effects; to put it the other way around, what is the contribution of the consumer in determining the actual use and effects of media products? This problem is often referred to as the question of the relative activity or passivity of media audiences. We also must consider the different functions that the consumption of media products serves for their users. What are the conditions under which people are able or unable to consume particular media products? Who can engage in particular acts of media consumption?

THE ROLE OF THE AUDIENCE

It is obvious that in some ways, consumption is an active process, even in the most apparently passive situations of media use. Consider the person—the couch potato—vegging out in front of the TV screen, eyes glazed, shoes off, reclining on the couch with a bag of potato chips in hand and a drink on the coffee table. The person looks passive. And yet, that person had to decide to watch television at this particular time, had to put the television on, had to get the bag of chips and the drink; maybe our couch potato read *TV Guide* to find out what was on or surfed through the channels to decide what to watch. And there's more.

A great deal of cognitive activity goes on. *Cognition* is the act of attending to and making sense of the world; it is the application of consciousness to the world. Even the couch potato is cognitively engaged with the television set: Couch potatoes have to focus attention on the screen, process the dots on the TV set into recognizable images, interpret those images as representations of some reality, fill in the blanks in the narratives presented by the television screen, and make sense of the messages coming from the screen. There is evidence that different people expend different amounts of mental effort to make sense of different programs. Nonetheless, this act of watching television can be said to be an active process because minds are engaged. The question is often raised whether the activity of watching television is as active, relatively speaking, as doing other things, such as reading a book, watching a live play, or writing a letter.

Another way the audience is active is in bending a medium and its messages to the audience's own purposes. In almost every instance, the producer of a media product has in mind some idea of about how the audience will understand and use the particular product. That is, the producer (which may be a corporation or an individual) intends for the product to have an effect. Indeed, researchers have to beware of what's called the *intentional fallacy*, the notion that what the creator of a message intended it to mean (its encoded meaning) is what the audience takes it to mean (its decoded meaning). Research on audiences and what they do with the media they consume clearly demonstrates that people are very creative—they have their own interpretations of media

BOX 9.1

Children and the Activity of Television Viewing

Researchers who watch children watching television in laboratory studies or in home observations find that children seem to be very actively involved in attending to the set: The children move in and out of attention, monitoring the set until something comes on that they want to watch. Indeed, the one programming style researchers have found that seems to elicit a "transfixed" gaze among children is cartoon shows. Moreover, there is considerable evidence (from postviewing interviews, as well as observational studies of children playing) that children have to actively work to make sense of television messages. This, too, suggests that television watching is an active process for children.

According to communication researchers George Comstock and Haejung Paik (1991),

The television experience cannot be described as either active or passive without reference to what each term is intended to denote. There is justification for both labels; no good rationale can be offered for giving either term precedence; and the appropriate term depends on what aspect of the experience is being described or emphasized. [Television watching] is typically passive in regard to involvement, but inherently active in regard to monitoring. (p. 23)

products, and they will often do very surprising and unpredictable things with them. Let's consider a range of different examples.

Think about the intentions of those who produce a newspaper. The newspaper's reporters and editors prepare newspaper stories to be read, to provoke thought, and perhaps even to persuade their readers to act in a particular way or to change their minds. But the purchasers may not act as expected. A study by Barnhurst and Wartella (1992) had college students write autobiographical essays about their memories of using the newspaper from childhood to adulthood. The authors found that

The newspaper played a role in a variety of activities—art projects, family, housework, do-it-yourself projects, and entertainment pastimes. Most of the uses mentioned for newspapers were predictable: hitting the dog with it, putting it in shoes that had holes, and the like. Few were at all unusual, but some students, like a White female frequent reader, implied that using the newspaper for anything other than reading was odd: "My parents have always found bizarre uses for the newspaper as well. My mother, a sincere plant lover, likes to spread newspaper over our countertops to shield them from soil when she repots her plants." Students reported making early use of newspapers as an implement (in 70 essays), an art medium (in 56 essays), and a protective covering (in 47 essays). These uses introduced a first frustration with newspapers: the ink rubs off. (p. 199)

A more consequential instance of the multiple and often unpredictable uses of the media can be found in many technological innovations. Industries introduce new technologies for a number of purposes, such as expanding their current markets or opening up new markets. As we have argued, in each instance, such new technologies are introduced to increase profit for the owners. However, in many cases, audiences use technologies in unintended ways, ways that had not been imagined and that often subvert the intentions of the producers. For example, audiocassettes have allowed people to make multiple copies for personal use and have allowed less scrupulous people to pirate recordings. Such practices have cut into the profit margins of the record companies. More sophisticated audio equipment has enabled the rise of new genres of popular music from rap to house music.

Perhaps the most important dimension of the audience's activity, at least as far as audience researchers are concerned, is the extent to which audiences make meanings for the media products they consume. In a study by Australian communication researchers Bob Hodge and David Tripp (1986) of children's use of television, they report a particularly striking example. One of the most popular programs among Australian grade school children in the 1980s was a program called *The Prisoner in Cell-Block H,* a minimalist, black-and-white, half-hour dramatization of everyday life in a woman's prison. This is not a program one would expect young children to embrace, and Hodge and Tripp wondered why it was so popular with children. They suggest that the children used the specific relationships and dramatic situations of the program to describe their own feelings about school and their everyday life. The program became a kind of secret code with which the children could talk to each other about particular teachers and classes, and about the experience of school, without fear of being understood by adult authorities. Although this example may seem extreme, audience researchers argue that television audiences give their own meanings to the programs they watch in order to fit the programs into their everyday life.

Think about your own experiences: When you listen to a song on the radio, or read a romance novel or a comic book, when you go to a movie on a date or watch a videotape in your room, or when you roam the Web on your computer, you help to determine or shape the meaning and significance of the particular media product. Your interpretation of a song does not necessarily match someone else's interpretation. Think of all the songs that have been taken to refer to drug experiences. In the late 1960s, many songs were assumed to be about drugs. Some of them, such as Canned Heat's "Amphetamine Annie" and the Jefferson Airplane's "White Rabbit," obviously were; others, such as the Beatles' "Norwegian Wood," were assumed to be by their fans; and still others, like Peter, Paul, and Mary's children's classic, "Puff, the Magic Dragon," were hotly debated. Today, debates rage about the Satanic meanings carried in some songs. Would you be surprised to learn that "Hotel California" by the Eagles and "Stairway to Heaven" by Led Zeppelin have a Satanic message, according to some critics? Audience researchers argue that the meaning of a media text resides in the audiences, not in the messages. However, it is not always easy to sort out and distinguish the contributions of the producer, the message itself, and the audience to the meaning of any given text.

Much of this audience research is based on Stuart Hall's (1980) distinction between encoding and decoding. Hall argued that the production and the reception of media messages were two relatively autonomous or independent processes within the larger *circuit of communication*. Thus, there was no basis for assuming that how a particular audience or audience member interpreted a text would correspond to the meaning that the producer of the message intended or hoped to communicate. Of course, this encoded meaning did define a *preferred meaning* and presumably, at least some of the elements of the text would push the audience in the direction of the preferred meaning. But this cannot guarantee that this process will be successful. Decoding is not a matter of misunderstanding but of the nature of communication as a struggle, from different social positions, over the meaning of the text. How a particular audience interprets a text is determined in complex ways by its social position, by the interests and resources it brings to the text.

Hall's original work was directed toward the study of network public affairs programming; consequently, he assumed that the encoded meaning of these texts would support the dominant ideology of the society on the particular issues that defined the topic of the text. He then identified three broad possibilities for decoding. An audience's decoding can assent or correspond to the encoded or preferred meaning. Or a decoding can explicitly oppose the dominant ideology encoded into the text, at least on the particular topic of the text. Or a decoding can negotiate a position somewhere between assent and opposition, bending the text to the experiences and values of the audience. It is important to remember that these categories of decoded meaning— preferred, oppositional, and negotiated—were developed to talk about texts where politics was a central and visible aspect of a message. These categories are less useful if one is talking about an audience's decoding of texts where such explicit political commitments are more difficult to identify.

The significance of media products in everyday life includes a broader range of uses and effects than just questions of the material use of a medium (such as using newspapers to wrap fish) and the meanings of particular messages. Consider the Madonna wannabes who construct elaborate images of themselves and a sense of their own identity (who they are, who they want to be, and how they want to be seen by others) through media products. In *Fast Times at Ridgemont High,* a new student in the high school remarks that another student looks exactly like Sheena Easton. Her friend points to a number of different groups of students, both male and female, who seem to have taken on the identity of their favorite rock star or actor. Researchers are beginning to look at the ways in which the media provide the resources with which audiences construct their sense of their own identity. This surely is a media effect, but it is one that requires the active involvement and investment of the audience in the process.

Another example opens up yet another dimension of media effects and uses: soap operas. For real soap fans, just watching a favorite soap is not enough. They want to talk to other fans about the trials and tribulations of the TV characters, they want to actively be involved in predicting the characters' futures, and they often refer to the experiences of these characters to make sense of their own lives. Television critics have long attempted to understand this powerful relationship. But it is very common for people to be fans of particular genres of television, movies, books, or music. People derive very real and complex pleasures and emotional experiences from media consumption. It is the emotional relationship to soaps that seems to dominate the fan's experience; it is the pleasure derived from particular media tastes that provides the foundation for other effects of media. All consumers derive some kinds of pleasure and emotional satisfaction from their media use; and like the meanings we give to media products, the pleasures and emotions we experience as consumers are often quite unpredictable. They vary not only individually but, as we shall see, across different social groups of consumers.

We have introduced here several of the major perspectives employed by audience researchers in understanding the place of the media in everyday life. In the rest of this chapter, we will elaborate each of these perspectives. First, we will consider one of the oldest and most commonsensical research perspectives, which looks at the social and psychological functions that media use serves for their audiences. This approach has been called *functionalism* or the *uses and gratifications perspective*. Second, we will investigate the *affective* or emotional experience of media audiences. Third, we will look at the *social context* of media use.

FUNCTIONS OF THE MEDIA

Perhaps the most commonsensical way to think about the mass media is to ask what functions they serve. For individuals, the functions of media can be thought of as the satisfaction or gratification of individual needs. For the society as a whole, the functions of media can be thought of as the purposes served by media in the society. A function can refer to a purpose, a consequence, a requirement, or an expectation. Denis McQuail (1987) gives the following example: "The term 'information function' can refer to three quite separate things: that media try to inform people (purpose); that people learn from media (consequence); that media are supposed to inform people (requirement or expectation)" (p. 69).

It is important to separate a requirement from an expectation: for example, although we might expect and hope that the media inform the audience, as contemporary presidential campaigns have demonstrated, this is not a requirement for the continued existence of the society. Another distinction is that some media functions are *manifest*, visible on the surface and easily recognizable, and others are *latent*, hidden deep below the surface of everyday life and difficult to identify. For example, news broadcasts inform the public about presidential candidates; that is a manifest function. But the character of the news coverage may also more subtly shape people's attitudes and assumptions about the nature of the political process itself (M. Robinson, 1976). That is a latent function of news coverage. Similarly, the manifest function of listening to music may be to relax us, to give us something to dance or exercise to, and the like. But music may also serve a latent function: it may shape our expectations about romance, and it may increase our tolerance for noise.

Functionalism is a perspective that assumes the existence of a closed system, whether a society or an individual or even an ecosystem, which has requirements for its continued survival. Media functionalism looks at the uses the media serve in the systems of society and individual lives.

SOCIAL FUNCTIONS

One of the earliest typologies of the social functions of the media was offered by Harold Lasswell (1948) in the 1940s. He wrote that the mass media served three major functions for the society: surveillance of the environment, correlation of the various parts of the society, and transmission of the social heritage from one generation to the next. In the 1950s, sociologist Charles Wright (1960) added entertainment as a social function of media. Denis McQuail (1994) added a fifth category, which he called *mobilization*, or the ability of the mass media to bring people into particular processes of change and development.

It's clear that these social functions of media are not always realized when any given media product is considered. There is no simple and direct relationship between specific acts of media consumption and any predictable function. Moreover, many acts of consumption involve multiple and sometimes even competing functions. For example, many

245

of the television programs that are on the surface "mere" entertainment may entail other social functions as well. The genre of "socially relevant entertainment programming" includes such programs as *All in the Family*, *Maude*, *Hill Street Blues*, *Murphy Brown*, and *Life Goes On*.

INDIVIDUAL FUNCTIONS

For individuals, the functions of media can be thought of as the motives or reasons why individuals use the media products they do and the sorts of satisfactions they receive from the use of these products. One of the earliest studies of the functions of media for individuals was conducted in the early 1940s by Herta Herzog (1944), a sociologist at Columbia University's Bureau of Applied Social research. She studied the motivations and gratifications of radio soap opera listeners. Her interest was to try to understand why women became such ardent fans of the radio soaps, serialized dramas about the trials and tribulations of people's relationships. The goal of the study was to determine what satisfactions listeners said they derived coupled with a psychological evaluation of these listeners' claims: The functional approach sought to account for why audiences attended to particular content on the assumption that the act of attending served some function for the individual. Herzog found that such programs served two overarching functions for these women: They provided emotional release from the women's everyday lives, and they served as a source of advice concerning real life problems. What sort of lessons did soap operas provide? Herzog found that the lessons of the soaps often applied in unlikely situations. For example, one woman reported going to the doctor before she started her diet because someone on the soaps had done so. The chief lesson Herzog identified was that if one remains calm and does nothing, everything will somehow come out all right in the end—perhaps a useful lesson.

In 1959, Elihu Katz, one of the founding figures of communication research and still one of the most active and influential figures in the field, relabeled the approach *uses and gratifications*. For Katz, uses and gratifications research would empirically test some of the critiques of popular culture that had been made in the 1950s: were audience tastes being debased? Were audiences being entertained? What did people do

BOX 9.2

Social Functions of the Media

Information

- Providing information about events and conditions in society and the world
- Indicating relations of power
- Facilitating innovation, adaptation, and progress

Correlation

- Explaining, interpreting, and commenting on the meaning of events and information
- Providing support for established authority and norms
- Socializing
- Coordinating separate activities
- Consensus building
- Setting orders of priority and signaling relative status

Continuity

- Expressing the dominant culture and recognizing subcultures and new cultural developments
- Forging and maintaining commonality of values

Entertainment

- Providing amusement, diversion, the means of relaxation
- Reducing social tension

Mobilization

- Campaigning for society's objectives in the sphere of politics, war, economic development, work, and sometimes religion

with the media? What uses and gratifications did people find in mass-produced news and entertainment?

The assumptions of the uses and gratifications model as proposed by Katz and expanded in work with two British communication researchers, Jay Blumler and Michael Gurevitch, are the following:

1. The audience is active and hence use of media is goal-directed.
2. Audience members have expectations of what certain kinds of content have to offer them and these expectations help shape their selections. That is, particular audience members can take the initiative in linking their needs to the ability of particular media products to gratify those needs.
3. The media compete with other sources of need satisfaction (such as reading, talking with friends, taking a walk, sleeping). The needs potentially satisfied by the mass media are only part of a wider range of human needs.
4. People are sufficiently aware of their needs, media choices, and the gratifications they receive from media use to be able to tell researchers what motivates their media behavior. (Katz, Blumler, & Gurevitch, 1974)

The major work on uses and gratifications research for the past 25 years has been to catalog the various uses and gratifications that audience members report obtaining from their media consumption.

THE CRITIQUE OF FUNCTIONALISM

Although uses and gratifications research has provided useful empirical evidence about audiences' consumption of the media, there have been serious criticisms of its theoretical assumptions and research programs. First, this approach ignores the social dimensions of media consumption and reduces media use to an individual psychological relationship. Yet, we know that media consumption is very often *socially situated*, that is, it is something engaged in with others. In fact, uses and gratifications research offers no way of understanding the connection between individual psychological needs and social structures and processes. At best, the individual is conceptualized in terms of specific social roles, which apparently carry their own socially induced needs and tensions.

BOX 9.3

Individual Functions of the Media

Information

- Finding out about relevant events and conditions in immediate surround-ings, society, and the world
- Seeking advice on practical matters or opinion and decision choices
- Satisfying curiosity and general interest
- Learning, self-education
- Gaining a sense of security through knowledge

Personal Identity

- Finding reinforcement for personal values
- Finding models of behavior
- Identifying with valued others (in the media)
- Gaining insight into one's self

Integration and Social Interaction

- Gaining insight into circumstances of others; social empathy
- Identifying with others and gaining a sense of belonging
- Finding a basis for conversation and social interaction
- Having a substitute for real life companionship
- Helping to carry out social roles
- Enabling one to connect with family, friends, and society

Entertainment

- Escaping, or being diverted, from problems
- Relaxing
- Getting intrinsic cultural or aesthetic enjoyment
- Filling time
- Emotional release
- Sexual arousal

McQuail (1987, p. 73) provides a useful summary of the typical list of uses and gratifica-tions.

Second, the key term—function—of this approach remains ambiguous. Functional activities have many different meanings in the literature: as a useful activity, as an appropriate or normal activity, as a necessary activity, and as a valuable activity. Nor is it clear how to determine whether an activity is useful, normal, necessary, or valuable. And for whom? How do we define the "society" within which such decisions are to be made?

Third, uses and gratifications research offers no account for the origin of needs or the relations among them. Instead, it often slips into deterministic accounts that are inconsistent with the notion of an active audience. Finally, uses and gratifications theory suffers from two more general problems facing any functionalist theory: it is circular and conservative. It is circular because the only way to tell that a need is being gratified is to assume that the gratification provides evidence for the existence of the need. That is, if watching television distracts me from my problems, I must need such distraction. This perspective is thought to be conservative because the system of needs assumes that the existing society is capable of satisfying any individual's needs—in this way, the status quo becomes the definition of the normal and only structure of society.[1] In short, uses and gratifications research allows no possibility for social criticism or social change.

THE SOCIAL PSYCHOLOGY OF CONSUMPTION

If uses and gratifications research fails to adequately describe the psychological relationship between a media product and its audience, perhaps looking more directly at the psychological state of the audience would be more helpful. Here we are going to consider some of the dimensions of an individual's psychological state, recognizing that such states are always in part the product of social conditions and relationships. In particular, we are concerned here with the *affective dimensions* of a person's psychology. Every affective state, such as feeling happy or being blue, varies in intensity and differs in character; thus, you can be happy rather than sad, satisfied rather than desirous. You can also be more or less happy, more or less sad, more or less satisfied. We will consider three affective or noncognitive dimensions—emotions, moods, and pleasures—and their relationship to media use briefly.

First, let's consider emotions. Media products try both to manipulate our emotions and to use emotions to produce some other effect (such as when advertisers use emotional appeals to try to get us to buy a product). Audiences, in turn, clearly use the media to produce emotional experiences for themselves. Many of us seem to enjoy going to movies that make us cry or cringe in fear or laugh at other people's foibles.

Interestingly, audiences do not seem to tire of such emotional uses of media products, even of the same product. People will watch a movie over and over, each time experiencing the same emotions, no matter how prepared they may be for the particularly moving scenes. On the third or fourth screening of *Aliens*, audiences still scream at the same points even though, after the first viewing, they know what is coming. Similarly, audiences cry at all the same moments in *ET*, every time.

In fact, audiences sometimes seem to use the media to learn about their emotional lives or to produce certain emotional states. Simon Frith (1981), the leading writer on popular music in England, has argued, for example, that the narratives of popular songs provide ways for fans to make private experiences public through a musical language of emotions. We learn how to feel about romance or the breakup of a romance by listening to a shared set of musical texts.

Think about your own use of music: When you are in love, there are particular songs that you play which capture and interpret your intense feelings. Conversely, many music fans create a "hate tape," which is full of songs expressing and making sense of the anger and rage they feel at another person when that person has deserted them. Country music is particularly overt in its constant narration of emotions and love stories.

Sometimes the emotional dimension is itself used for other purposes. For example, the popularity of horror films as a dating activity among adolescents and young adults is partially the result of a boy's desire to impress his date by demonstrating his ability to withstand the shock and horror of the film. He has to assume that females are the weaker sex, and thus unable to cope with the grotesque and shocking horror of such movies.

BOX 9.4

Television Commercials and Emotions

We've all experienced the feel-good feeling of watching a Kodak film ad where children, parents, and grandparents gather together to relive fond memories. That ad says little about the particular advantages of using Kodak film. Instead, it tries to make the viewer feel nostalgic and warm, tearful. The use of emotional appeals in advertising is not new. But does it work? Does it help us feel good about the product or even remember the product name?

In a series of laboratory studies on viewers' memory for television commercials, communications researcher Esther Thorson (1989) and her colleagues have been able to demonstrate that the use of emotional ads is very successful in increasing viewers' memory of the ads and in reducing counterarguing to the ads. What Thorson finds is that "emotion adds to the richness of memory traces" as viewers watch emotion-laden advertising and "when this occurs, counterarguing and other information from noncommercial sources is eliminated," increasing the likelihood that a viewer will remember the advertisement and evaluate it very positively (p. 403).

The second affective state is mood. One of the most successful media products of the past few years has been MTV. When Robert Pitman first conceived of a 24-hour music video channel, he described it as a mood enhancer. What does this mean? What is a mood? Did you ever wake up on the wrong side of the bed? Conversely, have you ever awakened feeling wonderful? In both cases, the cause of your mood is likely to be entirely unknown, but what is clear is that your entire day, and everything that happens to you during the day, is colored by that state of feeling, that mood. Things that might have made you happy yesterday now only make you angry, or vice versa. Here again we can use music as an example, for as many critics have commented, music is one of the most powerful means of affecting people's moods. The omnipresence of background music testifies to the power of music. One psychologist described the affective dimension of music listening this way:

> Why, when I first saw the Grand Canyon and the Piazza San Marco and the Alps, did I feel that things had all been more moving in Cinerama?

Why? Because both God and Man forgot to put in the music . . . in one sense, it's no surprise that music grabs us—it's supposed to. But once you look at the process, it seems quite miraculous that people can bowl one another over just by jiggling sound waves. (Rosenfeld, 1985, p. 48)

Think about the power of music in your life: think about the lullabies that parents sing to their children or the ritual music that every society has (Elgar's *Pomp and Circumstance,* played at almost every graduation, or Mendelssohn's *Wedding March* or the hymns of religious services). Recall the enormous power that you feel in a rock club or concert. Think of how you sing to yourself in the shower, on the street, while you are working, when you feel lonely or happy or afraid. In fact, many writers on popular music would agree with Robert Pitman's assumptions about music use: Music fans are in fact highly sophisticated in their ability to choose different music in order to manipulate their moods. You can use music to get yourself out of a bad mood, or to work off negative energy, or to wallow in your misery.

Music can construct socially shared moods that enhance people's commitment to action. The civil rights movement is perhaps the best-known instance of this use of music in recent generations. Protesters in the 1950s and early 1960s would sing songs, not only to gird themselves for protest marches and the upcoming battles but also to cope with their fears and to spread an affective blanket over the group. In many cases, this intensity brought new recruits into the community of civil rights protesters. "We Shall Overcome" is emblematic of this movement, just as "Solidarity Forever" was emblematic of an early twentieth-century union movement. Of course this has been true for ages and applied as well to war songs, and both the suffragette and the abolition movement.

Finally, let us turn our attention to the question of pleasure. If you ask most people why they watch particular television programs, or read particular novels, or listen to particular musical genres, they are likely to answer that they enjoy them, that is, they get some pleasure out of them. Pleasure is a deceptively simple notion. But it is in fact a very complex phenomenon, and we actually know very little about the mechanisms of the production of pleasure. The term pleasure covers a number of different relationships. The various ways in which pleasure is derived from media use signals the complexity of people's affective relationship to the media. Consider some of the different meanings of

253

pleasure and the different ways pleasure is accomplished. There is, for example, the comfort of escaping from or forgetting negative situations, the sense of reinforcement that comes with identifying with a particular character, the thrill of sharing another person's emotional life, the stature of expertise and collecting, the euphoria of vegging out, the release that comes from relaxation and putting aside troubles and stress, the fun of breaking rules, the satisfaction of doing what you are supposed to, the fulfillment of desires and needs, the exhilaration of shocking others through "rebellion," and the relief of catharsis.

All of these are involved in the normal and common relationship to media products. People engage with specific products because in some way and form, they are entertaining, they provide a certain measure of enjoyment, they are pleasurable. Think about your own pleasures in media use. Do you derive some pleasure out of every encounter with media? Are they always the same pleasures? Are there particular media products that regularly elicit the same kinds of pleasure?

One of the most heated debates about media today concerns the political implications of media pleasures. There are several positions on this issue. At one extreme are the critics who would morally police media use and excise pleasurable material they find objectionable. These people argue that particular pleasures are both evil and politically dangerous. These kinds of attacks have been made against popular culture throughout its history. The constant attacks on rock and roll since its inception—attacking the sexual energy of the music and often identifying it as "Black" music—provides one of the clearest examples.

At the other extreme, some critics argue that pleasure itself is a form of political resistance to the pressures of the dominant institutions and values of modern society. John Fiske (1989), a contemporary media critic, argues that the very fact that pleasure is derived from popular culture makes popular culture threatening to the status quo of the cultural mainstream. Fiske assumes that pleasure is always disruptive of social structures and cannot be controlled or regulated by them. Therefore, it is quite understandable why popular culture would always be the object of serious attack. And those attacks further prove that taking pleasure in popular culture is itself an act of resistance.

In between these two extremes are a number of positions that we need to briefly consider. Some people, especially feminist critics such as Janice Radway, argue that women who consume serial narratives, such

BOX 9.5
Attacks on Rock and Roll

As soon as rock became a national hit in the mid-1950s, ministers, politicians, and educators launched campaigns to have it banned. Its sexuality, it associa-tion with Black music and culture, its supposed violence, its volume, its lack of quality, its appeal to youth, all became the subject of attacks. Many cities banned rock and roll concerts in the 1950s, and newspapers printed editorials attacking its lyrics, its sexual rhythms, and the violence it seemed to stimulate. Rock was blamed for juvenile delinquency, it was linked with the devil and the communist threat, and it was accused of trying to turn "America's children" into animals, which in the racist language of the time, often meant that it made White kids act like Black kids.

All of this came to a head in a series of congressional "Payola" hearings held in 1958 and 1959, in front of the Special Committee on Legislative Oversight.

The subtext of this hearing was a battle between ASCAP (American Society of Composers, Authors, and Publishers) and BMI (Broadcast Music Incorpo-rated). These two organizations controlled music publishing and song licensing. ASCAP represented the traditional music publishing industry and had largely closed its doors to the new sounds of rhythm and blues and rock and roll, which BMI had welcomed. So the hearings were, at one level, a battle between com-peting economic interests in the music industry. The explicit topic of the hearings was *payola*: a practice widely practiced (and still practiced) throughout the mu-sic and radio industries by which a record company or representative would pay a radio station or disc jockey to play its record on the air. Because radio exposure was quite important to the marketing of records—and had become even more important since the 1950s—and because there were more records than could be played, the practice was considered normal and acceptable. ASCAP accused BMI of subverting "good music" by using payola to promote the horrible sounds of rock and roll. The interesting thing about the hearings was that the vast ma-jority of the testimony was given over to attacks on rock and roll music.

The result of the so-called Payola hearings was not an end to the practice of payola but a large-scale dismantling of the radio system that had grown up around rock and roll. Many of the best rock disc jockeys (Alan Freed was only the most famous) lost their jobs; many radio stations changed their format and either gave up rock and roll or started to separate the choice of music to be played (programming) from those who were playing it (and who knew and loved it).

The attacks on rock and roll all but disappeared in the 1960s and 1970s, surfacing as a major issue only occasionally, such as when then Vice President Spiro Agnew called upon radio stations to stop playing rock music as it advo-cated drugs and revolution. Some religious leaders continued to attack the mu-sic, and fundamentalist Christians accused rock and roll (as well as rock and roll musicians) of advocating and participating in Satan worshipping and using

(continued)

255

---

backmasking (the practice of recording a message backward on a record) and subliminal messages to influence listeners against their will.

However, in the mid-1980s, the attacks on rock took on a new seriousness and visibility, and legitimate spokespeople took up the cause. In 1986, Allan Bloom, a professor at the University of Chicago, published *The Closing of the American Mind,* a best-seller that seems to lay the blame for America's problems at the doorstep of rock music.

Also in 1985, four women who were married to key figures in the government, including Tipper Gore and Susan Baker, formed the Parents' Music Resource Center (PMRC), which advocated the voluntary labeling of records and videos. The PMRC did not attack all rock music, only music produced since 1970, and its leaders advocated giving parents more information and authority to decide what records their children could purchase and listen to. In September of that year, the Senate Commerce Committee held hearings on the problem of pornography in rock lyrics. Although no official consequences resulted, the music industry responded to the pressure by adopting a voluntary labeling program, which has not proven very successful.

At the same time, local and federal officials have been involved in a number of court cases that have charged rock groups (and record sellers) under obscenity laws. Local cities are increasingly trying to regulate the appearance of rock groups, and even the American Medical Association has recommended that doctors monitor children's tastes in music as a sign of psychological problems. For a fuller description of these attacks, see *Anti-Rock* and *You Got a Right to Rock.*

SOURCES: Grossberg, 1992; Martin & Segrave, 1988; Rock and Roll Confidential, 1991.

---

as soap operas and romance novels, are able to derive particular pleasures from texts that are in many ways oppressive to them. For example, the narrative of romance novels may reinforce images of weak women dominated by strong and powerful men. Radway's (1984) research demonstrates that pleasure goes beyond this dominating narrative. Radway found that regular readers of romance novels often interpret the narrative to give the woman more power in the relationship, and thus, construct a more pleasurable image for themselves of the role of women in contemporary life. She also found that for many of these women, the act of reading romance novels (sometimes more than a dozen novels a week) provided them with the only occasion for their own time, time when they were not responsible to other members of their family and to various domestic demands. In fact, Radway interprets this as a kind of resistance to the fact that women who do not work outside the home are constantly subject to the demands of others. By maintaining their right to enjoy romance reading, they refuse to define themselves as the object of other people's demands.

Another position argues that the political implications of pleasures can be understood only indirectly. Pleasure has to be judged in context. Consider Lawrence Grossberg's (1992, 1997) argument about the historical significance of the pleasures of rock and roll music. Grossberg argues that the pleasures of listening to rock and roll music are "empowering," that is, that they energize audience members and provide them with a sense that they can act in the world and accomplish something. To use a very specific example: Grossberg points to the apparent paradox of dancing to rock music. The more you dance, the more exhausted you become, the more you feel like dancing, and the more you can dance. The music actually generates an energy that keeps its audience going. These pleasures, this empowerment, however, have no direct political implications. What one does with the energy, with the feeling that some action is now possible, will be defined by the social context. Thus, Grossberg argues that precisely because rock music is energizing, it can be used by conservative political forces as easily as by liberal political forces. Both Lee Atwater, head of George Bush's first campaign for president and ex-chairman of the Republican National Party, and Bill Clinton, when he ran for president in 1992, mobilized the power of rock and roll to attempt to involve people in their political campaigns.[2]

THE SOCIOLOGY OF CONSUMPTION

Consumption is a social activity, that is, it involves people doing a certain kind of work (buying and using media) in particular places, often with other people. Consequently, consumption is implicated in many different relations of power with others and with institutions. In this section, we will consider some of the contexts and consequences of the social nature of the activity of consuming media.

THE GEOGRAPHY OF MEDIA CONSUMPTION

Think of all the places you consume the media: in your room, in common spaces like a living room, in your car, in sports bars or music clubs, outdoors on the beach or by the pool or on the streets, in class-rooms, as you walk through malls and department stores, at your workplace, in restaurants, in subways, trains, and buses, and in count-less other places. Where you consume the media has an important in-fluence on how you consume them, and it might also be said that the media themselves shape the geography of everyday life.

We can make some sense of this broad array of sites of consump-tion: Media are consumed in public spaces, private spaces, and transi-tional spaces. Another way of dividing these sites might be to differen-tiate between those places in which the media are the primary activity (movie theaters, for instance) and those places in which media are back-ground (Muzak and music videos in stores).

A third aspect of the geography of consumption is whether the presence of a medium brings people together or sends them off into personal spaces. James Carey (1969) and Denis McQuail (1994) have called these differences *centripetal* and *centrifugal*. For example, movies can be thought of as having a centripetal force, because in viewing a movie, the audience is brought together. The personal stereo has a more centrifugal impact, because it is used alone. We should note that some-times the force of a medium is largely the result of the technology itself (the personal stereo cannot easily be shared), whereas at other times, the force is the result of how people use a particular technology (for example, when TV is viewed in a community center).

The most important private space of media consumption is the home. It is in the home, for instance, that children first become intro-duced to media. Most people's first memories of the newspaper is see-ing their parents read it. Television is in nearly every American home. Magazines and books for children are found in their homes. And video brings movies and special children's programs into the home.

The media technologies that first came into the home—the book, the phonograph, the radio, television—were thought to have a cen-tripetal force within the private space of the home. That is, the family gathered around the medium; media use was a shared, communal ac-tivity. At one time, middle-class families read or made music together in their sitting room. Similarly, early phonographs and crystal set ra-dios were found in American living rooms. Television, when it came along in the late 1940s and 1950s, replaced the radio as the central focus of family activities in living rooms. Today, "home theaters" are common. There are multiple reasons for these trends. First, the devices often were large and/or expensive, intended for such communal use. Second, such use legitimated the new technologies and helped to allay fears that their use would undercut traditional family relations. For instance, media historian Lynn Spigel (1992) has found the early advertising for television sets (on television and in magazines) often quite self-consciously created the image of the family gathered around the television set in the living room in order to encourage families to buy this new technology as a family activity.

In every case, as the technologies have become cheaper, smaller, more mobile, and more personal, their effects became more centrifugal. The transistor radio, for example, enabled teenagers in the 1950s to listen to their radio (and thus to rock and roll) in the privacy of their own bedrooms. And by the 1980s, more than three quarters of American households had more than one television set, so that children often had their own set to use.

It is also interesting to observe how over time, different media have become more or less appropriate to different spaces in the home. Increasingly, middle-class and upper middle-class American families tend to locate the largest television set in a family room or play room, which is differentiated from the living room where guests are entertained. But the main music system is likely to remain in the living room; there may be others in the playroom and in bedrooms. This distinction seems to be based on the assumption that music can serve as background, even for socializing, whereas television demands focused attention. As we shall see, this assumption is often false.

It is also important to recognize that the introduction of media technologies into the home has reshaped the geography of domestic space and life as well. Today, the use of large-screen television and sophisticated surround-sound stereo systems requires rooms typically larger than those designed for suburban homes. The proliferation of electronic media has resulted in new electrical codes and requirements for wiring houses. And some have speculated that putting small-screen televisions in the kitchen has led to the rebirth of "breakfast nooks" and "eat-in kitchens" in newer homes.[3] Also, the availability of headphones for everything from televisions and stereos to electronic keyboards has made it less important to insulate the walls between rooms for sound.

It is surprising that when we think about the context of media consumption, we typically think about individuals consuming media in private places. Nonetheless, the fact of the matter is that an enormous part of actual media consumption takes place in public spaces. There are social rules regarding such consumption, which each of us has to learn about. Have you ever taken a preschool child to a movie? They don't know the rules about keeping quiet, not standing up, not annoying the people around them. The ongoing debates about the noise levels of music played on car radios or boom boxes suggest that the rules of such public media consumption have not been socially agreed upon yet.

We can distinguish several different forms of public spaces for media consumption. Some spaces or buildings are designed for media consumption or for activities in which media consumption is an integral part. The best examples are movie theaters, television and music bars, and concert venues. The activities that take place within such spaces often change with new technologies. Large-screen televisions and music videos have invaded bars and dance clubs and changed the ways people act in these spaces. Similarly, the invention of Diamond-Vision (those huge television screens used in arenas during concerts and sports events) has made possible larger audiences.

In some spaces, the media are intentionally provided as background to another sort of activity. The use of Muzak in a variety of public spaces—including workplaces—is a good example. Or consider the multiple television sets in department stores; these are to market the sets themselves, to baby-sit the children of shopping parents, to distract bored shoppers, and to advertise new products or sales. Most recently, television has invaded professional spaces: Chris Whittle, the creator of Channel One (a commercial news program for schools), also created first magazines and then video channels for doctors' and dentists' offices; and CNN designed a separate Airport News Network, with CNN programming but also with air time sold to advertisers seeking the largely upscale air travel market.

The media also exist in spaces that are between public and private: streets, transportation, parks, and so on. In fact, the presence of the media in such transitional places fundamentally transforms the nature of these spaces. The existence of car radios and transistor radios in the 1940s and '50s turned street corners and drive-ins into sites for a new

BOX 9.6

TV in Public

At some time, most of us have watched television in public spaces. Communication researcher Dafna Lemish (1982) conducted a participant observation study of the rules involved in watching television in public areas. She wanted to know what common knowledge people have about "how" to watch television in public: Should you talk to the person sitting next to you in the bar? Who has the right to change the channel? What are the guidelines or expectations about what can be done when watching television in public?

Lemish describes four rules of public viewing. She inferred such rules by observing hundreds of people viewing television in a variety of public places.

1. *A public viewer of television adjusts to the setting.* Clearly, shouting out advice to the football coach while watching a game in a bar was considered acceptable behavior, but it wouldn't be acceptable while watching the TV at a Sears store. Lemish noted that viewers adapted their behavior from public setting to public setting. This was the most obvious of all the rules she observed.

2. *A public viewer of television adjusts to other viewers.* Lemish observed television viewers trying to fit in to the social group watching television in any given setting. Fitting in involved being open for talking if other people in the group were talking about the program; keeping a safe and civil distance from other viewers (not encroaching on other people's space); and giving angry looks or even a "shush" to people talking too loudly in a group when the rest of the group was trying to watch the set.

3. *A public viewer adjusts to the television set.* Lemish observed that people walking by the television set would nod toward it or comment on the program; she watched viewers act as though the TV set itself was what she called a

communicative partner and not merely a physical object. For example, viewers would rarely leave the viewing area in the middle of a segment. While it could be argued simply that viewers were involved in the program or that they were showing respect for other viewers, this observer could not avoid the impression that viewers acted as if leaving in the middle was rude and inconsiderate. (pp. 765-766)

4. *A public viewer of television is open for television-related social interaction.* In fact, the "most observable and consistent aspect of the public context for viewing was the role television served in the initiation and sustaining of social interactions among participants." (p. 767). Indeed, television in public places most often served the function of allowing strangers to find a common topic—the program—to talk about, to initiate conversations that might have seemed awkward or even impossible without the presence of the television. People seem to expect that when watching television in a public place, it is acceptable for other viewers to approach them and talk about the show. In short, the act of watching TV was a public activity.

261

type of youth culture that was organized around music. An even more striking example took place in the early 1990s in eastern Europe, when radios were placed in apartment windows; people gathered in the streets to listen to the constant stream of revolutionary news. A different transformation has been achieved by the personal stereo, which has converted the public nature of transitional spaces into private, isolated bubbles of media consumption.

Indeed, every space and every place of everyday life is now a media space; no place is free of media messages and their complex patterns of consumption. The complexity of media consumption, however, owes much to the multiple forms of social relationships that define and shape media consumption.

MEDIA CONSUMPTION AND SOCIAL RELATIONS

One of the most common observations that people have made about the use of media in everyday life is that the media often function in conjunction with other activities and social relationships. Consider what you do when you are consuming media products. Maybe the television is on and you are . . . eating, sleeping, talking, doing homework, reading, exercising, cooking, making out, writing letters, doing chores, talking on the phone. Or music is playing and you are drinking, dancing, talking, or watching television. Clearly, what you are doing while consuming media products changes how you consume those products. The average viewer is unable to recall more than one or two stories from a newscast as little as a half hour after viewing; this finding is in part explained by the fact that TV watching is usually a *secondary activity*; that is, when we are watching TV, we are most often doing something else as well (See, for example, Robinson & Levy, 1986).

Our experience of consuming media products depends on whether that consumption is our primary activity or a secondary activity, and it depends as well on what other activities we are engaging in, how invested we are in the different activities, and how much the different activities compete with one another. For example, while we drive, we can pay attention to the music on the radio; while we read, we may not be listening carefully.

Sometimes producers of media products count on our doing several activities at once, and they may attempt to structure the media product in such a way as to enable us to do so. CD players that play multiple disks allow us to listen to music for hours at a time.

Equally important to the context of activities associated with media consumption are the social relationships that surround particular acts of media consumption. Sometimes we do indeed consume media alone. But most of the time, there are other people present (if not involved) with us. Consider four sets of social relations: familial, peer group, anonymous, and institutional. The first two are easily pictured, although their relationships to media consumption are the most complex. So let's consider first anonymous and institutional social relations and media consumption.

Anonymous Social Relations

As we consider media consumption in the context of anonymous social relations, we mean all of those occasions that involve the presence of strangers, such as viewing television in public places like bars, going to concerts or dance clubs, or reading a newspaper on a bus or subway. Typically, there are social rules that govern how we interact with those around us and with the media product. For instance, it is considered rude in our culture, or at least aggressive, to read over another person's shoulder or to get up and change TV channels in a public setting. In some music clubs, the space of each dancing couple has to be respected; at others, that space is intentionally and violently violated. Any music fan knows what is appropriate at a particular kind of concert. The presence of other people is often crucial to defining the setting and hence the activity of media consumption, despite the fact that the relationships are totally impersonal. It's clear, too, that the response of others to the media message may have an impact on how we perceive the message: For example, a comedy movie may be funnier in a theater when everyone is laughing than if we watch it on the VCR at home.

Institutional Relationships

Institutional relationships are the contexts of media consumption in which we are aware of the presence of other people who have power over us. Such hierarchical relations can be found at school with the teacher, at work with the boss, or at church with the preacher, or in any

---

BOX 9.7

Gender and Power in TV Watching

British communication researcher David Morley's (1986) observations of men and women watching television led him to note that *how* they watch says a great deal about power relations in families.

Men and women offer clearly contrasting accounts of their viewing habits—in terms of their differential power to choose what they view, how much they view, their viewing styles, and their choice of particular viewing material. However, I am not suggesting that these empirical differences are attributes of their essential biological characteristics as men and women. Rather, I am trying to argue that these differences are the effects of the particular social roles that these men and women occupy within the home. Moreover . . . this sample primarily consists of lower middle-class and working-class nuclear families (all of whom are white) and I am not suggesting that the particular pattern of gender relations within the home found here (with all the consequences which that pattern has for viewing behavior) would necessarily be replicated either in nuclear families from a different class or ethnic background, or in households of different types with the same class and ethnic backgrounds. Rather it is always a case of how gender relations interact with, and are formed differently within, these different contexts.

However, aside from these qualifications, there is one fundamental point which needs to be made concerning the basically different positioning of men

---

organization with an official representative present. Such relationships are often quite constrained and uncomfortable: The social relationship makes us self-conscious. Do you giggle at the wrong places? Are you too exuberant in your enjoyment? Are you embarrassed by the sexuality of your own response?

Media in the Family

As we have said, the family is an important media context; it is within the family that tastes about media products and notions of appropriate behavior with media are formed. Researchers studying the socializing influences of the media find that adolescent children of par-

and women within the domestic sphere. . . . The essential point here is that the dominant model of gender relations within this society (and certainly within that sub-section of it represented in my sample) is one in which the home is primarily defined for men as a site of leisure—in distinction to the "industrial time" of their employment outside the home—while the home is primarily defined for women as a sphere of work (whether or not they also work outside the home). This simply means that in investigating television viewing in the home, one is by definition investigating something which men are better placed to do whole-heartedly, and which women seem only to be able to do distractedly and guilt-ily, because of their continuing sense of their domestic responsibilities. More-over, this differential positioning is given a greater significance as the home becomes increasingly defined as the "proper" sphere of leisure, with the de-cline of public forms of entertainment and the growth of home-based leisure technologies such as video, etc. . . .

Masculine power is evident in a number of the families as the ultimate de-terminant on occasions of conflict over viewing choices. . . . More crudely, it is even more apparent in the case of those families who have an automatic con-trol device. None of the women in any of the families use the automatic control device regularly. A number of them complain that their husbands use the con-trol device obsessively, channel flicking across programs when their wives are trying to watch something else. Characteristically, the control device is the symbolic possession of the father (or of the son, in the father's absence) which sits "on the arm of Daddy's chair" and is used almost exclusively by him. It is a highly visible symbol of condensed power relations. (pp. 6-8)

ents who are well informed and interested in public affairs are them-selves better informed and more interested in public affairs than others of their age (Morley, 1986). This finding should not come as a surprise: These young people have been raised in homes with information-rich media environments (those, for example, with daily newspapers, news magazines, and lots of books), and they likely have modeled their par-ents' attitudes and values (that keeping up with the world is important) and behaviors (reading and paying attention to news). Furthermore, and also not surprisingly, researchers observing families' use of media in the home, specifically television use, have found that the relation-ships of *power* within the family are reproduced and structure the social relationships of media consumption in the home. In many households, the father often controls the remote control device. The older siblings in the household probably control what the kids will watch. Typically, the male's choice of program will dominate.

Peers and Media Use

Even at home, you may be consuming media with people other than your family. Whether you go to a movie on a date or with friends, whether you watch *Star Trek* with your roommate, whether you watch soap operas in a common lounge with fellow students, or whether you bring your best friend into your bedroom to hear the latest music and to learn the latest dance steps, peer relationships among children and young adults provide a major set of social relationships surrounding media consumption.

Research on adolescents (Morley, 1992; Press, 1991) has found that in questions of style such as what to wear; how to style your hair; what media to watch, read, and listen to, peers are more important than family for most adolescents. In many cases, adolescents define their taste in relation to media, and on the basis of media preferences, they distinguish their friends or peers from other peer groups. Think back to your high school. Can you remember the different cliques in your school? How did they dress? What music did they listen to? Did they ever socialize with one another? Numerous teenage movies, such as *Valley Girls* or *The Breakfast Club* or even *Buffy, the Vampire Slayer,* are based on these different peer group structures and the role that media consumption and style play in identifying adolescent subcultures.

These differences in social relationships and activities surrounding media consumption are not the same for all people. They vary along a number of dimensions: There are significant differences across the age span from childhood to senior citizens. Clearly, peer groups are more important to children and adolescents; older people tend to spend more time with the media by themselves or with one other person. These relationships also vary by social class, gender, race, and nationality. According to research by David Morley (1992) in Great Britain and Andrea Press (1991) in the United States, working-class family TV viewing tends to be more hierarchically structured than does middle-class family viewing.

FANS, FASHION, AND SUBCULTURES

When some individuals in the audience identify themselves with the media product or a particular media star or a particular style depicted in the media, they can be thought of as fans or as followers of media fads or fashions. No one is a fan of all the media products they consume, for being a fan entails a different sort of commitment, a different degree of investment in the media product. Fans use particular media products or celebrities to define their own identity. Fandom is a matter of degree: For some, it just means buying every Guns 'n Roses or Tupac album as soon it comes on the market, reading articles about these celebrities, and sharing the taste publicly. For others, fandom can become a matter of style, as they imitate the celebrity. For others, fandom defines a major part of their identity and a major activity of their life. The homeboy/hip-hop subculture, focused on music and clothing style, is one example.

Fandom can bring members of the audience together to celebrate their interest in some media star or product; in this way, fandom relates to a peer group. A whole collection of activities can be involved in being a fan: fan clubs, fanzines, and conventions. Some fan clubs go on long past the death of their celebrity: consider, for example, Elvis Presley fans.

During the 1940s and 1950s, movie magazines were popular vehicles for indulging fans' interest in stars. Since the 1970s, mainstream magazines such as *People* and *Us* as well as television shows such as *Entertainment Tonight* have joined in. These media outlets offer opportunities for audiences to follow the lives of their favorite stars. The talk show circuit of morning news shows and the late night talk shows offer opportunities both to create fans for budding stars and to feed the frenzy of fans. In a slightly different way, music magazines are available for the different sorts of fans within popular music.

The growing importance of celebrity and fandom as a part of people's identity is very much the result of media since 1900. In fact, it is only in the twentieth century that people began to find their images of heroes in the media. According to Leo Lowenthal (1961), who studied biographies appearing in American magazines from the 1800s to the 1930s, there was a major shift in the kinds of idols or celebrities in American popular culture, from *idols of production* to *idols of consumption* during this period. In the 1800s and early 1900s, most magazine biographies celebrated famous men of business, such as John D. Rockefeller, the founder of Standard Oil Company, or Andrew Carnegie of U.S. Steel. By the 1930s, after the rise of the movie and radio industries and the development of public relations experts, there was a shift in the types of people who became celebrities and heroes in popular culture. These new idols of consumption were people involved in various aspects of American entertainment and sports: movie stars such as Charlie Chaplin and Mary Pickford, radio stars such as George Burns and Gracie Allen, bandleaders such as Jimmy and Tommy Dorsey, and baseball players such as Babe Ruth. Long before there was Madonna and Sean Penn, there was Mary Pickford and Douglas Fairbanks, whose marriage and divorce riveted the nation. Long before people mourned the death of John Lennon, Americans cried at the unexpected death of Rudolph Valentino.

The transformation of the hero figures in American culture was not accidental. It depended to a large extent on the development of an industry designed to promote the media and to create fans. The 1930s and 1940s were the heyday of the Hollywood studio system, where stars were under contract with a single studio, such as MGM or Warner Brothers. The studio "made" stars not only by featuring them in films but also by using the studio's publicity agents to assure that the stars appeared in newspaper gossip columns, in magazine feature articles, and on radio shows.

The Hollywood system of today is far different. Stars no longer are under contract with studios, and publicity is handled by stars' own agents. The process of producing the seemingly endless amount of information about media stars and the film and television industry requires an industry of its own; publicists, creative managers, public relations specialists, and a variety of tabloid and other magazines are required to feed fans' interests. Although media producers may not be able to create stars as successfully as they have in the past, they are quick to exploit them when they arise. Most major stars are handled by a small number of major firms, such as CAA, MCA, and the William Morris Agency.

American presidential politics has followed a similar track in the same period. Until about 1960, the two major parties basically ran presidential campaigns. Since then, candidates have assembled their own campaign teams, complete with publicity agents, marketing and fund-raising experts, and pollsters, to compete in party primaries. Although they still need the party nomination, the campaigns are their own operation, not the party's.

Fans can also be fans of particular objects or styles. For example, over the years, the media promoted such unpredictable successes as coonskin caps, Hula Hoops, and pet rocks. Also, stars' "styles" of dressing and talking have started fashion trends. Television in particular has been a powerful source of such fads and fashions.

Although almost all of us have been caught up in various popular fads and been fans of some popular culture, for most of us, that is as far as it goes. But sometimes groups of youths have taken their relationship to popular culture and style one step further: They use their taste to define and mark their primary and most visible identity. What does this mean? A member of a subculture visibly displays his or her identification with the icon of popular culture. This presentation of self defines the fan's identity. Such identities are often disapproved of by parents, teachers, the media, and government, and sometimes even other youth. The punk, skateboard, and biker subcultures are easy to identify because of their relationship to popular culture, for example. (Notice that the yuppies were never a subculture in this sense, because a yuppie is not an identity that people took on for themselves and visibly wore in the face of social ostracism. Similarly, Trekkies are not a subculture although they may occasionally wear their identity visibly—such as when they dress up in costumes for conventions—because the identity of being a Trekkie is not always present for its owner—Trekkies have other lives and take on other social identities.)

Society's response to youth subcultures—whenever they are perceived as a potential threat to mainstream middle-class youth—takes the form of a moral panic. The presence of the subculture becomes seen as a sign of moral decay and as a threat to the stability of the society itself. In the United States, teenage and motorcycle gangs since the 1950s have been the most frequent and troublesome subcultures. Even in the 1990s, the question of gangs, gang membership, and gang colors still evokes powerful and often violent reactions across the country, as movies such as *Colors* and *Boyz 'n the Hood* represent and in some cases provoke.

BOX 9.8

TV Fads and Fashions

Here are some examples of fads and fashions that television has promoted over the years:

- In 1955, ABC's new family program, *Disneyland,* broadcast a miniseries on the life of Davy Crockett. In the seven months following the premiere of the program, $100 million worth of coonskin caps were sold (remember these were 1955 dollars); the price of raccoon skins went from 25 cents to $8 a pound.

- After Hopalong Cassidy migrated from radio to TV in the early 1950s, one million Hopalong trail knives were sold, at 98 cents apiece, in their first 10 days on the store shelves, and 4,000 bars of Hoppy soap were bought in one week. By the end of the 1950s, 108 manufacturers were producing Hoppy products, to the tune of $70 million a year.

- Among other achievements, *Howdy Doody* had three record albums in the Top 10.

- Mousketeers ears became the rage in 1955 after they were worn on *The Mickey Mouse Club.*

- Pat Boone made white buck shoes the "in" footwear between 1957 and 1960.

- Following the introduction of *Batman* on television in 1966, there were more than 300 Batman items for sale, including 25 different toy Batmobile models, cookie jars, crayons, costumes, and bubble bath.

- *Star Trek* has probably spawned more fads over a prolonged period of time than any television program. According to Michael Logan in *TV Guide* (Aug. 31, 1991), there have been six movies, nearly 100 novels including 28 consecutive bestsellers, 500 fan publications, a theme park, half a billion dollars in sales of *Star Trek* products, and, of course, *Star Trek: The Next Generation.*

- The "Fonzie" look (from ABC's 1970s hit *Happy Days*), with his leather jacket, thumbs up gesture, and "Aaay" expression, was placed on all sorts of objects in the 1970s.

- More recently, *Teenage Mutant Ninja Turtles, GhostBusters, The Simpsons,* and *Mighty Morphin Power Rangers* have all sparked their own fads.

SOURCE: Rosen, 1991.

Presumably, anyone can become a member of a subculture: If you have the right taste, if you look right, if you talk and behave according to the right codes, you too can be a punk or a homeboy or a surfer. But obviously not everyone chooses to take on such a visible cultural identity because it is usually seen not only as an act of rebellion but as an act of delinquency as well.

Sociologists argue that youth who participate in subcultures appropriate cultural products to construct an identity as an attempt to confront the contradictions they feel in their own lives. For example, poor kids might feel a real conflict between the optimistic promise of their youthfulness and the sense of hopelessness in which their economic position places them. Their style then becomes a sort of magical solution to the problem: the 1960s "mods" style (which copied Italian "modern" fashion) signaled British working class youth's desire to be upwardly mobile when that was almost impossible. Similarly, according to British cultural critic Dick Hebdige (1980), the late 1970s punk style in Britain and the United States represented youthful attempts to break down the hypocrisy of contemporary society by attacking its cultural codes.

THE AVAILABILITY OF MEDIA CONSUMPTION

It is a common myth in U.S. society that media consumption is equally available to all people: Because we have a "free marketplace" of media products, therefore everyone can consume. This assumption underlies the media institutions' defense of the current system of media production ("we give the people what they want"); it also underlies the process that makes the act of consumption into a site of resistance. Some feminists have criticized the position that consumption always involves resistance because it ignores the fact that consumption itself is a form of labor, it is something that some people (namely, women) have to do for the family. Moreover, of course, not everyone can afford to consume the products they desire.

There are two ways in which this inequality is structured: by the distribution of economic power or capital and by the distribution of cultural capital. Media consumption takes money and time; leisure

271

BOX 9.9

Dick Hebdige on Punks

British media sociologist Dick Hebdige (1980) wrote one of the classic interpretations of punk subculture. Here are a few excerpts:

> The most unremarkable and inappropriate items—a pin, a plastic clothes peg, a television component, a razor blade, a tampon—could be brought within the province of punk (un)fashion. Anything within or without reason could be turned into part of what Vivien Westwood called "confrontation dressing" so long as the rupture between "natural" and constructed context was clearly visible.
>
> Objects borrowed from the most sordid of contexts found a place in the punks' ensembles: lavatory chains were draped in graceful arcs across chests encased in plastic bin-liners (garbage bags). Safety pins were taken out of their domestic "utility" context and worn as gruesome ornaments through the cheek, ear or lips . . . "Cheap" trashy fabrics (PVC, plastic, lurex, etc.) in vulgar designs (e.g., mock leopard skin) and "nasty" colours, long discarded by the quality end of the fashion industry as obsolete kitsch, were salvaged by the punks and turned into garments . . . which offered self-conscious commentaries of the notions of modernity and taste. Conventional ideas of prettiness were jettisoned along with traditional feminine lore of cosmetics. Contrary to the advice of every women's magazine, make-up for both boys and girls was worn to be seen. . . . The perverse and abnormal were valued intrinsically. In particular, the illicit iconography of sexual fetishism was used to predictable effect. . . .
>
> Of course, punk did more than upset the wardrobe. It undermined every relevant discourse. Thus dancing, usually an involving and expressive medium in British rock and mainstream pop cultures, was turned into a dumb show of bland robotics. . . .

---

time is a luxury that is simply not available to the poor, the homeless, or people that have to work more than one job to subsist. In addition, some media are more expensive than others, and they are often outside the practical reach of some significant portions of the population. These sorts of considerations have given rise to policy discussions about the media rich and media poor, both in this country and around the world. As the United States invests more money in ever more expensive media

The music was similarly distinguished from mainstream rock and pop. It was uniformly basic and direct in its appeal, whether through intention or lack of expertise. . . . Johnny Rotten succinctly defined punk's position on harmonics: "We're into chaos, not music." (pp. 107-109).

The safety pins and bin liners signified a relative material poverty which was either directly experienced and exaggerated or sympathetically assumed, and which in turn was made to stand for the spiritual paucity of everyday life. . . . We could go further and say that even if the poverty was being parodied, the wit was undeniably barbed; that beneath the clownish make-up there lurked the unaccepted and disfigured face of capitalism; that beyond the horror circus antics a divided and unequal society was being eloquently condemned. However, if we were to go further still and describe punk music as the "sound of the Westway," or the pogo as the "high rise leap," or to talk of bondage as reflecting the narrow options of working-class youth, we would be treading on less certain ground. Such readings are both too literal and too conjectural. They are extrapolations from the subculture's own prodigious rhetoric, and rhetoric is not self-explanatory; it may say what it means but it does not necessarily "mean" what it "says". . . .

The punk subculture, like every other youth culture, was constituted in a series of spectacular transformations of a whole range of commodities, values, common-sense attitudes, etc. It was through these adapted forms that certain sections of predominantly working-class youth were able to restate their opposition to dominant values and institutions. However, when we close in on specific items, we immediately encounter problems. What, for instance, was the swastika being used to signify? (pp. 115-116)

The punk ensembles . . . did not so much magically resolve experienced contradictions as *represent* the experience of contradiction itself in the form of visual puns (bondage, the ripped tee-shirt, etc.). (p. 121)

technologies, are we increasing the gap and condemning the media poor to an ever downward spiraling social position?

The second way in which the inequality of media consumption is structured is by what the French sociologist Pierre Bourdieu (1984) has called "the unequal distribution of cultural capital." Cultural capital refers to the knowledge and sensibility that enables one to comprehend and appreciate particular cultural products. For example, Bourdieu argues that people may not enjoy high art (such as classical music, art films, avant-garde writing) because they either do not have the knowledge necessary to understand what is going on or because they do not share the aesthetic outlook embodied in such cultural traditions. Even aside from considerations of art, many media products and technologies require specific knowledge or cultural capital. Take, for instance, computers. The computer revolution is occurring with a number of social inequalities that cannot be explained in purely economic terms; for example, women have generally been slower than men to adopt and become expert with computers.

Sometimes cultural capital is not just a question of knowledge or expertise, but a matter of shared assumptions, shared values about the nature and function of cultural consumption. For example, Bourdieu argues that the middle class with its formal educational training (in the United States, typically a college education) judges cultural products in terms of aesthetic values (such as enlightening the human condition), whereas the working class tends to demand that culture embody strong moral principles as well as provide entertainment.

Thus, it is not surprising to find that media consumption follows the patterns of the distribution of economic and cultural capital in the country. Public broadcasting tends to attract richer, more highly educated, and older audiences than do the commercial networks. This is not a judgment about the quality of public broadcasting products or commercial television products. It is a description of the fact that consumption itself is socially determined even as it helps to determine and shape everyday life and our place in the social structure.

NOTES

1. Communication scholars John Stevens and William Porter (1973, p. 11) once quipped that audience research asking people what they liked to watch or read was like asking Chinese villagers if they liked rice. They would of course like rice, since they ate it every day and had little awareness of what other options were available.

2. During the 1992 political campaign, too, many commentators noted that Clinton's appearances on MTV, both with and without his saxophone, were an indication of his sophistication with the media, because they allowed him ac-

cess to an important bloc of potential voters, unmediated by the sharp questioners he faced on network newscast appearances.

3. Similarly, most college dormitories required rewiring in the 1980s because of increased student power consumption—for music systems, computers, and televisions, which earlier generations of students did not own in such numbers.

Media and Behavior

W hat do mass media *do* to us? What effects do they have on how we act? When Vice President Dan Quayle attacked the television program *Murphy Brown* in 1992 because Murphy had a child out of wedlock, he was arguing that a media portrayal directly and powerfully assaulted "family values" and that it influenced the behavior of its audience, encouraging unmarried women to have babies.

But as Joseph Klapper argued as long ago as 1960, the effects of media are not so easily proven. Klapper's position, which is often called the limited effects model of media influence, suggests that when (and if) media affect behavior, they do so through a web of other influencing factors, such as personality characteristics, social situations, and general climates of opinion and culture. Untangling this web of influence has occupied many researchers for years.

Nowhere is there more debate than in the realm of behavior about the power of the media to influence their audience. Since the beginning of media studies, some analysts have held that media strongly and directly affect the audience's behavior; others have argued for the more limited influence of media on behavior.

Vice President Quayle assumed that viewers would model—imitate—the undesirable behavior. Behavior—what people do—has always been the most important concern society has about mediamaking. Behavior *matters*. And it is concrete, observable, and measurable. For

277

example, a television commercial may try to convince you that Kodak can capture the memories of a moment. But in a very real sense, Kodak and its ad agency really do not care whether you believe this or not. What they care about is that you *buy Kodak film*—that you, in other words, *behave* in a certain way. Likewise, a politician calculates the impact of a televised speech in terms of how it will affect people's vote, another important behavior.

As each electronic medium was developing over the past hundred years, virtually the first question the public asked about it—and the first source of controversy—was how the medium would influence behavior (Wartella & Reeves, 1985). For example, when movies developed as a mass medium in the 1920s, people feared that movies would lead youth to "lewd and licentious" behavior; did movies lead teenagers to engage in sexual conduct that earlier generations had not? When television came along a generation later, people wondered whether television turned adolescents into "juvenile delinquents." They asked what effect the violent television shows, movies, and comic books of the 1950s had on the rise of aggressive behavior in children.

And just as the public raised concerns about the behavioral influences of each new media technology, social scientists have been studying the effects of media on behavior throughout the twentieth century; behavior has been a very active area of communication research: It has attracted psychologists, sociologists, and other social scientists to the communications field. For instance, in the late 1920s, an eminent group of social scientists was commissioned, in what came to be known as the Payne Fund studies, to examine film's effects on youth. One of the most widely cited volumes in this research was Herbert Blumer's (1932) *Movies and Conduct.* The 12 Payne Fund volumes stand as a model of how to study the behavioral effects of media.

BEHAVIORAL EFFECTS

In Chapter 1, we noted that a popular model for understanding mass media is Harold Lasswell's question, "*Who* says *what* to *whom* in what *channel* and with what *effect*?" To understand how media make behaviors, we need to clarify a few things about behavioral effects, for *effects* may be of very different sorts.

278

BOX 10.1

The Payne Fund

A history of research on children and media recalls the pioneering Payne Fund studies this way:

The 1933 Payne Fund studies—twelve volumes of research conducted by the most prominent psychologists, sociologists, and educators of the time—represent a detailed look at the effects of film on such diverse topics as sleep patterns, knowledge about foreign cultures, attitudes about violence, and delinquent behavior. These studies have not been cited much in the last 25 years, despite the fact that they represent a research enterprise comparable to the 1972 Surgeon General's Committee on Television and Violence. But at the time the Payne studies generated significant press attention, academic review, and critical comment, and were the basis of recommendations for government action on what the authors believed were significant social problems.

A major conclusion of the report was that the same film would affect children differently depending on the child's age, sex, predispositions, perceptions, social environment, past experiences, and parental influences. In this sense, the report was similar to the most current summaries of research about children and television. Further, the effects were said to be conditional on whether the criterion concerns were behaviors, attitudes, emotions, or knowledge about people and events. For example, Blumer's study of *Movies, Delinquency, and Crime* (Macmillan, 1933) concluded that the effects of film on criminal behavior may be diametrically opposed, depending on the diversity of themes presented and the social milieu, attitudes, and interests of the observer.

Although Blumer's contingencies were largely sociological, the conclusions of several other researchers involved affective and psychological differences. Dysinger and Ruckmick (*The Emotional Responses of Children to the Motion Picture Situation,* New York: Macmillan, 1933) studied emotional reactions and concluded, based on a physiologic measure, that children varied widely in emotional stimulation. They suggested that age differences in response were caused by varied abilities to comprehend information on the screen. For example, young children tended not to understand the romantic scenes to which adolescents responded enthusiastically. . . . [Also], the psychologists and educators on the Payne committee studied ideas and factual learning, social attitudes, emotions, sleep patterns, and moral development. (pp. 120-121)

SOURCE: Wartella & Reeves, 1985. For an overview of the Payne Fund studies, see Charters, 1933.

Effects are not just behavioral. Social psychologists studying persuasion usually divide attitudes into three components: the *cognitive* (the intellectual or knowledge) component, the *affective* (the emotional or evaluative) component, and the *conative* (intentional or behavioral) component. A media message may have an impact on one of these components but not on others. You might see, for example, a commercial for a deodorant that convinces you that it stops wetness (a cognitive effect), but you may not buy that deodorant. Nonetheless, the whole premise in persuasion is that usually *our behaviors are consistent with our existing cognitions and attitudes.* We behave in some way, in ways that are consistent with what we believe to be appropriate.

Media functions may be *manifest* (overt, obvious) or *latent* (implicit or unarticulated). A parallel idea is that media messages vary depending on the *intent* of their producers. A commercial maker's primary intention is to encourage the audience to buy a product, whereas an editor writing an endorsement for a political candidate is attempting to get voters to vote for the favored candidate. The important idea here is that media messages may have unintended consequences: The writers of *Murphy Brown* intended to entertain an audience; just as surely, they did not intend to promote out-of-wedlock pregnancies.

Perhaps historically, the most famous incident involving unintended consequences of a mass-mediated message was the 1938 CBS radio broadcast of the American Mercury Theater's dramatization of H. G. Wells's novel *The War of the Worlds.* Producer and actor Orson Welles's intention was to entertain, and he never dreamed he would promote a mass panic. Nonetheless, the episode raises several important ideas for us to keep in mind.

1. Messages may have unintended, and unanticipated, consequences.
2. Even when the vast majority of an audience is presumably unaffected by a message, given the *extent* of an audience and the vast amplificative power of media, a message may have important social consequences if even a few audience members are affected.
3. The episode reminds us that media impact may be evaluated on multiple criteria: We may assess a situation on its *effect*, or, conversely, on its *effectiveness*. Effect relates to the general impact of

BOX 10.2

The War of the Worlds

These are the opening paragraphs of a remarkable little book, Hadley Cantril's (1940/1966) *The Invasion from Mars*:

At eight P.M. eastern standard time on the evening of October 31, 1938, Orson Welles, with an innocent little group of actors took his place before the microphone in a New York studio of the Columbia Broadcasting System. He carried with him Howard Koch's freely adapted version of H. G. Wells's imaginative novel, *War of the Worlds*. He also brought to the scene his unusual dramatic talent. With script and talent the actors hoped to entertain their listeners for an hour with an incredible, old-fashioned story appropriate for Halloween.

Much to their surprise the actors learned that the series of news bulletins they had issued describing an invasion from Mars had been believed by thousands of people throughout the country. For a few horrible hours people from Maine to California thought that hideous monsters armed with death rays were destroying all armed resistance against them; that there was simply no escape from disaster; that the end of the world was near. Newspapers the following morning spoke of the "tidal wave of terror that swept the nation." It was clear that a panic of national proportions had occurred. The chairman of the Federal Communications Commission called the program "regrettable." (p. 3)

An estimated six million people heard the broadcast; probably fortunately, CBS's main competitor, NBC, was running a far more popular comedy-and-variety program at the same time. As Cantril notes, "Had the program enjoyed greater popularity, the panic might have been more widespread" (p. 56). Survey evidence suggests that upwards of a million people were upset by the broadcast.

The format of the broadcast was a "pretend" radio variety program, interrupted periodically by news reports detailing first the sighting by scientists of an explosion on Mars, then the landing of a spacecraft in New Jersey, then a journalist's eyewitness account of the havoc wreaked by the invaders. According to a survey by the American Institute of Public Opinion at Princeton, some 28% of the survey respondents who heard the broadcast took the news accounts to be real.

In retrospect, anyone listening to that broadcast today, or reading a transcript of it, is astonished that people found it to be real—the news network and many of the places mentioned in the broadcast are fictitious (others, however, were real); there were disclaimers at the beginning and middle of the broadcast, and Welles himself closes with the following:

(continued)

BOX 10.2 continued

This is Orson Welles, ladies and gentlemen, out of character to assure you that the *War of the Worlds* has no further significance than as the holiday offering it was intended to be. The Mercury Theatre's own radio version of dressing up in a sheet and jumping out of a bush and saying "Boo!" (p. 42)

Cantril's research team found not only survey evidence that people believed the broadcast; telephone calls went up in several parts of the country, and in Northern New Jersey, where the cataclysm supposedly was occurring, phone traffic was up 39% over a normal Sunday evening.

First, let us note that the large majority—almost three quarters by the best estimate—were not taken in by the broadcast. But by the best estimate as well, perhaps a million people were. *Why* were people taken in, and *who* was most likely to be?

Cantril suggests that the nature of radio listening (and the same is true today of television drama) had something to do with it; much listening is inattentive, and only when listeners heard journalists and witnesses in the fictional account screaming and panicked did they pay close attention—thus missing the disclaimers. Moreover, we need to recall that the broadcast occurred in 1938, as the world was edgy about world events. War would break out in Europe less than a year later. Radio then, as TV now, was viewed as a credible medium for fast-breaking "hard" news.

Who was, and who was not likely to be taken in? Those more likely to be upset were *proximate* to the purported event—those in northern New Jersey and New York (the creatures were advancing on Manhattan), and "social categories" were used to explain credulity as well: those of lower socioeconomic status and education were more likely to be duped. Cantril suggests that such people were less able to do "reality checking" for the broadcast.

We would ask readers to bear a couple of points in mind: First, the majority of listeners were *not* adversely affected by the broadcast. But second, because of the vast amplificative power of the mass media, even a small minority, in percentage terms, can translate into hundreds of thousands, even millions.

Could it happen again? A good question, perhaps, but one hard to answer. On the negative, we would note that virtually every mass communicator in the country knows some details of the *War of the Worlds* panic and virtually all would be wary of any attempt to repeat the experience; furthermore, much of the public knows of it, too, and would be as well. But on the other side, Abraham Lincoln had it right, 130 years ago, when he said that "You can fool some of the people all of the time, and all of the people some of the time. . . . "

a message or series of messages; effectiveness evaluates whether a message or series accomplished the goal its producers intended.

As communication theorist Denis McQuail (1987) notes, media may lead to a number of different kinds of changes. They may:

1. Cause *intended* change (conversion)
2. Cause *unintended* change
3. Cause *minor* change, of, for example, form or intensity of response
4. *Facilitate* change
5. *Reinforce* what exists (no change)
6. *Prevent* change

The first three of these are fairly self-explanatory, but the last three bear some comment. To say that media messages may facilitate change is to argue that although other social forces are the prime cause of a change, media messages make the changes easier or faster. For example, few would argue that media coverage of the civil rights movement in the South in the early 1960s caused the members of Congress to pass the 1964 Civil Rights Act, but many have argued that this coverage facilitated the passage of the act. At the beginning of the chapter, we noted Klapper's statement that the most usual effect of mass media is *reinforcement*, or lack of change, and that his view is frequently called a *limited effects model* of communication influence. In some views, reinforcement of the status quo and/or the prevention of change can also be thought of as a profound—perhaps *the* most significant—effect of mass communication.

We also need to think about behavior making on several different time scales. The first time scale is the frequency of exposure to the message.

1. Short-term message exposure occurs when you are exposed to a message once, such as when you watch a TV show. You are amused while you watch it, but you neither think about it nor act on it later.

283

2. Intermediate term message exposure is exposure to a series of related messages, such as a product campaign or "social marketing" of anti-drug messages or the United Way.
3. Long-term media message exposure occurs after many cumulative exposures to related messages over time. For example, the argument that TV violence leads to aggressive behavior, or that pornography leads to violence against women, is asserting that these effects occur after repeated exposures to similar messages over time.

Moreover, the effects of media on behavior can themselves be either transitory (lasting a short time, such as only during or shortly after exposure, as when you buy a new brand of toothpaste after seeing an ad for the new product), or persistent, lasting a long time.

LEVELS OF ANALYSIS

Social acts can occur at different social levels or levels of analysis. Although we are most comfortable thinking of behavior as something *people* do—the individual level of analysis—behavior has meaning at higher levels of analysis as well. Organizations, institutions, and societies all act. When Congress passes a law, it has acted. Media may have impacts on how organizations, institutions, and societies behave. The problem, however, is that it is not always easy, concrete, and evident to observe and assess how each of these higher levels behaves. Therefore, we account for social behavior in terms of how individuals in the social unit have acted.

For a bill to become a federal law, a majority of the members of the Senate and the House of Representatives must vote in favor of it, and the president must sign it. If the president does not sign the bill, it can still become law if two thirds of the members of both houses again vote for it. To account for the behavior of Congress, then, we look at the behavior of its individual members, and when they formed a majority in voting the bill up or down. The majority is an *aggregated* measure. We think of, and use, aggregated social measures all the time, as when we think of "the average American" or suggest that television has "caused" a decline in achievement test scores. However, a complete account of the "behavior of Congress" must note the existence of a minor-

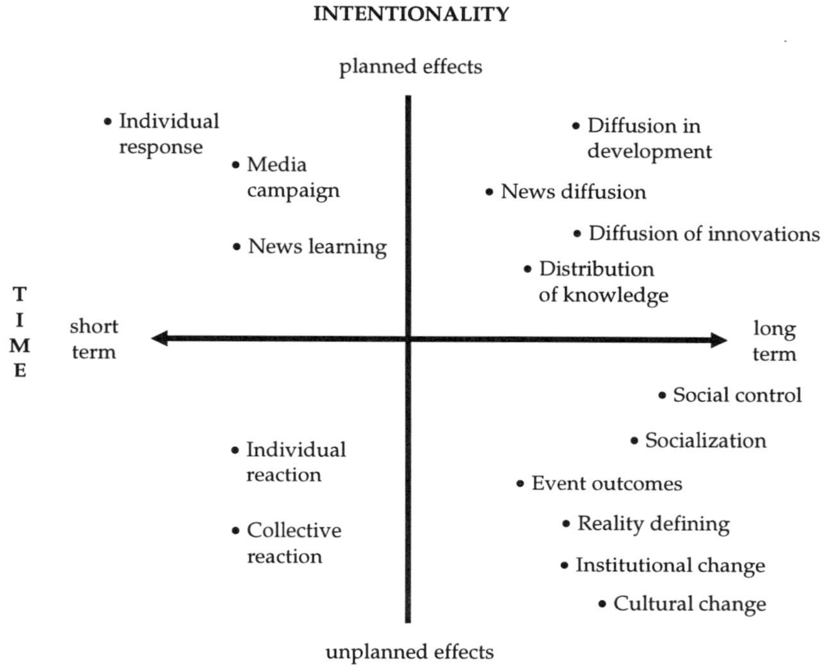

INTENTIONALITY

planned effects

Figure 10.1. A typology of media effects: Effect can be located on two dimensions, that of time span and that of intentionality.
SOURCE: McQuail, 1994, p. 336. Reprinted with permission.

ity as well, for when we talk about social aggregates, the nonmajority behavior may well be more significant than the behavior of the major- ity. For example, the vast majority of the *War of the Worlds* listeners did not take the broadcast as news of an invasion from Mars; but the minor- ity who did were sufficient to cause a mass panic. To hold to a limited effects model of communication influence is not to suggest that the be- havioral effects of mass media are themselves necessarily limited. In an election campaign, the vast majority of voters are uninfluenced by any single media message—a commercial, a candidate speech, a debate, a candidate endorsement. But if the election is a close one (let's say that 49% are predisposed to vote for Candidate A and 49% for Candidate B), what happens at the margins—the potential impact of media messages on the remaining 2%—looms large indeed.

MODELS OF BEHAVIOR MAKING

To understand how media affect behavior, too, requires that we specify the *mechanisms* by which media may have effects. For the individual, the minimal model for behavioral effects assumes a stimulus, a receiver, and a response. This is the familiar stimulus-response model of the psychologist:

Stimulus Message → Individual Receiver → Reaction

This model is the first and most enduring model of media effects considered by media scholars. It is often called either the *bullet theory* or *direct effects* theory of media influence. This unelaborated model of media effects argued essentially that media messages directly influence audiences' behavior. It is this model that represents the underlying fear of critics of mass media during the first third of this century, that is, that media messages can have a direct influence on the mass of the audience.

Over the years, much media research has gone into elaborating and correcting this model. First, it was noted that different people responded differently to the same messages. This phenomenon led to the development of theories about individual differences in media effects on behavior, and the assertion that some people may be more susceptible to the influence of media messages. As long ago as the 1950s, communication scholars Elihu Katz and Paul Lazarsfeld (1955) posited that there are individual differences in media effects because some audience members selectively attend to and remember media messages. Sociologists Melvin DeFleur and Sandra Ball-Rokeach (1975) add the *social categories* perspective, which holds that there are groups in the social world who tend to react to any particular media message in similar ways. Such groups may be characterized by age, sex, income level, or religious affiliation. DeFleur and Ball-Rokeach offer the *social relations* perspective as another type of individual difference in response to media: For some members of the audience, the influence of media messages is dependent on an opinion leader who tends to shape a group's opinion or reaction to the message.

Various theories also have been developed of *how* media influence people's behavior. Among the theories we want to describe here are:

social learning theory, theories about imitation/contagion, and theories of social reality as a mediator of the effects of media messages on audiences' behavior.

Social Learning

In 1941, two psychologists, N. E. Miller and John Dollard, proposed that people can learn new behaviors through their observation of others' behaviors. They called their theory *social learning theory*. They argued that imitative learning occurred when people are motivated to act like others, when people can observe others performing the behavior to be imitated, and when such imitative learning is somehow reinforced. In short, they offered a traditional stimulus-response learning model, that is, that in the presence of a modeled behavior (or stimulus), an observer if motivated will make copied or patterned acts (imitation) of the model's behavior (a response), and such responses are more likely to be learned when they are reinforced.

Miller and Dollard's notion of social learning, however, wasn't terribly helpful in understanding media effects, because their model still relied on adequate reinforcement to ensure that media audiences could learn to imitate a media actor's behavior. What mattered then was whether or not an imitated behavior was reinforced and whether such reinforcement occurred in the everyday life of the audience member. Thus, the ability of the media to influence audience behavior was still thought to be dependent on "who" the audience member was and the various social relationships in which that person was involved. That is, media effects depended on the various theories about the audience described above.

However, by the early 1960s, social psychologist Albert Bandura offered a revised social learning theory or observational modeling theory, which is a more powerful theory to account for imitative or observational learning. Bandura argued that actors in the mass media (and he and his colleagues studied primarily film and television programs) are so attractive that audience members want to be like the media actors. Therefore, media characters or models can influence the behavior of audience members simply by existing, because they are so attractive. Furthermore, Bandura argued that once an audience observer imitates or models the observed media behavior, the sheer act of acting like a media character reinforced the behavior. Indeed, Bandura believed that the best way to teach new behaviors, particularly to children, is to present the behavior you want the child to learn, and the child will imitate that behavior. In a series of early controlled laboratory experimental studies called the *Bobo doll studies,* Bandura and his colleagues demonstrated that children can and do learn new behaviors by observation.

Let's consider the classic Bobo doll experiment. Bandura wanted to study two different effects: first, whether observing a filmed behavior could teach children that behavior, and second, if such observation motivated the children to be like the film model. He showed nursery school children a film of a person hitting a Bobo doll, an inflated plastic clown doll with a sand base, which rocked back and forth when punched. According to Bandura (1965),

> The film began with a scene in which a model (an adult male) walked up to an adult-size plastic Bobo doll and ordered him to clear the way. After glaring for a moment at the noncompliant antagonist, the model exhibited four novel aggressive responses, each accompanied by a distinctive verbalization. First, the model laid the Bobo doll on its side, sat on it, and punched it in the nose while remarking, "Pow, right in the nose, boom, boom." The model then raised the doll and pummeled it on the head with a mallet. Each response was accompanied by the verbalization "Sockeroo . . . stay down." Following the mallet aggression, the model kicked the doll about the room, and these responses were interspersed with the comments, "Fly Away." Finally, the model threw rubber balls at the Bobo doll, each strike punctuated with "Bang." This sequence of physically and verbally aggressive behavior was repeated twice.
>
> For one group of children, the film ended there. For another group, in the model-rewarded condition, the film went on to show a second adult appear and reward the adult who had been hitting the Bobo doll with soft drinks and candies and informing the model that he was a "strong champion." A third group of children in the "model-punished" condition saw a film which showed a second adult appearing on the scene, shaking his finger, and saying, "Hey there, you big bully. You quit picking on that clown. I won't tolerate it." (pp. 590-591)

Bandura wanted to see how much spontaneous imitation or copying of the filmed characters' actions toward the Bobo would occur. So after each viewing condition, the children were taken into a room with various toys, including a Bobo doll like the one in the film, three balls, a mallet, a pegboard, plastic farm animals, and dolls with a doll house. Bandura argued that this set of toys allowed the children to either imitate the aggression on the film or engage in various nonimitative play behaviors. Each child was left alone in this playroom or laboratory for 10 minutes while experimenters observed through a two-way mirror.

Bandura found that the spontaneous modeling or imitation of the film actor's behavior toward the Bobo doll occurred in the playroom setting for those children who had seen the film with no consequence and those who had seen the model rewarded. Boys were more likely to imitate than girls. However, the children who had seen the adult punished were not likely to imitate the film character's actions toward the Bobo doll. But Bandura argued that these children had learned the behavior anyway. He went on to demonstrate this by having a second test. He had an experimenter enter the playroom after 10 minutes and offer the children fruit juice and stickers as treats if the children could reproduce what they had seen the film character do to the Bobo doll on the film. Even the children who had seen the model punished on the film were able to reproduce the film actor's behavior toward the Bobo doll. Thus, Bandura concluded that filmed portrayals of new behaviors could be learned through observation of the behavior. However, seeing the model punished for a certain behavior decreases the likelihood of such imitative learning (this Bandura called an *inhibitory effect*), whereas seeing a model rewarded (or even not punished) for making an aggressive behavior increases the likelihood that the viewer will imitate the behavior (this Bandura called a *disinhibitory effect*). Moreover, Bandura used the term *vicarious reinforcement* to refer to the idea that audience members are reinforced in the viewing situation itself and that observation of a media behavior is sufficient for learning of the behavior to take place, provided that the audience member engages in the following four steps in the process of observing the model.

1. Attentional processes. The audience member must be able to attend to and understand the various parts of the behavior being modeled by the media character.
2. Retention processes. The audience member must be able to remember what he or she sees the model do and be able to recall it at the time of copying the behavior.

3. Motoric reproduction processes. The audience member must be able to physically reproduce the actions of the media model.
4. Motivational and reinforcement processes. The likelihood that an audience member will model what he or she observes a media character doing is dependent on the audience member's desire or motivation to act like the media character.

The social learning theory, although subject to considerable criticism for the initial laboratory studies and their highly artificial nature, has been a powerful theory offered to account for children's learning from the mass media. It is important to know that social learning theory predicts that viewers can model media portrayals and that it has been the most widely used theoretical perspective in debates about the effects of television and film violence on children.

Contagion

Probably the most controversial "effects" of mass media are cases in which the media are presumed to have led to antisocial "panic" or "copycat" behaviors. We'll mention just four here.

In the 1970s, the plot of a made-for-TV movie, *The Doomsday Flight*, had extortionists demanding ransom for a commercial jetliner on which they had placed an atmospherically controlled bomb, which armed itself as the plane rose and would detonate when the plane descended below 5,000 feet. In the movie, the extortionists were foiled when the plane flew to Denver, the "mile high city," but several copycat extortion attempts followed the film. Moreover, similar copycat crimes occurred in other nations when the film aired there.

In the 1970s, NBC aired another TV movie, *Born Innocent*, which featured a depiction of the rape of a young girl. The parents of a young girl in San Francisco raped in similar fashion sued the network. The suit failed because the parents were unable to prove that the movie was the cause of the rape.

In two episodes in the 1980s, murderers committed crimes by doctoring Tylenol painkillers with the deadly poison cyanide; in each case, copycat crimes followed the news of the initial killings.

Following the urban riots of the late 1960s and again after the 1992 Los Angeles riot, a chorus of critics charged that media depictions, es-

pecially television news, either led to or fanned the flames of subsequent disorders.

Rock and roll lyrics have been blamed for suicides, news of suicides
has been blamed for other suicides, reported terrorist and hijacking attempts have been blamed for subsequent ones, Halloween candy tainting has been blamed on news reports of similar tainting, and so on.
These episodes are all terrifying, socially significant and clear threats to
social order. Given the importance of the problem, such contagion has
led to extensive research.

In each of these cases, note that a tiny fraction of the audience is
affected—that is, behaves by copying—but that tiny fraction can cause
enormous harm. *In principle,* there is no reason to discount the ability of
the media to cause such effects; they are quite consistent with the stimulus-response and social learning theories. Nonetheless, it is quite difficult to generalize about the way in which media can lead to such contagion, because so many other factors may be involved.

In one sort of action, an individual—usually, we would suspect, a
mentally unbalanced one—mimics a stimulus from a media message.
The problem is that such individuals might be set off by any stimulus
at any time, and so it is quite difficult to demonstrate that the media
messages "caused" the behavior. Admittedly, in the case of copycat
crime, it is abundantly clear that media reports are at least one among
several contributing agents. Research studies by the sociologist David
Phillips (1982; Phillips & Hensley, 1984/1985) have purported to show
that both news and soap opera portrayals of suicide lead to subsequent
rises in suicide, vehicle fatalities, and airplane crashes (which Phillips
asserts are copycat murder-suicides); his controversial research has
been challenged by other researchers, on both theoretical and methodo-
logical grounds.

The second class of examples—urban disorders and some terrorist
attempts—involve collective or group behavior. Here the best evidence
again is that media depictions do not themselves cause subsequent rioting, although they may well influence the timing or form of rioting
behaviors. The urban-disorder research suggests that personal and social contacts are far more influential in individuals' deciding to participate in riots. And, as Denis McQuail (1987) argues, in news coverage of
riots and terrorism, consideration of the alternative course of action—
that media should cover up such incidents—forces us to reflect on the

possibility that such a cover-up would lead to rumor-generated mass hysteria among those able to observe disturbances in their own areas.

"Social Reality" as Mediator of Behavior

How one perceives a media message—how one interprets a message as a statement about the world—has a profound impact on how one responds. When producer Norman Lear's *All in the Family* made its debut in 1971, the show became an immediate source of controversy. The main character, Archie Bunker, was an out-and-out bigot; and Lear's intention was clearly to ridicule him. But the critics suggested that, in fact, Archie would be seen by highly prejudiced people as a sympathetic character, thus reinforcing their prejudices. In other words, the critics were suggesting a process of *selective perception*. Several research studies, in fact, found this—racially prejudiced individuals saw Archie as sympathetic and were reinforced in their attitudes and values, whereas less prejudiced individuals saw just the reverse (Brigham & Giesbrecht, 1976; Vidmar & Rokeach, 1974). Moreover, one study of the program found that highly prejudiced individuals were more likely than others to avoid watching the program altogether (Wilhoit & deBock, 1976). Their choice is an example of *selective exposure*.

Selective perception speaks to the ability of individuals to mold their own view of reality from media content. Not all media portrayals, however, are equally subject to selective interpretation. Some are more concrete and unambiguous than others. But portrayals of reality do influence behavior. The simplest and most mundane example is that we listen to a weather forecast in the morning to decide how warmly to dress and whether to pack an umbrella.

Some commentators argue that the media's greatest impact is its influence on our pictures of the world. In other words, the behavioral effects of the media may indeed be quite limited, as Klapper suggests, under ordinary circumstances. But great media power may reside elsewhere—in media's ability to shape our cognitions and beliefs. Political scientist Bernard C. Cohen (1963) captured this idea in commenting on the power of the press: "It may not be successful much of the time in telling people what to think, but it is stunningly successful in telling its readers what to think *about*."

In telling us about the world—what is true, what is important, what aspects of problems are critical, what positions various groups have on particular issues, what other people are thinking and doing, and what they think are appropriate ways of behaving—the media have the potential to exert enormous influence. The potential is great for an obvious reason: People have just three ways to learn. These are personal, direct experience; interpersonal interaction; and media. An overwhelming share of what we know of the world comes from media sources. If you've never been to Kenya (or Russia or France), virtually everything you know about Kenya comes from a media source.

Are beliefs and cognitions related to behavior? A particularly vivid example comes from research by Alexander Bloj, a Syracuse University graduate student (reported in McCombs & Shaw, 1974). His research topic was flying on commercial airliners. Bloj examined an airline's ticket sales records for five years and related these to news reports of commercial airplane crashes involving fatalities and skyjackings. When a skyjacking or crash occurred, ticket sales went down. Furthermore, during those same weeks, sales of flight insurance went up. Because we almost never learn of air crashes firsthand, the effect virtually certainly is media-generated. In this example, the effect is concrete, in large part for two reasons. First, selective perception is unimportant: There's basically only one way to read the news that an airliner crashed and people were killed. Second, individuals' attitudes are likewise unimportant, because virtually everybody has the same strong belief that dying in an airplane crash is a lousy idea. Reports of crashes and skyjackings remind us that flying can be a risky business.

PERSUASIVE COMMUNICATION RESEARCH

One major area of theorizing about media effects concerns advertising and its influence on buying. How does advertising work? What are the mechanisms involved in getting us to buy those jeans, that cola, the right face cream, which we see advertised on television, in magazines and newspapers, on billboards, and now even at movie theaters? Communications scholar Michael Schudson (1984) titled his book on advertising effectiveness *Advertising: The Uneasy Persuasion*. Schudson's argument is that advertisers are "uneasy" in the sense that the evidence on the "effectiveness" of advertising to actually get people to buy products is not at all clear; how precisely advertising works may be more art than science, may be more rules of thumb than clear knowledge. Theories have been developed that attempt to describe the process of persuasion. In fact, this literature is enormous; the social psychologist William McGuire (1989) found over 7,000 published articles relevant to the study of persuasive communication. Let's consider some of the current well-regarded theories of how persuasion operates.

THE McGUIRE "PROCESS" MODEL

McGuire has himself contributed a model of the persuasion process; he offers a general description of the different steps necessary for persuasion to take place:

1. *Presentation:* A persuasive message must be presented to the audience member.
2. *Attention:* The audience member must attend to the message.
3. *Comprehension:* He or she must understand the message.
4. *Yielding:* The person must yield to, or accept or agree with, the persuasive argument presented in the message.
5. *Retention:* After receiving the message and leaving the communicative situation, the audience member must remember the persuasive message.
6. *Overt Behavior:* The audience member needs to behave in the expected way.

For McGuire, each of these steps must be followed for an advertisement or any other message intended to persuade an audience to do something to be effective.

The effectiveness of this process is dependent, however, on the various components of the persuasion process—the source of the message, the manner in which the message itself is constructed, the channel through which the message is sent, and the receiver or audience for the message. This general model of the steps and components of the persuasion process is useful in describing the persuasion situation, but it does not show how to create the most persuasive message.

THE THEORY OF REASONED ACTION

Other theoretical models have been advanced to address persuasion. One of the most widely known of these is Ajzen and Fishbein's (1980) *Theory of Reasoned Action.*

According to this theory, the best predictor of behavior, such as buying a particular brand of car, is the person's *intention* to engage in the behavior. A person's intention is, in turn, determined by a person's *attitude toward the behavior* and by what Ajzen and Fishbein call a *subjective norm,* or the person's perceptions of how other people they value think he or she should behave. And underlying a person's own attitude about buying a new car and a person's subjective norms about car buying are a deeper set of beliefs about the sorts of cars that are appropriate for the person, beliefs perhaps about environmental pollution, beliefs about whether and how cars may express deeper personality characteristics, and a whole set of beliefs a person holds that underlie their particular attitude toward buying a particular car.

Because this theory assumes, then, that most behavior is ultimately determined by sets of underlying beliefs, it follows that to affect someone's behavior (such as persuading them to buy a certain brand of car) is accomplished by changing these underlying beliefs. Changes in underlying beliefs lead to changes in attitudes and norms, which in turn lead to changes in intentions to behave and ultimately to behavior. Thus, a key tenet of the theory of reasoned action is that media messages intended to change behavior must be designed for and aimed at the underlying beliefs that are associated with behavioral intentions in the audience or population of interest.

INFORMATION-PROCESSING APPROACHES

Other theorists have focused on how the audience makes sense of the persuasive message—how they process the information. These theorists hope to gain insight into how to change the audience member's underlying beliefs about some object or behavior. According to this *information processing approach* to persuasion, it is necessary to determine how an individual processes a persuasive message, how that person's initial knowledge relevant to the message is represented or "remembered," how the message influences the person's selection of information from the message, and how the individual is transformed or changed in response to the message, from an initial state of knowledge about the object of persuasion to final knowledge state. A number of what are called *cognitive response theories* have been developed, arguing that the best way to predict how a persuasive message will be understood by the recipient or audience member is to understand the thought that occurs to people when they are exposed to the message. That is, what are you thinking about when you watch a Shaquille O'Neill advertisement for Pepsi Cola? These thoughts (or cognitive responses) are assumed to be indicative of how you are interpreting the persuasive message.

One particular cognitive response theory is Petty and Cacciopo's extended work on responses to persuasive messages. They have found, for instance, that the degree to which an audience member perceives that a message is personally important and relevant (what's called *high involvement* with the message) determines how the person *processes* the persuasive message. An advertisement, for instance, in which an audience member is highly involved (such as seeing an ad for a new car just when you are thinking about buying a new car) leads the involved person to scrutinize the information and arguments of that persuasive message more than an uninvolved person. This is called the *central* route to information processing. For messages that are not personally involving, audience members will use simpler, less taxing strategies to make sense of and respond to the message, maybe just focusing on the source of the message or the expertise of the person making the claims; this is called *peripheral* processing. Cacciopo and Petty argue that both forms of processing may lead to attitude and behavior change. Attitude change through the central route, however, is more difficult to accomplish because the person to be persuaded is fully engaged in thinking about and even arguing with the persuasive message, because she or he *cares* about the attitude object. Attitude change through the peripheral route is usually easier, because the person is not really engaged. But attitudes changed through the central route are more persistent and harder to change subsequently than less involving ones.

These various theories of how to develop a persuasive message have become increasingly important in planned information campaigns, particularly in the rise of health information campaigns, a topic we will take up in the next chapter.

In this chapter, we have tried to introduce you to some of the major theories of how media might influence individuals' behaviors. You probably have noticed that some of these theories, such as Bandura's (1977) social learning theory or Petty and Cacciopo's (1986) cognitive response theory, have been developed to theorize about media influences in specific areas, such as effects of violence portrayals on aggressive behavior in the case of Bandura, and advertising influences on product-purchasing behavior in the case of Petty and Cacciopo. Although we have reviewed various aspects of how to conceptualize media influences on behavior in general, it is the case that most theories of behavior influences of media have been developed to examine either a specific type of media content (e.g., violence, pornography, political reporting, advertising, etc.) or a special domain of people's behaviors (for example, aggressive behavior, product purchasing, health behaviors, voting, etc.). Also, it is clear that much of the research on media influence on individuals has been directed over the years to studies of media content that is thought to be a social problem, such as pornographic films or magazines. The next chapter will examine research on media influences in specific domains of behavior.

Debates Over
Media Effects

S tudies of media and behavior have been heavily tied to public
fears about the effects of various media on their audiences. Indeed, the thousands of studies that have been conducted throughout
this century to assess the power of media to influence behavior fall into
categories that represent strong public concerns: Does viewing television violence cause viewers to be aggressive? What are the effects of
pornographic images on their audiences? What influence does television have on the social behavior of children? How effective are advertising and other persuasive media messages? How can we design information campaigns to influence people's behavior? These questions
have occupied much of the research on media and individual behavior.
This chapter will consider each literature separately, and we will begin
with the most visible public issues regarding media influence, the effects of violent programming.

VIOLENCE IN THE MEDIA AND AGGRESSIVE BEHAVIOR

American society is frequently reported to be one of the most violent in
the world. Just as frequently, media violence is claimed to be, if not *the*

cause, then a major contributing cause to real violence. This is a sweeping charge, and one that no American citizen should take lightly. Since 1993, the entire issue of the effects of television violence has come under heavy scrutiny in Congress, the press, and the public arena. This concern about media violence is not new, however.

At least since the early days of film at the turn of this century, media violence has been an ongoing concern of the American public. It surfaced in the 1930s after the publication of the Payne Fund studies of film effects on youth and led to the creation in 1934 of the Hays Office, a self-regulation arm of the film industry. It surfaced in the 1950s in concerns over comic book violence and again led to self-censorship of violent comics by the comic book industry. And over the 50 years of American television, violence has been the most enduring concern of critics of television programming.

Public debates around the issue of media violence have fueled a variety of government investigations into the topic. Since 1950, these debates have led to congressional investigations such as the Harris Subcommittee hearings of 1952, the Hendrickson-Kefauver Subcommittee hearings of 1954-1955, and the Dodd Senate Subcommittee hearings of 1961-1964. Major federal government commissions, including the National Commission on the Causes and Prevention of Violence (Baker & Ball, 1969), the Surgeon General's Scientific Advisory Committee on Television and Social Behavior (Rubinstein, Comstock, & Murray, 1972) and its 10-year follow-up (Pearl, Bouthilet, & Lazar, 1982), also issued reports. More recently, Senator Paul Simon of Illinois held hearings in Los Angeles in the summer of 1993 and in Washington in December of 1993 about the issue. Each of these investigations prompted considerable research; it is estimated that more than 3,000 studies since the 1950s have been conducted to study the effects of violence on audiences.

However, the causes of violence in American life are multiple. Most of us generally accept the notion that violent behavior is a complex problem formed of many influences. Racism, poverty, drug abuse, abusive family relationships, gangs, guns, mental illness, and the frustrations of poverty can all lead to violence and aggressive behavior. As psychologist Rowell Huesmann (1986) has argued, aggression is a syndrome, an enduring pattern of behavior that can persist from childhood through adulthood. Is media violence one of the contributory causes as well? What evidence is there for this position?

Clearly, a number of factors contribute to violence in American society; and although any one act of violence can be found to have a particular cause (let's say the aggressor was on drugs and incompetent to
judge his actions), it is the persistent fact of violence throughout our
society that has worried Americans. To ignore television, film, gangsta
rap, and other media violence would be a grave oversight.

For instance, violence tears across the television screen through
many types of programs, from music videos and entertainment shows
to reality programming and the evening news. By the time the average
American child graduates from elementary school, he or she will have
seen over 8,000 murders and more than 100,000 other assorted acts of
violence (Huston et al., 1992). In 1985, the American Psychological Association (APA) held that indeed television *can* cause viewers to act aggressively. More recently, in its overall review of television and behavior, the APA Task Force on Television and Society reaffirmed this view
and asserted that media violence can contribute to two other outcomes,
desensitization of viewers to violent actions and fear of being the victim
of violence (Huston et al., 1992).

Strong evidence from survey research consistently shows that
heavy viewers of violence on television are more likely to engage in
aggressive behavior than are light viewers. Moreover, viewers of violent television express more willingness to use violence to resolve real
interpersonal conflicts (Huston et al., 1992, p. 54). However, these correlational studies simply say that television violence viewing is *associated with* holding favorable attitudes toward the use of violence and
aggressive behavior. Such studies alone are not sufficient evidence that
media violence *causes* aggression. Furthermore, correlational evidence
does not provide evidence of the direction of the causal relationship. It
might be that people inclined to act violently are more likely to watch
television violence, and so it is their predisposition toward violence
that leads to viewing violent TV, and not the other way around.

The social learning studies with Bobo dolls described in Chapter 10
were designed laboratory experiments or field experimental studies. In
experiments, the direction of causality can be demonstrated. When the
hundreds of such laboratory studies are reviewed, in particular, those
involving children and adolescents, there is support for the claim that
viewing television violence "can lead to increases in aggressive attitudes, values, and behavior" (Huston et al., 1992, p. 55).

Perhaps the most compelling evidence comes from longitudinal, or panel studies, which study people repeatedly over time. One such longitudinal study examined children at age 8 and then restudied them again at ages 18 and 30. This study found a clear relationship between the amount of violence on television that children watched at age 8 with the aggressive behavior of these same youth at age 18, and the seriousness of criminal acts of these same people at age 30. According to the researcher, L. R. Huesmann (1986),

> Aggressive habits seem to be learned early in life, and once established, are resistant to change and predictive of serious adult antisocial behavior. If a child's observation of media violence promotes the learning of aggressive habits, it can have harmful lifelong consequences. Consistent with this theory, early television habits are in fact correlated with adult criminality. (pp. 129-130)

In addition, viewing television violence may cultivate or shape positive attitudes toward violence and may activate other aggressive thoughts. Leonard Berkowitz and his colleagues assert that many media effects are immediate, transitory and short-term. When people watch television violence, it activates or *primes* other semantically related thoughts that may influence how the person responds to the violence on television. Viewers who identify with an actor on television may imagine themselves acting like that character, carrying out the character's aggressive actions. Research evidence suggests that exposure to media aggression does indeed prime other aggressive thoughts, evaluations, and behaviors, such that viewers of violence report a greater willingness to use violence in interpersonal situations (Berkowitz, 1984). Furthermore, viewing television violence may lead to disinhibition of aggression—greater willingness to use violent means—among children and adults who are already predisposed to react to conflict in aggressive ways. In other words, viewing lots of violence leads people to ignore other factors in their everyday life that normally inhibit them from reacting violently. For example, the presence of adults in a room inhibits children from punching each other; the threat of having people catch you in the act keeps you from hitting your teacher or boss.

Media violence may also influence even those viewers who do not themselves behave violently or have positive attitudes toward using

302

violence, and in two different ways, desensitization and fear, or "scary world" effects.

Research has demonstrated that prolonged viewing of media violence can lead to emotional desensitization toward real world violence and the victims of violence, which in turn can lead to callous attitudes toward violence directed at others and a decreased likelihood to take action on behalf of the victim when violence occurs (Donnerstein, Slaby, & Eron, 1994).

Studies by George Gerbner and his colleagues (Gerbner, Gross, Morgan, & Signorielli, 1990) have demonstrated that heavy viewers of television violence become fearful of the world, afraid of becoming victims of violence, and over time, they engage in more self-protective behaviors and show more mistrust of others, an outcome sometimes known as the *scary world syndrome.* To the extent that viewers equate the fictional world of television, with its overrepresentation of violence, as the same as the real world they live in, heavy viewers tend to see their world as a fearful and crime-ridden place. It is likely that both fictional and reality programs (including crime-saturated television news) contribute to this fear-inducing influence on viewers of television.

Although there is strong agreement on these points, there is not unanimity. Yet, over several decades, various research reviews have overwhelmingly concluded that television violence is *a* cause of real world violence; it may not be *the* cause. And it cannot be dismissed as having no impact on the behavior of audiences. As we will highlight in Chapter 13, the evidence implicating media violence in the social problems associated with violence in the real world has led to the current television ratings system and the introduction of program-blocking devices for home television receivers.

THE INFLUENCE OF PORNOGRAPHY

Somewhat akin to the violence controversy has been the public and legal discussions of the influence of sexually explicit media materials on viewers and consumers of print and audiovisual media. As in the violence controversies, public debate about sexually explicit pictures and other media is long-standing and recurring. The Comstock laws, which prohibited the selling of sexually explicit materials (defined as what would offend the sensibility of a young girl), go back to the late 1800s. And throughout the twentieth century, many U.S. Supreme Court cases have tried to define what is "obscene" and therefore not protected by the First Amendment of the U.S. Constitution. Obscene materials can be regulated and their sale punished. The debate, however, is wider than over what is truly obscene—because the courts have punished only very graphic materials. Public concern includes other sexually explicit or pornographic[1] content as well, and much of the debate relies more on moral, religious, and ethical grounds than on social and scientific ones. Extensive study of the influences of such material on audiences has been undertaken.

Beginning in the 1970s, some feminist writers began to connect the distribution of pornographic materials to crimes against women in general—and to rape in particular. They assert that pornographic images turn women into objects and that users of pornography are more likely than nonusers to sexually abuse women. As Robin Morgan (1980), a feminist author, has said and written repeatedly, "Pornography is the theory, and rape the practice."

Much of the recent research on the behavioral effects of pornography has attempted to turn this assertion into researchable questions. Communication scholars Neil Malamuth and Edward Donnerstein (1984) and their colleagues have done a large number of studies on the behavioral effects of pornography. In a recent review of the psychological effects of television, a committee of the American Psychological Association summarized the research in this area on *adult* viewers by discussing the findings of the effects of various types of sexually explicit materials, types identified in the federally funded Report of the Meese Commission on Pornography of 1986.

- Erotica or sexually explicit materials (such as X- and R-rated films), which are not violent or degrading to women: "Current research," the APA report said, "indicates that there are no antisocial effects from exposure to such images" (Huston et al., 1992, p. 50).

- Nonviolent sexually explicit materials that are degrading to women: Typically available only on pay cable channels (such as the Playboy channel) and through video rental stores or catalog sales, these materials often show men with large sexual appetites raping women and depict women as the objects of uncontrollable male desires. Such images have not been shown to have a consistent effect on their viewers. "Some studies of long-term exposure have found negative effects on attitudes and perceptions about women for both male and female viewers . . . , whereas other studies (the majority) have found no effects," the APA report said (Huston et al., 1992, p. 50).

• Violent pornography, in which women are sexually assaulted and shown actually enjoying the violent encounter: Such material is typically only found in the video marketplace and is X-rated or unrated. This material has especially come under scrutiny. According to the APA review,

> Men exposed to this material can become sexually aroused, they report callused attitudes about rape, and in laboratory studies they increase their aggression against women. Current research indicates that these attitude and arousal patterns may have some relationship to real-world aggression against women. . . . Two issues are important, however. The first is that these effects seem to occur most readily in those who already have certain callused attitudes about rape. Second they can occur *without any sexual content* in the material. In other words, it is the violence or the message about violence that is important, not simply the sexual nature of the materials. (Huston et al., 1992, pp. 50-51)

• Nonexplicit sexual aggression against women: Such material includes a wide range of images including some on network television, which may simulate sex under the bed covers or show a rape scene in a "tasteful" way. Interestingly, exposure to such materials "sometimes reinforces antisocial attitudes about rape, particularly in individuals with preexisting callused rape-related attitudes," the APA report (Huston et al., 1992, p. 51) said.

• Sexualized violence against women: Seen in R-rated movies or videos, such material sometimes shows graphic violence against women but typically not rape (more often torture or murder). These materials may be found in video stores or on pay movie channels. According to some studies, heavy exposure to such materials may desensitize their viewers, whether men or women viewers, to the severity of rape and sexual violence. Viewers of such materials in one study were found to have reduced emotional reactions afterward toward the supposed victim of a violent rape.

In brief, the APA report (Huston et al., 1992) suggests that pornography absent violence generally does not induce antisocial effects, although it may reinforce antisocial attitudes among those who already have them. Sexualized violence, on the other hand, does seem to lead to antisocial effects.

MEDIA AND CHILDREN

The violence controversies have focused heavily on children who view film and television violence, as well as on those who read violent comic books. More recently, concerns have been raised about the sexually explicit nature of television programs, films, and music that children can access. These concerns about children, who have historically been one of the earliest segments of the mass audience to adopt and use any new medium—from film to radio and television to video games, videotapes, and the Internet—have led to ongoing studies of how media influence children's behavior.

Children are thought to be particularly susceptible to the power of the media. Why? Because of their naiveté and inexperience. Children are thought to have less information about the world and fewer defenses to resist the power of media images and persuasion. Indeed, the titles of books, especially about television and children, conjure up a fragile child, gullible, with eyes glued to the television screen and easily overwhelmed by the powerful mass medium.

Children are not born with the inherent abilities to make sense of the sorts of codes and genres, the messages, of most of the mass media, including television. Even though children are introduced very early to media (television, video, newspapers, books, and even magazines and movies as preschoolers), children's abilities to interpret those messages change steadily over the course of childhood. Not until the early teenage years do children's understandings of a given television message resemble adult interpretations. In short, children have to learn to make sense of television's codes and content. (See also Chapter 5.)

So, what do we know about the impact of such media? First, we know that children can learn new behaviors from watching television and movies. This has been demonstrated across a wide range of behaviors, both violent and more positive or prosocial behaviors (such as altruism or learning to share or help others, and self-control). Bandura's Bobo doll experiments, which we described earlier, are the classic example of such studies. We will consider children's learning in these domains: the effects of planned educational programming on children's learning of school-related knowledge and behaviors, children's learning about people and how they should behave, and children's learning about consumption.

The 1969 development of *Sesame Street* marks the standard of educational programming for children that incorporates a planned curriculum (teaching preschoolers about their numbers, letters, grammar) and is entertaining. The popularity of Jim Henson's Muppets, along with the quickly paced and cleverly written magazine format of this program, was immediate. *Sesame Street* is now available in at least 67 countries in the world; it has affiliated magazine and book series featuring the Muppets and live characters, and it has won every U.S. and international award for children's television. Over the years, *Sesame Street* has been shown to teach children of different social classes and both sexes the planned curriculum, such as their letters and numbers (Ball & Bogatz, 1970; Bogatz & Ball, 1972). A recent study demonstrates that regular viewers of *Sesame Street* learn new words and improve their vocabulary from such viewing (Rice, Huston, Truglio, & Wright, 1990; Wright & Huston, 1995).

Since the success of *Sesame Street*, other planned educational programs, such as *Where in the World is Carmen Sandiego, Bill Nye the Science Guy, Square One Television, Reading Rainbow, Gullah Gullah's Island, Blues Clues,* and *The Magic School Bus,* have been found both to increase children's interest in the educational content of programs and to teach some of the planned curriculum. In addition, other children's shows, which focus less on teaching cognitive skills but more on such positive behaviors as helping others and sharing toys, can be successful. The most important evidence here comes from a study of preschool children's effective learning of such helping or prosocial behaviors from watching *Mister Rogers' Neighborhood*. Furthermore, recent evidence is that preschool viewing of planned educational shows has a long-term positive influence on children's overall educational attainment, However, the entire nature of the relationship between television and school performance is not wholly clear (see Huston et al., 1992).

Does watching television throughout the grade school years help children in school? Does it depend on both the type of programs the children view and the amount of time they spend watching? The evidence is mixed. There is no clear relationship between amount of television viewed during the grade school years and such school achievement measures as reading ability, scores on achievement tests, and so on (Huston et al., 1992). A major national study of the effects of *Channel One*'s 10-minute daily news broadcast demonstrated relatively little student learning about public affairs. The argument the researchers made was that Whittle's program may be high on entertainment values (fast pace, short segments) but not attentive enough to those production characteristics that aid the student's learning from the programs (Johnston, 1995). In fact, it is probably not reasonable to expect a strong relationship between television viewing overall and children's school performance. The relationship depends on which programs children watch and what other activities in their life reinforce television and other media use.

But children do learn other sorts of information and expectations about people and places from watching television and using other media. Many have described television for young children as "a magic window" on the world, which brings into the child's home an array of people and places not part of the child's everyday experience. Children learn about how fathers, mothers, and families are to behave from watching television; they also build up expectation of African Americans and other races and ethnic groups, as well as information about the world outside of their experience. Television can be a powerful teacher (Liebert & Sprafkin, 1988).

One part of everyday life children learn about from TV is the world of advertised products, for television aggressively advertises to children. Kids are an attractive audience, because they spend an estimated $15 billion a year on their own and influence an additional $160 billion spent by their parents (Hamilton, 1997). Since the 1970s, analyses of the products advertised to children on television has shown that the majority of advertising during children's programs is for food products (one half of all these ads are for cereals, candy, snack food, and fast-food restaurants—that is, mostly for products high in sugar and fat). After food products, toys make up the second largest category. And these

BOX 11.1

Television's Forms

Television as a communicative medium has certain characteristic visual and auditory production and editing techniques. In a series of experimental studies, Huston, Wright, Rice, and their colleagues have examined the impact of the forms of television on children's attention to and learning from television.

The use of slow motion, cuts, pans, zooms, pacing, dialogue, auditory distortion, and animation are production techniques used in television, and researchers describe these as forms, or formal features. These forms influence both what is communicated and how child viewers interpret messages communicated.

Two kinds of forms can be distinguished: *perceptually salient* forms and *reflective forms.* Perceptally salient forms are those that have their greatest impact in drawing children's attention to the television set when they are not watching but *are* in the room with a set on. Perceptually salient forms include such television production techniques as fast pacing, strange voices, and high levels of visual and auditory special effects—such as distortions of visuals or voices. Reflective forms, on the other hand, include such production techniques as zooms, singing, and moderate levels of action. They are called reflective forms because they are thought to encourage repetition and elaboration of the program content.

According to this research, perceptually salient and reflective forms are associated with different kinds of programs on television. Moreover, they influence children's learning from the programs in different ways. For instance, researchers found that many of the perceptually salient forms, in particular the fast pacing, high-action formal features, are associated with many of the Saturday morning children's cartoon shows. In contrast, educational television shows, such as *Mister Rogers' Neighborhood* and *Sesame Street,* are more likely to use a lot of reflective forms. They have also found that the more reflective forms, in particular, high amounts of dialogue and slower pacing, are associated with children's learning from the content. Perceptually salient production techniques seem to be good at bringing children's attention to the set when they aren't watching, as both educational programmers and advertisers have learned.

SOURCE: Rice, Huston, and Wright, 1982.

commercials tend to rely on animation, fast pace, and repetition of the product's name. According to the APA report (Huston et al., 1992),

Objective information about the product is scarce in advertisements. Instead, commercials rely on verbal assertions about the subjective qualities of the product (e.g., "it's delicious") and descriptions of the physical components of the product (8% by weight). Advertisements to children stress such food qualities as taste, texture, appearance, fun associations, and accompanying prizes as reasons for choosing foods. Nutritional information is usually brief or nonexistent. Products are sometimes lauded for making the consumer strong, but "being good for you" is rarely stressed. In fact, advertisements often imply that a healthy food is unpalatable by saying it tastes great despite the fact that it is healthy. (p. 72)

And what do we know about the effects of such advertising?[2] First, children only gradually come to understand that commercials are trying to sell something. That is, below the age of about 5 or 6, the majority of children do not understand the *persuasive intent* of advertisements and hence cannot criticize the advertiser's motives. Even older children, those under the age of 12, have not yet mastered a full and wary understanding of advertising and the nature of persuasive appeals. However, advertising's appeal to children declines as they grow older and become more mature, wary, and experienced viewers of such advertising, having bought products advertised and been disappointed with them.

Advertising does influence children's requests to parents for advertised products, and the more advertising children watch, the more they tend to request such products. There is some evidence that such product requests can lead to parent-child conflict. There is, however, little evidence that watching lots of advertising teaches children generally about the world of the consumer (what's known as consumer socialization), saving as well as spending, or a range of what are considered useful consumer practices such as comparison shopping. In summary, advertising can be successful with children, and its success is higher with younger rather than older children.

Evidence of advertising's influence on young children, coupled with a belief that young children are not an appropriate audience for advertising messages, led to passage of the 1990 Children's Television Education Act. One part of this federal law limits the amount of advertising during children's programs to 10 minutes per hour on weekends and 12 minutes per hour on weekdays.

Television is still the medium that most children spend the most time with. Considerable evidence indicates that television can teach a wide range of information, attitudes, expectations, and behaviors to child viewers. The concern is not whether television *can* teach children things, but rather what it *is* teaching them.

INFORMATION CAMPAIGNS

If you have ever been involved in an organization trying to raise funds or recruit new members, you know that a considerable share of the resources of any group are given to publicity, to spreading information about the group to the community to inform people that the group exists. What effect can information campaigns have on people? Can media campaigns succeed in influencing people's attitudes, beliefs, and behavior?

For much of the past 50 years, communication scholars have thought—erroneously we might add—that mass media are only marginally successful in informing the public and in changing behavior. Two very influential articles, Hyman and Sheatsley's 1947 review, titled "Some Reasons Why Information Campaigns Fail," and Star and Hughes's (1950) report of the failure of an information campaign about the United Nations in Cincinnati, Ohio, have often been cited as evidence that mass media alone cannot affect people's knowledge about new events or products, or their attitudes or behavior. Indeed, the results of these two studies stuck with us a long time. Only since the late 1970s has evidence been amassing of the success of well-constructed information campaigns in actually affecting their audiences' behavior. It's now commonly thought that well-constructed information campaigns can be successful.

Since the 1970s, a variety of media campaigns have specifically aimed at promoting health issues, such as campaigns encouraging the use of seat belts, promoting heart-healthy lifestyles, informing people about the causes and prevention of cancer, and disseminating information about consequences of smoking, alcohol use, and illegal drug use. Dozens of health information campaigns have been evaluated over this time and shown to be successful.

A *communication campaign* is a set of communication activities that is purposive, with specific intended outcomes, that is aimed at a large audience, and that typically has a specified time limit. Rogers and Sto-

311

BOX 11.2

The Campaign for a Drug Free America

In the mid-1980s, a volunteer coalition of members of the advertising community created the Partnership for a Drug Free America. The goal of the Partnership was to create and distribute antidrug advertisements (done without charge by members of the advertising community and broadcast free as Public Service Announcements or PSAs on radio and television stations as well as printed in newspapers and magazines) as part of national efforts to reduce the sale of and use of illegal drugs, particularly marijuana, cocaine, and crack.

Perhaps the best-known advertisement of the Partnership is the "This is your brain on drugs" spot showing an egg sizzling in a frying pan. All in all, by the end of the 1980s, the Partnership advertising campaign was ranked as the 11th largest campaign (in terms of overall media coverage) in U.S. history.

The specific aims of the Partnership campaign are to decrease acceptance of drug use, increase social disapproval of use, increase awareness of the risks associated with illegal drug use, and, over time, decrease the use of and demand for illegal drugs. In 1987, Gordon S. Black Associates set about to study the impact of this campaign in getting its message across. A first wave of studies, called baseline studies, was conducted in 1987 to see what initial knowledge of drug use existed in the population of adolescents, college students, and adults, as well as their attitudes toward drugs and their use of illegal drugs. Then in 1988, follow-up surveys were conducted to see if the Partnership ad campaign produced any changes in the initial (or baseline) knowledge about, attitudes toward, and use of illegal drugs. More than 8,000 people were interviewed in each wave.

The findings suggested that indeed the Partnership campaign was having some effect: Between the first and second waves of data collection, many of the attitudes and orientations toward illegal drug use had become "distinctly more antagonistic toward drug use. The changes are most pronounced in the college sample, followed by children (ages 9-12), and somewhat less, but important, change among the adult and teenagers" (p. 175). The greatest changes in attitudes and orientations were found in those communities with the highest exposure to the Partnership ad campaign, suggesting that indeed the ad campaign was having an effect on people's attitudes toward, and beliefs about, drug use.

SOURCE: Black, 1991.

---

rey (1987) use this definition in their review of dozens of such campaign evaluation studies. They argue that for information campaigns to be successful, they should follow several rules:

1. Adopt a strategic approach to the information campaign that involves considerable formative research, that is, research on the intended audience and how they already perceive the topic of the information campaign.
2. Design and target the media messages to the intended audiences (what's known in market research as market segmentation).
3. Set realistic goals for the campaign—decide whether providing more knowledge about a topic, such as knowledge of how one can contract the HIV virus, or getting people to change their behavior, such as getting men to use condoms—is the goal of the campaign.
4. Finally, media campaigns have been most successful when they are complementary to community-based or more interpersonal intervention efforts, as when newspaper and television messages are coupled with getting local health care workers to provide information as well.

Since the 1970s, research on campaigns such as those to encourage people to stop smoking or use seat belts and to inform them about HIV/AIDS suggests that well-formulated, persuasive campaigns rooted in strong theoretical formulations of how to accomplish attitude and behavior change offer the greatest likelihood of success. And these in turn must adequately "target" or design their messages for a particular group or segment of the population. (See Rice & Atkin, 1994; Rogers & Storey, 1987).

The history of media research on information campaigns suggests that media power and influence is often counterbalanced by audiences who resist, reformulate, and selectively retain media messages. Media campaign designers must hold realistic expectations about the goals of a media information campaign. For instance, expecting a media campaign to increase awareness and knowledge about the health risks associated with a high cholesterol diet may be a very realistic goal. However, expecting a media campaign alone to bring about direct and massive behavior change to low cholesterol diets among the entire population is unrealistic; to accomplish that would doubtless require additional intervention, most likely of an interpersonal nature.

The nature and types of impact that the media have are an immensely important policy question. We *care* about what the media may do to people because public behavior is a significant policy question: None of us wishes to live in a cruel, violent, or lawless society.

To argue that a television depiction is corrosive of public values, to suggest that media portrayals promote violence or that listening to pop music can sanction suicide, is an opening argument for regulating or suppressing of media content: It suggests that we can solve the problem by rooting out the offending material. To this, we would offer several observations.

Our review should suggest that the media may have many different impacts on public behavior. At the same time, several generations of research on the impact of the media suggest that it is quite difficult to be specific about the effect of any content, indeed any *class* of content on its audience. The same content, indeed, may have different effects on different segments of the audience. Moreover, by its very nature, most social science research must be highly qualified about its findings: It is very difficult to speak definitively about media impact.

Our discussion of causation has, we hope, made it clear that most behaviors have multiple causes; television alone, or recorded music, or movies, or newspapers, or all the media together, are rarely if ever a necessary and sufficient cause of public behavior; they operate in a larger social system that itself mediates most social behavior. Thus, the argument for media regulation usually ignores covariates that should not be ignored. In other words, it is likely that regulation of content would not alleviate most social problems. On the other hand, media factors may be the contributors that are the *easiest* to alleviate—certainly easier than eliminating poverty or abusive family relationships—and therefore cannot be ignored.

We are not saying, however, that society is helpless to make arguments about the impact of mass media, either pro or con. What we are saying is that the research record indicates caution. Arguments about media impact should be made, but we must recognize that the moral and cultural content of such arguments—what is good, desirable, and appropriate—should predominate. The effects research carries us only part of the way to their answers. Chapter 13 returns to the moral, ethical, and cultural context, or normative theory and media regulation.

NOTES

1. In other words, *obscenity* is material with sexual content that is legally prohibited, whereas pornography is a broader category, including legal and illegal material. What is obscene is decided by courts, whereas what is pornographic is open to public debate.

2. For supporting details, please see Ward, Wackman, and Wartella, 1977, *How Children Learn to Buy.*

PART IV

Media and Public Life

Media and Politics

Our next three chapters discuss the media and public life. There are big issues here: How do the media represent public life— how do they cover it as news, and what views of political reality predominate in such coverage? What role do the media have in political behavior, and how can we best describe the relationships between the public and media? In dealing with these, we will try to connect the answers to perspectives we have introduced earlier: seeing media and politics, media and public life, is best accomplished through multiple lenses, those of historical narrative, ideological frame, and studies of behavior.

A beginning point in this discussion must be a distinction; in the explicitly political realm, we will concern ourselves largely with media representations of reality. As we explain below, the principal influence of the media on public life is through the ways media present information—and the contexts within which they present it—how, in short, they treat the "real world," and how we, in turn, react to those presentations.

There are significant differences between the ways various media sectors approach reality: The news and information media attempt to represent it. Advertising and public relations practitioners try to focus attention on those aspects of reality that further their clients' interests. And producers of entertainment may use the "real world" as a source of raw material for fictional content, and, as we noted in Chapter 6, are usually bound by requirements of verisimilitude.

NEWS AND REALITY

From a contemporary vantage point, we couple the goal and purpose of journalism—the news and information function—with an attempt to represent political reality. Thus, we begin there, approaching news in three ways—through a quick history of the evolution of news as an idea, through a discussion of how news might be defined, and by returning to the question of how news gets made.

A THUMBNAIL HISTORY OF NEWS

Journalism historian Mitchell Stephens (1988) argues that it is impossible to find any society, past or present, without a "thirst for news." The members of all human societies in any historical epoch are marked by a "need to know" what is going on around them. But as Stephens, and virtually any other media historian will also tell us, *how* each society satisfies this need varies drastically. In "primitive" societies, everyone is a journalist, keeping up on what's happening through oral communication. Stephens observes that news in preliterate cultures could travel over great distances with breathtaking speed, as gossip can, even today. In such cultures, however, it is not wholly correct that everyone is his or her own journalist, for virtually every known culture has evolved "news specialists"—criers, drummers, messengers, and minstrels. Interestingly, these bearers of news are almost always adjuncts of commercial or political power: They carry news along trade routes or are the servants of the king or chief.

Over time and across cultures, societies vary in how they conceive of, gather, and disseminate news, and, as we note below, how news is gathered and disseminated is deeply related to how it is defined.

From the American colonial period through the first third of the twentieth century, newspapers were the principal means of news deliv-

BOX 12.1

Old News, New News

Below are the first few paragraphs from two front-page New York newspaper stories (we have modernized the orthography and spelling of the 1734 story):

The New York Weekly Journal

New Brunswick (NJ), March 27, 1734. (By) Mr. (John Peter) Zenger——I was at a public house some days since in company with some persons that came from New York; most of them complained of the deadness of trade. Some of them laid it to the account of the repeal of the Tonnage Act, which they said was done to gratify the resentment of some in New York in order to distress Governor Burnet, but which has been almost the ruin of that town, by paying the Bermudians about 12,000 pounds a year to export their commodities which might be carried in their own bottoms, and the money arising by the freight spent in New York.

They said that the Bermudians were an industrious frugal people, who bought no one thing in New York, but lodged the whole freight money in their own island, by which means, since the repeal of that Act, there has been taken from New York above 90,000 pounds and all this to gratify pique and resentment.

But this is not all; this money being carried away, which would otherwise have circulated in this province and city, and have been paid to the baker, the brewer, the smith, the carpenter, the shipwright, the boatman, the farmer, the shopkeeper, etc., has deadened our trade in all its branches and forced our industrious poor to seek other habitations, so that within these three years there has been above 300 persons have left New York; the houses stand empty, and there is as many houses as would make one whole street with bills upon their doors. And this has been as great a hurt as the carrying away the money and is occasioned by it, and all degrees of men feel it, from the merchant down to the carman. . . .

(continued)

ery for the nation. The newspapers of the early period in American history were quite different from today.

321

The New York Times By Serge Schmemann

JERUSALEM, Sept. 28 (1997)——Israeli and Palestinian leaders said today that they expected their meeting with Secretary of State Madeline K. Albright in New York on Monday would lead to the revival of long-stalled committee talks on such issues as the release of Palestinian prisoners and an airport in Gaza.

But both Israelis and Palestinians have cautioned against expecting that the new contracts would lead to a resumption of substantive talks on advancing the peace.

The meeting scheduled for Monday was preceded by several conciliatory gestures from both sides. Today, Prime Minister Benjamin Netanyahu told his Cabinet that he had spotted the "first, preliminary steps" by the Palestinian Authority to crack down on Islamic terror groups, which the Prime Minister has set as the condition for continuing the diplomatic process.

Mr. Netanyahu, who predicted that the Monday meeting would lead to the resumption of committee talks, also announced that he was releasing $17 million more of the tax money his Government has withheld from the Palestinians since a suicide bombing in July. . . .

If you find the 1734 story hard to follow, what *we* take it to say is that the correspondent is complaining that Governor Burnet's repeal of a trade act has led the city into a recession; this story was one of two that prompted the colonial government to bring seditious libel charges against Zenger; see Chapter 3.

The similarities and differences in these stories are worth comment. Both are political stories. Both rely on unnamed sources (Zenger appears to use anonymous sources to protect them from retribution; the *Times* story, because the names of the sources are incidental—although on other occasions the *Times* and most other contemporary newspapers *do* use anonymous sources for the same reason Zenger did).

The dissimilarities, however, are more striking. Note first that the 1997 *Times* story reports events that occurred the previous day. The 1734 *Journal* article report was written almost two weeks earlier. The delay in publication reflects the time it took to get the report back to New York and the fact that the newspaper appeared but weekly. An important stylistic difference is that the *Journal* article is written in the first person (*I* was at a public house. . . .), whereas the *Times* article is in the third person. Moreover, the 1734 article is discursive, with its information in no apparent particular order, whereas the 1997 article is in the inverted pyramid news form, with the most important information first, and information later presented in decreasing order of importance. But probably the most significant difference is in *point of view:* Zenger clearly is offering his own opinions, whereas Schmemann of the *Times* writes a descriptive account, and the first few paragraphs offer virtually no opinions (later in the story, there were statements of opinion, but they were offered by government sources, not by the writer).

Access to information was limited in two pivotal ways: the audience had limited access to newspapers, and newspapers had limited access to information. Early newspapers were expensive, beyond the reach of the average American. In the late 1700s, too, literacy rates were low, and much of the population lived on farms or in small towns. Because long-distance communication was slow, costly, and hazardous, news in early newspapers consisted of local stories, most usually written by the editor (who frequently doubled as the newspaper's publisher), texts of political addresses and proclamations and laws, clippings of stories from papers in other cities with whom the editor exchanged papers, and commercial notices. The most important of these—the most timely—were notices of the availability of goods on ships docking in the harbor or river. The bulk of the news in each paper concerned commerce, trade, and politics—the important concerns of the elites that read the newspapers. Each important town had multiple newspapers, and newspapers differentiated themselves mostly in terms of the "faction" or political party they represented. As the example in Box 12.1 suggests, the division between news and opinion—news on the front pages, opinion on editorial pages—that we now take for granted, was nonexistent. News *was* opinion, with facts selected to buttress the point of view of the editor and his political and commercial benefactors. Moreover, papers were small in size (typically four to eight pages), circulation (in the hundreds of copies, except in the largest cities), and staff: a "typical" newspaper about 1800 might have an editor-publisher-printer and one or two other employees to help him print and distribute copies of the paper; distribution was largely local.[1]

As we noted in Chapter 4, a variety of factors in the middle half of the nineteenth century transformed the newspaper from a "class" to a "mass" medium: increasing literacy of the population, a technological revolution that enabled the rapid and cheap production of thousands of copies of papers, the emergence of mass advertising to supplement the economic support of the medium, and increasingly rapid modes of transportation that enlarged the potential distribution area of newspapers.[2] Transformation to a mass medium was also accompanied by a gradual evolution in what news was—what was considered to be news and how news was gathered and produced.

Until roughly the end of the first quarter of the nineteenth century, news was largely commercial notices, transcripts, political dispatches, and essays. The evolution of the mass news press for the rest of the century was toward something more modern. The content of American newspapers slowly became "democratic," popular, fast, and "objective".[3]

More democratic: To say that the press became more democratic is to say that for both ideological and commercial reasons, the press first geared itself toward producing news that attracted and represented the tastes and interests of a wider, generally less elite audience, and second, actively promoted a post-Revolutionary ideology of democracy and interest of the common people over those of wealth and privilege. Sociologist Herbert Gans (1979) has noted that the press even today promotes a value he calls *altruistic democracy*: briefly, that popular democracy is *the* valued form of government, and individuals (and the press) have responsibilities for, and the right to, preserve and extend it.

More oriented toward the popular: We've noted that newspapers evolved from a class to a mass medium. This evolution was in both audience and content. The content became less focused on politics and more on crime, human interest, and sensational content (this is not to say that sensationalism in the press was new; journalism historian Mitchell Stephens (1988) finds it in the ancient Greek, Roman, and Chinese precursors to newspapers. The important point, however, is that newspapers began to compete for a mass audience on the basis of the popularity and attractiveness of their content.

More event-centered and timely: News becomes more timely as news-gathering technologies allow for this to happen. We noted above that a 1734 newspaper features a "lead story" by John Peter Zenger that is more than a week old, whereas "modern" newspapers tell what happened yesterday. Two years stand out as pivotal in accelerating the speed at which news is delivered: the first American telegraphed news item (announcing the Whig presidential ticket) in 1844, and the 1963 launch of the Telstar communications satellite. As we noted in Chapter 2, the telegraph for the first time separated time from space, information from transportation. News could be known virtually instantaneously anywhere there were telegraph wires. Communications satellites allow for instantaneous transmission of visual images anywhere on earth.[4] In part, the technologies help account for why news becomes event-centered rather than discursive: A reporter on the scene of an event "covers" that event and transmits a report to a newsroom, rather than digesting it and other events for later writing. And media compete with each other to bring the latest news to audiences first.

More "objective" and less partisan: Whereas early American big-city newspapers were largely the creatures of parties and interest groups bent on promoting their own point of view, modern mass news purveyors—newspapers, television networks, and news radio largely deal in "objective" news. By objective, we mean two things: first, that media become more neutral, less likely to take political positions on their own, and second, that *news* itself becomes less politically colored. In other words, news becomes "facts," whereas opinions and values, when expressed in media, are labeled and compartmentalized as commentary, editorials, and news analyses.

Media historian Donald L. Shaw (1967) has written that the development of the first great American telegraph wire service, the Associated Press (AP), is in large part responsible for news's becoming less partisan and more objective after 1848. Serving varied newspapers with varied political allegiances required the AP to develop a news style that would be acceptable to all, and this led to an objective, "just-the-facts-ma'am"[5] AP news style that in time came to be imitated by newspapers and later, other news media.[6] The notion of objectivity was important not just to the development of journalism, but also to other professions and especially to science (Schudson, 1978). The early twentieth century saw what historians call the Progressive Era, an era of popular reform, in which many writers and thinkers popularized and glorified science, *scientific management* (the rise of efficiency experts), and the importance of the expert.

NEWS TODAY

To describe what news is today requires us to do two things. First is, finally, to *define* what we mean by news, anyway. Second is to describe how news is made.

325

BOX 12.2

Coming Into Their Own

The *New York Times* has described "defining moments" for various news media, times when a medium "came into its own" as a purveyor of news. Their defining moments include the following:

Newspapers: April 13, 1861

Newspaper circulation shoots up during the Civil War, beginning with the siege of Fort Sumter in Charleston Harbor. The *New York Herald*'s readership grows from 77,000 in 1860 to 107,520 the day after Fort Sumter is attacked.

Radio: December 8, 1941

Sixty million people tune into President Franklin D. Roosevelt's address asking Congress to declare war on Japan the day after the bombing of Pearl Harbor.

Network television: November 22, 1963

CBS, NBC, and ABC drop regular programming to broadcast news the day President John F. Kennedy is assassinated. From 4 p.m. until 11 p.m., more than half of America's 51.6 million homes with television tune into these broadcasts.

Cable television: January 17, 1991

When the United States and its allies bomb Baghdad in the Persian Gulf war, CNN, with Peter Arnett filing reports from the Iraqi capital, reaches a record audience for a cable network, with 12.9 million households (a 22.7 Neilsen rating) tuning into the network.

The Internet: July 4, 1997

The National Aeronautics and Space Administration (NASA) reports 45 million "hits" on its website and mirror sites in the week following the landing of its Mars Pathfinder robot explorer.

SOURCES: *New York Times*, July 14, 1997 (national edition), pp. C1, C5, citing Frank Luther Mott's (1941/1962) *American Journalism*, NASA, CNN, and the A. C. Neilsen Co.

Defining News

The *Webster's New World Dictionary* defines news as "1. New information about anything; information previously unknown. 2. Recent happenings, especially those broadcast over the radio, printed in a newspaper, etc. 3. reports of such events, collectively." A widely used news reporting textbook adds two other definitions: "News is information about a break from the normal flow of events, an interruption in the expected," and "News is information people need in order to make rational decisions about their lives" (Mencher, 1984, p. 72).

Defining news is also asking what makes something newsworthy or worth reporting to audiences. Following a reporting textbook tradition, author Melvin Mencher, a former reporter and longtime professor at the Columbia University Graduate School of Journalism, lists seven factors that determine the newsworthiness of a potential story:

1. *Impact*: The significance, importance, or consequence of an event or trend; the greater the consequence, and the larger the number of people for whom an event is important, the greater the newsworthiness.
2. *Timeliness:* The more recent, the more newsworthy. In some cases, timeliness is relative. An event may have occurred in the past but only have been learned about recently.
3. *Prominence:* Occurrences featuring well-known individuals or institutions are newsworthy. Well-knownness may spring either from the power the person or institution possesses—the president, the Speaker of the House of Representatives—or from celebrity—the late Princess Diana or fashion designer Gianni Versace.
4. *Proximity:* Closeness of the occurrence to the audience may be gauged either geographically—close by events, all other things being equal, are more important than distant ones—or in terms of the assumed values, interests, and expectations of the news audience.
5. *The Bizarre*: The unusual, unorthodox, or unexpected attracts attention. Boxer Mike Tyson's 1997 disqualification for biting off a piece of Evander Holyfield's ear moves the story from the sports pages and the end of a newscast to the front pages and the top of the newscast.
6. *Conflict:* Controversy and open clashes are newsworthy, inviting attention on their own, almost regardless of what the conflict is over. Conflict reveals underlying causes of disagreement between individuals and institutions in a society.
7. *Currency:* Occasionally, as we noted concerning child abuse in Chapter 6, something becomes an idea whose time has come.

The matter assumes a life of its own, and for a time assumes momentum in news reportage.

Other textbooks add "human interest" as another dimension, although one can argue that it figures in Mencher's proximity, prominence, the bizarre, and currency categories.

Presumably, the more categories or dimensions any potential news story fits into, the more newsworthy it is. Years ago, journalism folklore suggests, a British journalist was asked for a definition of news, and he replied using a similar categories approach. News, he said, is anything with mystery or sex or religion or the Royal Family. "I guess that would mean," he quipped, "that the most newsworthy story in the world would begin, 'Oh my God, the Queen's pregnant. I wonder who did it?' "

Making News

A *second* approach to defining news begins by noting that many journalists and communication researchers have discovered that reporters and editors have a hard time defining news for themselves— news is just something "they know when they see it." A reporter might say, "I can't really define it, but tell me a story, and I'll tell you if it's news." Communication researcher John Dimmick (1974) once performed a very elaborate experiment, asking working reporters and editors to tell him how newsworthy a group of stories—ones he had constructed using categories or dimensions of news approach like the one above, and then statistically analyzed the journalists' answers. What he found, using the powerful statistical approach of factor analysis, was that no categories really explained how the journalists selected the stories they did. "A possible interpretation, of course," he wrote, "is that for the newsmen-subjects, the single dimension is 'news'" (p. 35).

So perhaps the way to figure out what news is to describe what journalists *do* to make news. In other words, we describe the structure and process by which news gets made. Sociologist Gaye Tuchman (1973) began doing research in newsrooms by asking journalists to define news. She got puzzled "I don't know" looks from reporters and editors. And so she took a slightly different approach, which was to ask how reporters worked on stories. When she did so, she found that journalists tended to classify stories into a relatively small number of categories—"hard" and "soft" news—that is, "breaking" stories about current events and feature stories that were less time-bound. Moreover, hard-news stories were further subdivided into "spot" stories—news that develops unexpectedly and quickly (a fire or a plane crash); "developing" stories, or spot-news stories that continue to develop over time, requiring follow-up stories; and "continuing" stories, or stories known about in advance, which, like developing stories, require a news organization to devote a reporter to the story for an extended period (a trial, a presidential candidate's campaign tour). An interesting feature of this classification system is that not only does it describe the way journalists think about their work, it also describes the way the news organization itself can organize reporters to cover the news: Some reporters can be assigned in advance to cover developing and continuing stories; others can be shifted around to cover the spot stories that develop without warning; and when there's time, the news organization can have reporters spend time on "soft" news or feature stories. Tuchman calls this "routinizing the unexpected."

Because news is "new information," it very much is, as Tuchman and many, many others note, "unexpected." But as Tuchman notes, journalists' conceptions of what news is and how it's covered also clue us in to the way news becomes routinized, or made predictable (sort of). Only a fraction of the news stories in any newspaper and in any newscast are unanticipated events that "break" without warning. The rest can be predicted in advance. News is made predictable by several structures and processes; together, they help answer the question: where does news come from, and who gets to make it?

First, consider individual news stories, and who gets to make them. There are essentially three origins for stories:

> Naturally occurring "events" such as disasters, floods, earthquakes, fires, and airline crashes are inherently unpredictable, and journalists must respond after the fact. News stories about disasters follow a predictable pattern: early reports, which frequently overestimate the severity of the disaster, rely on everyday people, because they're frequently the only witnesses; later stories, assuming the story is newsworthy enough to become developing news over several days, tend to rely on officials—mayors and governors, insurance company repre-

sentatives, disaster relief agency officials, and the like—
another way that news becomes routinized.[7]

Created and "subsidized" news is more frequent than unpredicted news. It occurs because a person, group, or organization either does something public and newsworthy (e.g., files
an important lawsuit, passes a law, breaks a law, opens or
closes a plant) and/or seeks and gets press attention. We will
discuss both these in a bit more detail below.

"Enterprise" news is made when journalists act rather than react,
as they do to accidents and disasters. This is so-called enterprise news, in which an editor or reporter takes the initiative
on a story. There are two main cases: beat coverage and investi-
gative journalism. We will discuss both in a bit more detail below.

In two of our three types, news doesn't "just happen" but rather it
is made. Billions of events occur daily, and only a tiny fraction of them
can become news. Tuchman (1978) uses the metaphor of a "news net."
Not knowing in advance exactly where news might come from, journalists strategically organize themselves to be in places where news is
most likely to happen, hoping to catch news in their net. Coping with
too much potential news is too costly, not only in terms of money but
in psychic costs as well. Walter Lippmann (1922) observed long ago that
without perceptual filters and routines to winnow through a mass of
potential news, journalists would "die of excitement" (p. 222). Much
journalistic work, particularly on newspapers, magazines, and network television, is organized around a beat system; that is, reporters are
assigned to a particular topic or specialty—city government, the police
and courts, the White House. Most beats are *geographic*—reporters
cover places and the people who occupy them and make news there
(science, environment, medicine, the arts are exceptions)—and that
most of these places are official. In fact, several content analyses of the
news show that two thirds to three quarters of all sources quoted in the
news are public officials (Brown, Bybee, Wearden, & Straughan, 1987;
Gans, 1979; Whitney, Fritzler, Jones, Mazzarella, & Rakow, 1989). In
part, officials "make news" because they do newsworthy things, and in
part, they make news simply because journalists are known, familiar,

and accessible to them, and vice versa (see also Chapter 3). By extension, nonofficials are relatively *dis*advantaged in their ability to make news; they have to work harder to capture journalists' attention, or they fall between the holes in the news net. Furthermore, official news, because of its familiarity to reporters and editors, starts off with a presumption that it is legitimate—it's news because that's the way news is.

There is one major potential problem for journalists who spend much of their time covering public officials. Journalists fear "going native": that is, there's a risk of journalists adopting the goals and values of the people they cover, rather than keeping an objective distance. Sociologist Mark Fishman (1980) noted that journalists who cover officials virtually inevitably also frame their news stories according to what he calls the "bureaucratic phase structures" of the organizations they cover. That is, the organization's routine decides for them when something is news. Think, for example, about crime stories: When do we get news about crime, and where does information in the story really come from? Virtually all crime stories are about the commission of a crime (police report) and when a person is arrested (arrest report), charged with the crime (arraignment), brought to trial, convicted or acquitted, and, if convicted, sentenced. In other words, news is organized in exactly the same way as the criminal justice system "organizes" crime. And because it is organized that way and follows the same routines, the coverage tends to assume or take for granted the official organizational ideology.

It is, however, possible that anyone can "make news." As we noted above, public officials are relatively advantaged in making news, and others are less so. Recall our discussion of resource dependence in Chapter 3: Journalists want access to news and can offer publicity; potential news sources often have information that, if known, would be newsworthy, and they may want several different things. Public officials may want to inform the public about new programs. They may be engaged in conflict with other officials (a Republican president versus a Democratic congress, a state senator who wants to increase the income tax versus a governor who does not) or others in the public and may want publicity for "their side" of the issue. Social action groups likewise want to promote their side of an issue and seek press attention as well.

In a classic study of the *New York Times* and *Washington Post*, researcher Leon Sigal (1973) discovered that about two thirds of stories in those papers originated from news releases, handouts, and documents provided by news sources to reporters; in other words, the initiative for the story was with the source, rather than the reporter. Potential sources who go to the trouble of providing information to journalists in a form they can use with relatively little reportorial "legwork" or in-house editing work of their own will have greater success in making news than others. The past few years have seen the development by large corporations and public relations agencies of *video news releases*, VCR cassettes and satellite links provided directly to stations; particularly in smaller TV markets, stations have frequently aired such news releases without acknowledging their sources. Communication researcher Oscar Gandy (1982) refers to such tactics as *information subsidies*. Clearly, the ability to shape news this way favors groups that are already advantaged—companies and organizations able to do skilled public relations or to hire others to do it for them.

But anyone who has ever visited any newsroom knows that for every news release used, dozens of others end up in the wastebasket. What makes the difference? Several things do, and each of them also applies to making news more generally.

Timing is important. It's better to have information arriving in newsrooms at slack times—at the beginning of the cycle (as editors get started on the day) and especially on weekends; on weekends, there's less official news to cover. It's also better to focus on topics of current interest (recall that Mencher mentioned currency as a news value).

Those who angle news toward satisfying one or more of those values are more successful at making news than are others. Sociologist Herb Gans (1979) has argued that for "ordinary people" to attract the attention of the news media, they frequently have either to demonstrate or resort to violence (the conflict value) or engage in odd or unusual activities (the bizarre value). And media scholar Todd Gitlin (1980) has suggested that this can have the impact of altering a social movement that is trying to attract the public's attention through the media. Gitlin argues that the Students for Democratic Society (SDS) evolved in the 1960s from being a left-liberal mainstream social action group to a radical and violent one because media accounts of its activities focused on one aspect of its work—demonstrations against the Vietnam War—rather than its full agenda of civil rights and antipoverty work. Media coverage attracted to the SDS antiwar activists willing to be violent, people far less interested in peaceful action. Finally, prominence as a value is attractive to journalists. The already-famous and powerful again are advantaged in making news.

Another powerful resource is expertise. To help them make news, journalists often turn to sources who are in a position either to know what's going on (present or former public officials, topic specialists in universities, interest groups and think tanks) or who are believed to have valuable insights into current events. The key characteristics of a media expert are not only expertise but also accessibility and reliability. The accessibility factor favors experts in places where journalists are concentrated, especially in the key news centers of New York and Washington. The reliability factor favors people who have already been in the news and whose information has been solid and who can deliver a quick, understandable "sound bite." Because journalists are always in a hurry, they tend to rely on sources who appear in what researchers Mark Cooper and Lawrence Soley (1990) refer to as the "Golden Rolodex," the list of sources already known about.

What may become news also depends on the news cycle—what's news for a particular day, for a newspaper or TV evening newscast, or a particular week or month for a magazine. Again, the potential number of stories is mammoth. Perhaps 20% of the news stories that the typical daily newspaper has in hand during a day will appear in the paper; at major dailies such as the *New York Times, Los Angeles Times,* or *Washington Post,* perhaps 5% will; and at the network evening newscasts, perhaps 1% will (Whitney & Becker, 1982). Where do these stories come from, and how do editors decide which ones to use?

Where do stories come from? At large newspapers, the networks, and newsmagazines, many stories come from the organization's news staff. Each has several hundred reporters, most of them covering specific beats. But at both large and small news operations, the large majorities of stories come from wire services, such as the Associated Press, and supplementary news services, most of them organized by newspapers (the *New York Times,* the Gannett news service), and, in the case of broadcasting, from the parent network for each station as well. These are supplied to newsrooms either by high-speed computer links or satellite feeds.

What becomes news? Much of this news is redundant: A paper or station may have several stories about the same news event, and in this case, it will most likely use the version prepared by its own staff member. If there is no in-house version of the story, an editor making selection decisions relies on several determinants to "decide what's news." First is to follow cues provided by news suppliers: at the beginning of each news cycle, for example, the Associated Press runs a "menu" alerting editors to the most important stories it will transmit. It may follow cues from opinion leaders within the news media themselves, especially the *New York Times, Washington Post,* the major newsmagazines, and the networks; these processes are sometimes called *intermedia agenda-setting.* (See the discussion of agenda-setting later in this chapter.)

These and other forces lead to a great deal of *standardization* of news. You have no doubt noticed that the front page of your daily newspaper is not terribly different from the news you see on television or hear on the radio, particularly in terms of what stories you see in a given day. There are several reasons for this: first, newsmen and women are constrained by the values they share for what news is. Second, each works for an organization with routines that constrain what news is. Third, each organization operates in a larger news environment in which other organizations are influencing their own news decisions (competition, we have noted, often leads to standardization rather than to differentiation[8]); moreover, in that environment, each relies on other, common suppliers, of news, such as the wire services. Finally, each lives in a social and cultural environment that exercises its own influences on reporters, editors, and the organizations for which they work.

News as report. The dictionary definition notes that news is not the event itself, but the *report* of an event. News is not only "made" by newsmakers, but "raw" occurrences must be made into stories. Each medium imposes its own demands on what a story is. TV stories, for example, demand a visual element; print media stories frequently are structured (and have been for more than a century) in "inverted pyramid" style; that is, with the most essential information at the beginning of the story and less essential detail and explanatory information further down. A useful exercise, always, is to compare across different media to see how they have structured their stories.

At another level, stories must be structured in terms of their content. We have noted that many news stories feature conflict. Conflict is important and frequently interesting; moreover, conflict serves journalistic interests. Because what's news in an event or issue is frequently unknown and ambiguous, journalists can employ conflict in the interests of their value of objectivity; an objective story is one that covers "both sides" (or "all sides") of an issue. Gaye Tuchman (1972) has pointed to objectivity as a "strategic ritual" for journalists: by quoting both sides in a story, the journalist can remain detached and nonpartisan. But as Tuchman further notes, the routine practices of journalists usually mean that the "sides" quoted tend to be the usual, and usually powerful, sources of news. Journalistic objectivity then, meets the standards suggested in Chapter 7 to describe an ideology (see also Glasser, 1985; Hackett, 1984).

NEWS AND REALITY, TODAY AND TOMORROW

News is supposed to be a representation of reality, something even some of its most vocal critics suggest. For example, critical scholar Todd Gitlin (1979) admits that journalists seek "truth—partial, superficial, occasion- and celebrity-centered truth, but truth nevertheless" (p. 263). But what can a 10-second sound bite capture "the truth" of? How we interpret how well journalism succeeds in truth seeking is a matter of perspective. Those of us who adhere to the first (reality as apparent) or second (reality as differing from appearances) views of reality tend to believe that the relationship between news and reality is fairly close. Faced with information that news tends to advantage the already powerful and advantaged, those holding one of these two views might well answer, "Well, yes; journalists are doing no more than reflecting the world in which they, and we, live." Faced with the same set of circumstances, those who hold the third view (reality as socially constructed and its ideology-and-hegemony cousins) would conclude something slightly different: that journalists reflect, uphold, and support the existing power relationships of the society.

The summer 1997 movie hit *Men in Black* had a running joke that the most reliable source of news and information about human contact with space aliens was the supermarket tabloid newspapers. The joke is funny because the movie—based on a comic book—is a sheer fantasy, but within the parameters of the fantasy, supermarket tabloids *could* be a reliable source of information. We note this because the lines between reality and "unreality" are far less clearly drawn than the preceding pages might suggest. During the 1990s, on television, in motion pictures, and in magazines, and in a variety of ways, the genres of the real and unreal have blurred,

All media bear some relationship to reality, but not all do so as directly as do news media. Most fictional programming is, of course, fantasy, but as we noted early on, entertainment producers must aim for the appearance of reality, so that the audience will willfully suspend its disbelief and thus be entertained.

Advertising presents a separate set of concerns. In the first place, advertisers are watched over by the Federal Trade Commission, the Food and Drug Administration, and the National Advertising Review Board of the self-regulatory Council of Better Business Bureaus. All prohibit outright lying and deception. But the reality of much advertising, especially for many consumer products, is that the products within a particular category are far more similar than they are different. Still none of us expects to hear any time soon a commercial that says, "Our pain reliever works just as well as half a dozen others, and it might cost a little more because we advertise." Rather, when the products in a category are not very different, the creative genius of the advertiser is either to find what advertiser Ted Bates called a "Unique Selling Proposition" for the product, some characteristic that differentiates that product from others, or else to create an image for the product that associates the product with an emotion or image that the audience-market desires. Is this reality? It is not deceptive; it is in the interstices.[9]

By the same token, ethical public relations practitioners—those who, for example, belong to the Public Relations Society of America and adhere to its code of ethics—will not purposefully lie to the public or the media. At the same time, they are obligated to present clients in the best possible light, to advance the client's goals. Is this reality, deception, or something in between?

MEDIA AND POLITICS

We have spent as much time as we have on the relationships between news, information, and reality because they are so important to the sort of society we have. As we further detail in the next chapter, reliable information is the cornerstone of a civil, public society, something the framers of the U.S. Constitution clearly understood. For a citizenry to make intelligent choices, it must have access to the day's intelligence before it can act. The next few pages outline the influences that media have on how we make up our minds and then act politically.

Media clearly perform important functions in politics. First, by the time we are teenagers, media are our most important source of political information (Atkin, 1981). Second, media serve as potential sources of persuasion and decision making, both directly, through endorsements and editorials, and indirectly, as a vehicle for candidates' and parties' speeches, platforms, and advertisements. Finally, information and persuasion may lead to behavior or political activity.

POLITICAL BEHAVIOR

Media effects on politics have been studied extensively, not only because they are socially important, but also because they're easy to study: As we noted about other campaigns in the previous chapter, political campaigns have a reasonably definite beginning and a very definite end—election day—and that end is a concrete, measurable behavior: People either do or do not vote, and if they do, they vote for a named candidate. There are, of course, other forms of political behavior —volunteering time to campaigns, contributing money, trying to persuade others. And there are likewise strong individual differences in how much the American public actually engages in each of them: On average, about half of Americans vote in presidential elections, fewer than a quarter in presidential primaries; one in five wear campaign buttons or display posters, and only about one person in nine has worked in a political campaign or given money to one.[10]

Why is there so much variation in how people do—and do not— behave politically? There are a number of causes: level of political interest, strength of political attitudes and opinions, amount of political

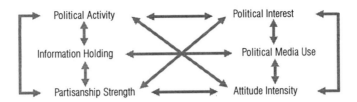

Figure 12.1 The reciprocal relationship of media use and political attitudes and behavior.

information, degree of attention to politics—largely through the media, and strength of partisanship. Moreover, these are deeply interrelated—mutually causal—so that a person "high" on one of these variables (a strong partisan) is likely to be high on others as well as politically well-informed), and those low on any one variable are likely to be low on others as well.

INFORMATION

Moreover, we've noted before that the media serve as the principal source of political information, determining how well we are informed about politics (or most other matters). The average American, it is safe to say, is *not* well informed about politics: At the height of the fall electoral campaigns, for example, fewer than half can name any candidate for U.S. House of Representatives from their district or both candidates for U.S. Senate from their state (Neuman, 1986). But as with political behavior, there are profound individual differences in what, and how much, we know about politics.

Communication researcher Philip J. Tichenor and his colleagues have postulated, and they and many others have found a great deal of evidence to support, what they call the *knowledge gap hypothesis* (Tichenor, Donohue, & Olien, 1970; see also Gaziano, 1983). It suggests that in the development of any social or political issue, the more highly educated segments of the population know more about the issue early on and, moreover, acquire information at a faster rate than the less-well-educated. In other words, the information-rich get richer, and the gap between them and the information-poor widens over time. Why should this occur? Just as the causes of variation in political behavior are multiple, the causes of knowledge acquisition are, too. Level of education predicts not only what and how much we're likely to know on a given topic at any given time, but also how interested in and motivated we are to learn about that topic. It also predicts the quality and quantity of media attention we pay to it, and how able we are to learn new information about that topic, a notion that E. D. Hirsch (1987) has labeled *cultural literacy.* Tichenor and other scholars, however, point out that whereas knowledge gaps are widespread, they are not inevitable: gaps can close. They do so particularly when issues "heat up" to an extent that all segments of the public are likely to learn about them—when, in other words, issues become so important that they generate interpersonal discussion and saturation media coverage, motivating people usually not interested in the topic to pay attention, and to learn. Extensive research on how people learn about timely events supports this: We're more likely to learn about the most intensely newsworthy events—a presidential assassination attempt, the crash of a spacecraft—from other people rather than from the media. We learn about the most newsworthy events from other people because those people want to talk about what they know. To the extent that we're likely to hear about unimportant things at all, we learn them from other people, simply because the media do not report on them. We're more likely to get intermediately important news from the media because the media do report on them but people aren't likely to focus conversations on them.

PERSUASION AND DECISION MAKING

How persuasive are the media in political questions? Much of the communication research literature suggests that the effects are quite limited, for it is often difficult to separate the effects of media—the messengers—from the messages and their initial sources—candidates, parties, and interest groups. At the same time, a half-century of research does help us understand the process of political communication effects.

Fifty years ago, the first large-scale studies of the impact of media on politics were conducted by the legendary Paul F. Lazarsfeld and his Columbia University colleagues (Berelson, Lazarsfeld, & McPhee, 1954; Lazarsfeld, Berelson, & Gaudet, 1948). In two communities in two presidential elections, they conducted panel studies, or repeated surveys of the same samples, to ascertain when potential voters made up their minds for whom they would vote. The panel design allowed them to speculate on what led these potential voters to the decisions they made. They initially suspected that mass media messages would be enormously important in vote decisions, but they found in each study that this was simply not so. In each, as a matter of fact, solid majorities of voters had made up their minds for whom they would vote *even before the candidates were officially nominated.* Their explanation for this was simple and straightforward—a social categories one: blue-collar families said they would support the Democrat, white-collar ones, the Republican. Moreover, they found two other important things: First, among those who had not made up their minds at the beginning of the campaign, relatively few cited any media source as the determining influence on their vote. Far more cited the influence of other people. Second, voters who make up their minds early in a campaign are different in several respects from those who make up their minds later on.

THE "OPINION LEADER" CONCEPT

Surprised by their failure to find large-scale media effects, Lazarsfeld and his fellow researchers followed up on those who had identified "other people" as their sources of a vote decision. They found that these other people were not a random assortment, but the same names cropped up as sources. In their voting studies and subsequent research, they did find a "media effect" of a sort: these other people, whom they dubbed opinion leaders or influentials, were not remarkably different demographically (or, in social categories terms) from the people they influenced, but they were different: As Elihu Katz and Lazarsfeld (1955) explain it,

> Who or what influences the influentials? Here is where the mass media re-entered the picture. For the leaders reported much more than the non-opinion leaders that for them, the mass media were influential. Pieced together this way, a new idea emerged—the suggestion of a "two-step flow of communication." The suggestion is basically that ideas, often, seem to flow *from* radio and print [remember that this is the '40s, before TV] *to* opinion leaders and *from them* to the less active sections of the population. (p. 32)

340

The two-step flow model proved a very important one for understanding communication influence and was heavily studied for many years. As a "trickle-down" theory, it suggests that media influence is limited, because most people (the less active) can be affected only indirectly. At the same time, media do play an important role in political influence. Subsequent research on the model, however, has modified it, and how we understand its importance, considerably.

We now believe that the model is general, not restricted to politics: We find examples of opinion leadership on virtually any topic—popular music, buying computers, fashion, food, and so on. And there are variations, topic by topic, on the relative influence of opinion leaders and of the media.

By the same token, opinion leadership is not general. We see few generalized opinion leaders. Think of your own conversations with others: You're likely to discuss what are good movies, good cars, good cameras, or good manners with different people. Moreover, in the original conception, opinion leadership was taken to be an "ideal type": Either you were an opinion leader or you were a follower. More realistically, there are probably degrees of leadership, so that a person sometimes leads and sometimes follows.

The idea of "ideas" in the model is too simple. Katz and Lazarsfeld say "ideas . . . flow," but the media (and opinion leaders) transmit two distinct things: information and attempts to influence or persuade. Most usually, it would appear, opinion leaders gather information from the media to craft persuasive arguments. The relative importance of media and interpersonal influence is subject to a wide range of variation: Extensive research on the diffusion of innovations—how people learn to do new things—shows that both media and opinion leaders serve important functions. Media, for example, may make us aware of and/or interested in some idea, but we may be hesitant to try it out, to buy it, or otherwise to behave in accordance with what we have learned, particularly if the behavior implied by the idea is risky or expensive (e.g., buying a computer). For that, we need the advice of an opinion leader, who is more likely to be knowledgeable and experienced.

The flow need not be two-step. It can be multistep (from the media to one person, to another, to another, and so on), two-step, one-step (directly from the media) or *no*-step: some ideas find no popular resonance at all and drop from sight. A one-step flow suggests direct media influence—from the media to the individual, without the intervention of an opinion leader. And given the vast variety of topics and issues to which we are all exposed, and the unlikelihood that we will discuss most of them with another person, the potential for the two-step flow model to come into play is vastly restricted: We don't talk about it, and hence the model does not apply.

In politics, for example, repeated surveys have found that even during the course of a presidential election campaign, roughly half of all potential voters simply do not discuss the elections with other people. Then, the only source of potential influence on such people is the media. Communication researcher John Robinson (1976a), for example, notes that in the 1968 presidential election campaign, more voters surveyed said they were aware of having seen a newspaper endorsement than reported having been subject to any interpersonal attempt to persuade them how to vote. Thus, absent any interpersonal discussion, the media may emerge as the sole source of political influence.

WHEN VOTERS DECIDE

Lazarsfeld and his colleagues, and again this has been verified in subsequent research (Chaffee & Choe, 1980; Whitney & Goldman, 1985), also found that there are important differences in voters that relate to when they reach their vote decisions. *Early deciders,* those who make up their minds early, tend to be strong partisans, likely to identify with a major party, to be interested in politics and to pay close attention to political media, to be better informed about politics in general and in the campaign and candidates in particular, to be likely to discuss politics, and to eventually vote. Moreover, like all other voters, once they've made up their minds, they are unlikely to change them. *Campaign deciders* are less partisan—more likely to be political independents, are somewhat less interested in politics than early deciders, and lower in routine attention to political content in the media, but somewhat more likely to follow political news during the campaigns (motivated, we would guess, by a desire for information on which to base a vote choice); they are intermediate in the amount of political discussion in which they engage and in their ultimate likelihood of voting. *Late* or *last-minute* deciders are lowest on all these measures—the least partisan, the least likely to follow politics in general or the campaign in particular, to discuss politics, and, for that matter, to vote.

What does this typology tell us about media impact? Something subtle. Early deciders pay close attention to media, and so we might guess that the potential effect of media on them would be great. But because they've already made up their minds, media messages have little impact on their political decisions. Because they make up their minds during the campaign, campaign deciders, on the other hand, are open to influence by media because they lack the strong partisan ties early deciders have and because they pay closer attention to media (and especially candidate debates) during the campaign. But because they discuss the campaign with others, they're likewise open to interpersonal influence. The last-minute deciders are the most perplexing, and at the same time, most interesting of all: because they don't discuss the campaign or follow it closely in the media, are unlikely to watch televised debates, and lack the political party ties that tell them how to choose, it's not clear what leads them to a choice (in fact, fewer of them vote than in the other categories; some of them flip coins; still others resort to *latent partisanship,* voting for candidates of parties with which they very weakly identify). But political scientist Philip Converse (1962) has suggested a paradox: Even though late deciders pay the *least* attention to media politics, they are the *most* susceptible to media influence, for they have so little else on which to base vote decisions. For this reason, last-minute saturation advertising, particularly on television (and during or between entertainment programs) may be very effective.

ENDORSEMENTS AND ADVERTISING

Media messages make evaluative statements in efforts to persuade and to influence behavior, most usually in two ways, through *endorsements,* in which a medium urges voters to support a particular candidate or referendum position, and *political advertising,* in which third parties—the candidates, political parties, or others—urge a course of behavior.

Over the years, the U.S. print press has become decidedly less partisan, and declining numbers of newspapers endorse candidates for office, particularly for the office of president. However, many papers, including most of the largest ones, do endorse candidates, and whether endorsements have an impact is an important question. The answer is yes, but, particularly at the presidential level, the effect is modest in size. The most careful statistical study of the effects of newspaper endorsements on presidential voting, conducted by John Robinson over five presidential elections (1956-1972), indicated that the presence of an endorsement made an average three percentage point difference in the vote for endorsed candidates. Although that's not a large difference, we've previously noted that in close elections, a small difference can have a large effect. However, Robinson (1976b) found the largest endorsement effects (an endorsement persuading voters to vote for a supported candidate) in the two landslide elections (Lyndon Johnson's 1964 victory over Goldwater, Richard Nixon's 1972 win over George McGovern) among the five he studied; in short, he found the largest effects when it made no political difference. It is generally suspected, however, that in lower level races—for city and county offices and judicial seats—where voters tend not to be well informed about candidates, the effects of endorsements may be somewhat greater, simply because the fact that a newspaper endorsed a candidate may be one of the only things that a voter may *know* about the candidate.

We earlier cited Michael Schudson's (1984) book, *Advertising, the Uneasy Persuasion*, noting that when Schudson interviewed advertising researchers, they were unable to give him any clear idea of how much impact advertising has. That applies to political advertising as well as to consumer products. At the aggregate level, there is scanty evidence that the amount of money spent on candidate advertising is itself directly related to whether candidates win or lose, once incumbency accounted for (that is, incumbents tend to be reelected, and they also tend to be able to raise a lot more money).[11] Nonetheless, there is evidence that some advertising, in some contexts, can be effective, and so we will take a brief closer look.

One perhaps unanticipated impact advertising has on elections is information. Political scientists Thomas Patterson and Robert McClure (1976) found in a study of one presidential election that advertising, in fact, contributed more to the public's knowledge of candidates and issues than even the news did, and although subsequent studies have generally found that news is more informative than advertising, the fact remains that advertising's contribution to knowledge is impres-

---

BOX 12.3

Negative Political Ads

Perhaps the most famous television political commercial of all time was the 1964 "Daisy" commercial, created by political consultant Tony Schwartz. Showing a little girl plucking the petals off a daisy and moving to a close-up of her pupils, a voice-over counts down (10 . . . 9 . . . 8 . . .) followed by a quick cut to a view of a nuclear explosion. Then, on a black background, came an appeal to vote for President Lyndon Johnson. The ad never even mentioned Johnson's opponent, Senator Barry Goldwater, but the "message" was unambiguous, suggesting that Goldwater was a dangerous warmonger who might lead the country into a nuclear holocaust.

First runner-up would be the 1988 "Willie Horton" commercial, in which the Bush campaign showed a still picture of an African American man who raped a woman while he was on furlough from a Massachusetts prison, during the time Bush's Democratic opponent, Michael Dukakis, was governor of Massachusetts. The voice-over blamed the act on Dukakis, although in fact, the furlough program had become law while Dukakis's predecessor—a Republican—was governor.

Both ads became controversial—and newsworthy: The ads were replayed many times, not as paid advertising, but in news programs (the Daisy commercial, in fact, aired only *once* as a paid commercial, on the NBC *Movie of the Week*). Each ad thus helped form the political debate of the respective campaigns.

But can we be sure of the commercial's impact? No. In the first place, it becomes impossible to separate the impact of the commercial as a commercial from the impact of the news coverage of the political issue. In each case, only minorities of the electorate ever saw the commercials as commercials. Moreover, at a very aggregate level, poll data tend to discount the effect: In both of these cases, the percentages of likely voters expressing a preference for the eventual winners *at the time the commercial first aired* were virtually identical to the fraction of the popular vote the winner received two months later in the presidential election.

---

sive, particularly among less active voters. Political candidate advertising, however, differs from most consumer-product advertising in several respects. What we're being sold is a candidate and/or his or her ideas and promises about what public policy should be, rather than some product we will use and later discard. Moreover, the behavior sought is a vote, not a sale. Finally, political advertising, unlike consumer-product advertising, tends to be *comparative* and frequently *negative*: The candidate tries to persuade people to vote for her or him by finding something to criticize in an opponent's past or record. (When was the last time you saw a product ad that tried to sell you something by pointing out how awful the competition was?)

Despite the fact that polls show large majorities of the public find negative political ads distasteful, politicians use them frequently because they think they work, and historians often point to ads that appear to have had profound impacts on campaigns, such as the "Daisy" ad in the 1964 Goldwater-Johnson election and the Willie Horton commercial in Bush's 1988 victory over Michael Dukakis. But negative ads may have several different impacts on individual voters. A voter may believe the ad and form a negative impression of the candidate, which is the ad's intent; at the same time, however, it may also translate into a negative impression of the sponsoring candidate, although usually the negative belief about the target candidate is somewhat more important (which is why negative ads appear to work better in two-candidate general elections rather than in multicandidate ones; in multicandidate races, if Candidate A attacks Candidate B, they may both "lose" while Candidate C emerges unharmed). In general, however, we can never be quite sure how successful negative advertising really is with individual voters. A secondary effect of negative ads is more easily documentable: They tend to focus political debate, particularly in the news media, on the issues the negative ads have raised.

We now turn to several related models of communication influence, which bear some similarities. Each suggests that major impacts from the media may flow not from intentional efforts to persuade (what we think), but by changing our cognitions (what we think *about*). These are the ideas of *agenda-setting, priming, third-person effects,* and the *spiral of silence.*

THE AGENDA-SETTING MODEL

The news media by and large do not set out to persuade, but to inform. In telling us what to think about, we are first of all suggesting that the media *set the public agenda,* that is, they tell us what issues are important for public debate. The idea behind agenda setting is quite simple: The media, over time, by featuring some issues prominently and some issues less prominently and still other issues not at all, give us a sense of what issues are important, or, in the research literature, senses of the issue's salience. By salience, we mean the amount of public or political importance an issue possesses—the "light and heat" it generates.

Media cue us as to the importance of issues in different ways: We get a sense of the importance of an issue in media by its prominence (Is it at the top of the front page, or buried somewhere inside? Is it the first item in the evening news, or near the end?), and by the extensiveness, both of stories in a given day and of the duration of coverage over time—Is there one story, or is there a main story and one or more related *sidebar* stories? How long and detailed are the stories? Does artwork—photos, charts, or graphs—accompany the story? Does the issue receive treatment over many days, weeks, months?

Communication researchers test for agenda-setting impact by obtaining measures of the media agenda and the public agenda and then comparing the two. For example, we might content-analyze a sample of news media to see which issues received how much coverage and then rank-order those issues. The economy might rank first, crime second, drugs and drug abuse third, and so on. We would then look at survey or polling data on what Americans described as important problems. If the two lists looked similar, we might conclude that the media set the agenda for the public, and when researchers have done such analyses, they usually conclude this. (For good reviews, see McCombs & Gilbert, 1986; Rogers & Dearing, 1988).

However, we should ask: who's to say that it doesn't work the other way around—that the *public* sets the *media* agenda? And isn't it also quite possible that something else—for example, what's happening in the real world—sets *both*?

We can design studies that elaborate both questions. To test the relative strength of the public and media agendas on each other, researchers rely on a technique called *cross-lagged correlation*: measures of the public and media agenda are taken at two points in time, and the impact of the media agenda at the first time point is correlated with the public agenda at the second time point, whereas the impact of the public agenda at the first time point is compared with the media agenda at the second. Researchers have found that the impact of the media on the public agenda is virtually always greater than the opposite: In other words, the media do more to set the public agenda than the public do to set the media agenda (although there is a noticeable effect of the public on the media). Answering the second question—does something else, the "real world," set both agendas?—requires a different research strategy. Researchers use not only measures of the media and public agendas, but also some "real world" indicators as well, such as unemployment and inflation rates, crime rates, wartime casualty rates, and so on. A number of analyses have found that the closest correlations are between the media and public agendas—closer than between the real world and media agendas *or* between the real world and public agendas, although, as before, each does of course somewhat influence the other (Rogers & Dearing, 1988).

But the relationships between the media and public agendas in research studies are never perfect—the lists are never identically ranked. In other words, the power of the media to set the public agenda is somewhat constrained or limited, and in ways—by things—that are instructive. Among the limitations are the following:

1. *Individual differences:* The strongest agenda-setting effects have been found in experimental research studies, which suggests that a major condition for obtaining the effect is *attention* (that is, in experiments, subjects are expected to pay attention, but under naturalistic conditions, some people do and others don't) (Iyengar & Kinder, 1987). And as we noted in discussing knowledge effects more generally, the sorts of things that lead one to attend to the news are related to levels of education, interest, and the like. Indeed, in the experimental studies, the strongest agenda-setting effects generally were among people who did not usually follow news closely. Moreover, David Weaver (1980) and others have noted that an individual's "need for orientation" on an issue—one's recognition that an issue may be important, coupled with a belief that one doesn't know enough about it—is a strong predictor of agenda-setting effects.

2. *Media differences:* It should be fairly obvious that not all media present precisely the same agendas at the same time, and logically people's agendas should correspond to the media to which they *do* pay attention. On average, however, most major national media do present very similar news and hence news agendas, as we argued earlier in the chapter.

3. *Issue differences*: Issues differ in two principal ways. The first is *content;* some issues concern problems facing a society or group, whereas others more specifically focus on policy proposals (legislation or executive orders) or solutions to problems. Second is the kind of *impact* issues may have on the public or society. Some issues are obtrusive ones, affecting nearly everyone, and affecting them in pretty much the same way (inflation, when it is high; gasoline shortages); others are selective, affecting some people deeply, while affecting others far less so (noise pollution); still others are remote, directly affecting small numbers of people (U.S. foreign policy toward Malawi) (Lang & Lang, 1983). In general, agenda-setting effects are greatest on remote issues and smallest on obtrusive ones.

4. *Salience differences:* There are different kinds of salience. *Social* salience is our sense of an issue's impact on the larger society. *Interpersonal* salience is what we think is important to the people with whom we're in regular contact—what we talk about with others. *Individual* salience is what we personally think is important. In general, agenda-setting effects are greatest on social salience and least evident on individual salience.

In these sections, we are discussing political media impacts on individuals. As we noted earlier in the chapter, agenda setting, as well as the effects we discuss next—priming, third-person effects, and the spiral of silence—occur at higher levels of analysis, as we noted in Chapter 3. As noted, intermedia agenda setting occurs when a "prestige" medium's agenda becomes the agenda for local media.

PRIMING

The *priming* effect is a close cousin of agenda setting, and in fact, it was described by researchers conducting agenda-setting studies. Like agenda-setting, priming is a metaphor. Here, the metaphor is of priming a pump—adding enough liquid to the pump to get it started working on its own. It is described by political psychologist Shanto Iyengar (1991) this way:

> The so-called "priming effect" refers to the ability of news programs to affect the criteria by which individuals judge their political leaders.

Specifically, researchers have found that the more prominent an issue is in the national information stream, the greater will be the weight accorded it in making political judgments. While agenda-setting reflects the impact of news coverage on the perceived importance of national issues, priming refers to the impact of news coverage on the weight assigned to specific issues on making political judgments. For instance, after watching news stories on the increased budgetary outlays for the Pentagon under the Reagan administration, viewers were not only more likely to cite the arms race as an important national issue, but were also likely to give more weight to their evaluations of President Reagan's performance on arms control when rating his performance overall. (p. 133)

Note that priming blurs the line between "what to think" and "what to think about": Agenda-setting tells us an issue is important, and priming suggests we evaluate a political leader or group based on its performance for this issue, but agenda setting does not necessarily shape our attitudes on that criterion. To follow the Reagan example: If we already thought that a military buildup was a good thing, we would then evaluate Reagan more favorably; if we thought it was bad, we would evaluate him less favorably.

Both agenda setting and priming are largely inside-the-head psychological models; they affect how we *behave* only to the extent that we *act on what we "know" or believe*. (Perhaps the best example is the commonly noted effect that tourism declines in areas after terrorist attacks. While the odds that, if we visited such a country, we would be a victim of an attack are very low, the news coverage raises the salience of risk.) We'll now turn to two other models that have a bit more to say about behavior.

"THIRD-PERSON" EFFECTS

Public opinion researcher W. Phillips Davison (1983) coined the term *third-person effect* to try to describe how, in some cases, media messages may have an impact on our behavior but little or no impact on our attitudes. He began his classic article on the effect with a historical anecdote about the World War II battle of Iwo Jima in the Pacific. A historian friend of Davison's had asked him if he could give a good explanation for the fact that Black soldiers did not fight in that battle because they were kept from the battle by superiors who had heard a Japanese propaganda radio broadcast urging them not to fight. Why, the historian asked, did the commanders withdraw the Black troops, when they had no evidence that the Black soldiers had been persuaded by the broadcast? Davison responded by formulating his third-person model.

All of us, Davison suggests, go through a little mental calculation when we see or hear media messages. First, we calculate whether we personally believe or are affected by them (first person). We then calculate whether our friends—people like us—are affected (second persons). Finally, we calculate whether "other people"—those about whom we are likely to know little or nothing (third persons)—are affected. A usual response, he says, is to believe that we, and others like us, will not be affected, but that other people will be. A simple example: How much does advertising affect *you*? How much does it affect other people? Reams of survey data tell us that most people believe that advertising messages generally don't have much impact on them, but the same people believe that other people are more affected than they are. As Davison points out, it's possible that we either underestimate effects on ourselves, or overestimate impacts on others, or both, but he and we believe that more often than not, we overestimate effects on others.

There is likely a fair degree of generality to the third-person model. Each of us finds ourselves in situations in which, before doing or saying something—that is, before we behave—we calculate what others think or believe. Indeed, this is a component—subjective social norms—in the Ajzen and Fishbein attitude-and-behavior-change model presented in the last chapter. Reporters, for example, in writing a "second-day" story on new developments in a story since the day before, have to calculate how much the audience is likely to remember (they usually calculate, based on experience, that it won't remember much). Political operatives must calculate how much impact the speeches and ads of opponents have had on voters and respond accordingly. What the third-person model suggests is that when we must behave, and when that behavior depends on our estimate of how others have been influenced by a message, and lacking information (usually we are) about how much these others have been affected, we are likely to overestimate the influence of media messages.

351

Political scientist Bernard Cohen (1963) observed that this phenomenon helps to explain the power of the news media in political affairs. The media are not powerful in policy matters necessarily because they shape public opinion:

> Lacking any other *daily* link to the outside, any other *daily* measure of how people are reacting to the ebb and flow of foreign-policy developments, the policy maker reaches for the newspaper as an important source of public opinion, as the instrument of "feedback." In fact, many officials treat the press and public opinion as synonymous, either explicitly equating them or using them interchangeably. (p. 233-234)[12]

THE SPIRAL OF SILENCE

The *spiral of silence* model introduced by the German social scientist Elisabeth Noelle-Neumann (1974, 1984) is similar to Davison's third-person model. It too argues that media messages alter people's, and society's, behavior. But the behavior that interests Noelle-Neumann is how and when people are willing to express their opinions.

She argues that a "fear of isolation" is very important in motivating people, that we dread putting ourselves in a position where other people will shun or make fun of us. So before we are willing to let other people know what we think on some issue, we perform a mental calculation quite similar to the one Davison suggests; that is, we try to assess what other people think on a topic before we let them know what *we* think. If we think that they are likely to agree with us, or if we think that more and more people feel the same way, then we go ahead and speak out. If we think, however, that they disagree with us, or that the opinion is becoming unpopular, we do not speak out; moreover, Noelle-Neumann suggests that we are each endowed with a *quasi-statistical sense* that allows us to intuit "public opinion," or the predominant opinion of others. As we walk through any neighborhood, Noelle-Neumann says, we'll likely observe one of two situations—that almost all the houses are neat and tidy, with well-trimmed lawns, or that almost none are. Why? Because in the former case, there is social pressure to conform to a community standard that overwhelms any personal desire to be lazy. Many researchers have noted that in presidential elections in which there are more than two candidates, the third-party candidates go into a nose-dive shortly before the election. Noelle-Neumann would explain this in trend terms: People supporting the third-party candidates learn from the media that their candidate has no chance, and they desert. Indeed, the spiral of silence model is a media model only because the media serve as the primary sources of our information about the distribution of public opinion and about trends in that opinion.

As outlined above, the model is an individual level model, describing what goes on in our heads. But the model is also a social level model, describing the dynamics of public expression and opinion. If, as Noelle-Neumann suggests, people *do* decide whether to express themselves based on their view of predominant opinion or trends in opinion, then *over time*, those favoring the majority opinion should express it willingly and those favoring the minority position should prefer to remain quiet. If this occurs, the majority opinion will be expressed loudly and frequently, whereas the minority position will "spiral into silence."

Although there is both historical and research support for the spiral of silence, it, too, does not always occur, which is a good thing, too, or we would eventually devolve into a society in which there was never any expressed difference of opinion. Why does it sometimes work, and sometimes not?

1. *Individual differences:* "Willingness to express" is an attribute on which people differ, regardless of topic or predominant opinion; some people are simply more outspoken than others. Willingness to express an opinion is also a function of opinion intensity—how strongly someone holds an opinion: People who hold strong opinions may well express them regardless of their perceptions of how others feel.

2. *Perception of predominant opinion (and future trends):* The model's assumption that people are able to figure out what others think on all issues is almost certainly not always correct. Social psychologists have written extensively on pluralistic ignorance, or uncertainty about the distribution of opinions of others. If we are uncertain about the opinions of others, the model may not apply. If we are uncertain, the theorists say, we generally react in one of two ways: In general, we may have "looking-glass perceptions," believing that others feel the same way we do, or, if we believe the topic to be touchy or controversial, we may exercise a conservative bias, thinking that others are more conservative or restrictive than in fact they are (Taylor, 1982).

3. *Perceptions of "others'" opinions.* The model assumes that in our mental calculation, we have some generalized other, or, in Davison's terms, third person, in mind. In fact, most of most people's public or political talk is not to a generalized mass audience. Before a more specialized audience, someone might believe that the opinion expressed will be a majority one, even if it's not a majority opinion in the mass audience. In other words, most of our discussion is among friends or people whose views we think we know pretty well, and who we think are likely to agree with us. When we don't think this, however, the model is more likely to apply.

The social reality models we have discussed—agenda setting, priming, third-person effects, and the spiral of silence—have several aspects in common: All of them suggest that behavioral impacts such as how we vote or whether we give money or speak aloud may result from media-induced changes in beliefs or cognitions. Each also suggests that media impact does not result from a single message, but from the cumulative impact of media messages over time. And whereas research to date has confirmed each model, one cannot argue that any one of them works equally effectively all of the time, even at the individual or personal level.

This chapter has focused on two aspects of politics and the news media, how media cover news, and how their impacts affect people. We turn next to two other aspects of people and the media—the media and the people as a public, and public considerations of how the media ought to behave, or normative theories of the media.

NOTES

1. Our characterizations here are necessarily general and overly simple; for a more complete characterization of early newspapers, see Nerone (1987). Nerone in particular notes that the degree to which newspapers were partisan before 1840 was highly variable; many papers, particularly in larger cities, were, but others were more objective by present-day standards. He also notes that changes in the newspaper were evolutionary, occurring slowly and undramatically, rather than revolutionary.

2. In the United States, however, unlike Europe, the newspaper has remained largely a local phenomenon almost to the present. Among American newspapers, only a handful—the *Wall Street Journal, USA Today,* and the *New York Times*—have an appreciable circulation outside the cities in which they are

produced. In Europe, however, the principal newspapers are national—produced in the capital and distributed throughout the nation. The "mass" newspaper evolved in Europe at the same time as the national railroad system, enabling metropolitan newspapers to be on breakfast tables the next morning throughout the country. The size of the United States, however, did not allow this, and what "national" newspapers we do have emerged as national only in the 1970s and 1980s, when communications satellites and commercial jet aviation made it economically feasible to print national papers in satellite printing facilities across the country.

3. In general, see Edwin and Michael Emery (1984), Schudson (1978), and Nerone (1987). It might be noted that historians disagree over the pace at which, and reasons why, these changes occur, but they tend to concur *that* they did.

4. Although Telstar was used to televise the funeral of President John Kennedy in 1963, routine TV news usage of satellites did not come into being until the 1970s. The Vietnam War is often called "the first televised war" and writer Michael Arlen dubbed it "the living-room war." But, for most of that war (from 1960 to 1969), the TV images were on film flown from Vietnam to California and aired two days after the events were filmed.

5. This slogan was a favorite of Lieutenant Joe Friday (Jack Webb, also the show's producer) on the 1950s and '60s TV show *Dragnet*. The *message* was that if the witnesses he and his partner were interviewing would stick to the facts, the police could interpret them and more quickly and efficiently catch the criminals.

6. One aspect of news style that is indisputably an AP legacy is the inverted pyramid style of constructing news stories, with the most important facts first and less central ones later in the story, the "who-what-when-where-followed-by-why-and-how" or "5 Ws and H" formula.

7. Tuchman (1973) has noted that even unpredicted stories, especially when they are obviously big news, are quickly covered in ways that allow reporters and editors to apply routines to them.

8. In their memoirs, many journalists have commented on the "second-guessing" that their own editors do when the staff journalist's story is different from the other versions: that is, the staff journalist is asked to account for "why your story is different from what the AP (or the *New York Times* or ABC) says." And reporters agree that over time, this serves as a powerful standardizing influence, not to be too different from what other journalists are writing.

9. Sisello Bok (1978) is the standard work on truth and deception and gray areas in between, and is highly recommended to anyone who is considering any media career.

10. The Gallup Poll, May 1988 and November 1986. *The Gallup Opinion Index* is published monthly and available in most research libraries.

11. A study of the 1988 elections by political communication researcher Michael Robinson found that in 60 primaries that year, the biggest spender won the primary only 40% of the time (Kolbert, 1992).

355

12. Cohen (1963) wrote this in the year that network TV news went from 15 to 30 minutes, which occurred at about the same time that, in Roper Polls, the public shifted from finding newspapers a more credible news medium to believing that television was. We've no doubt that if Cohen rewrote his book today, he would substitute *television news* or *the press* for *newspapers*.

The Media and the Public

W e talk about "the public" throughout this book, for no term in
understanding mass media is more vital. The next two chapters focus on the public. In the present chapter, we will try to delineate
what we mean by the public, talk a bit about where contemporary ideas
of the public come from, show how different notions of the public lead
us to different questions, and set the stage for the next chapter on issues
of how the media *ought to* operate.

DEFINING THE PUBLIC

In ordinary language, we think of *public* in a variety of ways. Among
the most common:

> Public as the not-private, that which goes on in the open, observ-
> able by and accessible to others, as in "open to the public";
>
> Public as general, pertaining to or emanating from all citizens, as
> in *public interest* or *public opinion*;
>
> Public as communal, or governmentally owned or regulated, as
> in *public television* or *public utilities*.

Public implies openness, community, citizenship, discussion, debate. And the relationship between media and public can be discussed on several levels by reference to these terms.

The media clearly serve public functions in two essential ways. First, the media have become the key instrument of "public-ness" in our first sense: that is, they bring information and issues out into the open—they constitute *publicity*. When the news media argue that trials—the O. J. Simpson trials, the Oklahoma City bombing trials—and military operations—the Gulf War—should be open to media access, they assert "the people's right to know." They argue that the public can hold its own institutions accountable only to the degree that public (governmental—our third sense of public) business is conducted "in public" (our first sense). Second, media constitute a key portion of what we sometimes call *the public sphere,* the multiple forums in which issues and controversies can be debated (our first and second senses of public), something essential in a democracy if what we mean by democracy is the manifestation of the public will.

For the *public will* to have much meaning, we have to have some sense of how we might know what that will is—what the public wants and needs—and how we might find that out. For now, we will note that the public can be thought of in a variety of ways, ways that are related to how the public is *represented*—as individuals (or as aggregations of individuals), as groups or publics, or through the usual political form of representation, the government ("We, the people . . ." are the opening words of the U.S. Constitution.)[1] The very idea of a public is intertwined with the idea of a democracy.

CREATING THE PUBLIC

The notion of democracy is an ancient one, dating from the golden age of Greece; its modern manifestation, however, dates from the Enlightenment, roughly dating from the 1700s, and especially in Britain and Holland, and slightly later in France.[2] Prior to this period, the notion of the public—in the sense of a body of citizens capable of expressing public opinion—is virtually absent—and for good reason: As we note in the next chapter, Europe was ruled by coalitions of kings, feudal lords, and the hierarchy of the church. Real power and authority rested in very few hands, and the opinions of anyone else (if they had them and dared express them) mattered for little. Such dissent as existed was usually ruthlessly suppressed.

THE RISE OF THE PUBLIC

From the mid-1700s to the present, there has been a gradual shift toward greater democracy. It arises first with the gradual empowerment of the bourgeoisie, an urban upper middle class whose claim to political voice and power was based on its accumulating wealth and knowledge, not on the traditional claims to power of title and land held by the nobility. As the bourgeoisie gradually gained political stature, they begin the development and transformation of the public sphere. Public debates, over justice, equality, and a hundred other questions, spring up in the coffeehouses of London and Amsterdam, and in the *salons* of Paris, meetings of intellectuals in the mansions of the recently rich. And even at this early juncture, the media—newspapers, journals, and books—are important carriers of the information and opinion that formed the bases of debate.

We must emphasize, however, that in the middle to late 1700s, the public was still a rather small segment of the whole population. If we take citizenship—the right to vote—as a rough indicator of membership in the public, as an index of publicness, we may remind ourselves that at the founding of the United States, the first modern republican democracy, its 1789 Constitution extended the right to vote only to property-owning (and in most states, White) males. In the United States, as in Europe, the next 150 years would see the expansion of the voting franchise to include almost everyone as a citizen—as part of the public. Sometimes this extension was accomplished peacefully, sometimes only after bloody conflict.

THE DECLINE OF THE PUBLIC

As this story is frequently told, especially by those familiar with the important work of Jürgen Habermas, a scholar of the German critical theory Frankfurt School, the "transformation of the public sphere" divides roughly into a classical and a modern period. In the classical period, the expansion of the public sphere was an ideal time, when public debate was robust, eloquent, well-reasoned, and vigorous: competing viewpoints found public forums—the pulpits, stump-speaking political debates such as the classic Lincoln-Douglas debates of 1858, well-attended town meetings, a flourishing newspaper press. Recall from the previous chapter that newspapers were individually partisan and partial but, in the larger cities, at least, collectively represented wide ranges of viewpoints (Habermas, 1962/1989; Postman, 1985). In this formulation, however, there is what media scholar Peter Dahlgren (1995) calls a "second act," a modern period characterized by decline:

> The second act traces the decline of the bourgeois public sphere in the context of advanced industrial capitalism and the social welfare state of advanced democracy. With mass democracy, the public loses its exclusivity; its socio-discursive coherence comes apart as many less educated citizens enter the scene. The state, to handle the growing contradictions of capitalism, becomes more interventionist; the boundaries between public and private, both in political economic terms and in cultural terms, begin to dissipate. Large organizations and interest groups become key political partners with the state, resulting in a "refeudalization" of politics which greatly displaces the role of the public. The increasing prevalence of the mass media, especially where the commercial logic transforms much of public communication into PR, advertising and entertainment, erodes the critical functions of the public. The public becomes fragmented, losing its social coherence. It becomes reduced to a group of spectators whose acclaim is to be periodically mobilized, but whose intrusion in fundamental political questions is to be minimized. (p. 8)

In other words, this criticism suggests that in the present day, the public itself has become disenfranchised: Although citizens may still vote, fewer see a reason to do so, and fewer actually do so; Christopher Lasch laments "the transformation of politics from a central component of popular culture into a spectator sport" (cited in Schudson, 1995, p. 189)—and at that, a spectator sport with declining attendance, as networks prune their coverage of the presidential nominating conventions further and further back, and news media rely on "lite" coverage and attention-grabbing graphics rather than substantial political coverage. The American political system, suggest distinguished journalists Haynes Johnson and David Broder (1996), echoing an argument made by Walter Lippmann (1922) almost 75 years earlier, has gotten so large, cumbersome, and dominated by organized special interests that it is unable to come to terms with fundamental social problems such as health care, and its journalism is unable to explain those problems and policy questions to citizens. Television coverage of politics devolves into 10- to 15-second sound bites, and pundits trying harder to score points on each other than to broaden public debate. At the same time, Harvard political scientist Robert Putnam (1995, 1996) strikes a responsive chord with an argument that America's "social capital" is eroding, largely because people are staying home to watch TV, rather than joining organizations, talking with each other, and participating in politics.

Such scholars argue that the classical unity of *audience* and *public* has dissolved. Whereas once the public constituted the audience for serious political media, today, the public is eroding, as audiences have become no more than markets, commodities, "eyeballs" to be bought and sold and traded.

IS THERE A PROBLEM OF THE PUBLIC?

The story told by Habermas, Dahlgren, Lasch, Putnam, and many others has not gone unchallenged. There are two strong arguments against it. First is that the classical public sphere cannot be painted in such rosy hues as its proponents suggest. Second is that the public is a flexible concept, one that is constantly being reinvented.

Media scholar Michael Schudson (1995) points out that the American public of the 1800s may have turned out for political debates and lengthy speeches, but we have scant evidence that the majority of attendees spent all that time carefully weighing the speakers' arguments.

The longing of contemporary critics of our political culture to stand in the sun for three hours to listen to political speeches is selective. If there is nostalgia for the Lincoln-Douglas debates (not that they left any words, phrases, or ideas that anyone can recall), there is no hankering for dramatic readings of Edward Everett's hours-long address at Gettysburg. Instead, it is Abraham Lincoln's sound bite-length address that has left a lasting impression. As it happens, not long ago, people did listen to literally hours of political addresses, interspersed with music, at antiwar rallies in the 1960s. If it is any measure, I can say from personal experience that there is a big difference between attending a rally and actually listening to the speeches.

Schudson (1995) notes further that the percentage of eligible voters who actually vote is an unreliable index of public participation. Across the course of American history, voter turnout has cycled up and down, with downward cycles occurring regularly when different groups are newly enfranchised—immigrants before World War I, women between the world wars, African Americans in the South, and 18- to 21-year-olds since the 1960s. As he notes, if one's standard for a democratic public is that it incorporates all individuals, then contemporary America is far more "democratic" than at any other period (see also Calhoun, 1992). Finally, he notes, critics who argue that the level and quality of public and political discourse was higher at some past point are likewise being selective: As many critics have pointed out, political discourse in the preceding two centuries, although it indeed featured strong and well-crafted arguments, also contained slanders, mudslinging, and sloganeering that we would find familiar today. Moreover, critics have seen the public in decline for a long time. Walter Lippmann, for example, in *Public Opinion* in 1922 and in *The Phantom Public* in 1925, French sociologists Gustav LeBon (1977) and Gabriel Tarde (1901/1969) in books at the turn of the century, and Alexis de Tocqueville (1835, 1840) in *Democracy in America* in 1835 all expressed reservations about the ability of mass or general publics to govern themselves rationally (see also Peters, 1995).[3]

A second challenge suggests that classical understandings of the public must change with the times, that traditional ways—both structures and narrative forms—of political expression are changing. The Internet is often held up as a technology capable of reinventing the public. In an essay contesting Putnam's notion of declining social capital, *Time* magazine essayist Richard Stengel (1996) suggests that Internet chat rooms and interest-group websites are augmenting traditional public forums, and MIT research scientist Janet Murray (1997) argues that Internet discourse is evolving narrative forms with which an increasingly computer-literate public feels comfortable.

Arguments about the decline of the public are inherently moral and political. As such, they are contests over readings of history and weighing of evidence and thus incapable of settlement (see, for example, Whitney & Wartella, 1988). There is no denying, however, that in these times, the very notion of publicness is strongly tied to the mass media, and the public has a strong stake in what the media say and do. In the remainder of this chapter, we will explore two further issues—the relationship of the contemporary public to the media and the question of how the media should relate to the public.

REPRESENTING THE PUBLIC

In understanding the ways the media and the public interact, we return to our levels of analysis argument. We are the public, and have relationships with the media, in four ways: as individuals, as aggregates, as members of organized groups, and as citizens ("We, the people").

THE PUBLIC AS INDIVIDUALS

We relate to the mass media as individuals every time we make a choice about what to watch, which magazines or audio tapes or books we buy, which movies we pay to go to, and so on. In this, we either are or are not the audience. But audience and public are distinct concepts: The audience is a market or commodity, but as part of the public, our range of concerns is wider. When we're part of the public, we put on a different hat: We think not only of ourselves and our own interests, but of a public interest, what we think is good and right and fair not just for ourselves but for our fellows. In other words, our public selves are *social* selves, and our public opinions are expressions of what content and conduct we think is good or bad, moral or immoral, ethical or unethical, tolerable or intolerable.

Clearly, most of our judgments about media are private or shared only among close friends (Did you see *Melrose Place* last night? What do you think of the new Wallflowers?). But occasionally, we may be moved by a social judgment to want to weigh in using some more public form—a fan letter or call, a congratulatory letter, or complaining call. The best estimates are that fewer than one in five Americans have ever written or called any mass medium to express an opinion (about one in four have communicated to an elected official). Moreover, workers in the news media inherently distrust the feedback they get from individuals, especially if it's critical (and most of it is) (Gans, 1979). Why? First, they believe that such feedback is unrepresentative—that people

363

who react strongly are somewhat different from those who do not (and after a while, they begin to recognize "repeat offenders," people who repeatedly write and call in). Second, most know from experience that many calls and letters arise not spontaneously from individual sentiment but from organized campaigns by interest groups. Their judgments about "what the public thinks" are in most cases much more shaped by organized *aggregate* measures of feedback—polls, surveys, ratings, and sales data—which rarely show the same patterns of public reaction as do individual responses.

THE PUBLIC AS AGGREGATE

When a producer or editor responds that a letter writer is "not representative," essentially he or she is arguing that an individual's expressed opinion is different from what the editor takes public opinion to be. More often than not, that judgment of public opinion is based on some *aggregated* or accumulated evidence: *how many* individuals have responded or behaved in a countable way—how many have bought a magazine? News magazine editors usually judge the popularity of an individual issue as some mixture of the newsworthiness of the news in a given week and the presumed appeal of the cover subject and cover story. How many calls or letters, pro or con, does an issue generate? (We'll give an example in a moment.) Most especially, what do polls, surveys, ratings, and other interview-based research tell them? There's a subtle but essential difference between the individual response (what one letter writer says, specifically) and aggregated individual responses (how many individuals, counted up, respond in roughly the same way), and that difference is that the individual voice and inflection is lost, while some sense of representativeness is gained.

Furthermore, as previously noted, different modes of aggregation may produce different representations of public opinion. One such example comes from the October 1983 invasion of Grenada, when President Reagan decided that the news media would not be present when U.S. troops landed on the island. The press raised a furor, citing the people's right to know, but as *Time* magazine (Henry, 1993) reported, the news media found their calls and mail running from 3 to 1, up to 99 to 1, in favor of the Reagan administration, against the news media. "It may well be," *Time* quotes former *Washington Post* ombudsman Robert McClosky, "that the public reacted cumulatively with a judgment that the press had it coming" (p. 76). Over the next 18 months, however, a number of polls and surveys, many of them commissioned by the media, found that in fact the public, at least as measured by polls and surveys, was reasonably supportive of the news media (Whitney, 1987).

So what *do* polls and surveys, as measures of aggregate public opinion, tell us about what and how the public thinks about the media? There's no quick and easy answer to that question, but several dimensions of public attitudes and beliefs are notable.[4]

In general, the public is inclined to be favorable toward the media; a variety of opinion polls have found that on average, a majority of the public finds the media reasonably fair, reasonably accurate, and reasonably believable. When it comes to the news media, people to a great extent value the press's performing a "watchdog" function, scrutinizing the performance of other institutions, especially government.

When it comes to specifics, however, the public *is* critical of the media. Majorities fault the media for invading people's privacy, believe the media should not report the results of election-day exit polls before polling places close, find the media sensationalistic, believe that the news media focus too heavily on bad news and find the media *biased.* Extensive research on how people think the media are biased shows, however, that somewhat fewer than half of them see this bias in political or ideological terms (among those who do, two thirds are likely to say the media have a liberal bias, but a third see them as conservatively biased). *More* people say that the bias is toward special interests, big business, government, and especially advertisers. And when people are questioned about the accuracy of stories they say they know something about firsthand, they give the media lower marks than they do in general.

The public both does and does not make distinctions between and among media; their expectations of how media *should* perform, that they should be truthful and impartial, are similar, but they do not believe all media meet these standards equally well. The public has a slightly higher opinion of their own media (the newspapers they usually read and local TV and radio) than of national media or "the media" in general) and a slightly higher opinion of television and radio than of print media. Abundant survey evidence suggests that most do not find

---

BOX 13.1

Public Opinion About the Media: A Sampler

These are selected results from opinion surveys about the news media. All results are from national polls of Americans age 18 and older, with sample sizes of 1,000 or greater and sampling errors of ±3% or less.

1. From 1991: *How would you rate the honesty and ethical standards of people in these different fields—very high, high, average, low, or very low?* (percentage saying high or very high):[a]

Pharmacists	60	Business executives	21
Medical doctors	54	Building contractors	20
Dentists	50	Senators	19
College teachers	45	Local political officeholders	19
Engineers	45	Congressmen	19
Police officers	43	Real estate agents	17
Funeral directors	35	State political officeholders	14
Bankers	30	Stockbrokers	14
TV reporters, commentators	29	Insurance salesmen	14
Journalists	26	Labor union leaders	13
Newspaper reporters	24	Advertising practitioners	12
Lawyers	22	Car salesmen	8

2. From 1939: *Do you feel that the news story (in newspapers) itself is almost always accurate as to its facts, is usually accurate as to its facts, or is not accurate in most instances?*[b]

Always accurate:	23.3%
Usually accurate:	45.1%
Not accurate:	24.7%
No opinion:	6.9%

3. From 1985: *In general, do you think news organizations get the facts straight, or do you think that they are often inaccurate?*[c]

Accurate:	55%
Inaccurate:	34%
No opinion:	11%

4. From 1984: *For each of the following types of media, I will read a description, and I would like you to tell me if you think it applies to that medium* (in percentages):[d]

	The newspaper you read	Nationally influential newspapers	Local TV News	Network TV News	News magazines	Radio	Supermarket tabloids
Accurate	77	73	78	81	81	78	29
Fair	86	79	77	82	76	79	32
Too negative	27	34	42	31	38	32	55
Arrogant	27	34	42	25	39	37	60
Politically biased	52	62	71	54	61	60	49
Invades people's privacy	33	45	62	52	58	54	66
Patriotic	75	78	75	80	76	77	46
Sensational	43	41	52	48	57	52	60
Reports the news intelligently	85	83	88	85	90	87	32

5. From 1990: *Do you feel the media should be protected . . .* [e]

	Not Protected at all	Protected sometimes	Protected Absolutely
When reporting about the sexual habits of public figures?	42%	38%	19%
When journalists criticize political leaders?	22%	41%	32%
When journalists report stories about national security without government approval?	45%	37%	17%
When distributing recordings that portray sexual themes, drugs, or religious cults?	62%	24%	13%

a. From *The Gallup Poll*, 1988, p. 115).
b. From a *Fortune* magazine poll reported in Erskine, 1970-1971, p. 641.
c. Gallup poll for the Times-Mirror Corp., June-July 1985, reported in Times-Mirror Corp., 1986, p. 20.
d. Gallup poll reported in Alter, 1984.
e. Wyatt, 1991.

either supermarket tabloids or "tabloid TV" credible—at least this is what they tell pollsters.

When the media and media practitioners are compared with other institutions, media usually come out in the middle of the deck—that is, when pollsters ask people to compare media, and media professionals, to other institutions and other professionals, media usually end up in the middle of the rankings. Usually, nonprofit and public service professions rank above media, political and commercial ones rank below.

Public assessment of the relationship between media and government shows some paradoxes. Although the public usually finds the media more believable than government officials and has a slightly higher general opinion of the media than of government, at the same time, a majority always sides with the government on questions of executive secrecy and particularly national security matters.

The public makes distinctions between kinds of media it would *restrict*, giving widest leeway to news and political content (except for national security matters) and least to entertainment content, particularly that which offends some people's sensibilities—materials containing profanity, sexual themes, and the like. In almost all cases, however, a significant fraction of the public would allow more censorship than the law currently allows, making the media less free to say and print what they now can.

Finally, and recently, the public has taken the media to task for what it sees as excessive cynicism and negativism in the news media. Quoting a 1995 study by the Times Mirror Center on the People and the Press, author James Fallows (1996) notes that "the public goes so far as to say that the press gets in the way of society solving its problems, an opinion that is even shared by many leaders. . . . Two out of three members of the public had nothing or nothing good to say about the media" (p. 46; see also Starobin, 1995).

Opinion researchers Andrew Kohut and Michael Robinson speak of a "riddle of two-mindedness" in the public.

> How is it possible for the public to be so "two-minded" about the press? How can it express such overall favorability, so much willingness to believe the press, then proceed to question the fairness, the independence, even the manners of newspeople and news organizations? (quoted in Times-Mirror Center, 1985, p. 4)

The answer seems to be that people perceive a need for news, information, and entertainment; they value the watchdog function, but at the same time have strong convictions that the media do not measure up to high standards of accuracy, fairness, honesty, and impartiality. People, to paraphrase the political scientist V. O. Key, are not fools.

368

THE PUBLIC AS "PUBLICS"

John Dewey (1927) has argued that to think of the public as some mass or aggregate—everybody—is not useful in understanding how a society works; he preferred to think of publics of like-minded individuals, concerned with and communicating with each other about a common interest or problem. As early as 1835, Tocqueville (1956/1981) was able to note in his classic *Democracy in America* that Americans were, far more than contemporary Europeans, joiners of voluntary associations, to promote all manner of interests. Tocqueville also took note of the fact that newspapers furnished the means of communication between members of such groups, that "hardly any association can do without newspapers" (p. 69). The newspapers of that day were less mass media and were more specialized publications issued by what were then called factions to allow publics both to speak among themselves and to recruit others to their point of view. Today, there are an estimated 35,000 voluntary associations, from the National Rifle Association to almost every school's PTA, and 40,000 private charitable foundations giving $30 billion per year, in the United States.[5] Most of the time these voluntary groups go their own way, doing their own business. But at every level, from the local to the national, public associations interact with the media, either to further their own ends, as when the National Rifle Association and Handgun Control, Inc., purchase ads to further their conflicting positions on gun control, or when they attempt to influence the media and the government to take positions consistent with their own. This influence can take several forms.

First is what communications researcher Oscar Gandy (1982) calls *information subsidy,* as groups (interest groups, businesses, and the government itself) feed information via news releases, videotapes, reports, and press conferences to the news media and to talk shows, information supporting that group's point of view.

Second is *lobbying and persuasion,* both directly to the media and indirectly, through attempts to influence public policy. A variety of civil rights groups, for example, successfully lobbied the federal Equal Employment Opportunity Commission and especially the Federal Communications Commission to insist that they provide better employment opportunities to ethnic minorities in the 1960s and 1970s. And the efforts of Action for Children's Television, a social action group active in the 1970s and '80s, were instrumental in the 1990 Children's Television Act, which restricted the amount of commercial time broadcasters could air during children's programs. More recently, a consortium of activist groups successfully lobbied the Federal Communications Commission in 1997 to persuade the television networks to revise the V-chip TV ratings from an age-based to an age- and content-based system.[6] Recently, too, interest groups have employed the Internet and E-mail with organized campaigns to reach political leaders, so successfully that some complain that "Astroturf" lobbying has replaced traditional "grassroots" lobbying.

Third is *confrontation* with the media to influence their content, as when the National Council of Catholic Bishops and other Catholic groups vehemently protested TV producer Norman Lear's 1972 script on the CBS program, *Maude*, in which the 47-year-old character accidentally became pregnant and had an abortion. That protest eventually led virtually all the program's sponsors to pull their advertising and 21 of 198 local affiliates to drop the program for the episodes dealing with the abortion.[7] On the other hand, the 1997 Southern Baptist Convention boycott of Disney appeared to have few immediate consequences for the company. Whether one views such efforts as good—democratic free expression aimed at winning the hearts and minds of the wider public—or bad—bluenosed attempts at censorship of ideas—usually depends on where one stands on the issue at hand.

Three points stand out in this quintessentially American exercise: First, social action, through protest, boycotts, and lobbying, can have profound consequences; it is almost indisputable that interest groups have been instrumental, particularly since the 1960s, in toning down if not eliminating stereotypical portrayals, especially on television, of African Americans, women, gays, and other social groups. One consequence, however, is that television executives, as we noted in Chapter 4, have increasingly followed the L-O-P—least objectionable programming—dictate, preferring bland content to controversy.[8] Second, however, the elevating of offensive depictions to the status of controversy not infrequently leads to *celebrity* for the offenders: it's likely that attempts to stifle the Martin Scorcese film, *The Last Temptation of Christ*, and 2 Live Crew's recording, "As Nasty as I Wanna Be," in fact increased interest in and sales of these media products. Third, it's easy to argue that suffering the discomfort of having to defend oneself from would-be censors is a fair price for media to pay for their freedom of speech and press.

THE PUBLIC AS CITIZENS

We've noted that democratic theory presupposes that government is the creature of the public. In essence, this means that majority public opinion *should* translate into public policy and law, including policy and law about the media. However, a recurrent theme in recent political campaigns is that government, especially in league with other powerful institutions, frustrates rather than enacts the public will. This assertion requires several qualifications. First, there is in fact some empirical evidence that much more often than not—although clearly not always—policy changes *can* be attributed to changes in public opinion, at least as measured by opinion polls.[9] Second, the Constitution provides the government, the media, and the public some insulation from the whims of the public. On the government side, the Constitution requires extraordinary majorities for amending the Constitution itself and makes the election of the president indirect, through the Electoral College, rather than direct, through popular election. Also, the Bill of Rights, the first 10 amendments to the Constitution, enumerates the rights of the people that are to be off limits to government.

Sometimes, the public needs protection from public opinion, especially to protect the rights of minorities, be they racial, ethnic, or opinion minorities. U.S. history, unfortunately, is replete with examples of violence against the media, much of it waged by opinion majorities and aimed at suppressing unpopular minority sentiments (Nerone, 1990).

For example, in the nineteenth century, a mob in Alton, Illinois, incensed at the writings of abolitionist editor Elijah Parrish Lovejoy, seized the press from his newspaper office and tossed it in the Mississippi River. When Lovejoy purchased another press and began anew, a second mob threw it in the river and murdered Lovejoy. And in 1898, a White supremacist mob in Wilmington, North Carolina, burned to the ground the office of a newspaper sympathetic to Blacks, killing more than a dozen Blacks in the process. Although not all violence against the press is conducted by local majorities, and although not all opinion majorities resort to violence to suppress unpopular opinion, the govern-

371

ment, largely through the courts, has the obligation to protect individuals' (and the media's) First Amendment rights. However, when majority opinion becomes strongly dominant and deeply held—as occurred in the 1798 Alien and Sedition Acts, in "Red scares" in the 1920s, 1930s, and 1950s, and during most U.S. wars—the courts have on occasion yielded to the dominant opinion and curtailed freedom of expression.

Episodes of violence are extreme forms of the urge to censor. We are all free to choose what we will read and listen to, and we all have the right to attempt to persuade others of the correctness of our own opinions and taste. The trick is to balance our rights, whether we are in the majority or minority, against the rights of others.

MEDIA RESPONSE TO THE PUBLIC

So far in this chapter, we have largely concerned ourselves with the public side of the media-public equation. Now we turn to the media side. At the end of the century, the media find themselves in unsettled circumstances: the readership and viewership of the "massest" of the mass media—daily newspapers, newsmagazines, network television—are in a slow but steady decline, public confidence in the media—news and entertainment media alike—is slipping, and political leaders from Dan Quayle and Bob Dole to Bill Clinton and Janet Reno garner sustained applause when they suggest that the media assault family values, promote violence, and pander to base instincts.

A number of responses have come from the media industries. Time-Warner's Warner Records sold its share of a "gangsta rap" label, Interscope Records, in 1995, and Disney added a Jesuit priest to its corporate board after controversy over its Miramax Films division's release of *Priest*, a film about a gay Roman Catholic priest (Streisand, 1997). Under extreme pressure, the broadcast and cable networks—with the notable exception of NBC—in 1997 instituted a "voluntary" program-rating system to be coupled with the V-chip screening device.[10] The American Society of Newspaper Editors in July 1997 announced a three-year "credibility initiative" and the newspaper publishers' trade association, the Newspaper Association of America, has begun an advertising campaign to bolster the reputation of the newspaper press (Peterson, 1997).

The 1990s also saw the beginning of a more grassroots movement dubbed "civic" or "public" journalism which through a variety of approaches is attempting to reconnect media to the communities which they serve. In one experiment, the Columbus, GA, *Ledger-Enquirer* organized community discussion groups that led to a civic association; in others, newspapers have used focus groups and surveys to determine what issues local citizens think are most important and have then crafted their election coverage around those issues rather than the more traditional approaches of deciding for themselves or focusing on issues nominated by the candidates themselves. Still others have formed community boards to discuss newspaper play and coverage with editors (Charity, 1995; Merritt, 1995). While the movement has come under criticism both within journalism and without, for allegedly compromising press independence and objectivity and for being little more than a marketing device, and while it has less than enthusiastic support from a majority of journalists, it does represent one effort to recognize—and to remind their publics—that the media do have a stake in public life.

"The public" has a variety of meanings, meanings that have evolved over time, and meanings that have real-world consequences for the way that media operate. The public view of the media as reflected by public opinion and public action suggests a recognition both of the power and importance of the media and of their shortcomings, and recent events suggest some media recognition of the need to address these shortcomings.

However, a full discussion of the public nature of the media requires us to discuss more fully the frameworks in which the debate about how the media *ought* to perform, a topic to which we turn in the next chapter.

NOTES

1. A good general discussion of how public opinion is represented is in Herbst (1993).
2. Important sources are Eisenstein (1978), Ginsberg (1986), Calhoun (1992), and especially Habermas (1962/1989).
3. It might be noted that de Tocqueville and Lippmann were both writing in periods in which the composition and definition of the public was being transformed—in de Tocqueville's case by the opening of what was then the West (west of the Atlantic states but east of the Mississippi) and the increasing

political empowerment of tradesmen, small merchants, and yeoman farmers, and in Lippmann's case, by immigrants from central and southern Europe.

4. The discussion that follows draws from the following: Alter, 1984; Erskine, 1970-1971; Gallup Poll, 1988; Times-Mirror Corp., 1985; Wyatt, 1991.

5. Foundation estimate from National Public Radio's *Morning Edition*, July 28, 1997.

6. In the fall of 1997, age ratings were TV-Y for programs considered good for children, TV-Y7 for those good for kids over age 7, TV-G for programs acceptable to general audiences, TV-PG for parental-guidance programs, TV-14 for programs suitable to audiences age 14 and older, and TV-M for programs suitable to adult audiences; in addition, programs were rated with letters V for Violence, S for Sexual situations, D for adult dialogue, N for Nudity; the ratings were voluntarily adopted by all broadcast and cable networks except NBC and Black Entertainment Television (BET) for entertainment programming but not news or sports.

7. Montgomery (1989) has a good account of the *Maude* controversy and other episodes of protests against television through the 1980s.

8. The coming out of Ellen DeGeneres on ABC's *Ellen* is an exception, but it ignited its own controversy when the network inserted, in the fall 1997 premiere episode, a parental advisory. DeGeneres protested the advisory and the TV-14 rating as evidence of the network's acquiescence to a view of homosexuality as a deviant lifestyle.

9. See Page and Shapiro (1983, 1992). In the earlier work, the authors argue that in two thirds to three quarters of all cases they examined, from the 1930s to the 1970s, changes in public opinion led to changes in public policy; such changes were *most* likely on large-scale domestic issues and most likely in the later time periods (i.e., the 1960s and '70s) and *least* likely for "low-salience" issues—ones less likely to get extensive media coverage. On such issues, they argue, special interests rather than the mass public probably dominate policy.

10. The V-chip provision of the 1996 Telecommunications Act required broadcasters and cablecasters voluntarily to create their own ratings system or face having the Federal Communications Commission impose one on their programming.

Normative Theories of the Media

Q uestions about the proper role and function of media are as old as the media themselves, and systematic approaches to their answers are referred to as normative theories of the media. The media, beginning with the printing press, were born into Western society in a system we have earlier described, and that we can characterize as an authoritarian normative approach. But for most of their existence, questions about how they ought to perform have been answered by resort to other, newer, theories, first the libertarian, and later the social responsibility and materialist models.[1]

The beginnings of the modern Western press, and later all mass media, are tied to the political ferment of the late 1700s and the philosophy of the Enlightenment—and the foundations of the American revolution. The Enlightenment brought forth a view of human freedom and human nature that characterizes modern Western history, including key concepts that relate directly to how media should operate.

First and foremost is the assumption that humans are rational creatures, capable of setting aside base emotions and choosing between right and wrong, between what is false and what is true.

Second is the concept of liberty, reflected in the first few words of the American Declaration of Independence—"all men are created equal and endowed by their Creator with certain unalienable rights," including liberty. *Liberty* in this context is freedom *from* intrusion by government.

Third, that there *is* such a thing as truth, that it *is* discoverable by people through a process of reasoning, rather than being handed down by God. English poet and philosopher John Milton put it this way in a 1644 essay called *Areopagitica:* "Let [Truth] and Falsehood grapple. Whoever knew Truth put to the worse in a free and open encounter?" In more modern terms, truth emerges from the competition between ideas. Rational people will be able to discriminate between the true and the false.

CLASSICAL LIBERALISM

This overall philosophy of society comes to be called *classical liberalism* in economics or *libertarianism* in theories of freedom of expression. One should not, however, confuse this form of liberalism with its current everyday usage: A classical liberal philosophy is closer to modern conservatism or libertarianism, which emphasizes individualism and minimal government roles in society. Classical liberalism was, however, quite consistent with the then-developing theory and practice of economics we know today as capitalism (epitomized by the 1776 publication in England of Adam Smith's *The Wealth of Nations*). We see the two *merge* in a familiar metaphor, "the free marketplace of ideas."

The idea of a free marketplace of ideas assumes equivalence between the world of commerce and the world of ideas: As products compete, ideas do, too. In free competition, the good and useful drive out the bad and worthless. Thus, the driving spirit of liberal capitalism suggests that free people, left to their own initiative, will make economically and intellectually profitable choices. And "left to their own" largely means that the state, the government, will not interfere. In the realm of expression, this idea is embodied in the First Amendment to the U.S. Constitution: "Congress shall make no law abridging freedom of speech, or of the press. . . . " If the government does not interfere in expression, the free marketplace will assure that good ideas will drive out bad ones, and truth will prevail.

According to common wisdom, this philosophy has prevailed, at least in England and the United States, from the late 1700s to today. The history of *formal* or *government* control of media (remember that until the twentieth century, mass media were exclusively print media) is largely one of decreasing state or government control. Moreover, media became more abundant in the same period, with rising literacy, rising wealth, and increasing technological sophistication. In 1900, there were 2,226 daily newspapers in America, with every major city having more than one and the largest cities having half a dozen or more. And these newspapers competed with each other not only for news, but also in the realm of ideas, staking out different positions on the political spectrum. Although we have substantially fewer (about 1,500 daily newspapers) today, we also have other kinds of news media: radio, television, and on-line news services such as Bloomberg and CNN.

Nonetheless, between the 1880s and 1940s, cracks began to appear in the conceptual foundation of classical liberal capitalism, both in its notions of rationalism and in the assumption that the marketplace is free.

The popularization of Darwinian theories of evolution and Freudian ideas in psychology and psychoanalysis gradually led to a widespread questioning of the nature of human nature. If the theory of evolution is substantially correct, humans are animals, not, as biblical authority would have it, direct descendants from God. Freudian psychoanalysis emphasizes the degree to which human behavior is motivated not by rational but by irrational impulses. The work of Karl Marx similarly challenged the concept that human thought is rational and logical. For Marx, human thought is determined by the material and economic relations of social life.

Events of the first half of the twentieth century seemed to validate this revised, negative view of human rationality. The incredible carnage of the First World War (in which more soldiers died than in the Second World War, Korea, Vietnam, and the Persian Gulf War combined) seemed wholly senseless. Fifteen years later, there seemed no accounting for how a cultivated and civilized nation such as Germany could democratically vote into power an Adolf Hitler. And another 10 years later, the world was staggered by the horror of the Holocaust.

Substantial cracks also appeared in the idea of a free marketplace. In the commercial and industrial arena, the same time period, roughly the 1880s to 1930, saw not a free marketplace but its opposite—the formation of trusts, combines, and cartels. Oil, railroads, meatpacking, and steel were consolidated into *monopolies,* in which one firm controls all or almost all of the trade, or *oligopolies,* in which a small number of firms control a commercial sector. A monopoly becomes almost wholly free to charge what it will and to treat workers as it will. There is no competition, and any effort by outsiders to establish competition can be suppressed by the monopoly, which can control necessary resources and make the cost of attempting to compete prohibitively expensive.

An oligopoly can operate in much the same way if the companies agree to charge the same prices and otherwise limit competition. And, as noted, oligopoly characterized a number of key American industries until the government began to intervene with antitrust legislation in the first two decades of the twentieth century. For such legislation to pass, however, required a widespread public recognition that in the commercial arena, the possibility of competition did not guarantee a free marketplace. It also required a recognition that the government might have to intervene to promote competition in some instances, whereas in others, the government might actually promote monopoly, as in the telephone industry and other utilities. Government grants of monopoly, however, were always accompanied by government regulation of the prices such monopolies could charge.

Changes in the media landscape also challenged the idea of a free marketplace of ideas. The early part of the century saw the development of motion pictures and radio. Movies were virtually born as a monopoly, or rather as a cartel. A small number of people, of whom the inventor Thomas Edison is the most notable, held the patents on motion picture cameras and projectors and thus could control who could make motion pictures. (A major reason Hollywood became the American movie industry center was that "outlaw" moviemakers moved there to be beyond the reach of the agents of the New York-based movie trust. When the trust was broken up, Hollywood remained the center because the weather and scenery were more conducive to outdoor filming year-round.)

Radio was different. Even in the 1910s and 1920s, the technology for rudimentary radio transmission and reception was fairly widely available, so much so that hundreds of radio stations began operating.[2] But radio transmission (and the same, later, is true of television) relied on peculiarities of the electromagnetic spectrum: Only on a finite number of spaces on this spectrum can clear signals be transmitted and received. As more stations came on the air in the 1920s, their signals began to interfere with each other, and reception became difficult—the airwaves became the biblical Tower of Babel. The solution for individual radio operators was either to increase the power of the transmission, to tell listeners that a station was moving its broadcast to a different place on the dial, or to go off the air. But this was only a temporary solution for any one operator, and these strategies compounded the problem for the operators and the audience. By the mid-1920s, radio operators appealed to the federal government to clean up the mess—to regulate the airwaves so that some voices, at least, could be heard. In 1927, Congress passed the Federal Radio Act to regulate radio broadcasting, and it was refined with further regulation in 1934 as the Federal Communications Act. This regulation (remember that classical liberal capitalism presupposes little or no government interference) assigned particular frequencies and power levels to individual license holders and, significantly, *limited* the number of stations on the air.

Thus, the regulation explicitly—and for the first time with regard to a U.S. medium—recognized limits on numbers of voices. In theory, then and now, anyone can publish a newspaper, a magazine, or a book. But in regulating broadcast media, the government was left with the question of who should be allowed to have a broadcast license and who should not. The early Federal Radio Commission emphasized three criteria: adequate financial means to put and keep a station on the air, the technical ability to reproduce an adequate broadcast signal, and operation of the station in the "public interest, convenience, and necessity." This last criterion was meant to assure that, because not everyone could have a station, those who did would operate for the public benefit. These criteria favored, early on, those with significant financial means. The more financial resources a potential station owner could demonstrate—to buy equipment, to create programming—the higher the likelihood that the applicant would get a license. Furthermore, to assure that once on the air, broadcasters would continue to serve the public interest, licenses were to be renewed every six years. Renewal required demonstrating that the licensee had lived up to his or her public interest obligations. Thus, for the first time, the government found itself—and at the invitation of those to be regulated—applying a very

379

different formula for how media ought to operate: Classical liberalism urges a negative conception of regulation—that the government should take no role, make no law. Broadcasting requires a positive or affirmative role—that the government must intervene, as a referee to decide who can use a medium.

At the same time, the print media were changing too. Improved technology had led to lower production costs. Two phenomena served to nationalize media—the rise of modern marketing and advertising of national brands, and the development of transcontinental communication systems, first the telegraph, later the telephone.

The telegraph gave rise to national news or wire (as in telegraph wire) services, of which the largest and most important is the Associated Press (AP). The AP is a cooperative service owned by newspaper publishers, which gave a local monopoly to its members: Only one daily newspaper in a city could belong to it, and thus one newspaper would have a substantial advantage over its competitors in the gathering of national and international news. The one-paper-per-city rule ended in the 1940s after the Supreme Court ruled that it violated antitrust law.

Advertising had come to play a more important role in newspapers and magazines, and circulation—the price the customer pays for the product—a less important one. As this happened, the advertiser became a more important influence on what appeared in the newspaper and the reader or subscriber became less important. Newspapers had to pay more attention to the demands of advertisers.

All together, the strategies publishers learned from their counterparts in other industries, and technological and economic changes within the publishing industry, created an important trend that continues to this day: the consolidation and concentration of print media into smaller numbers of companies, with, in newspapers particularly, smaller numbers of newspapers. We earlier noted that in 1900, there were 2,226 daily newspapers. By 1950, U.S. population had doubled, but the number of daily papers had shrunk to 1,900; by 1990, population had gone up another 30%, but the number of daily newspapers declined to under 1,750, and by 1997, it is estimated that there are just under 1,500 daily newspapers (Bogart, 1989). In other words, whereas broadcasting has a physical limit on the number of operators or possible channels, economic and technological constraints began in the early decades of the twentieth century to limit the number of voices the public could hear, especially in the print media.

By the mid 1990s, the case of on-line communication via the Internet and World Wide Web and the spectacular growth of this form of communication raised anew questions of media regulation. Anyone can set up a web page, anyone can use (for minimal cost) electronic mail, and anyone can access information that may or may not be appropriate to all users, especially children. This new form of communication, without national boundaries, clear ownership, or standards for conduct, has posed a challenge regarding how to think about a free marketplace of ideas. This medium offers an unprecedented opportunity to increase the number of voices in the marketplace. Yet, with so many voices speaking contradictory words, what is credible and who is to be believed? Will the Internet, in the long run, undergo the consolidation and concentration that other media have seen? It is becoming clear that the notions of liberalism's view that truth will win out in an open marketplace of ideas may be severely put to the test by on-line media.

What does this media history and media economics have to do with normative theories of media performance? Everything. The historical challenge makes us question how the media are organized economically as well as what they say to us. The basic argument between supporters and challengers of classical liberalism's conception of media performance has to do with how well the media serve the public. Liberalism as a theory of media performance is predicated upon classical liberal economic theory. Does a capitalist system of media organization allow for the widest variety and diversity of viewpoints, or does it limit cultural and informational products along particular lines?

This thinking suggests several subquestions, as well: first, as consumers of media, do we have access to the widest possible variety of ideas and to truthful, intelligent, and comprehensive accounts of society? Second, to what extent do we and others have access to media to express our own ideas, to promote points of view about which we may care deeply? In other words, are we free and able to be producers of ideas as well as consumers? These questions of consumption and production are pivotal in a debate about how well a liberal capitalist system performs.

The strongest argument on the liberal side is the sheer volume of the media. In the United States, there are 1,500 daily newspapers, 8,000 weekly newspapers, 11,000 magazines, almost 11,000 radio stations, almost 1,500 television stations, 2,500 book publishers annually issuing almost 60,000 book titles, and seven major motion picture studios. There are four major television networks, two major U.S. news wire services, and dozens of other newspaper-affiliated news services, five major recording companies (and numerous independent companies), and countless other media and ancillary services—newsletters, film processors, shoppers (free circulation newspapers), computer networks, syndication services, cable television systems in virtually every community, and on and on. The output of this system—millions of words, sounds, and images every day—is literally incalculable.

This media system, by accident or design, produces an astounding variety of material. On the consumption side, its beauty, the libertarian argument goes, is that of the free marketplace of ideas. These media compete with one another in a very direct sort of way. As consumers, we are wholly free to buy what we want, not to buy what we don't want; to "vote" with our TV remote controls, our radio dials, with the videocassettes we choose to rent; to buy products and vote for politicians if we like their ads or to boycott them if we do not. Moreover, the system is democratic, and, even better, pluralistic—if you or I don't like and don't buy something like the *National Enquirer*, that's fine. If the product can't find a market, can't find an audience, it will cease to exist. But if other people do like it and buy it, then they're free to do so, and if enough others do so, then it will remain available.

On the production side, the argument for the libertarian model is that the producer is remarkably free to produce whatever he, she, or it wants. If a media product can find an audience, the product will be produced. To be profitable, the producer must "give the audience what it wants," and if he, she, or it does so, then all obligations have been met, save one: As with any other product, no media producer may knowingly produce anything that is dangerous to the audience. On the production as well as on the consumption side, this process is viewed as both democratic and pluralistic. If there is too much competition in some media sector, the producer is free to shift to another one, to try to find an audience. If the producer fails, it is only because the audience won't buy—the audience is supreme.

However, we have already suggested that as an overall theoretical model and for practical and economic reasons, this rosy picture cannot go unanswered.

CHALLENGES TO CLASSICAL LIBERALISM

SOCIAL RESPONSIBILITY THEORY

A social responsibility position is the mainstream counterpoint to the liberal capitalism viewpoint. Shortly after World War II, a blue-ribbon Commission on the Freedom of the Press (1947), largely funded by *Time* magazine publisher Henry Luce and chaired by the very respected president of the University of Chicago, Robert Maynard Hutchins, was convened to discuss the state of American media. The panel was frankly worried that economic, cultural, and technological trends, and particularly the decreasing number of editorial voices in the nation's press, were leaving the nation less well served by its media than it should be. In its 1947 report, the Commission observed, among other things, that the media spent too much effort on the trivial and sensational, that the press was not meeting its responsibility to provide "a truthful, comprehensive, and intelligent account of the day's events in a meaningful context." The press should be providing a forum for the exchange of ideas, presenting the widest variety of views. The press should avoid stereotyping and provide a representative view of the society. This could be accomplished, the Commission said, if the press were more responsible, if its practitioners were better trained, and if it effectively regulated itself. If it could not, the Commission suggested, then the government might have to establish its own media and more directly intervene to assure that the press was responsible—a departure from the libertarian notion.

In another departure from libertarianism, the Commission suggested that the media should be a "common carrier" of ideas. The press had obligations to present different ideas. This departed significantly from the libertarian idea that the media are wholly free—free, if they wish, to promote only those ideas of their own choosing.

Note that the intellectual seeds for such a social responsibility position are planted by the case of broadcasting, where government intervention was necessary to allocate channels. The very idea that government had a role in assuring a free and responsible press—at least in the United States—was born of the necessity of assuring an open marketplace.[3]

As might be expected, the print press greeted the Commission report with hostility and derision, but its ideas over time have gained ground. Since 1947, the American press has professionalized itself considerably, with far larger proportions of media producers having received university and college training in communications or journalism and more of them subscribing to some social responsibility notions, especially that they have obligations to be fair, truthful, and objective and to provide balanced representations of the society and its varying opinions. At the same time, virtually none of them would subscribe to a notion that government control or ownership of media would enhance free expression.

In fact, the social responsibility school of thought is not that far from libertarianism. The two viewpoints share, to some degree, two key assumptions that more radical critics will question—the general rationality of the audience, its ability to separate truth from falsehood, and the assumption underlying *this* assumption, that of an independent, discoverable truth in the first place. The main point of divergence is over the matter of the role of government, with libertarians insistent that the government have no role and social responsibility advocates maintaining that government should remain in the background, prodding media to be responsible through self-regulation.

There are other approaches to the question of how media should operate, however, that diverge more fundamentally from the liberal tradition than the social responsibility doctrine does.

MARXIST CRITIQUE

In 1846, Marx wrote in *The German Ideology* (1970, p. 64) that "in every epoch, the ruling ideas are the ideas of the ruling class." In this century, much of the criticism of the media economy has been shaped to some degree by Marx and his followers. On examination, Marx's quote goes to the heart of the assumption of the discoverability of truth by asking the degree to which, as both consumers or producers, the average person has a chance to see the truth.

BOX 14.1

The Fairness Doctrine

As we noted in earlier chapters, the histories of the print media and of the broadcast media travel along different tracks, and the regulatory environment of each differs. At about the same time as the Hutchins Commission was writing its report, the Federal Communications Commission, which regulates broadcasting and telecommunications, was writing a policy that came to be known as the Fairness Doctrine. When the FCC issued it in 1949 as an advisory to broadcasters, the set of regulations was to guide radio and television station operators in dealing with issues of controversy: After all, the "scarce-channel" logic goes, if not everyone can have a radio or TV station of their own, then broadcasters have an affirmative obligation to see that all views are represented. This is a prototypical example of social responsibility theory in action.

Basically, the Fairness Doctrine required some degree of balance in the presentation of controversial issues. If a broadcaster supported one side in a controversial issue (say, in a prolife editorial during a newscast, or in giving or selling air time to a group), then the broadcaster was obligated to make time available to others to present other sides of the issue. Later, the FCC extended the doctrine to require that if a personal attack were made on an individual, a station was required to inform the individual and offer air time for a reply.

From its earliest days, the Fairness Doctrine was vigorously criticized by the broadcast industry. The argument was the libertarian one, that as far as possible, government should keep its hands off the free marketplace: Let the broadcasters, in a competitive environment, be the ones to decide what should be seen and heard. The effect of government regulation in this area would be, they argued, not that "all sides" would be heard on controversial matters, but that broadcasters would be discouraged from allowing *any* sides to be heard, that broadcasting would steer away from any matters of controversy. Moreover, they argued, channels are not that scarce, and new technologies are making more and more channels available to the audience.

In the deregulatory political climate of the 1980s, the anti-Fairness Doctrine arguments won out at the FCC. In August 1987, the Commission voted unanimously to suspend—but not repeal—the Fairness Doctrine, effectively relieving broadcasters of direct legal requirements to be fair, although they are still bound, broadcasters argue, by moral and ethical social responsibility requirements to be so. (It should be noted, too, that the *equal time* rule, requiring broadcasters to provide equal amounts of time in comparable parts of the day to all legally qualified candidates for political office, remains in effect.)

Marxism is based on two major sets of arguments. First, Marxism offers an interpretation of the principles of the capitalist economy. Second, it emphasizes the relations between the economy, politics, and the various forms of communication and culture.

According to contemporary Marxists, it is important to recognize that the mass media are implicated in the various structures of capitalism at a number of different levels. The media involve the production of goods, hardware as well as programming. The media are a major source of advertising and the promotion of other goods. The media help to create and shape our desires for certain lifestyles, images, and commodities. And the media package and commodify the audience so that it can be sold to advertisers. The audience has to be large, but it also has to be the right kind of audience, and it has to be in the right frame of mind.

Moreover, we have to remember that the media play a very central role in contemporary society: They shape our desires for goods, they control the information we receive around the world, they organize our leisure activities, and they provide many of the interpretations of reality we use in our everyday lives.

Consequently, like any other industry, the media industries must attempt to control and rationalize both the production and the consumption processes, trying to make people's tastes consistent and predictable. The media industries attempt to limit the uncertainty of both supply and demand, in order to maximize their own efficiency and profits.

The nub of the critical argument is that some sectors of the society and economy have so much access to the resources to put forward their ideas that others essentially have none. On the production side, the critical argument is that those who have access to the means of production will use those means to promote points of view that either forward their own interests or at least bolster the status quo. Moreover, the critical counterpoint argues that on the consumption side, we are thwarted from receiving ideas that seriously challenge the existing order. Although the libertarians, this argument goes, may be quite right that we have available a great *variety* of media fare, there's not much *diversity* there (Glasser, 1984/1985). What's the difference?

Variety suggests lots of material that is superficially, but not basically, different. Suppose all car manufacturers built basically the same car—say a four-door, five-passenger, four-cylinder, automatic transmission model—but allowed us to choose among 500 different colors

BOX 14.2

Variety and Diversity in Children's Television

How much variety and diversity of programming is there in the media? This question was addressed in a study of children's programming in a midwestern community. The study was prompted by arguments made at the Federal Communications Commission throughout the 1980s: that the growth of new technologies, such as cable television, video, pay television, and satellites was increasing the diversity of programming available to children and therefore no single broadcaster in a community had a responsibility to program for child audiences. The study asked: Beyond over-the-air broadcast television, what sorts of programming are available for children in one media marketplace, Champaign-Urbana, Illinois? A survey of all audio-video programming available to children in this one community was conducted to test the proposition that there indeed is both variety and diversity.

Program variety in children's programming refers to the amount of broadcast, cable, and videocassette rentals of children's product in this one community. Program diversity, on the other hand, is measured by the number of different genres or types of programs that could be delivered through any of the different media delivery systems, such as over-the-air broadcast television stations, cable channels, or videocassette rentals. In particular, two genres of program have been the focus of much public debate about children's television: animated toy-related programs (such as *Teenage Mutant Ninja Turtles* or *Ghostbusters*) and educational/informational programming, or those programs designed to educate children and provide them with information about science, history, culture, and so on (the best example here is *Sesame Street*).

So, how much variety did the researchers find in this one community? First, children's programming was available on all television, cable, and pay cable services during weekdays and weekends, and in fairly large amounts: On broadcast television, researchers found 52 hours on weekdays and 21 hours on weekends (even though Saturday morning is thought to be children's time). And basic cable services in the community aired 149 hours of children's shows during weekdays and 36 hours on weekends (thanks to the inclusion of Nickelodeon, the children's channel on cable). However, there were relatively few children's videos available for rental: Only 9% of all videotapes available in the community's 17 video rental stores could be classified as children's video.

Aside from variety, which the children do seem to have, do they have diversity of programming? Only if their families could afford cable ($18 a month—$216 a year—at the time):

(continued)

BOX 14.2 Continued

The most striking characteristic of these data is their clear indication that there is no diversity of children's programming on commercial television. All the weekday commercial children's programs are cartoon; two thirds of these are toy related. Public television provides the only alternative genres: educational and variety children's programming such as *Sesame Street* and *Captain Kangaroo*. Weekend commercial television provides minimal diversity: Only 3 of the 28 commercial children's programs over the weekend are not cartoons.

A very different picture emerges, however, in the analysis of children's program offerings on cable television. Although cartoon programming still predominates, composing more than one half of all basic cable children's offerings, there is much more diversity. Nearly all of the seven categories of genres (including: animated toy, animated non-toy, live action comedy or drama, quiz, variety, exercise, instructional, or other) are represented on cable services.

It appears that Champaign-Urbana children with access to basic cable and pay cable services are able to receive both a variety and a diversity of children's programming that far exceed that provided by the broadcast television stations in the community. . . . And unlike adult tapes, which tend to represent Hollywood film product, children's video tapes (with the exception of Disney movies and old cartoons) represent television-originated product. . . . Dominating this television product on videotape is toy-related programming. . . . Videotape rentals in Champaign-Urbana simply provide more of what is available on television and cable. Little educational programming is available for rent or purchase, and few stores carry a majority of non-toy related animated tapes. (pp. 51-54)

This study confirms what critics of children's television argued throughout the 1980s: that there was too little diversity in children's television provided by the traditional broadcasters. Such evidence helped to bring about the passage of the Children's Television Act of 1990, which, among other provisions, requires all broadcasters to identify their information/educational children's programming and which establishes a National Endowment for Children's Television to encourage and fund the production of more educational television. As of Fall 1997, it is too early to tell whether, in this one community or nationwide, the act's requirement that broadcasters air and label educational and informational programming for children has had much of an impact on variety and diversity.

SOURCE: Wartella, Heintz, Aidman, and Mazzarella, 1990.

of paint. That would be a lot of variety. Diversity suggests fundamental difference. Diversity in motor vehicles would include motorcycles, minivans, vans, pickups, two-door sports models, convertibles, sedans, station wagons, and so on. And real diversity would not only offer us private transportation but comfortable and efficient public transportation. So what if we have 35 channels on our cable television if all we can see during prime time is situation comedies, cop shows, and bland old movies? So what if we have competing television news, but we can't tell the difference between one station or network and another? So what if we have competing newspapers if all the competitors ignore or trivialize the same groups—African Americans, women, the young—and keep their politics close to the political center?

The critical counterpoint argues that economic structures foreclose true diversity of ideas. The critical argument comes in two main forms, the political economic and the cultural. Political economic criticism focuses on the ownership of the means of production as the mode of control of the social order. "Freedom of the press belongs to those who own one" is a quotation variously attributed to Mohandas Gandhi and to the American press critic A. J. Liebling. Cultural criticism focuses on the processes by which dominant forms of thought (ideologies) support the existing social order and suppress social change.

THE POLITICAL ECONOMIC ARGUMENT

We have noted the great number of different media in the United States. Press critic Ben Bagdikian (1997) has pointed out that if American daily newspapers, magazines, radio and television stations, and book publishers were owned by separate individuals, there would be 25,000 different owners (a large number, yes, but still only one out of every 10,000 Americans). But there are not 25,000 different owners. Today, Bagdikian says, just 10 corporations dominate the output of daily newspapers and most of the sales and audience in magazines, broadcasting and cable, books, and movies. They are Time Warner, Disney, Viacom, News Corporation Ltd. (Murdoch), Sony, Tele-Communications Inc., Seagram (ownership positions in TV, movies, cable, books and music), Westinghouse (CBS), Gannett, and General Electric (NBC). "In the last five years," Bagdikian notes, "a small number of the country's largest industrial corporations has acquired more public communications power—including ownership of the news—than any private business has ever before possessed in world history" (p. xii). Together, these companies "have created what is, in effect, a new communications cartel within the United States" (p. ix).

Not only do a relatively small number of people head these corporations, a very small number effectively control them. Although the directors of these corporations constitute a larger number than the chief officers of the companies, there are interlocks between these boards; that is, the same people tend to sit on boards of a number of corporations, both within media and in other pivotal sectors of the economy, and they are the same *types* of people, drawn from a very small upper stratum of the society.

Media concentration has continued to accelerate. In the first edition of his book in 1984, Bagdikian said 50 corporations dominated U.S. media, through ownership and control, and at the time, companies tended to concentrate on one medium, such as Gannett in newspapers or RCA, which then owned NBC, in broadcasting. By the third edition in 1990, he argues, the number of dominant owners was 23, and today, as noted, he says it is now ten, with two of the biggest deals concentrating media ownership and power occurring in the past two years, the $19 billion acquisition of ABC/Cap Cities by Disney and the purchase of Turner Broadcasting by Time Warner, which created the world's two largest media corporations.

Many of the dominant media firms are not *just* media firms but part of larger multinational corporations with diverse interests. Columbia is a unit of Sony, CBS is owned by Westinghouse, and NBC is owned by General Electric. To what extent can the media perform other functions—information and entertainment—adequately if their major role is to make money? A corollary question is the extent to which a media enterprise will be subject to the corporate goals and interests of a parent company. For example, questions have been raised about whether network news programs adequately cover stories that negatively portray their corporate owners, and there have been numerous suggestions of the possibility of both corporate and self-censorship. Can NBC and CBS, whose parent companies have strong financial interests in power generation, including nuclear power, be counted on to report fairly and in depth about utilities and their regulation? Perhaps the news divisions are sufficiently insulated from corporate influence, but the appearance of a conflict of interest may erode the confidence of the public in their credibility.

Media economics in general, the political economic argument goes, are driven by a *logic of capitalism,* a pursuit of maximal profit, in which advertising plays a primary role. We noted that the *Saturday Evening Post* was driven out of business, not because it failed to attract readers, but because it was deserted by advertisers. The liberal point argued for the supremacy and democracy of the audience as voter. The death of mass magazines, entertaining and informing large audiences, is a counterpoint. But, you may argue, the vitality of specialized magazines supports the libertarian argument. Yes, but only to a point, that point being where some profit exists. It is worth observing that among the thousands of magazines in this nation, there is none called *Old and Poor* or *South Central Los Angeles.*[4] Furthermore, as Bagdikian (1997) points out, the corporate logic of capitalism extends into the news coverage of the largest media, who instantly take note of any drop in the stock market that would jeopardize the minority of Americans who have significant investment holdings, but who paid little attention from 1987 to 1994 when the real buying power of the minimum wage declined by 35%.

And it is worth remembering that there are millions of people, even in America, who simply cannot afford to purchase any media products. If a medium cannot attract advertisers, and its potential audience cannot afford to buy it, it probably does not exist. As Box 14.2, on variety and diversity in children's television, points out, variety and diversity exists only for kids whose parents can afford cable TV, premium cable channels, VCRs, and videocassette rentals. Moreover, the Gulf War produced still one further example: By the time of the cease-fire, the networks had lost millions of dollars, both because of extra programming costs associated with news coverage (NBC alone spent almost $45 million to cover the war), money that the networks then had to recoup by cutting back on news coverage the rest of the year, and especially because advertisers would not advertise on the news specials that replaced the usual entertainment fare. Noted Howard Stringer, president of the CBS Broadcast Group,

> One of the great ironies is that advertisers pulled commercials because they were afraid the coverage would include a lot of people being

killed. But there are more people routinely killed across the spectrum
of American television in a given night than you saw in any of the coverage of the war. (quoted in Carter, 1991, p. C1)

Thus, the political economic argument against liberal capitalism focuses on ownership of media production and the power that ownership
and control exercises over both individuals' ability to produce messages they would like others to see and hear and individuals' abilities
to receive or consume messages as well. Where the liberal point emphasizes openness and variety, the political economic counterpoint answers, "only if there's a profit in it." And increasingly, the number of
independent voices through which ideas can be expressed with any real
hope of reaching more than a few eyes and ears is declining.

THE CULTURAL ARGUMENT

The cultural argument points to the logic of capitalism argument,
as well. But instead of focusing on the ownership of the means of production, it looks at the programs—the messages—that are produced.
The cultural argument suggests that a media system such as America's
runs to simple-minded and superficial content not only because capitalist media producers are bent on making a profit at all cost, and the
surest way to profit is noncontroversial programs that avoid offending
anyone. Rather, it begins by looking at why the media industries' products—television programs, films, news, music, and so on—are different
from other capitalist commodities.

What is unique about the products of the media industries? The
cultural argument starts with the fact that the media make meanings
and organize those meanings into systems or codes. These codes interpret the world; they make it meaningful and comprehensible. But the
cultural argument goes one step further. It argues that we only use
some of these codes to interpret our reality. In other words, certain
codes of meaning are not only intelligible, they are also assumed to be
descriptions of the world. As descriptions, they appear obvious, commonsensical, and even natural. They are assumed to be simply neutral
and objective descriptions of how things are, and of how they are supposed to be. Because we live within these systems of representation, we
experience the world according to their codes of meaning (Hall, 1980).

There is nothing outside of them that allows us to measure or judge their truth. As we noted in Chapter 7, such systems are called ideologies, or systems of meaning by which people live. They define how we experience the world, what we take for granted. Ideologies define what we take to be common sense; their truth appears obvious and even natural, unconscious and often unchallengeable.

Every society has to maintain itself; it has to continuously reproduce the things necessary for its existence. One way of doing that is through force and the active suppression of opposition. A more efficient way involves getting people to accept a way of thinking and seeing the world that makes the existing organization of social relations appear natural, inevitable, and proper.

Ideologies are, then, not merely particular systems of representation or ways of seeing. They are also ways of excluding and limiting, for they set the boundaries on what we are able to understand and accept into the realm of the possible. Finally, ideologies are not neutral. Obviously, they are connected to the struggle of one group or another to maintain or challenge particular social organizations, particular relations of power. On this view, culture involves constant struggles between competing ideological codes, each attempting to gain the upper hand, to somehow win people into seeing the world in terms of its particular meanings, to experience the world on its terms. Obviously, although some ideological codes are explicitly linked to political positions and philosophies (we can think of the ideologies of communism and capitalism, or of the Democrats and the Republicans), the cultural argument makes ideology into a much more pervasive and common feature of our lives.

This cultural or ideological argument does not suggest that no space is left for alternative views. What it does suggest is that when they appear in the mainstream media, such views are likely to be clearly identified as "controversial," and hence suspect, and, consistent with the more materialist critics' thinking, that they likely will be crowded out by profit-seeking producers who would rather avoid controversy in the first place. Another common strategy is to rewrite controversial events or positions so that their content is transformed from a challenge to the dominant values into a reaffirmation. For example, during the protests of the 1960s, news media reporting on demonstrations would often emphasize that the very fact of such protests confirmed that our

393

society was free and equal. In the process, the actual object of the protest (for example, the war in Vietnam or the disproportionate number of Blacks serving in the armed forces) was forgotten or ignored (Gitlin, 1980).

Thus, our ability to produce messages is constrained by the taken-for-granted assumptions of normality by those who operate the media system, at the same time that the fare we have available to consume is caught up in the same assumptions. The job of cultural critics is to unmask the ideologies inherent in various media products: the news, advertising, films, the Internet.

NORMATIVE SOLUTIONS: WHAT SHOULD BE DONE?

What do such normative theories ultimately have to say about the context in which media should operate?

A strict, radical libertarian would argue that the media should be free to publish and broadcast what they wish, that sovereign, rational consumers should determine their fate. The government should have no role in the media, except perhaps to foster and encourage their economic success and to referee frequency allocations, as it does in broadcasting and cellular communications.

A strict, radical Marxist, either of a cultural or a political-economic stripe, would argue the opposite—that media should be created by and owned by the public—with the state or government serving the necessary function of allocating the means to produce media to the people.

There is, however, a lot of territory in between. Social responsibility theorists argue for a tripartite division of responsibility for media performance. Ownership of media would remain private, with both owners and the professionals who actually create and distribute media messages invested in a set of values emphasizing their responsibility for fair, accurate, and complete presentations to, and about, all constituent groups of a society. The role of the state and the government is in three areas: It should prevent flagrant abuses by the media—in false advertising, libel, and profoundly harmful communications. It should correct the marketplace's tendency toward ownership concentration and foster competition. And it should assure that where the marketplace cannot adequately serve underrepresented groups and points of view, publicly owned media will do so. Furthermore, the position usually argues that educational institutions have an obligation at all levels, and particularly in primary and secondary education, to teach media literacy. The social responsibility position emphasizes, too, that the public has a role, through citizens' groups and through personal feedback to media outlets, to assure that the media know what the public thinks of them, and the jobs they are doing.

NOTES

1. The classic treatment of the decline of authoritarianism and rise of libertarianism is Siebert (1965). We should note that other models or theories exist, primarily development-communication models in emerging nations, but we will focus on those in developed economies.

2. A "patents trust" involving the British Marconi Company, General Electric, the Radio Corporation of America, AT&T, Westinghouse, and others, also operated, allowing for these companies to gain an upper hand both in making radios and in radio broadcasting, once the commercial potential of the medium was assured by the late 1920s.

3. In almost all of the rest of the industrialized world, radio broadcasting began as a public, that is, government-owned, monopoly system and would remain so until well after the institution of television, which likewise emerged as a public system.

4. Our thanks to Professor Robert Reid of the University of Illinois for this example.

Media Globalization

S o far, this book has considered the media within a national (primarily American) context, but developments since the 1970s require us to broaden that context. For both economic and technological reasons, the world is becoming a smaller place; to put it simply, nations and individuals worldwide are more closely connected by communications than they have ever been before. This trend toward globalization is certain to continue and likely to accelerate, and it has had and will continue to have profound ramifications for the world of the twenty-first century. Furthermore, cultural and political differences between the nations and regions of the globe remain substantial; in many cases, international communication heightens conflicts as much as it reduces them.

CONDITIONS UNDERLYING INTERNATIONAL COMMUNICATION

One of the defining experiences of the end of the twentieth century has to be the globalization of communication and culture. The fact is that people virtually worldwide can and do observe the same events in "real time": the Olympics, the World Cup championship, the Academy Awards, and significant historical events. Moreover, wherever we travel, the same cultural references—in music, film, television—are likely to greet us. Culture travels across national borders in surprising but predictable ways. This doesn't happen by either magic or chance. Certain conditions make it possible for a viewer in one part of the world to watch something taking place on the other side of the world.

TECHNOLOGY

International television is possible because information can be bounced off communications satellites 26,000 miles above Earth from virtually any place on the globe to any other. At one end, a television camera captures the image, which is recoded as digitized information, fed by a satellite uplink transmitter to the satellite, amplified by the satellite, and repeated. It can then be received at a ground station (NBC in New York) and disseminated through a network (up to another satellite and back down again or along terrestrial fiber optic or copper cables or along microwave relays) to a television station or cable company, and thence into a home television set, which decodes the signal and recodes it as a visual image.

INFRASTRUCTURE

Somebody (many bodies, actually) worked on the various stages necessary for the broadcast. Some people had to produce the event that provided the image to be broadcast; other people had to produce, broadcast, receive, and distribute the image; and still other people had to work on the various materials and technology necessary for each of these stages. Most likely, most of these people work in specific media organizations. The internationalization of the media is accompanied by the internationalization of media organizations. CNN, NewsCorp, Sony, and McCann Erickson are all global media corporations.

STANDARDS

Technology and organized infrastructure imply common standards. Standards make modern technology viable. In the 1870s, before time standardization, if one traveled by rail from New York to St. Louis, virtually every stop would have a different local time. Not surprisingly, the railroads, anxious to make usable timetables, were the chief architects, in 1883, of the four standard time zones. The federal government did not make them official until World War I.[1] Into the twentieth century, standards for transportation, communications, and industry were predominantly national. A rail traveler doing a tour of Europe well into the present century would have to debark from a train at each national border and board a new one because the gauges (distance between the two rails) of the track were different; a German train could not travel on French tracks. Today, that is no longer true. In a few cases, even language has become standardized: all international commercial pilots and air traffic controllers, for example, are required to use English.

Electronic information technologies virtually demand international standards—of time, hardware, software, format. Even the electromagnetic spectrum must be allocated: radio frequencies are assigned to commercial users, the military and government, and ships at sea.[2] For nations and transnational corporations to arrive at international standards demands a high degree of international organization and integration.

CULTURE

An international telecast of the Olympics, or of anything else, has cultural considerations. For an event to become a televised event requires a degree of common understanding about the event itself— about what one is watching, why it is significant, what the standards for interpretation and judgment are. Why is it that people from very different national cultures can watch and enjoy the Olympics every four years? Why is it that people in so many countries enjoy American country music, whereas American audiences for the music of other nations are comparatively small?

There remain significant cultural differences across national borders. To a great extent, however, and particularly in the industrial countries, cultural differences between nations are declining rapidly, as commerce and communications increasingly internationalize. At some level, it seems that intercultural diversity—differences between cultures—is decreasing while intracultural diversity—differences within nations and cultures—is increasing (Hennessy, 1985).

That intercultural diversity is decreasing may be seen at different levels, from the introduction of American football into Europe and European football into America, to the earth-shattering international events of the 1990s—the reunification of Germany, the breakup of the Soviet Union. The normative centerpiece of this internationalization of culture is democratization and a movement toward a capitalist economy, elements, as we have already suggested, that are inextricably intertwined. This movement toward intercultural homogeneity, however, is not proceeding at the same pace worldwide; some parts of the world are attempting to prevent such international influences on their cultures.

At the same time, there is an apparent trend toward intracultural diversity, marked by the fragmentation of the media audiences, by the proliferation of ethnic styles and tastes. Part of the increase may be due to immigration and the representation of diverse cultures in the media. Part of the increase may be illusory, the result of the marketing of exotic cultures to make a profit.

Mass communication is intimately connected with cultural diversity. Before the advent of electronic media (and the power of the ideology of the free market), any nation predisposed to keep "foreign" messages and ideologies out could do so with relative ease, merely by closing its borders, inspecting all goods coming in, and censoring what it wants. In the pre-electronic era, transportation and communication were functionally identical. Electronic media, however, do not respect national boundaries. Although it is possible to jam radio signals (and somewhat easier to jam TV transmissions) and to control telephone and data transmission lines and satellite downlinks, newer media technologies make any border more porous to foreign ideas. When transistor radios are affordable to the majority of the world's population, when easily duplicated audiocassettes can be surreptitiously passed from one family to another, when fax machines, photocopiers, and computer printers become available to intellectual elites in a society, then official state censorship (whether explicit or through regulation) begins to crumble. Official authority can be challenged, new images and ideologies shared, and resistance organized. One factor often cited in the challenges to various political-economic systems (such as the collapse of the Soviet Union) is the circulation of messages not sanctioned by the state by pirate media. But communication technologies also can accelerate the trend toward intracultural diversity, as new media technologies allow for as much specialization as the market will bear. In a technologically intensive world, hyperspecialization of media is the order of the day. Thus, communication technologies can pull in both directions, toward increasing integration of the world and toward increasing diversity.

ECONOMICS

The British media scholar Anthony Smith (1991) notes that the globalization of media has been under way for a century, ever since international media became a possibility as the telegraph made international news agencies (wire services) a practical reality.[3] From 1887, the news services operated as a cartel. The American, British, French, and German agencies were essentially guaranteed a regional monopoly within the geopolitical spheres of influence of each of these colonial powers. Although each of these agencies was privately owned, most had close ties to their governments: The Reuters agency, for example, exchanged use of government cables for assurances that the British government would be favorably treated. As a cartel, the arrangement effectively excluded other agencies from entering the market, but it likewise kept the participating partners out of business outside their own spheres and forced the participating agencies to rely on each other for news accounts outside their own region.

The cartel arrangement broke down when the geopolitical spheres of influence shifted as a result of World War I; more important, the partners grew unhappy with the performance of the others as news suppliers. Each accused the other of biasing reports toward its own national interests. In 1934, the Associated Press (AP) withdrew from the cartel, and the period between the wars saw the establishment of national agencies in virtually every major country. Since then, the market for the world news provided by agencies has become dominated by three firms: The American AP, Britain's Reuters, and the French Agence France Presse. Video news is likewise dominated by cooperative agreements among a handful of players: CNN, the BBC, the three American networks, and the European VisNews.

As this history exemplifies, from early times, the international flow of media messages has been subject to concentration of control. In addition, the international trade in media messages has always faced arguments about the relationship between media messages and the biases of their producers.

The big jump in the globalization of media has occurred since World War II, and it has become most pronounced since the 1980s. We see two general trends. First, the dominant media corporations are exclusively First World firms, not all American; many of them are transnational firms with global interests. Examples include Germany's Bertelsman, Japan's Sony Corporation, France's Hachette, and the United States' Time Warner, the world's largest media corporation. Second, the major media firms worldwide are vertically integrated—they attempt to control all aspects of production—as well as horizontally integrated—they attempt to control multiple media.

At the same time, many of the economic trends that characterize the internationalizing of the media industries have come to characterize most if not all of the major economic industries and forces of the world (from manufacturing to banking). Transnational corporations have challenged the ability of nations to regulate economies, and consequently, global markets have an increasing power over nations. Moreover, the fall of communism and the apparent success of capitalism, combined with the unregulated power of global financial exchange, has resulted in the domination of an ideology of free markets and the inevitability of economic inequality.

NEW PROBLEMS

These trends raise several unsettling questions. First, foreign ownership has been a concern since the Federal Communications Act of 1934 specifically forbade foreign nationals from owning American broadcast stations, fearing that they would use such stations for foreign propaganda. This sword cuts both ways: American worry when the Japanese company Sony buys Columbia Pictures, but the fact that American movies dominate the world motion picture market and that American TV programs likewise are seen worldwide raises serious concerns for the leaders of other countries.

A related concern is that the media giants may owe no loyalty to anyone except their investors, who are scattered over the world and increasingly care only about short-term profit. Moreover, the economic clout of the largest operators give them extraordinary political leverage with governments and regulatory agencies anywhere they operate.

As we noted earlier, economic concentration, nationally or globally, leads to the concentration of ideas: the free marketplace becomes less free. Furthermore, economies of scale and market dominance may effectively keep small entrepreneurs with different ideas from entering the marketplace.

These problems take on special urgency in developing nations. In international debates in the 1980s, especially in the United Nations Educational, Scientific, and Cultural Organization (UNESCO), representatives of these nations vociferously criticized Western industrialized nations and their media for dominating news, entertainment, and cultural programming worldwide. They argued that this threatened their political sovereignty and effaced their local culture. Many of these ideas were published in a UNESCO (1980) document, *Many Voices, One World*, which called for a "New World Information Order." This document was strongly opposed by the United States and other Western governments and media on the ground that it violated the free flow of information. Although the debates continued for more than a decade, the growth of media markets and the collapse of the Soviet Union have rendered the arguments moot. For instance, during the 1990s, privatized television has become the dominant model around the world, diminishing the power of public broadcasting systems. And multinational corporations have invested in media throughout the world.

The growing internationalization of media and culture, some critics argue, has replaced political forms of colonialism. As Western culture—through movies, books, television, music, and video—is distributed throughout the world, critics have become rightly concerned about the exportation of American culture, values, and structures of everyday life and their impact on other cultures. The term used by critics who fear that American culture is colonizing the world is *media imperialism*. Media imperialism involves two relations. First, it involves the transfer of money and/or resources from a dominated culture to the dominant culture. Many American media corporations have subsidiary companies in other countries, and the profits made by these subsidiaries all return home. Second, theories of media imperialism claim that American media products are overwhelming the media products of other cultures: that throughout the world, American media products drive out other nations' media products. The result is that American culture as depicted in its media products now dominates throughout the world, negating all alternatives and oppositions.

An alternative model proposed by European media scholars Roger Wallis and Krister Malm (1984) is that of transculturation. They argue that "through the trans-culturation process, music from the international music industry can interact with virtually all other music cultures and subcultures in the world, due to the worldwide penetration attained by music mass media during the past decade" (p. 301). That is, they argue that because culture is always changing and transforming itself into something new, the internationalization of media products simply expands the scope of these possible interactions and transformations. Rather than arguing that indigenous cultures (for example, African music) have a pure and essential identity that should be protected from the influence of American culture, they note that these cultures have always changed as a result of external influences, just as American culture has changed through its encounters with various international cultures. It is this transaction that characterizes the nature of global culture and that should be defended. Although Wallis and Malm do not defend the economic imperialism of media corporations, they point out that the global media culture has enabled African musicians, for example, to be recorded and reach wider audiences than ever before.

THEORIES OF HEGEMONY AND GLOBALIZATION

We are confronted here with very different evaluations of changes involving the media and their relation to the structure of power, based in very different descriptions of those changes. As we have been suggesting throughout this book that our descriptions of reality play an active role in constructing reality, the only way out of this dilemma may be to turn to the larger and more abstract questions of the nature of power and globalization in the contemporary world. First, we can consider the changing conditions and nature of power in contemporary society. We have already pointed out that power in modern societies is based less on force than on culture. The idea that power itself resides in culture defines hegemony. The dispute between media imperialism and transculturation can be understood, then, as an instance of the larger dispute between two theories of hegemony, which we will characterize as modern and postmodern.

Modern hegemony assumes that power operates through civil society and on behalf of a particular elite class. With the rise of the nation-state and democratic capitalist societies in Europe in the eighteenth and nineteenth centuries, state or government power could no longer be exercised solely through force—through police or the military or other physical means—simply because increasing numbers of the population became involved in political and cultural life. The government exercises its power through the institutions of civil society, those social institutions that appear to be free of direct political intervention by the government, such as the press, the schools, the church, leisure activities, and other entertainment media. The government, representing the ruling interests, attempts to win the population over to its way of seeing the world, to win a consensus around its ideology.

Modern hegemony is based on the division of society into two distinct groups or classes, one of which is always dominant: capitalists and workers, men and women, Whites and people of color.

Theorists of postmodern hegemony argue that modern hegemony no longer describes how power works. They argue that consensus is unnecessary for the maintenance of power. The dominant group does not have to get subordinated groups to agree to its vision of its world, to its ideology. Rather, subordinated groups simply have to agree to the "leadership" of the representatives of the dominant group.

Theorists of postmodern hegemony also argue that it is an oversimplification to see society organized simply in terms of a struggle between two coherent and opposing groups, the dominant and the subordinate. They argue instead that postmodern hegemony involves the ongoing construction of alliances among various and disparate fractions of the population, some of whom have little in common, to form a *power bloc.*

Postmodern hegemony is often constructed through processes that the French historian Michel Foucault (1977) describes as *discipline.* He argues that discipline involves the surveillance and regulation of people's behavior. The process of gathering large amounts of data on how people behave and using this information to control the "health of the social body" is a form of social control and power. Foucault argues that various institutions such as the school, the hospital, and the penal system produce knowledge that brings people under further surveillance and control. The implication of this argument is that the very forms of culture and even knowledge that characterize a society are always implicated in the making of power, the making of reality, and the making of history.

The distinction between modern and postmodern hegemony has broad implications, and operates as well in discussions of globalization. Modern theories of globalization conceive of globalization between two places: the West and the Rest. There are different versions of this model. For example, political scientist Benjamin Barber (1995) describes the contemporary world as a contest between the international capitalism represented by McDonald's and the forces of tradition represented by religious fundamentalism. One side is usually taken to embody the forces of homogenization, and the other the forces of differentiation. Too much attention to the forces of homogenization leads some critics to an extremely pessimistic view of global culture, and the prediction that all local cultures will be erased eventually. Too much attention to the local forces of differentiation leads some critics to a naively optimistic view that celebrates local cultural forms.

Stuart Hall (1991) has proposed a postmodern theory, arguing that globalization involves the transformation of every local culture into a hybrid that already includes elements from many different cultures. Globalization does not pit a dominant global culture against a local traditional culture. Rather, for Hall, the commonality of globalization is that every culture is a hybrid. Every culture remains different insofar as it is a variant of a common global culture. Globalization is a force of hybridization; our commonality is that we are different. This new global postmodern culture does not speak a single language or ideology. Thus, for Hall, both international capitalism and fundamentalism are forces working against globalization and toward domination.

This is a difficult theory to comprehend, but it is apparent to anyone who travels. Entering any big city around the world at first offers a common visual experience: skyscrapers, Coca Cola signs, Benetton shops, McDonald's restaurants, and CNN on cable. Many of the pieces that make up the kaleidoscope that is a city are universal. But each city is configured differently, and each city offers itself as a unique experience. Different languages, ethnicities, and religions will dominate any given city, but virtually every major city will have other minority languages, ethnicities, and religions, reflected and refracted through their food, their videos, and their music.

These theories of the globalization of culture demonstrate that the media cannot be separated from the larger context of social and historical relations. Many people will have been surprised in reading this book at the extent to which we have written about things other than media, things that on the surface would seem to have little to do with the media. Yet, that is just the point. If we are to understand society and our lives, we have to look at how media make our lives. If we are to understand the media, we have to understand how the context of our lives makes the media.

At a time when American society and the whole world are facing enormous challenges, the media are playing and will continue to play an important role in helping us come to terms with these changes. They will undoubtedly help us understand the challenges, define the values with which we attempt to meet them, and imagine the possibilities for their solution.

It would serve us badly to either underestimate or overestimate the media's role in these processes, and it would serve us badly as well to oversimplify the complex relationship between media and history. We cannot predict what new directions social life will take, but we can predict that the media will play an important part in shaping and interpreting those future directions.

The questions surrounding the media are, paradoxically, too important to be left to the media themselves. These are questions that are central to our lives and our future, and we need to find ways to integrate our understanding of mediamaking into everyday life. The challenge for all of us is to take the growing importance of the media and the knowledge we have of how they work and turn them into a force that we can use to realize a world of our own making.

NOTES

1. Carey (1989) notes that whereas a transportation technology demands standard time, a communications technology, the telegraph, that allows for instantaneous transmission (and coordination) makes it possible.

2. Some standards are more or less arbitrary. That is, one standard may not necessarily be "better" than another, only different, or one standard may be technically better on one dimension and another better on another. And different standards may for a time coexist: witness VHS and Beta-format video recorders, AM and FM radio, Apple and IBM-compatible computer-operating systems. There is a preference for standard systems; over time, one standard usually vanquishes another. The economic stakes are extremely high: for example, the failure of the technically superior Beta format to VHS, which consumers liked better because the tapes were longer-playing, is reported to have cost Beta's originator, the Sony Corp., more than a billion dollars.

3. This entire section owes much to Smith (1991).

References

Ajzen, I., & Fishbein, M. (1980). *Understanding attitudes and predicting social behavior.* Englewood Cliffs, NJ: Prentice Hall.

Alter, J. (1984, October 22). The media in the dock. *Newsweek,* pp. 66-68, 70, 72.

Althusser, L. (1970). *For Marx* (B. Brewster, Trans.). New York: Vintage.

American Society of Newspaper Editors. (1997, April). *Report on minority representation on American daily newspapers.* Reston, VA: Author.

Aries, P. (1962). *Centuries of childhood.* New York: Vintage.

Arnold, M. (1960/1869). *Culture and anarchy.* Cambridge: Cambridge University Press.

Atkin, C. K. (1981). Mass communication and political socialization. In D. D. Nimmo & K. R. Sanders (Eds.), *Handbook of political communication* (pp. 288-328). Beverly Hills, CA: Sage.

Bagdikian, B. H. (1997). *The media monopoly* (5th ed.). Boston: Beacon.

Baker, R. K., & Ball, S. J. (1969). *Violence and the media: A report to the National Commission on the Causes and Prevention of Violence.* Washington, DC: Government Printing Office.

Ball, S., & Bogatz, G. A. (1970). *The first year of* Sesame Street: *An evaluation.* Princeton, NJ: Educational Testing Service.

Bandura, A. (1977). *Social learning theory.* Englewood Cliffs, NJ: Prentice Hall.

Bandura, A. (1965). Influence of models' reinforcement contingencies on the acquisition of imitative responses. *Journal of Personality & Social Psychology, 63*(3), 590-591.

Barber, B. R. (1995). *Jihad vs. McWorld: How the planet is both falling apart and coming together and what this means for democracy.* New York: Times Books.

409

Barnhurst, K., & Wartella, E. (1992). Newspapers and citizenship: Young adults' subjective experience of newspapers. *Critical Studies in Mass Communication, 8,* 195-209.

Barthes, R. (1974). *S/Z: An essay* (R. Miler, Trans.). New York: Hill & Wang. (Original work published in 1970 by Editions du Seuil)

Baudrillard, J. (1983a). *In the shadow of the silent majorities.* New York: Semiotexte.

Baudrillard, J. (1983b). *Simulations* (P. Foss, P. Patton, & P. Beitchman, Trans.). New York: Semiotexte.

Baudrillard, J. (1988). *The ecstasy of communication* (B. Schutze & C. Schutze, Trans.). New York: Semiotexte.

Benjamin, W. (1969). *Illuminations.* New York: Harcourt Brace.

Berelson, B., Lazarsfeld, P., & McPhee, W. (1954). *Voting.* Chicago: University of Chicago Press.

Berger, J. (1972). *Ways of seeing.* London: Penguin.

Berkowitz, L. (1984). Some effects of thoughts on anti- and prosocial influence of media events: A cognitive neoassociationistic analysis. *Psychological Bulletin, 95*(3), 410-427.

Berman, M. (1982). *All that is solid melts into air.* New York: Simon & Schuster.

Black, G. S. (1991). Changing attitudes toward drug use: The effects of advertising. In L. Donohew, H. E. Sypher, & W. J. Bukoski (Eds.), *Persuasive communication and drug abuse prevention* (pp. 157-194). Hillsdale, NJ: Lawrence Erlbaum.

Bloom, A. (1986). *The closing of the American mind: How higher education has failed democracy and impoverished the souls of today's students.* New York: Simon & Schuster.

Blumer, H. (1932). *Movies and conduct.* New York: Macmillan.

Bogart, L. (1989). *Press and public* (2nd ed.). Hillsdale, NJ: Lawrence Erlbaum.

Bogart, D. (Comp. & Ed.) (1997). *Bowker annual library and book trade almanac* (42nd ed.). New Providence, NJ: R. R. Bowker

Bogatz, G. A., & Ball, S. (1972). *The second year of* Sesame Street: *A continuing evaluation.* Princeton, NJ: Educational Testing Service.

Bohannon, L. (1967). Miching Malecho: That means witchcraft. In J. Middleton (Ed.), *Magic, witchcraft, and caring.* Garden City, NY: The Natural History Press.

Bok, S. (1978). *Lying: Moral choices in public and private behavior.* New York: Pantheon.

Bourdieu, P. (1986). *Distinction: A social critique of the judgment of taste* (R. Nice, Trans.). Cambridge, MA: Harvard University Press.

Braudel, F. (1972). *The Mediterranean world in the age of Philip II* (Vol. 1; Sian Reynolds, Trans.). New York: Harper & Row.

Brigham, J. C., & Giesbrecht, L. W. (1976). *All in the Family*: Racial attitudes. *Journal of Communication, 26*(4), 69-74.

Brown, J. D., Bybee, C. R., Wearden, S. T., & Straughan, D. M. (1987). Invisible power: News sources and the limits of diversity. *Journalism Quarterly, 64*(1), 45-54.

Calhoun, C. (Ed.). (1992). *Habermas and the public sphere.* Cambridge: MIT Press.

Cantor, M. (1971). *The Hollywood TV producer.* New York: Basic Books.

Cantril, H., with H. Gaudet & H. Herzog. (1966). *The invasion from Mars: A study in the psychology of panic.* New York: Harper & Row. (Original work published by Princeton University Press in 1940)

Carey, J. (1969) The communications revolution and the professional communicator. In P. Halmos (Ed.), *The sociology of mass-media communicators* (pp. 23-38). Keele, UK: University of Keele.

Carey, J. W. (1989). *Communication as culture: Essays on media and society.* Boston: Unwin Hyman.

Carter, B. (1991, March 4). 3 networks retrench after war. *New York Times* (national edition), pp. C1, C8.

Chaffee, S. H., & Choe, S. Y. (1980). Time of decision and media use during the Ford-Carter campaign. *Public Opinion Quarterly, 44*, 53-69.

Charity, A. (1995). *Doing public journalism.* New York: Guilford.

Charters, W. W. (1933). *Motion pictures and youth.* New York: Macmillan.

Clark, D. G., & Blankenburg, W. B. (1973). *You & media.* San Francisco: Canfield Press.

Cohen, B. C. (1963). *The press and foreign policy.* Princeton, NJ: Princeton University Press.

Commission on Freedom of the Press. (1947). *A free and responsible press.* Chicago: University of Chicago Press.

Comstock, G., & Paik, H. (1991). *Television and the American child.* New York: Academic Press.

Converse, P. (1962). Information flow and the stability of partisan attitudes. *Public Opinion Quarterly, 26*, 578-600.

Cooper, M., & Soley, L. (1990, February-March). All the right sources. *Mother Jones*, pp. 20-27, 45-48.

Cornfield, M. (1988). The Watergate audience: Parsing the powers of the press. In J. W. Carey (Ed.), *Media, myths, and narratives* (pp. 180-204). Newbury Park, CA: Sage.

Dahlgren, P. (1995). *Television and the public sphere.* Thousand Oaks, CA: Sage.

Davison, W. P. (1983). The third-person effect in communication. *Public Opinion Quarterly, 47* 1-15.

DeFleur, M. L., & Ball-Rokeach, W. (1975). *Theories of mass communication.* New York: David McKay.

Derrida, J. (1981). *Dissemination.* (Trans. B. Johnson.) Chicago: University of Chicago Press.

de Tocqueville, A. (1835, 1840). *Democracy in America* (2 volumes) (G. Lawrence, Trans., J. P. Mayer, Ed.). Garden City, NY: Anchor Books.

de Tocqueville, A. (1981). Newspapers and public associations in the United States. In M. Janowitz & P. Hirsch (Eds.), *Reader in public opinion and mass communication* (2nd ed.) New York: Free Press. (Reprinted from R. D. Heffner, Ed., *Democracy in America*, 1956, New York: New American Library).

Dewey, J. (1925). *Experience and nature*. LaSalle, IL: Open Court.

Dewey, J. (1927). *The public and its problems*. New York: Holt & Rinehart.

Dimmick, J. (1974, November). The gate-keeper: An uncertainty theory. *Journalism Monographs, 37*.

Dominick, J., & Pearce, M. C. (1976). Trends in network prime time programming, 1953-1974. *Journal of Communication, 26*, 70-80.

Donnerstein, E., Slaby, R., & Eron, L. (1994). The mass media and youth violence. In J. Murray, E. Rubinstein, & G. Comstock (Eds.), *Violence and youth: Psychology's response* (Vol. 2, pp. 219-250). Washington, DC: American Psychological Association.

Eisenstein, E. (1978). *The printing press as an agent of change* (2 Vols.). New York: Cambridge University Press.

Emery, E., & Emery, M. (1984). *The press and America* (5th ed.). Englewood Cliffs, NJ: Prentice Hall.

Erskine, H. (1970-1971, Winter). The polls: Opinion of the news media. *Public Opinion Quarterly*, 630-643.

Ettema, J. S. (1982). The organizational context of creativity: A case study from public television. In J. Ettema & D. C. Whitney (Eds.), *Individuals in mass media organizations: Creativity and constraint* (pp. 91-106). Beverly Hills, CA: Sage.

Ewen, S. (1976). *Captains of consciousness*. New York: McGraw-Hill.

Fallows, J. (1996). *Breaking the news: How the media undermine democracy*. New York: Pantheon.

Fishman, M. (1980). *Manufacturing the news*. Austin: University of Texas Press.

Fiske, J. (1989). *Reading the popular*. Boston: Unwin Hyman.

Foucault, M. (1970). *The order of things: An archaeology of the human sciences*. New York: Pantheon.

Foucault, M. (1973). *The birth of the clinic: An archaeology of medical perception*. (Trans. A. M. Sheridan Smith.) New York: Pantheon.

Foucault, M. (1977). *Discipline and punish: The birth of the prison* (A. Sheridan, Trans.). New York: Pantheon.

Frith, S. (1981). *Sound effects: Youth leisure and the politics of rock 'n' roll*. New York: Pantheon.

Gabler, N. (1988). *A world of their own: How the Jews invented Hollywood*. New York: Crown.

The Gallup Poll: Public opinion 1991. (1988). Wilmington, DE: Scholarly Resources Inc.

Gandy, O. H., Jr. (1982). *Beyond agenda-setting: Information subsidies and public policy*. Norwood, NJ: Ablex.

Gans, H. J. (1979). *Deciding what's news*. New York: Pantheon.

Gaziano, C. (1983). The knowledge gap: An analytical review of media effects. *Communication Research, 10*(4), 447-486.

Gerbner, G., Gross, L., Jackson-Beeck, M., Jeffries-Fox, S., & Signorielli, N. (1978). Cultural indicators: Violence profile No. 9. *Journal of Communication, 28*(3) 176-207.

Gerbner, G., Gross, L., Morgan, M., & Signorielli, N. (1990). Living with television: The dynamics of the cultivation process. In J. Bryant & D. Zillmann (Eds.), *Media effects* (pp. 17-41). Hillsdale, NJ: Lawrence Erlbaum.

Ginsberg, B. (1986). *The captive public: How mass opinion promotes state power.* New York: Basic Books.

Gitlin, T. (1979). Prime time ideology: The hegemonic process in television entertainment. *Social Problems, 26,* 251-266.

Gitlin, T. (1980). *The whole world is watching: Mass media in making and unmaking the New Left.* Berkeley: University of California Press.

Glasser, T. L. (1993). Objectivity precludes responsibility. In A. Alexander & J. Hanson (Eds.), *Taking sides: Clashing views on controversial issues in media and society* (2nd ed., pp. 110-116). Guilford, CT: Dushkin. (Reprinted from *The Quill,* February, 1984)

Glasser, T. L. (1985). Competition and diversity among radio formats. In M. Gurevitch & M. R. Levy (Eds.), *Mass communication review yearbook* (Vol. 5, pp. 537-562). Beverly Hills, CA: Sage. (Reprinted from *Journal of Broadcasting, 28,* Spring 1984)

Goldman, N., & Hall, S. (1987). *Pictures of everyday life: The people, places, and cultures of the commonwealth.* London: Comedia.

Graesser, A. C., Millis, K. K., & Long, D. L. (1986). The construction of knowledge-based inferences during story comprehension. In N. E. Sharkey (Ed.), *Advances in cognitive science* (Vol. 1, pp. 125-157). New York: John Wiley.

Gramsci, A. (1971). *Selections from The Prison Notebooks* (Q. Hoare & G. Nowell-Smith, Trans.). New York: International Publishers.

Grossberg, L. (1992). *We gotta get out of this place: Popular conservatism and postmodern culture.* New York and London: Routledge.

Grossberg, L. (1997). *Dancing in spite of myself: Essays on popular culture.* Durham, NC: Duke University Press.

Habermas, J. (1989). *The structural transformation of the public sphere.* Cambridge, UK: Polity Press. (Original work published in German in 1962)

Hackett, R. (1984). Decline of a paradigm: Bias and ideology in news media studies. *Critical Studies in Mass Communication, 1,* 229-254.

Hall, S. (1980). Encoding and decoding in the television discourse. In S. Hall, D. Hobson, A. Lowe, & P. Willis (Eds.), *Culture, media, language.* London: Hutchinson.

Hall, S. (1985). Signification, representation, ideology: Althusser and the post-structuralist debates. *Critical Studies in Mass Communication, 2*(2), 91-114.

Hall, S. (1991). The local and the global: Globalization and ethnicity. In A. D. King (Ed.), *Culture, globalization, and the world-system.* London: Macmillan.

Hallin, D., & Mancini, P. (1985). Speaking of the president: Political structure and representational form in U.S. and Italian television news. In M. Levy & M. Gurevitch (Eds.), *Mass communication review yearbook* (Vol. 5). Beverly

Hills, CA: Sage. (Reprinted from *Theory and Society, 13*[6], 829-850, November 1984)

Hamilton, M. M. (1997, October 5). No allowance? No problem. Advertisers looking for new ways to reach the youngest consumers. *Austin* (TX) *American Statesman* (Washington Post News Service), pp. D1, D11.

Hassan, I. (1982). *The dismemberment of Orpheus: Towards a postmodern literature* (2nd ed.). New York: Oxford University Press.

Hebdige, D. (1980). *Subculture: The meaning of style.* London: Methuen.

Hennessy, B. (1985). *Public opinion* (5th ed.). Monterey, CA: Brooks/Cole.

Henry, W. A. (1993, December 12). Journalism under fire: A growing perception of arrogance threatens the American press. *Time*, pp. 76-77, 79, 82-86, 91, 93.

Herbst, S. (1993). *Numbered voices: How opinion polling has shaped American politics.* Chicago: University of Chicago Press.

Herzog, H. (1944). What do we really know about daytime serial listeners? In P. F. Lazarsfeld & F. N. Stanton (Eds.), *Radio research 1942-43.* New York: Duell, Sloan & Pearce.

Hirsch, E. D. (1987). *Cultural literacy: What every American needs to know.* Boston: Houghton Mifflin.

Hodge, B., & Tripp, D. (1986). *Children and television: A semiotic approach.* Cambridge, UK: Polity Press.

Huesmann, L. R. (1986). Psychological processes promoting the relation between exposure to media violence and aggressive behavior by the viewer. *Journal of Social Issues, 42*(3), 125-139.

Huston, A., Donnerstein, E., Fairchild, H., Feshbach, N., Katz, P., Murray, J., Rubinstein, E., Wilcox, B., & Zuckerman, D. (1992). *Big world small screen: The role of television in American society.* Lincoln: University of Nebraska Press.

Hyman, H., & Sheatsley, P. (1947). Some reasons why information campaigns fail. *Public Opinion Quarterly, 11,* 412-423.

Innis, H. A. (1950). *Empire and communications.* New York: Oxford University Press.

Iyengar, S. (1991). *Is anyone responsible? How television frames political issues.* Chicago: University of Chicago Press.

Iyengar, S., & Kinder, D. (1987). *News that matters.* Chicago: University of Chicago Press.

Jameson, F. (1991). *Postmodernism or the cultural logic of late capitalism.* Durham, NC: Duke University Press.

Johnson, H., & Broder, D. (1996). *The system: The American way of politics at the breaking point.* Boston: Little, Brown.

Johnston, J. (1995). Channel One: The dilemma of teaching and selling. *Phi Delta Kappan, 76*(6), 436-443.

Katz, E., Blumler, J., & Gurevitch, M. (1974). Utilization of mass communication by the individual. In J. Blumler & E. Katz (Eds.), *The uses of mass communications.* Beverly Hills, CA: Sage.

Katz, E., & Lazarsfeld, P. (1955). *Personal influence.* Glencoe, IL: Free Press.

Klapper, J. (1960). *The effects of mass communication.* New York: Free Press.

Kolbert, E. (1992, March 22). Political ads may wound, but not win races. *New York Times,* p. E4.

Kosinski, J. (1970). *Being there.* New York: Harcourt Brace & Jovanovich.

Lang, G. E., & Lang, K. (1983). *The battle for public opinion: The president, the press, and the polls during Watergate.* New York: Columbia University Press.

Lasswell, H. (1948). The structure and function of communication in society. In L. Bryson (Ed.), *The communication of ideas* (pp. 32-51). New York: Harper.

Lazarsfeld, P. F., Berelson, B., & Gaudet, H. (1948). *The people's choice.* New York: Columbia University Press.

LeBon, G. (1977). *The crowd: A study of the popular mind.* New York: Penguin.

Lemish, D. (1982). The rules of viewing television in public places. *Journal of Broadcasting, 26*(4), 757-781.

Lesser, G. S. (1974). *Children and television: Lessons from Sesame Street.* New York: Vintage.

Lichter, R., Rothman, S., & Lichter, L. (1986). *The media elite.* Baltimore: Adler & Adler.

Liebert, R. M., & Sprafkin, J. (1988). *The early window: Effects of television on children and youth* (3rd ed.). New York: Pergamon.

Lippmann, W. (1922). *Public opinion.* New York: Macmillan.

Lippmann, W. (1925). *The phantom public.* New York: Harcourt Brace.

Littlefield, H. M. (1964). The wizard of Oz: Parable on populism. *American Quarterly, 16*(1), 47-58.

Lowenthal, L. (1961). *Literature, popular culture, and society.* Palo Alto, CA: Pacific.

Lynd, R. S., & Lynd, H. M. (1929). *Middletown: A study in modern American culture.* New York: Harcourt, Brace & World.

Magazine Industry Market Place 1996. (1996). New York: R. R. Bowker.

Malamuth, N. M., & Donnerstein, E. (Eds.). (1984). *Pornography and sexual aggression.* New York: Academic Press.

Martin, L., & Segrave, K. (1988). *Anti-rock: The opposition to rock 'n' roll.* Hamden, CT, Anchor.

Marx, K. (1975). *Early writings.* (Ed. Q. Hoare.) New York: Vintage.

Marx, K. (1977). *Capital, volume 1.* (Trans. B. Fowles.) New York: Vintage.

Marx, K., & Engels, F. (1970). *The German ideology.* New York: International Publishers.

McCombs, M., & Gilbert, S. (1986). News influence on our pictures of the world. In J. Bryant & D. Zillman (Eds.), *Perspectives on media effects* (pp. 13-27). Hillsdale, NJ: Lawrence Erlbaum.

McCombs, M., & Shaw, D. L. (1974, August). *A progress report on agenda-setting research.* Paper presented to the Association for Education in Journalism, San Diego, CA.

McGuire, W. J. (1989). Theoretical foundations of campaigns. In R. Rice & C. Atkin (Eds.), *Public communication campaigns* (2nd ed., pp. 43-65). Newbury Park, CA: Sage.

McLuhan, M., with Q. Fiore (1964a). *The medium is the message* [audio recording].

McLuhan, M. (1964b). *Understanding media: The extensions of man.* New York: McGraw-Hill.

McNeal, J. U. (1992). *Kids as customers: A handbook of marketing to children.* New York: Lexington Books.

McQuail, D. (1987). *Mass communication theory: An introduction* (2nd ed.). Newbury Park, CA: Sage.

McQuail, D. (1994). *Mass communication theory: An introduction* (3rd ed.). Thousand Oaks, CA: Sage.

Mencher, M. (1984). *News reporting and writing* (3rd ed.). Dubuque, IA: Wm. C. Brown.

Merritt, D. W. (1995). *Public journalism and public life: Why telling the news is not enough.* Hillsdale, NJ: Lawrence Erlbaum.

Miller, N. E., & Dollard, J. (1941). *Social learning theory and imitation.* New Haven, CT: Yale University Press.

Montgomery, K. C. (1989). *Target: Prime time, advocacy groups, and the struggle over entertainment television.* New York: Oxford University Press.

Morgan, R. (1980). Theory and practice: Pornography and rape. In L. Lederer (Ed.), *Take back the night: Women on pornography* (pp. 134-140). New York: William Morrow.

Morley, D. (1980). *The "nationwide" audience.* London: BFI.

Morley, D. (1986). *Family television: Cultural power and domestic leisure.* London: Comedia.

Morley, D. (1992). *Television, audiences, and cultural studies.* New York: Routledge.

Mott, F. L. (1962). *American journalism* (rev. ed.). New York: Macmillan. (Original work published 1941)

Murray, J. H. (1997). *Hamlet on the holodeck: The future of narrative in cyberspace.* New York: Free Press.

National Television Violence Study. (1997). *Volume 1.* Thousand Oaks, CA: Sage.

Nelson, B. (1984). *Making an issue of child abuse.* Chicago: University of Chicago Press.

Nerone, J. (1987). The mythology of the penny press. *Critical Studies in Mass Communication, 4*(4), 376-404.

Nerone, J. (1990). Violence against the press in U.S. history. *Journal of Communication, 40*(3), 6-33.

Neuman, W. R. (1986). *The paradox of mass politics.* Cambridge, MA: Harvard University Press.

Noelle-Neumann, E. (1974). The spiral of silence: A theory of public opinion. *Journal of Communication, 24*(2), 43-51.

Noelle-Neumann, E. (1984). *The spiral of silence: Public opinion—our social skin.* Chicago: University of Chicago Press.

Ong, W. (1982). *Orality and literacy.* New York: Methuen.

Orwell, G. (1981). *1984.* New York: New American Library. (Original work published 1949)

Page, B., & Shapiro, R. Y. (1992). *The rational public.* Chicago: University of Chicago Press.

Page, B., & Shapiro, R. Y. (1983). Effects of public opinion on public policy. *American Political Science Review, 77,* 175-190.

Patterson, T. (1980). *The mass media election.* New York: Praeger.

Patterson, T., & McClure, R. (1976). *The unseeing eye.* New York: Putnam.

Pearl, D., Bouthilet, L., & Lazar, J. (Eds.). (1982). *Television and behavior: Ten years of scientific progress and implications for the eighties.* Washington, DC: Government Printing Office.

Peirce, C. S. (1958). *Selected writings.* New York: Dover.

Peters, J. D. (1995). Historical tensions in the concept of public opinion. In T. Glasser & C. T. Salmon (Eds.), *Public opinion and the communication of consent* (pp. 3-32). New York: Guilford.

Peterson, I. (1997, July 21). The newspaper industry is thriving, but several projects are exploring danger signs. *New York Times,* p. C9.

Peterson, R., & Berger, C. (1975, April). Cycles in symbol production: The case of popular music. *American Sociological Review, 40,* 158-173.

Petty, R. E., & Cacciopo, J. T. (1986). *Communication and persuasion: Central and peripheral routes to attitude change.* New York: Springer-Verlag.

Phillips, D. P. (1982). Airplane accidents, murder, and the mass media: Toward a theory of imitation and suggestion. In D. C. Whitney & Ellen Wartella (Eds.), *Mass communication review yearbook* (Vol. 3, pp. 97-120). Beverly Hills, CA: Sage.

Phillips, D. P., & Hensley, J. E. (1985). When violence is rewarded or punished: The impact of mass media stories on homicide. In M. Gurevitch & M. Levy, *Mass communication review yearbook* (Vol. 5). Beverly Hills, CA: Sage. (Reprinted from *Journal of Communication, 34*[3], 1984)

Pollak, A. W. (1991, July 23). Computer images are staking out star roles in movies. *New York Times* (midwest edition), pp. B1-2.

Postman, N. (1985). *Amusing ourselves to death.* New York: Viking.

Press, A. (1991). *Women watching television.* Philadelphia: University of Pennsylvania Press.

Protess, D. L., & McCombs, M. (Eds.). (1991). *Agenda setting: Readings on media, public opinion and policymaking.* Hillsdale, NJ: Lawrence Erlbaum.

Putnam, R. (1995, January). Bowling alone: America's declining social capital. *Journal of Democracy.*

Putnam, R. (1996, Winter). The strange disappearance of civic America. *The American Prospect, 24,* 34-49.

Radway, J. (1984). *Reading the romance.* Chapel Hill: University of North Carolina Press.

Rice, M. L., Huston, A. C., & Truglio, R., & Wright, J. C. (1990). Words from *Sesame Street*: Learning vocabulary while viewing. *Developmental Psychology, 26*, 421-428.

Rice, M. L., Huston, A. C., & Wright, J. C. (1982). The forms of television: Effects on children's attention, comprehension, and social behavior. In National Institute of Mental Health, *Television and behavior: Ten years of scientific progress and implications for the eighties: Vol. 2. Technical Reviews* (pp. 24-38). Rockville, MD: National Institute of Mental Health.

Rice, R. E., & Atkin, C. K. (1994). Principles of successful public communication campaigns. In J. Bryant & D. Zillmann (Eds.), *Media effects: Advances in theory and research* (pp. 365-387). Hillsdale, NJ: Lawrence Erlbaum.

Rivers, W., Peterson, T., & Jensen, J. W. (1971). *The mass media and modern society* (2nd ed.). San Francisco: Rinehart.

Robinson, J., & Levy, M. (1986). *The main source*. Newbury Park, CA: Sage.

Robinson, J. P. (1976a). Interpersonal influence in election campaigns: Two step-flow hypotheses. *Public Opinion Quarterly, 40*, 315-325.

Robinson, J. P. (1976b). The press as king-maker. *Journalism Quarterly, 51*(4), 587-594, 606.

Robinson, J. P. (1996, November). Remarks at Speech Communication Association, San Diego, CA.

Robinson, M. J. (1976). Public affairs television and the growth of political malaise. *American Political Science Review, 70*, 409-432.

Rock and Roll Confidential (Eds.). (1991). *You gotta right to rock* (3rd ed.). Los Angeles: Author.

Rogers, E. M., & Dearing, J. (1988). Agenda-setting research: Where has it been, where is it going? In J. Anderson (Ed.), *Communication yearbook* (Vol. 11, pp. 555-594). Newbury Park, CA: Sage.

Rogers, E. M., & Storey, J. D. (1987). Communication campaigns. In C. R. Berger & S. H. Chaffee (Eds.), *Handbook of communication science* (pp. 817-846). Newbury Park, CA: Sage.

Rosen, G. A. (1991, July 27). Fads. *TV Guide*, p. 18.

Rosenfeld, A. H. (1985, December). Music, the beautiful disturber. *Psychology Today*, p. 48.

Rothenberg, R. (1990, December 31). Time Warner's merger payoff. *New York Times* (national edition), p. 26.

Rubinstein, E., Comstock, G., & Murray, J. (Eds.) (1972). *Television and social behavior: Report on the U.S. Surgeon General's Scientific Advisory Commission on Television and Social Behavior*. Washington, DC: Government Printing Office.

Sapir, E. (1921). *Language*. New York: Harcourt, Brace and World.

Schudson, M. (1978). *Discovering the news*. New York: Basic Books.

Schudson, M. (1984). *Advertising, the uneasy persuasion: Its dubious impact on American society*. New York: Basic Books.

Schudson, M. (1995). Was there ever a public sphere? In M. Schudson (Ed.), *The power of news*. Cambridge, MA: Harvard University Press.

Shaw, D. L. (1967). News bias and the telegraph: A study of historical change. *Journalism Quarterly, 44*(1), 3-12, 31.

Shoemaker, P., & Reese, S. (1991). *Mediating the message: Theories of influence on mass media content.* White Plains, NY: Longman.

Shoemaker, P. J., & Reese, S. D. (1996). *Mediating the message: Theories of influences on mass media content* (2nd ed.). White Plains, NY: Longman.

Siebert, F. S. (1965). *Freedom of the press in England 1476-1776.* Urbana: University of Illinois Press.

Sigal, L. V. (1973). *Reporters and officials.* Lexington, MA: D. C. Heath.

Smith, A. (1991). *The age of behemoths: The globalization of mass media firms.* New York: Priority Press.

Sousa, J. P. (1906, September). The menace of mechanical music. *Appleton's Magazine.*

Spigel, L. (1992). *Make room for TV: Television and the family ideal in postwar America.* Chicago: University of Chicago Press.

Star, S., & Hughes, H. (1950). Report on an educational campaign: The Cincinnati Campaign for the United Nations. *American Journal of Sociology, 55,* 385-400.

Stark, R. W. (1962). Policy and the pros: An organizational analysis of a metropolitan newspaper. *Berkeley Journal of Sociology, 7*(2), 11-31.

Starobin, P. (1995, March/April). A generation of vipers: Journalists and the new cynicism. *Columbia Journalism Review,* pp. 25-32.

Stein, B. (1979). *The view from Sunset Boulevard: America as brought to you by the people who make television.* New York: Basic Books.

Stengel, R. (1996, July 22). Bowling together. *Time,* pp. 35-36.

Sterngold, J. (1997, October 7). Networks' lineups reflect their stakes in shows they offer. *New York Times,* pp. A1, C2.

Stephens, M. (1988). *A history of news.* New York: Penguin.

Stevens, J., & Porter, W. (1973). *The rest of the elephant.* New York: Harper & Row.

Streisand, B. (1997, July 14). It's a divisive world after all. *U.S. News & World Report,* pp. 45-46.

Tarde, G. (1969). The public and the crowd. In T. Clark (Ed.), *On communication and social influence* (pp. 277-294). Chicago: University of Chicago Press. (Original work published 1901)

Taylor, D. G. (1982). Pluralistic ignorance and the spiral of silence: A formal analysis. *Public Opinion Quarterly, 46,* 311-335.

Thorson, E. (1989). Processing television commercials. In B. Dervin, L. Grossberg, B. J. O'Keefe, & E. Wartella (Eds.), *Rethinking communication: Paradigm exemplars* (pp. 397-410). Newbury Park: CA: Sage.

Tichenor, P. J., Donohue, G. A., & Olien, C. N. (1970). Mass media flow and differential growth in knowledge. *Public Opinion Quarterly, 34,* 159-170.

Times-Mirror Center for the People and the Press. (1985, June-July). *The people & the press.* Los Angeles: Author.

Tuchman, G. (1972). Objectivity as strategic ritual. *American Journal of Sociology, 77,* 660-679.

Tuchman, G. (1973). Making news by doing work: Routinizing the unexpected. *American Journal of Sociology, 79,* 110-131.

Tuchman, G. (1974). Assembling a network talk-show. In G. Tuchman (Ed.), *The TV establishment.* Englewood Cliffs, NJ: Prentice Hall.

Tuchman, G. (1978). *Making news.* New York: Free Press.

Turow, J. (1982). Unconventional programs on television: An organizational perspective. In J. S. Ettema & D.C. Whitney (Eds.), *Individuals in mass media organizations: Creativity and constraint* (pp. 107-129). Beverly Hills, CA: Sage.

Turow, J. (1984). *Media industries.* White Plains, NY: Longman.

Turow, J. (1991). *Playing doctor.* New York: Oxford University Press.

UNESCO, International Commission for the Study of Communication Problems. (1980). *Many voices, one world.* New York: Author.

Vidmar, N., & Rokeach, M. (1974). Archie Bunker's bigotry: A study in selective perception and exposure. *Journal of Communication, 24*(1), 36-47.

Wallis, R., & Malm, K. (1984). *Big sounds from small peoples: The music industry in small countries.* New York: Pendragon.

Ward, S., Wackman, D. B., & Wartella, E. (1977). *How children learn to buy.* Beverly Hills, CA: Sage.

Wartella, E., & Reeves, B. (1985). Historical trends in research on children and the media: 1900-1960. *Journal of Communication 35*(2) 118-133.

Wartella, E., Heintz, K., Aidman, A., & Mazzarella, S. (1990). Television and beyond: Children's video in one community. *Communication Research, 17*(1), 45-64.

Weaver, D. (1980). Audience need for orientation and media effects. *Communication Research, 7,* 361-380.

Whitney, D. C. (1987). *The media and the people: Americans' experience with the news media, a fifty-year review.* New York: Columbia University, Gannett Center for Media Studies Working Paper Series.

Whitney, D. C., Fritzler, M., Jones, S., Mazzarella, S., & Rakow, L. (1989). Geographic and source biases in network television news. *Journal of Broadcasting & Electronic Media, 33*(2), 159-174.

Whitney, D. C., & Becker, L. B. (1982). Keeping the gates for gatekeepers: The effects of wire news. *Journalism Quarterly, 59,* 60-65.

Whitney, D. C., & Goldman, S. B. (1985). Media use and time of vote decision: A study of the 1980 Presidential election. *Communication Research, 12,* 511-529.

Whitney, D. C., & Wartella, E. (1988). The public as dummies. *Knowledge: Creation, Diffusion, Utilization, 10,* 99-110.

Whorf, B. (1956). *Language, thought and reality.* Cambridge: MIT Press.

Wilhoit, G. C., & deBock, H. (1976). *All in the Family in Holland. Journal of Communication, 26*(4), 75-84.

Williams, R. (1958). *Culture and society 1780/1950.* New York: Harper & Row.

Williams, R. (1965) *The long revolution.* Middlesex, UK: Penguin.

Williams, R. (1975). *Television: Technology and cultural form.* New York: Schocken.

Wright, C. R. (1960). Functional analysis and mass communication. *Public Opinion Quarterly, 24,* 606-620.

Wright, J. C., & Huston, A. C. (1995). *Effects of educational TV viewing of lower income preschoolers on reading skills, school readiness, and social adjustment.* Lawrence: University of Kansas Center for Research on the Influences of Television on Children.

Wyatt, R. O. (1991). *Free expression and the American public.* Washington, DC: American Society of Newspaper Editors.

Index

About the Authors

Lawrence Grossberg, is the Morris Davis Distinguished Professor of Communication Studies at the University of North Carolina at Chapel Hill. He has won the B. Aubrey Fisher Mentorship Award of the International Communication Association and the Distinguished Scholar Award of the National Communication Association. He is the author of four books (including *Bringing It All Back Home: Essays on Cultural Studies,* and *Dancing in Spite of Myself: Essays on Popular Culture*). He has co-edited nine books, and is currently the international co-editor of the journal *Cultural Studies.* He has published over 100 articles and his work has been translated into more than a dozen languages.

Ellen Wartella, Dean of the College of Communication and Walter Cronkite Regents Chair in Communication at the University of Texas at Austin, serves on editorial boards of seven journals; is co-author or editor of 11 books and dozens of articles on television's effect on children; consults with the FCC, FTC, and the U.S. Congress on television issues. She is co-principal investigator on a multisite grant from the National Cable Television Association to monitor violence on television. She received her Ph.D. from the University of Minnesota and completed post-doctoral study in child development at the University of Kansas and in media studies at Columbia University, New York. She sits on several nonprofit boards in Austin and nationally, including the Board of Trustees of the Children's Television Workshop, the producers of *Sesame Street*.

D. Charles Whitney has been a professor in the Department of Journalism at the University of Texas at Austin since 1993; he also holds an appointment as professor of radio-TV-film. He has also taught at the University of Illinois (1979-1993), the University of California at Santa Barbara (1992-1993, on leave from Illinois), the Ohio State University (1976-1979) and Stanford University (1975-1976). In 1985-1986, he was research director of the Gannett Center for Media Studies (now the Freedom Forum Media Studies Center) at Columbia University. His Ph.D. is in mass communication from the University of Minnesota, and his research specialties are in the sociology of mass media communicators and in political communication and public opinion. He is currently a senior researcher and University of Texas site manager of the Independent Television Violence Assessment Study, a three-year, $3.3 million investigation of violence on cable and network television; the study is conducted jointly by researchers at Texas, the University of California-Santa Barbara, the University of Wisconsin, and the University of North Carolina.

Send comments or questions to the authors, or hear what other readers have to say about this book, by visiting Sage's web page at:

http://sagepub.com/sagepage/mediamaking. html